Kansas and the West

Kansas and the West

New Perspectives

Edited by Rita Napier

University Press of Kansas

Published by the University Press of Kansas
(Lawrence, Kansas 66049),
which was organized by the Kansas Board of Regents
and is operated and funded by Emporia State University,
Fort Hays State University, Kansas State University,
Pittsburg State University, the University of Kansas,
and Wichita State University

Library of Congress Cataloging-in-Publication Data

Kansas and the West : new perspectives / edited by Rita Napier.
        p. cm.
Includes index.
ISBN 0-7006-1231-9 (alk. paper)—ISBN 0-7006-1232-7 (pbk. : alk. paper)
1. Kansas—History. 2. Kansas—Ethnic relations.
3. Kansas—Social conditions. I. Napier, Rita.
F681.5 .K35 2003
978.1—dc 21   2002154128

British Library Cataloguing in Publication Data is available.

Printed in the United States of America

10 9 8 7 6 5 4 3 2

Contents

Contents

Preface

The new approaches to studying history represented in this collection, which ask questions about race, class, gender, and environment, reveal a multitude of experiences and begin to explore and explain the importance of diversity. Recent scholarship has focused on new images and themes and calls for the reinterpretation of our past, incorporating as many people and ideas as possible. Rejecting a linear, progressive understanding of history, the new history hopes to provide a more complete, more inclusive view of the past. This book attempts to encompass that new vision.

The book is arranged into three roughly chronological periods, but it can also be explored thematically, since key themes recur in each period. One can, for example, follow the theme of environment and cultural adaptation or imposition in the essays by Richard White, Paul Sutter, and Donald Worster. Gender is prominent in the essays by Angel Kwolek-Folland, Michael Goldberg, Ann Schofield, and Caron Smith. Bill Cecil-Fronsman, Richard Sheridan, James C. Carper, Mary L. Dudziak, Michael Goldberg, and "Anonymous" offer new perspectives on politics in Kansas history. Race, class, economic development, the nature of work, and ethnicity and diversity are the subjects of still other selections. Most articles incorporate more than one theme. Each article is reprinted as originally published, with a few exceptions. Notes have been placed at the end of each essay. Where I found errors, I corrected them. Those articles that were considerably longer than the rest, I shortened, keeping both argument and evidence intact. Ellipses in the text indicate where these omissions have taken place. All changes were done with permission.

I am indebted to a number of people for help in producing this work. My good friend and colleague Ray Hiner patiently led me through revisions of my overview essay. Angel Kwolek-Folland and Betsy Kuznesof both critiqued the essay and offered excellent suggestions as well. Out of his vast store of knowledge of Kansas history, Virgil Dean suggested examples of excellent recent articles to include, patiently edited the first essay, and evaluated the entire manuscript. Discussions with Donald Worster informed my choice of essays and enhanced my knowledge of environmental history and the directions that field might take. My good friend John Wunder at the Great Plains Center encouraged my work and evaluated the entire project. As always, Sheryl Williams, curator of the Kansas Collection at the University of Kansas, was exceedingly helpful as I pursued my research. I want especially to thank the patient and skilled women of the College Word Processing Center for their extensive work on the manuscript.

INTRODUCTION

Rethinking the Past, Reimagining the Future

Rita Napier

In recent years western history has been a battleground of contested knowledge. Kansas is one of the disputed areas. Why do the stakes seem so high? Because the battles are being fought over the control of knowledge, and knowledge is the yarn out of which we weave the fabric of the future. Identity from our past is the talent and skill we bring to the task of weaving.

Reinterpretation of history is not new. Historians always are looking for new or previously unused manuscripts and new kinds of data that will cast more light on our shared past. Errors in past writing, people or topics left out, and new perspectives or research techniques from scholars in other disciplines may cause historians to revise history. The impact of momentous events in a historian's own time also can generate new research and writing. In recent years there has been significant reinterpretation of all fields in American history, none more so, perhaps, than the history of the American West.

Much change was generated by social and political events of the late 1950s and the 1960s. Historians began to recognize then that traditional western history left out many people, in particular women, African Americans, and ethnic groups of color. Civil rights issues, grassroots political movements, women's rights activities, and environmental

"Rethinking the Past, Reimagining the Future," by Rita Napier, *Kansas History* 24, 3 (2001): 218–247. Copyright Kansas State Historical Society. Reprinted by permission.

questions, among others, provided new perspectives on the past. Historians discovered new source material and new ways of using familiar documents such as the census. As a result, historians introduced a host of new topics, people, and perspectives that produced a new western history.

At stake are some of our most cherished myths, values, and stories of the West. America's sense of identity often is tied to the values found in western origin stories. For example, stories of cattle trails, army campaigns to conquer recalcitrant tribesmen, and pioneer farmers' battles to dominate and transform an often arid, treeless landscape have been favorite topics among historians of the West. However, some argue that we must transform our vision of the past to include people and perspectives ordinarily omitted from these stories. In some cases we are asked to question whether these traditional subjects had the significance given them by historians. To do so will lead to questions about the rightness of conquest, the importance of individuals over groups, the focus on elites rather than "ordinary" people, and triumphs rather than problems and failures.[1]

The purpose of this essay is to shoot a different vector on the new history by examining in detail one western state, Kansas. Studies over the past thirty-five years have transformed our understanding of the history of Kansas. Material on topics such as environment, gender, race, class, ethnicity, community, capitalism, westward expansion, and Native Americans is rich and challenges old assumptions. The new story is complex if yet incomplete. For those who read history as literature, there are intriguing new characters, previously unknown episodes, and a chance to look at the complexities, successes, and failures in the experience of life. These new ideas about the past are stimulating a rethinking of our history.

New issues have been raised. For example, do stories about cowboys, fur traders and trappers, wagon trains on overland trails, pioneer farmers, prospectors and mining rushes, and Indian wars in the nineteenth century tell the whole story of the Kansas or western past? Or Kansas and western identity? Do we need to look more closely at farm families, their daily lives, family relationships, gender, and work roles? Should we not include the stories of women, African Americans, ethnic groups, and wage workers as well as wild and woolly trappers? Indeed, is it not at least as important to look at profit-seeking cattlemen as at cowboys? Or poor people and environmental destruction as well as

2

prospectors and bonanza kings? And is not the twentieth century as crucial to our understanding as earlier centuries?[2]

The new history is not just the reverse of the old, however. Historians have begun to use a multitude of new sources that have created a very different picture of the West. Because it attempts to be inclusive, the new narrative incorporates greater diversity and is both different and more complex. Historians now include the full sweep of Kansas and western history, not just that before the turn of the last century. Some see the great stretch of prehistory as essential to the story as well. This longer view reveals some critical continuities obscured by the shorter span of much traditional history. For these reasons, the new adds both new topics and new perspectives. Its more analytical approach allows us to rethink the past and, perhaps, to reimagine the future. This essay addresses the change from the old western and Kansas history to the new and seeks to explore explanations historians have advanced by focusing on the history of Kansas.

THE COMPLEXITIES OF NATIVE AMERICAN LIFE

Native American history has been at the nexus of controversy. Historians before the 1960s uniformly regarded Indians—if they discussed them at all—as warlike savages who were obstacles to superior Euro-American expansion and settlement. In the 1930s Walter Prescott Webb, for example, equated Plains Indians with animals who were perfectly adapted to the harsh, arid Plains environment. Their exquisite adaptation made them formidable foes before industrialization made conquest possible. As obstacles to Euro-American expansion, they were superb horseman, expert buffalo hunters, cruel and barbarous foes, and excellent thieves, but eventually they would be conquered by six-gun toting Americans on horseback. More recently, historian Frederick Merk described Plains Indians as "wild" and "likely to rob or destroy small parties of Whites." According to Merk, "Indians north of Mexico were a primitive people" with a "backward society" that did not use the land properly and did not deserve to keep it.[3]

Kenneth Davis, writing about native peoples in Kansas history, shared this orientation. He wrote as late as 1976, "This generally open prairie, this timeless land, was very sparsely inhabited in 1776 by a primitive and timeless people who, because they were few and possessed tools of limited environmental destructiveness, had left few marks upon it." In this view historians echoed the beliefs of the Euro-American conquerors and ignored the perspective of native peoples.[4]

The new histories of Kansas and the West restore native peoples to a central role throughout. The stereotype of unchanging savages is disappearing. This inclusive approach describes more complicated, sophisticated native cultures and produces a more complex narrative with multiple perspectives embedded in it. It seems unlikely that historians ever again will resort to the old stereotypes when they describe native peoples.

In the new history Native Americans are central actors. Most historians now begin with the story of native origins and native life, at least ten thousand to twelve thousand years before Europeans entered this land. The story begins with explorers making their way over the land, creating mind maps of it, adjusting to great environmental changes, and generating their particular relationships with land, flora, fauna, and each other. Some evidence is available on their cosmologies as well. The native peoples of this place we would later call Kansas were a heterogeneous people who manipulated and altered the environment in significant ways. Both nomadic hunting and settled agriculture developed in Kansas. The agriculturalists transplanted tropical plants such as corn, beans, and squash and bred corn to adapt to the climate and environment of the Plains, which shows they recognized environmental possibilities and limits and created a method of adaptation to them. They also replanted highly desirable wild plants to make them more accessible. This agriculture successfully produced a surplus, stored in large underground pits, and made greater cultural development possible in the leisure time thus gained. The hunters were attracted to the uplands of the Plains occupied by great buffalo herds and chose to focus their economic, social, and religious life on bison and grass. They traded surplus meat and hides to the agricultural villagers for vegetables. Thus, a complex trading network existed well before Europeans entered the scene. When the horse came to the Plains, the native peoples readily integrated it into their cultures as a tool for more efficient hunting and packing and as a new inspiration in their religious thinking.[5]

The experience of native peoples with the horse illustrates the way they both altered the environment and adapted to it before direct contact with Europeans. Historian Richard White's essay on the Pawnee cultural landscape, for example, supplies us with some of our best evidence

of native manipulation of the environment. The Pawnees, agriculturalists who hunted buffalo on the Central Plains, were eager to acquire
horses, but they also wished to continue farming. Because of their adoption of the horse, the Pawnees had to find feed away from their villages
in the dangerous winter season when the tall prairie grasses had lost
their nutritional value. The Pawnees adapted by changing their seasonal
routine. They went on winter hunts to places where they could find nutritious buffalo grass and cottonwood bark and twigs as they searched
for buffalo. By firing dead grass in the spring, they also altered their environment for horse grazing by hastening green-up. The firing also
killed trees and shrubs in an area where timber was already scarce. The
land Euro-Americans found was hardly an unchanged "virgin" land.[6]

Just as the cultures and societies that developed in the thousands of
years before Europeans arrived were not unchanging, they were not simple. The Pawnees of the Central Plains, as anthropologist Gene Weltfish
has demonstrated, for example, understood and ordered their world
through a complex cosmology and a thorough understanding of the
natural world, both earth and the heavens. They used astronomy to calendar the year and to time their ceremonies and rituals. Based on their
cultural understanding of life, they ordered their complex kinship system in terms of perceived relationships to constellations of stars. Well-
thought-out household organization, divisions of labor, a system of
matrilineal descent, and political order created the stability necessary to
sustain a long-term agricultural society. Pawnee village life on the Central
Plains existed at least seven hundred years. Their elaborate culture was
made possible in part because of the leisure time created by a successful
economy. This was a long-term but hardly simple life on the Plains.[7]

Buffalo hunters on the Central Plains, too, had complex cultures
that do not fit the stereotype. The Cheyennes in western Kansas used
the stars to predict the solstice, calendar the year, and time the Sun
Dance. Their sense of sovereignty was based on a covenant with the
spirit keepers of the game and their right to hunt buffalo on a kinship
relationship. The Cheyennes preserved social order through a combination of public law, leadership behavior based on a value consensus,
appropriate kinship behavior, a tribal political system, and social os-
tracism. Although the Cheyennes were scattered in small groups a
good part of the year, clear, shared rules guided their behavior. These
hunters also produced a surplus and participated in an ancient trade
network on the Plains.[8]

The evidence showing that native peoples were neither savage nor primitive should not cause us to create a new ideal type. Like other human societies, those of native peoples had imperfections. Their adaptation to horses, buffalo, and grass was not a perfect one, as some historians such as Dan Flores and James E. Sherow have demonstrated. Equestrian tribes struggled to prevent numerous horse deaths in winter, and once they began to hunt buffalo for the market, the nomadic peoples in western Kansas contributed to the weakening of the great herds. The Cheyennes created public laws against acts such as homicide and incest because they were real problems; most tribes created ideals of generosity, self-control, and wisdom because they knew such behavior was not innate and that some would achieve it and others would not. The new western history challenged us to avoid dehumanizing stereotypes and seek to fairly depict the complexities of Native American life.[9]

EURO-AMERICAN EXPANSIONISM OR CONTEST FOR THE KANSAS PLAINS

The traditional interpretation of Native Americans also was central to how historians depicted expansionism. Until recently historians saw taking native lands and replacing them with "civilization" as part of a great American triumph story. According to intellectual historian and literary scholar Kenneth S. Lynn, for example, resettling the West "constitutes one of the great achievements in the history of human freedom." The "most spectacular achievement," he wrote, was "the extension of its [the United States'] principles of free democratic republicanism across the width of the entire continent." Like the famous historian of frontier expansion Frederick Merk, himself a student of Frederick Jackson Turner, Lynn saw expansion and resettlement as a great reform whereby an advanced civilization replaced backward people who seemed incapable of proper use of the land or of running effective governments. The earlier historians of Kansas generally shared this perspective.[10]

According to the new western historians, United States expansion into Kansas is no longer seen as a simple story of a triumphal march westward. Instead, they see it as a contested process in which Native Americans appear as legitimate sovereigns protecting their territory from unjust invasion. While military actions played a role in expansion,

scholars now see a number of reasons why Native Americans did not resist successfully. The ability of tribes to resist was severely hampered by
population losses from epidemic diseases such as small pox and
cholera and ongoing problems such as malnutrition. Historian William
E. Unrau has documented the series of epidemics suffered by the
Kansa Indians, for example, and the concurrent decline in their power.
The operation of the market and the practices of traders created a
credit dependency that also sapped native ability to resist political and
cultural pressures. Further, tribal divisions meant that the expanding
Euro-American population met divided resistance. Even so, expansionism and concomitant efforts to subsume native cultures were not
uncontested, as native peoples resisted when they could and accommodated when they could not.[11]

One of the ways historians have changed narratives of expansion, as
evidenced in the work of Richard White and others, has been to include Native American resistance and adaptations. One aspect of expansion was removal of native peoples from the land. In Kansas the
Munsees and Chippewas followed a strategy of both accommodation
and resistance to keep their land. Over and over again, argued historian Joseph B. Herring, they refused to move to Indian Territory (now
Oklahoma) as vociferously demanded by both missionaries and Indian
agents. At the same time, they tried to accommodate to other demands
as an argument for retaining land and residence in Kansas. One set of
strategies involved culture change. According to Herring, they accepted Euro-American-style clothing and agreed to send their children
to missionary schools. Another strategy was economic. They took up
the tools of their conquerors and began to cultivate farms. The two
small bands finally succeeded in resisting further expansion and removal, but the loss of culture and autonomy was great.[12]

The way new western historians have rewritten the narrative of the fur
trade adds another dimension to the understanding of expansion across
Kansas. They now emphasize the long period of time when the fur trade
anchored a new kind of economy and society. In Kansas French fur
traders married Kansa and Osage women who became key to the organization of hunting and trapping by their native kin. According to recent scholarship, native peoples also influenced methods of trading and
the value of goods transferred. Exchange of commodities typified trade,
not cash payments, and often followed native rules and practices. The
marriages resulted in distinctive communities like the one at Kaws-

mouth. These mixed-blood communities reflected adaptation by both the French and the native peoples and their offspring. Most lived by a combination of barter, based on trapping, and of growing small gardens. The majority was bilingual, although French was the main language. These novel mixed-blood communities were an excellent example of ethnic intermingling in the eighteenth and early nineteenth centuries that was a result of Euro-American expansion across Kansas.[13]

Other historians have rewritten the narrative of expansion in Kansas by emphasizing the mind-set of resettlers to control the world around them. That is, expansion and conquest represented more than taking the land and incorporating it into United States sovereignty. German immigrants to Kansas easily accepted the ideal of manifest destiny, argued Julie Wilson in a 1996 *Western Historical Quarterly* article, and, like other resettlers, saw victory in changing the wilderness to a garden, creating land uses bounded by newly drawn lines, and even attempting to change the climate of the state. Farmers and railroad companies alike tried to grow forests on the flat arid grasslands. According to this historical argument, even the introduction of new varieties and species, which destroyed indigenous crops and animals, can be seen as evidence of part of this larger process of conquest and domination.[14]

THE RESETTLEMENT PROCESS AND THE
CREATION OF A NEW KANSAS ECONOMY

When we turn to depictions of life after the United States took political control of Kansas and the West, the contrast between old and new history is equally stunning. In the traditional narrative, the economy was depicted as simple and isolated. Because of western isolation, economic decisions were made locally, influenced by local environmental conditions and local people who were primarily male. This perspective reflected an agrarian vision in which pioneer farmers were key figures. Work was simple and labor intensive. Farmers relied on muscle power and animal power to turn the prairies and harvest crops with simple tools. Although farmers might barter with neighbors for necessities or luxuries, held the influential western historian Ray Allen Billington, crop raising was primarily for subsistence not sale and profit. Because of the ready availability of land, most if not all of the men who went west could become farm owners, especially after passage of the Homestead Act.[15]

As the traditional version of the story continues, other economic activities reflected the same simplicity, isolation, and opportunity. For example, cowboys cooperatively rounded up cattle and shared the labor of branding calves and driving herds to market. Even if people wished to market what they produced, they could do so only in local areas because there was no transportation infrastructure tying them to a larger economy. Most travel was on dirt wagon roads or trails cut by the hooves of thousands of cattle. Few rivers beyond the Missouri were navigable. In such a primitive economy there were no urban areas and few towns. Exchange was based on local needs, local products, and the skills of individual farmers, but there was little specialization. The primary goal of each farmer was to provide subsistence for his family by transforming the wilderness into a civilized place. There was widespread access to potentially wealth-creating resources, and as a result, there were no great distinctions of wealth. Gradually a more complex economy evolved.

It is apparent from this description of the traditional histories of Kansas and the West that narratives focused on the significant economic activities of single, white men. Although African Americans and Hispanics were a large portion of cowboys, their labor, for example, was ignored. Women had few economic roles in the story as well.

Traditional interpretations also were exclusive in another sense. People with specialized economic roles were ignored. When a few historians began to discover the ubiquitous land speculator, cattle town businessmen, bankers, and commercial farmers, the older paradigm seemingly had no place for them. Instead of rethinking the paradigm, however, historians just plugged brief references to the new figures into the old story.

In the traditional version of Kansas and western history, the pioneer conquest of wild and often arid lands eventually led to the successful modern economy of the twentieth century. The hallmark of the economy was the evolution from simple to complex. Those who drove this change were celebrated as agents of progress. Indeed, a development paradigm shaped the historical narrative of that evolution. Thus, historians presented development as progress rather than analyzing it in terms of costs and benefits. The darker side of economic history was not a part of the traditional story. Some historians bemoaned the dependence this economic isolation and simplicity represented. Because the western economy was extractive, as in farming, any surpluses generated left the region to be processed and sold, thus transferring most economic power outside the region.

In contrast to the isolated, simple, subsistence economy depicted by earlier historians, the new history envisioned a complex economy with ties to other sections of the United States and to the larger world from the beginning. In this view, well represented in William Cronon's influential *Nature's Metropolis* and Richard White's *"It's Your Misfortune and None of My Own,"* the old was not so different from the modern West. Its economy had complexity at its heart from the beginning. There were several significant types of economy, many types of historical actors, a network of economic connections to the larger world, a wide range of occupations and statuses, and a hierarchy of wealth-holding skewed to the top. The contrast between this portrait of a complex economy from the beginning and the older view of a simple agrarian West is striking.[16]

In Kansas, as in the rest of the West, there were commercial, industrial, and agrarian economic activities. These major types of economic activities were not the product of an evolutionary process but were carried intact from East to West, and they continued to be influenced by financial control from the East. The range and character of major activities reflected economic complexity.

Commercial centers, towns, appeared from the beginning of resettlement, for example, not at the end of a long development process. Town builders in eastern Kansas planted a cash-based market economy at a number of places where existing trade from overland traffic, outfitting of immigrants, cattle trails, or other activity made it profitable. In western Kansas, where the railroad preceded settlement, the company established towns at regular intervals. In these towns specialists operated wholesale houses, ran retail establishments, acted as commission merchants, loaned money, processed local produce, opened boardinghouses and hotels, restaurants and saloons, and acted as skilled artisans. Land speculators, who often controlled town sites from the beginning, ensured that town lands were sold as commodities in a market exchange. These places of trade were inland economic nodes that tied the commerce of Kansas and the West to the urban financial and manufacturing centers of the East and established market-based transactions in the West.[17]

But in the new narrative these towns were not the only evidence of a commercial economy. Around them and along the railroad that often preceded resettlement, there was a surplus-oriented agriculture. Indeed towns stimulated the production of crops in their vicinity, and settlers who wished to farm commercially—and could afford higher land prices—sought land near them and along railroads. In addition some specialized forms of commercial agriculture appeared in certain areas such as bonanza farming and irrigated agriculture in western Kansas.

Commercialization encouraged specialization on family farms. Those farmers moved away from diversification to focus on a single marketable crop such as wheat. Cattle ranchers were commercial agriculturalists from the beginning in western Kansas. Their specialization made these entrepreneurs much more subject to the vicious boom and bust cycles of the market economy.[18]

Not all farms were thoroughly capitalist, however, nor were they completely hooked into the national or international economic network. Some were left out because they could not get their crops to market, but that dilemma was solved gradually with the extension of roads and railroads. Even so, in the late nineteenth century some "corporate" family farms chose a different path, according to historians such as Kathleen Conzen, "Peasant Pioneers," and John Stitz, "A Study of Farm Family Culture in Ellis County, Kansas." These families emphasized the connections between generations and followed the ideal of intergenerational cooperation and assistance. They aimed at perpetuating the family farm and farming as a way of life. Adults accepted responsibility for training children in the skills of farming. At the same time the essential labor of children contributed to the success and often the expansion of the farm. When the children were grown they would receive a piece of the farm or a dowry to assist them toward their own successful farm ownership. The adult child who received the main farmstead cared for elderly parents. These reciprocal relationships among three generations provided for the needs of all generations, including the social security of the aged. These were not subsistence farms, because some crops were sold; the primary goal was not profits solely, but the well-being of a family. Other examples of alternative attitudes and economic behavior suggest the economy was more complex than previously thought. Further research may reveal both added complexity and a better idea of how and why capitalism came to dominate.[19]

Major industrial activities also were carried to Kansas from the beginning. Initially far fewer people were engaged in industrial than in agrarian activities, but they pointed the direction the western economy would take. The railroad spearheaded industrialization in Kansas. From the 1860s through the 1880s railroad companies built shops every few hundred miles along the tracks and hired large numbers of wage workers to repair the rolling stock and keep tracks intact. Railroads often also operated underground coal mines along their routes to provide coal for fuel. In other areas, such as southeastern Kansas, industrial mining came hard on the heels of the removal of native peoples. Substantial capital was needed to operate underground and to process ore. In these cases large companies and corporations financed the heavily capitalized operations and made decisions, usually as absentee owners. This sector expanded at the turn of the century and became central to the economy in the twentieth century. World War II capped the trend by making Kansas and the West an urban, industrial region.[20]

Industrialization has taken a somewhat different turn in recent years in Kansas. Meatpacking was a major industry from the 1870s characterized by corporate organization, wage workers, dangerous conditions, and labor strife. It was an urban operation and contributed to the state's urbanization trend. Some of its key operations were in Kansas City, Kansas. Since the 1970s Kansas has been one of the pioneers in rural industrialization. Packing companies cut costs by bringing plants, feed lots, grain, and a supply of unskilled labor into closer proximity to each other. As Donald Stull and Michael Broadway pointed out, Kansas has "increased its share of the U.S. meatpacking employment since the 1970s and has had a gain of 3000 meatpacking jobs." Large packing companies deliberately placed plants in right-to-work states such as Kansas.[21]

Many workers, particularly in smaller cities and towns such as Garden City, Dodge City, and Liberal, were part of new ethnic groups from southeast Asia. They have experienced the meaning of unrestricted corporate control and hazardous work first hand. According to Stull and Broadway, managers speed up the line to increase production, and safety often is sacrificed. Productivity has increased, and so have accidents. In Kansas between 1980 and 1988, seventeen thousand workers in meatpacking were injured, and eight died. Since workers are unorganized and the legislature maintains the state's right-to-work status, they have little control over work conditions. The turnover rate is 72–96 percent annually, in meatpacking alone, conditions that seem to mirror those of nineteenth-century Kansas and the West. Obviously industrialization came early and determined a major trend in the character of the capitalist economy that continues today.[22]

This complex economy has had market capitalism at its center from the beginning. Why historians took so long to recognize its importance in Kansas remains something of a mystery, but recent studies, such as the one by Thomas Frank, "The Leviathan with Tentacles of Steel," have shown how increasingly pervasive its effect has been. Because capitalism is both an economic and a social system, it produced a much different economy and society from the one depicted in traditional history. In Kansas the promise of opportunity was experienced by many fewer people than previously thought. Land speculation not only established a market in land, it also intervened between the government and settlers to drive up the price. A large amount of public land went to railroad corporations and was available to settlers only at higher prices. Corporate mining relegated many men to low paying, dangerous wage labor rather than economic independence, and there was a much broader array of work and workers. Farmers, too, suffered from the vagaries of the market, as attested to by both the rise in tenancy in the 1880s and the Populist movement. With unequal access to the riches of the West came inequality in wealth and status, an effect that multiplied over time. This was especially true for people of color who regularly occupied the lowest paying jobs with little hope of mobility. In the face of great hopes of people for opportunity, this result seems tragic. The myth of opportunity has obscured the tragedy from us.[23]

THE ENVIRONMENT AND KANSAS HISTORY

Environmental history has been a major force in the new history. Historians such as Donald Worster and Richard White have taken a more analytical approach toward the study of development, and as a result they often have questioned the idea of progress in economic change. Another way that historians have altered perspectives is in recognizing that the environment was a major actor in Kansas history, in that it set the limits and possibilities of life there. Historians have sought, therefore, to understand how people have dealt with environmental parameters for life.[24]

Worster and others have shocked us into recognition that environmental control has been a central theme regardless of natural limits. They have documented the decimation or destruction of indigenous flora and fauna, the blocking of rivers, the pollution of air and water, the changing shape of the land itself. The Dust Bowl is an excellent case in point. After seventy-five years of farming experience in Kansas,

with research available on the character of the arid Plains environment, some still chose to engage in the Great Plow Up in the 1920s.
Using the new gasoline-powered tractor, farmers plowed up many acres
of prairie never before turned over. When drought came, as it had in
the past, and the winds blew, topsoil disappeared. Farmers had ignored
environmental limits with devastating effects. This aggressive attitude
toward the environment influenced water use as well. Jim Sherow
pointed out that use of the Arkansas River for both irrigation and industrial use caused decrease in river flow, falling ground water levels,
and narrowing of the river channel. People saw water, too, as an object
to be exploited, through engineering, to secure economic growth.
These studies of the human relationship to the environment also are
excellent examples of history that examines both the costs and benefits of development.[25]

For most of Kansas history, one primary cultural cause of all this destruction, according to some revisionist historians, has been the culture
of capitalism. In this culture, plants, animals, water, even the land itself
became objects whose value depended on profits they brought. Other
studies suggest an even broader cultural orientation to power and control. Most settlers saw themselves as an army and resettlement as a victory. As Julie Wilson pointed out, "They harnessed water power, subdued
the tall prairie grasses, and even developed 'artificial forests.'" It was a
common belief that, by plowing up the land and planting crops, they
could increase rainfall and change the climate. They sought, in other
words, to control even the climate. This attitude has persisted in the
twentieth century. Kansans, often in cooperation with the federal government, have built dams to control flooding, diverted rivers to irrigate
crops in arid areas, and reclaimed wetlands for suburban and industrial
development. Currently, irreplaceable fossil water from the Ogallala
aquifer is being pumped to irrigate corn crops and wash the carcasses of
thousands of cattle in the packinghouses in western Kansas.[26]

The environment has not just been acted upon as depicted in traditional history, however. In the new history the environment is seen as
an active force that sets limits and opens up possibilities for life. Studies of recurring droughts show environmental limits. In the drought
years of 1859 to 1861, for example, many farmers failed, and about
one-third of the population left Kansas, as revealed in the author's own
study, "Squatter City: The Social Construction of a New Community in
the American West." Instead of approaching the drought as evidence

of a new kind of environment about which to learn and adjust, most business and political leaders blamed failed crops on the farmers themselves. Because leaders could see no limits to the possibilities of the environment, the cause had to be incompetence. Other examples of the powerful influence of the environment include the death of masses of cattle after overstocking the grasslands, the failure of poor African-American exodusters forced to farm the thin soil of the Flint Hills uplands, or massive failures of farmers in the face of drought and grasshoppers in western Kansas in the 1870s and 1890s.[27]

"Pioneer settlers" pose a particularly interesting case for trying to balance costs and benefits because they hold such a powerful place in traditional history and popular imagination. The idea that there were great environmental costs in agricultural development can seem to be a harsh evaluation of settlers. The pioneers often are revered as people who persevered in the face of daunting hardship, to establish civilization in Kansas and the West on the one hand; and on the other, some environmental historians such as Worster and White point out that theirs also is the story of attempts to control and transform the environment by destroying indigenous grasses and animals and by exposing fragile topsoil to fierce Plains winds. We are the recipients of both traditions and must comprehend the cultural context of each.

A book such as *Sod and Stubble,* a classic story of pioneer life by economist and historian John Ise, allows us to appreciate the hardship in resettlement and the personal characteristics of the "pioneers" who persisted in spite of them. At the same time we can understand the ways settlers sought to control and change their environment. *Sod and Stubble* is an inspiring book about the daunting hardships, sacrifices, and courageous acts necessary to resettle north-central Kansas in the last thirty years of the nineteenth century. Henry and Rosie Ise struggled to grow crops such as corn and wheat on the arid Plains. They fought off the incursions of grasshoppers, the devastation of prairie fires, the power of death-dealing blizzards, and the desolation of drought to become successful German American farmers.

To Rosie, the Plains were a wonderful new world but also a wilderness characterized by the "raw, savage loneliness of the uninhabited prairie." She looked with approval on settlers' attempts to bring order to wilderness, to civilize it. Henry and Rosie replaced the natural grass cover with crops foreign to that country, brought cattle, chickens, and hogs to replace the wild animals, and even tried to change the climate by plowing the land and planting crops and trees they imported. Rather than seeing the natural order of the Plains or even interpreting the Plains as God's creation, they understood their acts of transformation, culturally, as God's will.[28]

Yet the powerful environment set limits to the changes they could make. Aridity made it extremely difficult to raise corn, and periodic droughts brought near starvation to some and failure to others. Invading grasshoppers ate crops down into the ground and finished up on curtains and wooden tools. The environment was a formidable foe, and long before the great Dust Bowl, with most of the natural grass cover destroyed, wind storms blew away the earth they had plowed.

The historian's challenge, of course, is to incorporate both these stories into a more inclusive and complex narrative—to seek a better balance of costs and benefits in our understanding of environmental change in both the past and the present. Environment as a topic helped shape the new approaches to the history of the economy, where efforts to dominate are no longer seen as progress. Historians weigh the costs and benefits of control of the environment as they look at industrial development and damage that may be irrevocable or at the culture of domination that has made adjustment difficult and insufficient. The new history of Kansas and the West, unlike most traditional history, reflects a profound respect for the power of the environment to shape human affairs.

THE ROLE OF THE FEDERAL GOVERNMENT

Kansans, like other westerners, have welcomed federal assistance but have opposed federal direction in their lives. Nevertheless, the role of the federal government has been strong in the state. Subsidies have been willingly accepted for the most part, but federal regulation continues to be resented. The major exception to this pattern was the Populist call for public ownership of major public utilities, such as the railroads.

Kansas was, of course, a creation of the federal government. The Louisiana Purchase in 1803 brought the land under federal ownership and jurisdiction. Congress carved the territory of Kansas out of that purchase in 1854, and in the territorial period federal involvement was necessarily heavy. The chief executive appointed territorial officials, and Congress funded the government. During the short territorial period, the federal government paid for and directed the army, land officers, and Indian agents.

Once Kansas became a state, federal involvement did not end. The role of the army in sweeping tribes from western Kansas is well known. Less well recognized is the ongoing presence of the Bureau of Indian Affairs (BIA) on the state's four remaining reservations and the fact that army posts such as Forts Riley and Leavenworth pumped money into the economy and assisted local development. The federal government gave an enormous subsidy of free lands to get railroads built. By failing to stop free use of the public grasslands by cattleman who appropriated them, the government in essence subsidized cattle ranching.[29]

Traditional history saw the role of the federal government phase out when public lands were in private hands and tribes were on reservations. In contrast, the new history points to a large and important role for the federal government in national parks and monuments, management of unsold public lands and national forests, reclamation, irrigation, damming rivers for flood control or hydroelectric power, and administration of Indian reservations. Unlike other western states, Kansas did not retain large amounts of public land administered by federal agencies. Nevertheless, the role of the federal government in the state at the end of the nineteenth century and the early twentieth century was strong.[30]

The BIA presence continued. The federal government subsidized highway development and began to regulate its character and quality after the invention of the automobile. Kansas resisted federal standards and control of highways, as Mary Scott Rowland showed in "Kansas and the Highways, 1917–1930," but accepted monies to build a modern system. Federal funding also built dams, subsidized irrigation, and reclaimed land in Kansas. For example, the Army Corps of Engineers built dikes to protect the bottoms of Kansas City, Kansas, so that the city could industrialize in that area.[31]

The Great Depression and the New Deal dramatically increased federal involvement in the lives of Kansans. Indeed, during the depression many farmers and bankers would not have survived without federal programs such as the Farm Security Administration and the Production Credit Association. Farm subsidies were crucial to the agricultural sector of the economy for most of the rest of the twentieth century. Social Security, including unemployment insurance, has touched most Kansans since the 1930s.[32]

One of the strongest influences of the federal government on Kansas came in World War II. While industry was important in Kansas before the war, federal subsidy of war industries stimulated great industrial development. Defense contracts bolstered the state's economy beginning in 1940. Credit allowed existing industries such as Boeing Air Craft Company and Beech Aircraft Corporation to expand rapidly. According to historian Robert W. Richmond, the federal government pumped fifty million dollars into the Kansas economy in 1940 alone.[33] The federal imprint was heavy for the entire war. Forts were expanded, munitions plants built, and smaller defense plants went up in many towns. This boost to industrialization irrevocably shifted the Kansas economy toward industrialization and urbanization. Industries encouraged then received further support as a result of the Cold War. Thus the federal presence in Kansas has been profound and long lasting.[34]

A COMPLEX SOCIETY

In traditional histories society was not an organizing concept. Historians tended to write in terms of atomistic individuals who represented a larger expansionist society, pioneers who laid the foundation for later development. Typically the individuals noted were white, male figures such as cowboys, pioneer farmers, prospectors, Pony Express riders, and desperados. Initially these men lived in isolation on farms and ranches except in special circumstances (or cases), such as mining camps or cattle towns. If women were present they were presented as a distinct minority, usually "harpies" and dance hall girls, but some histories noted the presence of pioneer women after the first phase of re-settlement. All these individuals operated in a world of extraordinary opportunity and equality where free grass or gold might bring a handsome fortune. At the least they could acquire farms from free land and become secure yeoman farmers. Failures moved on to try again on the next frontier. When complex society finally evolved, unique western history ended, according to this interpretation, best expressed in Billington's classic *Westward Expansion*.[35]

Groups, a more complex arrangement, did appear in the older narrative from time to time, but usually they were rudimentary and short-lived. The roundup, for example, was a brief, cooperative gathering where cowboys from different ranches separated cattle and branded them to establish ownership. Farmers who settled on isolated claims initially needed no social organization except rules that defined access to property such as claims. If these rules seemed to represent more complex social relationships, that was not explained. When there were sufficient numbers in an area, people did gather together to worship and begin to establish schools. Wagon train members might form an organization for protection, but it dispersed at the end of the trail. Ramshackle towns, outposts at the end of railroad lines, were "peripatetic Gomorrah's" moving with the track crews and disappearing when they completed the railroad. As in the case of individual settlement, the narrative line moved from simple to complex.[36]

When people came together in groups in this older story, some sought order while others were lawless. The older histories typically described them as egalitarian organizations to protect life and property in a social and legal vacuum. The ensuing conflict generated a typical western form of ad hoc social organization. When some squatters faced lawless claim jumpers, fights over claims, and lack of institutions to cope with them, they formed claims clubs, wrote rules, and administered rough justice. Here many historians found the seeds of a later order and democracy. Ranchers, too, appropriated sections of the public domain to run cattle and then defined range rights to give orderly if illegal access to land and water. When "roaring reprobates" threatened that tenuous social order, vigilantism, again a local, improvised, and impermanent social creation to bring order, solved the problem with guns and ropes, then dispersed. In this older story, the individual was supreme, and group organization fleeting. Indeed, it is this local creation of rules and behavior that constituted much of the argument for western uniqueness. When population grew, and permanent, complex organization became necessary, the old West began to disappear.[37]

Society in the old story also was relatively egalitarian. The old West was characterized by the individual search for new wealth in a new land where most if not all migrants could easily acquire it. Although historians mentioned the role of the market in the cattle kingdom, for example, they did not include the complex society of professional cattle drovers, hotel managers, bankers, and railroad managers associated with it. If most farmers got cheap or free farms in the land rush west, the rough economic equality led to greater social equality in this version. Historians did not see success and failure in the race producing a society structured by inequality of wealth.[38]

The social situation in the traditional story was simple in another sense as well. African Americans appeared only as unique figures such as York, the slave of William Clark of Lewis and Clark fame, who amazed Indians, or as frontier trappers such as James Beckworth who joined the Crow tribe. Chinese "coolies" made brief appearances as picturesque, pigtailed workers building transcontinental railroads. Conquered people tended to disappear from the narrative after conquest. Mexican Americans seldom reappeared as farmers, ranchers, cowboys, or even railroad and agricultural workers, after the Mexican-American War. The traditional story became a touchstone for vanished values, not a key to unlock our past or imagine a new future.[39]

Traditional histories of Kansas also are characterized by the same narrow focus and exclusivity. The story of the pioneering experience in the state mirrored the western synthesis previously discussed. Once past the colonizing period, historians focused on gubernatorial administrations and important political movements such as Populism and Progressivism, effectively excluding women and minorities from the story. Significant political activity was assumed to be at the state rather than the local level. This assumption produced an almost exclusive focus on state political and social elites and a very narrow definition of what was political.[40]

Since race was assumed not to play a key role in most state campaigns or in policymaking at the state level, it was seldom mentioned. Because of the unique connection of Kansas with the struggle over slavery, traditional historians did look at race in the 1850s but with a focus on white combatants, not enslaved people and free blacks. Likewise, historians narrated the story of the Great Exodus to Kansas but ignored the contributions of African American people in the larger Kansas society. Although the question of women's rights was debated almost constantly in Kansas, it received only peripheral attention from the traditional historians, and women's roles in the larger society were excluded. Industrialization, wage workers, and strikers all cried out for coverage, but were seldom—or only briefly—addressed. This narrow definition of the proper topics of history decidedly influenced Kansas history to be exclusionary and limited as well. As a result, supposedly well-educated people could exclaim that they had no idea there was segregation in Kansas when *Brown v. Topeka Board of Education* brought national attention in 1954.[41]

Because the new history strives to be inclusive, the population in this depiction is quite diverse. The new West is a place that is female as well as male, African American and Native American as well as Caucasian, and an ethnically diverse society as well. Society is a central part of the new story, and complexity is its hallmark. Instead of a simple, atomistic society of young, white males, early Kansas is a complex society structured by social characteristics of gender, race, class, and ethnicity. Rather than individuals waging a lonely war against the wilderness, we find groups of people, families, church groups, clubs and societies, even corporations, transplanting fundamental social forms that were useful both in resettling Kansas and in long-term structuring of Kansas society.

This diversity has been explored from a number of angles. One has been to determine where and how each of these groups fits into the larger picture of Kansas. Another has been to give voice to their perceptions and perspectives. Still another has been to look at the relationship among these different groups at important cultural crossroads.

Kansas society was not based on rough equality or open, equal access to prestige and power. Inequality in prestige and power has been apparent throughout Kansas history (including the "pioneer" period). Social status often was determined more by factors such as gender, race, class, and ethnicity than by individual ability, personality, or achievement. Access to participation was influenced in the same way. Because of conflicts between different social forms, the meeting of different ethnic and racial groups, and the unwillingness of individuals and groups to accept the place assigned to them, conflict often characterized this society.[42]

THE FAMILY AND GENDER AS DYNAMICS IN KANSAS HISTORY

Families, not individuals, were the essential and persistent unit of Kansas society. Elliott West pointed out that the family has been the center of society in central Kansas for the past eight hundred years. Members of families, acting in "mutual dependence," resettled and transformed society and economy. The majority of the population was made up of farm families.[43]

These families were the center of production and reproduction. Children and women helped in major farming tasks, herded animals, hunted and gathered, made salable products such as butter, cared for

21

chickens and gathered eggs, worked to bring home extra income, preserved food, and cared for the household. In this setting boys were
trained by fathers and girls by mothers in gender-specific roles. Children learned the cooperative behavior needed to make gender roles
work together for the good of the household. They also learned the necessity of reciprocal relationships between the generations that perpetuated farm families. Even after the decline of family farms and the
removal of much production from the household, the family remained
the key unit for reproduction, early childhood development, and so-
cialization. West's depiction of the family contrasts sharply with that
presented in the traditional story.[44]

This new work showed rather quickly that women were major players in a complex society from the beginning of the United States' territorial governance in Kansas. Indeed studying women and gender
opened a new window on Kansas and the West. Initially historians focused on restoring women to history, and they found them populating
farms, ranches, early towns, and mining camps from the beginning.
More recently historians such as Glenda Riley and Nicole Etcheson
have explored how gender structured society.[45]

Women were indisputably a part of what the old history called the pioneer period after Congress formed Kansas Territory. Sometimes they
were partners in the earliest resettlement efforts; at other times they arrived within the first year or two. As previously discussed, married cou-
ples with children, not single males, usually carved out farms, built
towns, opened mining camps, and built ranches. Women, sometimes
single or widowed, also came to Kansas as newspaper reporters, missionaries, schoolteachers, domestics, and even political campaigners.[46]

From the beginning women transplanted a complex society with the
family at its core, but they also started literary and debating societies
and the like to transmit culture, organized library associations to channel the behavior of youth, and fought for different moral standards in
places such as the cattle towns. Middle-class women were at the forefront of the temperance movement throughout the nineteenth century. In such groups as voluntary societies, those middle-class women
also trained themselves for public roles and fought to secure the right
to vote, campaign, and hold office in an unequal society.[47]

These women were important carriers and transmitters of culture to
Kansas. In the resettlement of western Kansas, women created "elegant
dugouts," as historian Angel Kwolek-Folland has pointed out. The

home was a woman's "autonomous cultural creation." This behavior fit nicely with the concept that, although a woman's place was in the private sphere of the home, she designed the cultural character of life there. Women believed that the physical home played a role in character development and change, and the home demonstrated that the family was "civilized." In dugouts women worked to "reproduce the visible symbols of home" important to the idea of civilization. To that end they furnished the dugout with linen, silverware, and fine china. They also furbished it with other objects of cultural significance: organs, bird cages, matching tables and chairs, good books, and flowers. By organizing and furnishing the home with objects that evidenced culture and refinement, Kansas women also transplanted the values and practices in the "essential ideal of the home."[48]

Another way that historians have expanded our knowledge of Kansas and western society is to use gender as a category of analysis. It is clear that gender provided one of the fundamental structures of Kansas society for most of its history. On farms women and men divided work by gender. Both believed that these specialized gender roles were necessary to run a family farm. Children were taught those roles from an early age as they were assigned chores. These gender divisions continued well into the twentieth century and some women resented them sorely. As Julene Bair writes about her 1950s experience in *One Degree West,* "I considered myself a tomboy and resented my brother's comparative freedom. My family and our society placed more value on men's work than on women's work."[49]

Gender also divided public and private worlds. Men negotiated the public world of business while women were more restricted to the private world of home. As historians point out, men generally went to town to market crops and controlled that income, while women's work was ordinarily unpaid labor. The same was true in towns and cities across Kansas. The main exception to this role was women in domestic service, often African-American and ethnic women. Censuses and city directories indicate few jobs were available to women; the ones that did exist were usually low paying and low status.[50]

The legal places defined for men and women in Kansas demonstrate another way that society was structured by gender. Initially the common law governed gender roles in territorial Kansas. It defined gender roles differently and unequally. When women married they became "dead in the law." They could not own businesses, sign contracts, sue or be sued. Any property a woman brought into marriage came under the control of her husband. Typically, the man would receive custody of children in a divorce, and the terms of divorce were generally easier for men than women. Single women had to have a legal "friend" in business situations or when dealing with property. In addition, women in territorial Kansas could not vote or hold office. By these legal definitions men and women did not have the same legal or political rights or the same access to political and economic power. This political and legal position also defined their social position as decidedly inferior under the law.[51] Women of different classes, ethnicities, and races were affected in different ways, however.

Another way of seeing the importance of gender ideology in structuring society is to look at major ongoing efforts to change it. Many women and like-minded men recognized how ideas about gender led to unequal places in social structure. Clarina Nichols and allies such as Augustus Wattles and the Moneka Women's Rights Association used the debates over the new state constitution in 1859 to secure greater legal equality for women. Nichols also risked arrest to prove the unfairness of child custody laws and decisions. In addition to more equality in this area of law, activists succeeded in getting more property rights for women and the right for them to vote in school board elections written into the Wyandotte Constitution. Lyn Bennett's study of divorce in Kansas suggests that the changes embodied in the constitution did not alter completely the unequal treatment of women in the courts.[52]

Four times in the nineteenth century and once in the twentieth, mostly middle-class women campaigned for greater political rights in Kansas society. The first campaigns in 1867 on two referenda to give the vote to women and African Americans failed after an arduous contest. In the 1880s women made the right to vote in municipal elections a moral reform by tying it to temperance, and they secured that suffrage in 1887. After an attempt, supported by the Populists in 1894, to attain complete suffrage failed, the Kansas Equal Suffrage Association spearheaded another attempt in 1911. The campaign succeeded in 1912. Not long after, the United States ratified the Nineteenth Amendment extending suffrage to women across the country. The fight for the Equal Rights Amendment in the 1970s reflected the continuing unequal structure of society in Kansas.[53]

Another more radical campaign to change gender ideology was conducted by the "sex radicals" in the 1880s, as explored by Hal Sears in

The Sex Radicals. This was a group led by Moses Harman, Elmina Slenker, and Lois Waisbrooker, who regarded marriage as a state-defined institution that harmed women. They published a newspaper, *Lucifer the Light-Bearer,* that printed letters about the abuse of women in marriage. Because the letters to Lucifer contained sexually explicit descriptions, the government prosecuted and convicted Harman of sending "pornography" through the federal mail. Harman also urged women to follow the example of his own daughter and leave both church and state out of their marriages. The "sex radicals" opened up the question of the inequality of women under the marriage laws.[54]

Each of these movements strove to change the gendered structure of Kansas society. Proponents thought the structure made women's social place inferior to that of men. More is needed, but in recent years stories of women's participation, legal restrictions on their rights, and all the fights to change the nature of society have become fundamental to the new narrative.

RACE, ETHNICITY, AND CLASS IN KANSAS AND THE WEST

Race, too, was a key ingredient in Kansas society in both the nineteenth and twentieth centuries. This may seem surprising since the older view depicted Kansas and the West as having few African Americans or other peoples of color. There also was the myth that, in Kansas, freedom for African Americans was won during the Bleeding Kansas period. This myth seems to have discouraged people from looking at community formation, discrimination, or the place of African Americans in the social structure.[55] But the new history presented a very different "take" on race and society.

In this view, race was crucial in structuring Kansas society. Discrimination ensured that African Americans were at the bottom of the social ladder. Although antislavery warriors rid Kansas of slavery in the 1850s, the state constitution they wrote created second-class citizenship for African Americans. Under the Wyandotte Constitution, African Americans could not vote in the new state, join the militia, bear arms, or serve on juries. In an election in 1867 to change the constitution so that they could vote and hold office, Kansas voters said no. During the Reconstruction Era there was a brief respite from the exclusion, but the old pattern soon returned.[56]

One sees this social structure quite clearly in the work of James C. Carper on school segregation. Although most Kansans believed that African Americans should receive free public education, they were divided over its form. With few exceptions, state legislatures over time established a legal basis for segregation in schools. Notably, even where the legislature did not allow it, communities segregated anyway. The recurring debates over school segregation show a deeply divided culture on the question of race and social relations. There was no fundamental change in this pattern of school segregation over time. If anything the divide deepened because African Americans gradually concentrated in cities where segregation in the elementary grades was permissible. This pattern was still firmly in place in 1954. Because education offered one of the best avenues for potential African-American social mobility, school segregation was a key factor in structuring and maintaining inequality in Kansas based on race.[57]

In spite of attempts to change this situation in some periods and places, segregation even deepened. At the University of Kansas, African Americans attended from 1870 on. They could not live in campus dormitories, were barred from dances, band, glee club and pep clubs, and often had to sit at the back of classrooms, but for a time at least, experienced some measure of integration in athletics, for example. In the early twentieth century, however, as Kristine M. McCusker and other historians have demonstrated, some leading figures there instituted new segregationist measures. Under Forest C. "Phog" Allen and with the support of Chancellors Frank Strong and Ernest H. Lindley, black athletes were excluded from varsity athletic teams, and black students were not allowed to use the previously integrated swimming pool. In 1927 Chancellor Lindley segregated the student cafeteria.[58]

Opponents of segregation did not keep silent and inactive. Court cases in 1881 and 1903 challenged but failed to halt segregation. In 1881 the Kansas Supreme Court held that segregation in smaller cities had not been authorized by the legislature but left segregation of primary schools in first-class cities intact. Many smaller cities, towns, and rural areas continued to segregate primary schools unless directly challenged. In 1903 segregation in Kansas schools was confirmed in *Reynolds v. Board of Education of the City of Topeka*. Soldiers and veterans of World War II attempted unsuccessfully to institute in Kansas the values they fought for in Europe. Then black Topekans and the NAACP finally succeeded in winning a case as part of the larger fight against segregation in 1954 in *Brown v. Topeka Board of Education*.[59]

Forms of discrimination continue in Kansas today. Numerous newspaper articles attest to ongoing de facto segregation in some schools and to the powerful role of race in structuring Kansas society. This new picture of race presents a very different Kansas and West. Clearly there has been a persistent structural inequality in Kansas society based in part on race, and we can only hope that the "new" historians of the twenty-first century will continue to enhance the narrative and deepen our understanding of this complex issue.

Ethnicity, too, has been central to Kansas society, but in ways different from gender, race, and class. Older histories saw ethnicity as a quickly passing phenomenon because immigrants adapted both to American life and to frontier wilderness life. They were then assimilated into the larger society. Thus the wilderness forged a homogeneous although unique society in the old story. One of the hallmarks of the society was its openness, its fostering of social mobility. This picture of ethnic groups obviously focuses on white ethnics to the exclusion of others, ignores pre-existing societies, and anticipates the rather rapid extinguishing of ethnic differences. These traditional histories presented the ethnic experience primarily from the point of view of the larger society and glorified assimilation of immigrants.[60]

The older story is based in part on the mistaken assumption that most immigrants came from western Europe. Between 1850 and 1890 most immigrants did indeed come from England, Ireland, Wales, Germany, and the Scandinavian countries. Germans from Russia represent an interesting exception to the pattern. Small communities as well as individuals also arrived from France, Holland, Belgium and Canada. Beginning in the 1880s, however, new migrations came primarily from eastern and southern Europe and Mexico.[61]

These new groups settled in the mining areas of southeastern Kansas and the industrializing cities of the Northeast. Mexicans, whose numbers increased in the twentieth century, moved to areas of sugar beet farming and processing, meatpacking, or railroad shops. Imagine the complexity when such diverse populations had to negotiate relations with each other as well as with members of the larger society. This diversity and complexity were intensified in the twentieth century by the addition of greater numbers of ethnic people of color from Latin America and Asia.[62]

The new history includes these diverse groups and incorporates their experiences and perspectives. In this way ethnicity offers a different look at Kansas society. Because most immigrants chose to live with people from the same countries who spoke the same language, they formed many rural communities characterized by their own symbols, institutions, and cultures, creating a pattern of diverse communities across the state. These communities retained their distinctiveness well into the twentieth century and many, such as the Mennonites, remain distinct. At the same time, some groups such as the Mexicans chose to form distinct sub-communities in larger towns and cities. Thus the making of a diverse and complex society has been an ongoing process.[63]

Newer studies gave us this perspective because they examined ethnicity in Kansas differently. Historians began with countries of origin to see how much of their culture and society emigrants were able to transport to Kansas. Linguists such as J. Neale Carman, who published his valuable research in the early 1960s, documented the persistence of languages. We began to pay more attention to the perspectives of immigrants themselves—to let them speak for themselves.[64] Finally, historians began to see that ethnic groups could accommodate to the larger society in some ways yet retain distinctive cultures in others.

One unusual example of this process comes from the work of historian Joseph B. Herring. He studied a wide range of Native American communities that used selective accommodation and resistance to prevent removal from Kansas. One group was led by the Kickapoo prophet Kennekuk, who fashioned a religion that exhibited Christian characteristics yet was based on deeply held native beliefs. A study of Potawatomi resistance to allotment by an anonymous author supports Herring's argument by showing how the Potawatomi used both old rituals and new practices such as petitions to resist.[65] Distinctive Potawatomi and Kickapoo communities remain on reservations in Kansas today.

When one looks at ethnicity after the resettlement of Kansas by Euro-Americans, one can see that immigrants chose to cluster with people of the same culture whenever possible. They added a pattern of large numbers of distinct communities to the society in both rural and urban areas in every county in Kansas and refute the idea of a single Kansas culture. Some of the better known of these were formed by Germans from Russia, Swedes at Lindsborg, or Czechs at Wilson, but Carman's linguistic maps show that community clustering was pervasive and included a wide range of ethnic groups.[66]

In Osborne County, for example, Germans with quite disparate origins formed a rural community in the 1860s described in marvelous detail by John Ise in *Sod and Stubble*. Some members of this community were first-generation immigrants from Germany mingled with second-generation sons and daughters of others. The community also contained Pennsylvania Dutch. In a different migration altogether, Mennonite Germans from Russia purchased a large amount of railroad land in the 1870s so they could cluster together and reproduce a pattern of villages with outlying fields. They successfully perpetuated a distinctive culture based on religion. Swedes formed a company in Chicago and founded an exclusive utopian community based on ethnicity and religion, with a particular concept of salvation at the center. Throughout the state, French, Welsh, Swedes, Bohemians, English, Italians, and other nationalities fashioned communities of ethnic people with their distinct languages.[67]

In cities, ethnic groups formed cohesive subcommunities. Instead of assimilating into the larger society, Germans in Atchison, according to Eleanor Turk, deliberately built a viable subcommunity within the larger society. The "unifying social center" of the Atchison German community was the Turnverein, a political and sport club. They established their own Catholic churches and schools, supported a German-language newspaper, and organized their own antislavery militia company. They even created a special holiday to celebrate the birthday of the German poet Schiller. These German people created a separate social structure with permanent institutions that were long-lived, according to Turk. After World War I their separateness and distinctiveness declined.[68]

At the same time, the Germans were connected to the larger community. Some ran for office; others formed a community-wide choral society. As noted above, they fought in the political conflict over slavery. This participation was not without conflict or cost. Newspapers tended to depict them as comical stereotypes. The issue of Sunday drinking at beer gardens became quite controversial, but the Germans were able to effect a compromise. Indeed they were critical of some social aspects of that community, in particular its marriage and child-rearing practices. Ethnic subcommunities like this appeared in many towns and cities and constituted a major aspect of a diverse nineteenth-century Kansas society.[69]

In the last third of that century several new groups came to Kansas, particularly to the southeastern mining regions and the urbanizing area around Kansas City, Kansas. Some were from the British Isles, but the majority came from eastern and southern Europe. Italians, Slovenians, Belgians, and French were mixed in the camps, making it difficult to form separate institutions such as schools or churches. Social forms beyond the family were dominated by the mining companies. Kansas City, Kansas, was an intensely polyglot area. By the early twentieth century more than twenty-five different ethnic groups populated the regions, including people from Greece, Mexico, Czechoslovakia, Yugoslavia, and Russia, living in their own neighborhoods near the major packing plants and other industries near the Kaw River. Specific churches such as St. Cyril and Methodius Catholic Church (Slovak) marked the neighborhoods.[70]

The importance of ethnicity did not cease with the nineteenth century, however. Several changes did occur in the patterns of ethnic origins. The new history recognizes the important role new groups such as Mexicans and Indochinese as well as the people from eastern and southern Europe played in Kansas history. As Robert Oppenheimer has pointed out, the largest Mexican barrios were in Kansas City, Topeka, Emporia, Wichita, and Garden City. Mexicans experienced discrimination because they were people of color as well as ethnic. "Until the 1950s, in virtually every Kansas town and city, Mexicans and Mexican-Americans remained segregated in movie theaters and were often restricted from some sections of city parks, churches, and other public facilities." Mexicans were concentrated in low-paying, unskilled work, such as railroad section gangs, sugar beet field labor, and meatpacking. Unlike other ethnic groups, Mexicans were fired from jobs and repatriated to Mexico during the Great Depression at the urging of Governor Clyde Reed.[71]

At the same time, Mexicans created their own communities with the Catholic church at the center. The sense of community was particularly apparent in the 1930s depression when Mexican workers split jobs among themselves. In Garden City one woman ran an open house, providing meals and shelter. Distinct Mexican communities remain today.[72]

More recently diversity has been enhanced by the immigration of Indochinese, whom Kansans also regarded as people of color. They formed subcommunities in meatpacking towns such as Garden City and Dodge City since the 1970s. The work of Donald Stull and Michael Broadway has explained their experience particularly in the packinghouses. In Garden City they work in unskilled jobs on the bloody cutting room floor where wages are low and the accident rates high. The character of their communities has yet to be explored thoroughly, but their cultures and their treatment by the larger society reflect long-term, persistent patterns in ethnicity in Kansas. Diversity and complexity continue to be major characteristics of Kansas society.[73]

Perhaps the most surprising part of the new story of society comes from the evidence on class. Not only did Kansas have a middle class, but a working class also helped define Kansas society, and it was a part of that society from the beginning of resettlement and before natives were removed. For example, the transcontinental railroad passed through Kansas by 1870, before resettlers came in many areas. During the next twenty years feeder lines webbed the state. Railroad companies immediately established shops every few hundred miles and populated them with wage workers to repair the running stock. Much of the work was hazardous. Gangs of unskilled wage laborers also worked out of these towns and repaired tracks.[74] This working class had parallels in other parts of the state.

In southeastern Kansas, mining began only a few years after the land was opened to resettlement. The miners lived in twenty polyglot mining camps. The 7,562 men employed there in the early twentieth century were idle about one-third of each year. The shared work culture fueled unionism and strikes. Here was a concentrated population of working-class people engaged in a high-risk occupation for low wages with little power to control their fortunes.[75]

Kansas suddenly became aware of the working class during strikes against the railroad in 1877 and 1883. At first, according to Joseph Tripp, the workers' demand for better wages received general support, but conflict soon became a confrontation between labor and capital. Further strikes, particularly the one in 1920–1921, affirmed the existence of a working class, and the creation of the Industrial Court demonstrated the statewide opposition to strikes. The "Red Scare" after World War I further enhanced mistrust of the highly ethnic working class, but, as historian Ann Schofield and others have demonstrated, the strikes show the importance of the work culture and the strength of union organizing in Kansas.[76]

One notable feature of the coal miner's strike was a women's march. In solidarity with the strikers, women from several ethnic groups joined together to protest the use of "scabs" to work the mines. They saw themselves as marching to protect the family wage. In their eyes, the struggle to earn a living wage was linked to American ideals of justice and democracy, but theirs was a working-class definition of those ideals. Other Kansans depicted them as a frightening "army of amazons."[77]

The working-class component of society did not disappear as the state moved toward mid-century. Rather it grew proportionately with urbanization and industrialization. Areas of particular importance were oil field development, airplane production, and meatpacking. The great expansion of federally subsidized airplane construction during World War II drew many new wage workers to Kansas. The state's economy became truly a mixed one as a result of these wartime developments, and industrial production became increasingly significant; nevertheless, the legislature affirmed its anti-union stance in 1956 by passing a right-to-work law. One can see its impact, as Stull and Broadway pointed out, in the accident-riddled meatpacking industry today.[78]

CONCLUSION

Society in Kansas was far more complex than that depicted in the traditional histories where social simplicity gradually evolved into intricacy. The new story depicts complexity and diversity from the beginning. Instead of an open, egalitarian society where the opportunity for social mobility was unlimited, there was a society structured by gender, race, class, and ethnicity. The inequalities in the structure were hotly contested at times, sometimes with success as in the case of the fight against women's legal and political disabilities. In the case of peoples of color, society has changed much less and even more slowly.

These differences between the older view of society and the newer one are emblematic of the larger differences discussed in this essay. The new history has brought us different stories, new actors, fresh images of Kansas. If they are not all pleasing, they do reflect a recognition that life past and present is complex, a study in shades of gray, rarely black and white. Kansas history has not always been a story of progress, but careful analysis will let us distinguish more carefully between what we can praise and what we need to correct. This new knowledge has yarn of many colors with which to weave our future.

NOTES

1. Important books and articles that represent this new perspective in western history include: Patricia Limerick, *The Legacy of Conquest: The Unbroken Past of the American West* (New York: W. W. Norton and Co., 1987); Richard White, *"It's Your Misfortune and None of My Own": A New History of the American West* (Norman: University of Oklahoma Press, 1991); Donald Worster, *Under Western Skies: Nature and History in the American West* (New York: Oxford University Press, 1992); Worster, *The Wealth of Nature: Environmental History and the Ecological Imagination* (New York: Oxford University Press, 1993); William G. Robbins, *Colony and Empire: The Capitalist Transformation of the American West* (Lawrence: University Press of Kansas, 1994); John Mack Faragher, "The Frontier Trail: Rethinking Turner and Reimagining the American West," *American Historical Review* 98 (February 1993): 106–17; John Wunder, "What's Old About the New Western History: Race and Gender," *Pacific Northwest Quarterly* 85 (April 1994): 50–58.

2. Elizabeth Jameson and Susan Armitage, "Editors' Introduction," in *Writing the Range: Race, Class, and Culture in the Women's West,* ed. Elizabeth Jameson and Susan Armitage (Norman: University of Oklahoma Press, 1997), 3–16; Patricia Limerick, Clyde Milner II, and Charles E. Rankin, eds., *Trails: Toward a New Western History* (Lawrence: University Press of Kansas, 1991); Valerie J. Matsumoto and Blake Allmendringer, eds., *Over the Edge: Remapping the American West* (Berkeley: University of California Press, 1999); Clyde Milner II, *A New Significance: Re-envisioning the History of the American West* (New York: Oxford University Press, 1996); Donald Worster, "New West, True West: Interpreting the Region's History," *Western Historical Quarterly* 18 (April 1987): 141–56.

3. Walter Prescott Webb, *The Great Plains* (Boston: Ginn and Co., 1931), 47–84; Frederick Merk, *History of the Westward Movement* (New York: Alfred A. Knopf, 1978).

4. Kenneth Davis, *Kansas: A Bicentennial History* (New York: W. W. Norton and Co., 1976), 7, 12–15.

5. Donald L. Fixico, "Ethics and Responsibilities in American Indian History," *American Indian Quarterly* 20 (1996): 29–39; Preston Holder, *The Hoe and the Horse on the Plains: A Study of Cultural Development Among North American Indians* (Lincoln: University of Nebraska Press, 1970); Gene Weltfish, *The Lost Universe: Pawnee Life and Culture* (Lincoln: University of Nebraska Press, 1965, 1977); Richard White, "The Cultural Landscape of the Pawnees," *Great Plains Quarterly* 2 (Winter 1982): 31–40; Elliott West, *The Way to the West: Essays on the Central Plains* (Albuquerque: University of New Mexico Press, 1995).

6. White, "The Cultural Landscape of the Pawnees," 31–40; James E. Sherow, "Workings of the Geodialectic: High Plains Indians and Their Horses in the Region of the Arkansas River Valley, 1800–1870," *Environmental History Review* 16 (Summer 1992): 61–84; Dan Flores, "Bison Ecology and Bison Diplomacy: The Southern Plains from 1888 to 1950," *Journal of American History* 78 (September 1991): 465–85.

33

7. Weltfish, *The Lost Universe,* 10–60, 79–87, 166; Waldo Wedel, "Native Astronomy and the Plains Caddoans," in *Native American Astronomy,* ed. Anthony F. Aveni (Austin: University of Texas Press, 1977).

8. Karl Schlesier, "The Rise of the Tsitsistas," in *Wolves of Heaven: Cheyenne Shamanism, Ceremonies, and Prehistoric Origins* (Norman: University of Oklahoma Press, 1987), 74–87; John I. Moore, *The Cheyenne Nation: A Social and Demographic History* (Lincoln: University of Nebraska Press, 1987); Karl Llewellyn and E. Adamson Hoebel, *The Cheyenne Way: Conflict and Case Law in Primitive Jurisprudence* (Norman: University of Oklahoma Press, 1941); West, *The Way to the West,* 15–17, 19, 67.

9. Webb, *The Great Plains,* 47–84; Moore, *The Cheyenne Nation,* 172–73; Flores, "Bison Ecology and Bison Diplomacy," 482–83; Sherow, "Workings of the Geodialectic," 58–83.

10. Kenneth S. Lynn, "Extending the Republic," *Times Literary Supplement,* March 12, 1982, 272; Frederick Merk, *Manifest Destiny and Mission in American History: A Reinterpretation* (New York: Vintage Books, 1963); Davis, *Kansas: A Bicentennial History,* 101–6.

11. Holder, *The Hoe and the Horse on the Plains,* 68–69; Donald J. Lehmer "Epidemics Among the Indians of the Upper Missouri," *Reprints in Anthropology* 8 (1977): 105–11; William E. Unrau, "The Depopulation of the Dheghia-Siouan Kansa Prior to Removal," *New Mexico Historical Review* 48 (October 1973): 313–28; Richard White, *Roots of Dependency: Subsistence, Environment, and Social Change Among the Choctaws, Pawnees, and Navajos* (Lincoln: University of Nebraska Press, 1983), 145–46, 189–92, 204; Joseph B. Herring, *The Enduring Indians of Kansas: A Century and a Half of Acculturation* (Lawrence: University Press of Kansas, 1990).

12. Joseph B. Herring, "The Chippewa and Munsee Indians: Acculturation and Survival in Kansas, 1850s–1870," *Kansas History: A Journal of the Central Plains* 6 (Winter 1983–1984): 212–20. The Prairie Band of Potawatomis also were no strangers to the power of white expansion or the need to find strategies to resist. See "The Prairie Potawatomi Resistance to Allotment," *Indian Historian* 9 (Fall 1976): 27–31.

13. Sylvia Van Kirk, *Many Tender Ties: Woman in Fur-Trade Society, 1670–1870* (Norman: University of Oklahoma Press, 1980); John Mack Faragher, "American, Mexican, Metis: A Community Approach to the Comparative Study of North American Frontiers," in *Under an Open Sky: Rethinking America's Western Past,* ed. William Cronon, George Miles, and Jay Gitlin (New York: W. W. Norton and Co., 1992), 90–109; Charles E. Hoffhaus, *Chez Les Canses: Three Centuries at Kawsmouth: The French Foundations of Metropolitan Kansas City* (Kansas City: Lowell Press, 1984).

14. David Emmons, *Garden in the Grasslands: Boomer Literature of the Central Plains* (Lincoln: University of Nebraska Press, 1971); Julie Wilson, "'Kansas Uber Alles!' The Geography and Ideology of Conquest, 1820–1900," *Western Historical Quarterly* 27 (Summer 1996): 171–87.

15. A major book that reflects the older perspective is Ray Allen Billington, *West-*

ward Expansion: A History of the American Frontier (New York: Macmillan Co., 1960). For Kansas, see William Frank Zornow, *Kansas: A History of the Jayhawk State* (Norman: University of Oklahoma Press, 1957); Davis, *Kansas: A Bicentennial History;* Robert W. Richmond, *Kansas: A Land of Contrasts* (Arlington Heights, Ill.: Forum Press, 1974).

16. William Cronon, *Nature's Metropolis: Chicago and the Great West* (New York: W. W. Norton and Co., 1991); White, *"It's Your Misfortune and None of My Own,"* 236–97.

17. Rita G. Napier, "The Spirit of Speculation: A Study of Town Site Preemption and Land Use in Four Frontier Kansas Towns" (master's thesis, American University, 1969); Cronon, *Nature's Metropolis;* Robert R. Dykstra, *The Cattle Towns: A Social History of the Kansas Cattle Trading Centers Abilene, Ellsworth, Wichita, Dodge City and Caldwell, 1867 to 1885* (New York: Alfred A. Knopf, 1968); John W. Reps, *The Forgotten Frontier: Urban Planning in the American West Before 1890* (Columbia: University of Missouri Press, 1981).

18. Donald Worster, *The Dust Bowl: The Southern Plains in the 1930s* (New York: Oxford University Press, 1979); Gilbert C. Fite, *The Farmer's Frontier, 1865–1900* (New York: Holt, Rinehart and Winston, 1966); George E. Hasse and Robin Higham, eds., *Rise of the Wheat State: A History of Kansas Agriculture, 1861–1986* (Manhattan, Kans.: Sunflower University Press, 1987); H. Craig Miner, *West of Wichita: Settling the High Plains of Kansas, 1865-1890* (Lawrence: University Press of Kansas, 1986), 52–66, 119–31; Homer E. Socolofsky, *Landlord William Scully* (Lawrence: University Press of Kansas, 1979).

19. The best general description of corporate family farms, although not in Kansas, is Kathleen Conzen, "Peasant Pioneers," in *The Countryside in the Age of Capitalist Transformation: Essays in the Social History of Rural America,* ed. Stephen Hahn and Jonathan Prude (Chapel Hill: University of North Carolina Press, 1985). John Stitz describes this kind of family farming in his dissertation "A Study of Farm Family Culture in Ellis County, Kansas, and the Relationship of the Culture to Trends in Farming" (Ph.D. diss., University of Kansas, 1983). The author's students at the University of Kansas have located contracts in county courthouses made by corporate families to cement the relationships between generations.

20. James H. Ducker, *Men of the Steel Rails: Workers on the Atchison, Topeka and Santa Fe Railroad, 1869–1900* (Lincoln: University of Nebraska Press, 1983); Thomas R. Walther and Robert K. Ratslaff, "Industrialization on the Frontier: A Case Study, Crawford County, Kansas, 1870–1914," *Red River Historical Review* 6 (Fall 1981): 15–23; John G. Clark, *Towns and Minerals in Southeastern Kansas: A Study in Regional Industrialization, 1890–1930,* State Geological Survey of Kansas, Special Distribution Publication 52 (Lawrence: University of Kansas, 1970); Richmond, *Kansas: A Land of Contrasts,* 270; White, *"It's Your Misfortune and None of My Own,"* 496–531.

21. Eva Lash Atkinson, "Kansas City's Livestock Trade and Packing Industry,

1870–1914: A Study in Regional Growth" (Ph.D. diss., University of Kansas, 1971); Margaret Walsh, *The Rise of the Midwestern Meat Packing Industry* (Lexington: University Press of Kentucky, 1982); Donald D. Stull and Michael J. Broadway, "The Effects of Restructuring on Beefpacking in Kansas," *Kansas Business Review* 14 (Fall 1990): 10–16.

22. Stull and Broadway, "The Effects of Restructuring on Beefpacking in Kansas," 14–15.

23. Worster, *Under Western Skies*, 13–14; Napier, "The Spirit of Speculation"; Paul W. Gates, *Fifty Million Acres: Conflicts over Kansas Land Policy 1854–1890* (Ithaca, N.Y.: Cornell University Press, 1954), 106–52; Ann Schofield, "The Women's March: Miners, Family, and Community in Pittsburgh, Kansas, 1921–22," *Kansas History: A Journal of the Central Plains* 7 (Summer 1984): 159–68; Thomas Frank, "The Leviathan with Tentacles of Steel: Railroads in the Minds of Kansas Populists," *Western Historical Quarterly* 20 (February 1989): 37–54; Dykstra, *The Cattle Towns*, 11–111; Randall Woods, "Integration, Exclusion, or Segregation? The 'Color Line' in Kansas, 1878–1900," *Western Historical Quarterly* 14 (April 1983): 181–98.

24. Richard White, "American Environmental History: The Development of a New Historical Field," *Pacific Historical Review* 54 (August 1985): 297–335; "A Round Table: Environmental History," *Journal of American History* 76 (March 1990): 1087–147; Donald Worster, "Doing Environmental History," in *The Ends of the Earth: Perspectives on Modern Environmental History,* ed. Donald Worster (New York: Cambridge University Press, 1988), 289–307; William Cronon, "The Uses of Environmental History," *Environmental History Review* 17 (Fall 1993): 1–22.

25. Worster, *The Dust Bowl;* Wilson, "'Kansas Uber Alles!'" 170–87; Richard White, "Animals and Enterprise," in *The Oxford History of the American West,* ed. Clyde A. Milner, Carol A. O'Conner, and Martha A. Sandweiss (New York: Oxford University Press, 1994), 237–73; James E. Sherow, "The Contest for the 'Nile of America': *Kansas v. Colorado* (1907)," *Great Plains Quarterly* 10 (Winter 1990): 48–61; Sherow, *Watering the Valley: Development Along the High Plains Arkansas River* (Lawrence: University Press of Kansas, 1990).

26. Emmons, *Garden in the Grassland;* Annette Kolodny, *The Lay of the Land: Metaphor as Experience and History in American Life and Letters* (Chapel Hill: University of North Carolina Press, 1975); Wilson, "'Kansas Uber Alles!'" 172–73; Worster, "The Dirty Thirties: A Study in Agricultural Capitalism," *Great Plains Quarterly* 6 (Spring 1986): 107–16; Eugene D. Fleharty, *Wild Animals and Settlers on the Great Plains* (Norman: University of Oklahoma Press, 1995); Jay Antle, "Against Kansas's Top Dog: Coyotes, Politics, and Ecology, 1877–1970," *Kansas History: A Journal of the Central Plains* 20 (Autumn 1997): 160–75; Michael A. French, "'The Strategic Middle Route': Planning and Developing the Fairfax Industrial District, 1922–1946" (seminar paper, University of Kansas, 1993), private collection of Rita G. Napier, Lawrence, Kans.; Stull and Broadway, "The Effects of Restructuring on Beefpacking in Kansas," 11.

27. Rita G. Napier, "Squatter City: The Social Construction of a New Community in the American West" (Ph.D. diss., American University, 1976); Joseph Hickey, "(Pap) Singleton's Dunlap Colony: Relief Agencies and the Failure of a Black Settlement in Eastern Kansas," *Great Plains Quarterly* 11 (Winter 1991): 23–36; Miner, *West of Wichita,* 52–66, 119–31. For an earlier study of recurring drought and dust, see James C. Malin, "Dust Storms: Part One, 1850–1860," *Kansas Historical Quarterly* 14 (May 1946): 129; ibid., "Part Two, 1861–1880" (August 1946): 265; ibid., "Part Three, 1881–1900" (November 1946): 297.

28. John Ise, *Sod and Stubble* (Lincoln: University of Nebraska Press, 1968), 2, 9, 14, 15, 67, 70, 74, 115, 254.

29. James Clifton, *The Prairie People: Continuity and Change in Potawatomi Indian Culture, 1665–1965* (Lawrence: Regents Press of Kansas, 1977); William Dobak, *Fort Riley and Its Neighbors: Military, Money, and Economic Growth, 1853–1895* (Norman: University of Oklahoma Press, 1998); Homer Socolofsky and Huber Self, *Historical Atlas of Kansas* (Norman: University of Oklahoma Press, 1988), 31.

30. White, *"It's Your Misfortune and None of My Own,"* 57–59.

31. Mary Scott Rowland, "Kansas and the Highways, 1917–1930," *Kansas History: A Journal of the Central Plains* 5 (Spring 1982): 33–51; Paul G. Sutter, "Paved with Good Intentions: Good Roads, the Automobile, and the Rhetoric of Rural Improvement in the Kansas Farmer, 1890–1914," ibid., 18 (Winter 1995–1996): 284–99; French, "'The Strategic Middle Route,'" 16–19, 22–28.

32. Peter Fearon, "From Self-Help to Federal Aid: Unemployment and Relief in Kansas, 1929–1932," *Kansas History: A Journal of the Central Plains* 13 (Summer 1990): 107–23; R. Douglas Hurt, "Prices, Payments, and Production: Kansas Wheat Farmers and the Agricultural Adjustment Administration, 1933–1939," ibid., 23 (Spring–Summer 2000): 72–87; Richmond, *Kansas: A Land of Contrasts,* 252–54, 258–59.

33. Richmond, *Kansas: A Land of Contrasts,* 270; French, "'The Strategic Middle Route,'" 28–30.

34. Richmond, *Kansas: A Land of Contrasts,* 270; Peter Fearon, "Ploughshares into Airplanes: Manufacturing Industry and Workers in Kansas During World War II," *Kansas History: A Journal of the Central Plains* 22 (Winter 1999–2000): 298–314; Patrick G. O'Brien, "Kansas at War: The Home Front, 1941–1945," *Kansas History: A Journal of the Central Plains* 17 (Spring 1994): 6–25.

35. Billington's *Westward Expansion* is a major but certainly not the only example of this approach.

36. Webb, *The Great Plains,* 255–60; Allan Bogue, "The Iowa Claims Clubs: Symbol and Substance," *Mississippi Valley Historical Review* 45 (September 1958): 231–53; Billington, *Westward Expansion,* 647.

37. Bogue, "The Iowa Claims Club," 231–53; Billington, *Westward Expansion,* 680–83, 623–24.

38. Billington, *Westward Expansion,* 1–11, 748.

39. Billington's 1960 edition of *Westward Expansion* does not even have an index entry for women; there are no references to Mexicans after the war with Mexico; and, once Indians were forced onto reservations, references to them virtually disappear from this major textbook on western history.

40. For example, chapter 11 of Richmond, *Kansas: A Land of Contrasts,* covers political campaigns and the administrations of governors James M. Harvey, Thomas A. Osborn, George T. Anthony, John P. St. John, George W. Glick, John A. Martin, Lyman Humphrey, Cyrus Leland, Lorenzo D. Lewelling, and John W. Leedy.

41. This conclusion is based on a survey of textbooks in Kansas history. See, for example, Richmond, *Kansas: A Land of Contrasts,* 61–78, 170, 171, 192, 214, 227, 297–98; Davis, *Kansas: A Bicentennial History,* 76, 89, 97, 117–118, 143, 150, 152, 154, 181.

42. No one source summarizes society in the new history of Kansas. This interpretation is based primarily on a survey of articles published during the past thirty-five years. Representative articles and relevant books are cited in notes 42–77.

43. Elliott West, "The Story of Three Families," *Kansas History: A Journal of the Central Plains* 19 (Summer 1996): 112–23.

44. Elliot West, *Growing Up with the Country: Childhood on the Far Western Frontier* (Albuquerque: University of New Mexico Press, 1989), 247.

45. Nicole Etcheson, "'Labouring for the Freedom of the Territory': Free-State Kansas Women in the 1850s," *Kansas History: A Journal of the Central Plains* 21 (Spring 1998): 68–87; Julie Roy Jeffrey, *Frontier Women: The Trans-Mississippi West, 1840–1880* (New York: Hill and Wang, 1979); Glenda Riley, *The Female Frontier: A Comparative View of Women on the Prairie and the Plains* (Lawrence: University Press of Kansas, 1988); Ann Schofield, "An 'Army of Amazons': The Language of Protest in a Kansas Mining Community, 1921–22," *American Quarterly* 37 (Winter 1985): 686–701.

46. "Letters of John and Sarah Everett, 1854–1864," *Kansas Historical Quarterly* 8 (February 1939): 3–34; ibid. (May 1939): 143–74; ibid. (August 1939): 279–310; ibid. (November 1939): 350–83; Riley, *The Female Frontier;* Joanna Stratton, *Pioneer Women: Voices from the Kansas Frontier* (New York: Simon and Schuster, 1978).

47. Dykstra, *The Cattle Towns,* 239–92; Nancy G. Garner, "'A Prayerful Public Protest': The Significance of Gender in the Kansas Woman's Crusade of 1874," *Kansas History: A Journal of the Central Plains* 20 (Winter 1997–1998): 214–29; June O. Underwood, "Civilizing Kansas: Woman's Organizations, 1880–1920," ibid., 7 (Winter 1984–1985): 291–306; Michael Goldberg, "Non-Partisan and All-Partisan: Rethinking Woman Suffrage and Party Politics in Gilded Age Kansas," *Western Historical Quarterly* 25 (Spring 1994): 21–44.

48. Angel Kwolek-Folland, "The Elegant Dugout: Domesticity and Moveable Culture in the United States, 1870–1900," *American Studies* 25 (Fall 1984): 21–38.

49. West, *Growing Up with the Country,* 88, 115–17, 138–43, 257–59; Julene Bair, *One Degree West: Reflections of a Plainsdaughter* (Minneapolis: Mid-List Press, 1991).

50. White, *"It's Your Misfortune and None of My Own,"* 277–78; Riley, *The Female Frontier.*

51. Joseph G. Gambone, ed., "The Forgotten Feminist of Kansas: The Papers of Clarina I. H. Nichols, 1854–1885," *Kansas Historical Quarterly* 39 (1973): 243, 422–29.

52. Gambone, "The Forgotten Feminist of Kansas," 12–28, 422–29; Lyn Bennett, "Reassessing Western Liberality: Divorce in Douglas County Kansas, 1867–1876," *Kansas History: A Journal of the Central Plains* 17 (Winter 1994–1995): 274–87.

53. Goldberg, "Non-Partisan and All-Partisan"; Ellen Dubois, *Feminism and Suffrage: The Emergence of an Independent Women's Movement in America, 1848–1869* (Ithaca, N.Y.: Cornell University Press, 1978), 79–104; Marilyn Dell Brady, "Populism and Feminism in a Newspaper by and for Women of the Kansas Farmers' Alliance, 1891–1894," *Kansas History: A Journal of the Central Plains* 7 (Winter 1984–1985): 280–90; Martha B. Caldwell, "The Woman Suffrage Campaign of 1912," *Kansas Historical Quarterly* 13 (August 1945): 463–72.

54. Hal Sears, *The Sex Radicals: Free Love in High Victorian America* (Lawrence: Regents Press of Kansas, 1977).

55. This assessment is based on a survey of Zornow, *Kansas: A History of the Jayhawk State;* Richmond, *Kansas: A Land of Contrasts;* Davis, *Kansas: A Bicentennial History.*

56. Richmond, *Kansas: A Land of Contrasts,* 71, 164; Davis, *Kansas: A Bicentennial History,* 150, 152, 154; Dubois, *Feminism and Suffrage.*

57. James C. Carper, "The Popular Ideology of Segregated Schooling: Attitudes Toward the Education of Blacks in Kansas, 1854–1900," *Kansas History: A Journal of the Central Plains* 1 (Winter 1978): 254–65; Mary L. Dudziak, "The Limits of Good Faith: Desegregation in Topeka, Kansas, 1950–1956," *Law and History Review* 5 (1987): 351–91.

58. Richard B. Sheridan, "Charles Langston and the African American Struggle in Kansas," *Kansas History: A Journal of the Central Plains* 22 (Winter 1999–2000): 268–83; Kristine M. McCusker, "'The Forgotten Years' of America's Civil Rights Movement: Wartime Protests at the University of Kansas 1939–1945," ibid., 17 (Spring 1994): 29–30.

59. Dudziak, "The Limits of Good Faith," 357–62; McCusker, "'The Forgotten Years' of America's Civil Rights Movement," 31–37.

60. Billington, *Westward Expansion,* 745–58, emphasizes the Americanization of foreign immigrants in the nineteenth-century West; Richmond, *Kansas: A Land of Contrasts,* 153–61, is less theoretical but describes the same immigrants as being absorbed into Kansas economy and society and as contributing to their development. He also notes the partial assimilation of Mexican migrants.

61. Carroll D. Clark and Roy L. Roberts, *People of Kansas: A Demographic and Sociological Study* (Topeka: Kansas State Planning Board, 1936), 50–51.

62. J. Neale Carman, *Foreign-Language Units of Kansas* (Lawrence: University of Kansas Press, 1962), 110, 244, 306–7, 41, 40.

63. Every county map in ibid. shows ethnic clustering. For southeastern Kansas, see 110–15; for northeastern industry and ethnic settlement, see 306.

64. James C. Juhnke, *A People of Two Kingdoms: The Political Acculturation of the Kansas Mennonites* (Newton, Kans.: Faith and Life Press, 1975); Carman, *Foreign-Language Units of Kansas.*

65. Joseph B. Herring, "The Prophet Kenekuk and the Vermillion Kickapoos: Acculturation Without Assimilation," *American Indian Quarterly* 9 (Summer 1985): 295–307; Herring, *The Enduring Indians of Kansas;* "The Prairie Pottawatomi Resistance to Allotment," 27–31.

66. Carman, *Foreign-Language Units of Kansas,* offers a linguistic map for every county in Kansas.

67. Ibid., 226–27; Ise, *Sod and Stubble,* 37; Norman Saul, "The Migration of the Russian-Germans to Kansas," *Kansas Historical Quarterly* 40 (Spring 1974): 38–62; Emory K. Lindquist, *Smoky Valley People: A History of Lindsborg, Kansas* (Lindsborg, Kans.: Bethany College, 1953), 33–50.

68. Eleanor L. Turk, "The Germans of Atchison, 1854–1859: Development of an Ethnic Community," *Kansas History: A Journal of the Central Plains* 2 (Autumn 1979): 146–56.

69. Ibid.

70. William S. Powell, "European Settlement in the Cherokee-Crawford Coal Field of Southeastern Kansas," *Kansas Historical Quarterly* 41 (Summer 1975): 150–65; Carman, *Foreign-Language Units of Kansas,* 306–7.

71. Michael J. Broadway "The Origins and Determinants of Indochinese Secondary In-Migration in Southwest Kansas," *Heritage of the Great Plains* 20 (Spring 1987): 19–29; Robert Oppenheimer, "Acculturation or Assimilation: Mexican Immigrants in Kansas, 1900 to World War II," *Western Historical Quarterly* 16 (October 1985): 431, 432, 433, 436, 442–44.

72. Oppenheimer, "Acculturation or Assimilation," 445–46.

73. Stull and Broadway, "The Effects of Restructuring on Beefpacking in Kansas," 10–16.

74. Ducker, *Men of the Steel Rails,* 3–13.

75. Schofield, "An 'Army of Amazons,'" 686–701.

76. Joseph F. Tripp, "Kansas Communities and the Birth of the Labor Problem, 1877–1883," *Kansas History: A Journal of the Central Plains* 4 (Summer 1981): 114–29; Schofield "An 'Army of Amazons'"; Richmond, *Kansas: A Land of Contrasts,* 216–17.

77. Schofield, "An 'Army of Amazons.'"

78. Fearon, "Ploughshares into Airplanes," 298–314; Richmond, *Kansas: A Land of Contrasts,* 255, 296; Stull and Broadway, "The Effects of Restructuring on Beefpacking in Kansas," 15.

PART ONE

Native Americans, Dispossession, and Resettlement

The Central Plains is an ancient land with thousands of years of human presence—a fact long ignored in traditional approaches to writing western history. The nineteenth-century ideology of Manifest Destiny assumed the West was an uninhabited land, one ready to be settled, tamed, and incorporated into the larger American nation. This perspective dominated not only the settlement of the West but also many of the histories of that process. With the emergence of Native American studies, however, our understanding of settlement in the West, and Kansas in particular, has become much more complex. What the new history shows us is that the transplanting of Euro-American culture and society to this area in the nineteenth century was only one step in a long history of peopling the region.

Long before the area we now call Kansas became a state, it was home to diverse Native American peoples, each with distinct economic, social, and cultural traditions. Those traditions were not part of a static, unchanging worldview but were adaptable to various pressures and changes in the region's physical and cultural environments. There has been in recent years a remarkable growth in scholarship focused on the traditions and experiences of the area's first inhabitants, both before western expansion brought Euro-Americans to the region and after this convergence of cultures took place.

Since historians began including Native Americans as central actors in their stories, our understanding of the interactions between Native and Euro-Americans has changed dramatically. In particular, we learn about the goals that Natives held in dealing with Euro-Americans, their attitudes about being encouraged or forced to change their cultures, and their interest in retaining the land held by their groups. Native American peoples throughout the region increasingly faced these pressures as more Euro-Americans moved to the area and as the federal policy of Removal became more widely implemented. The process of Removal elicited a wide array of responses from Native peoples, ranging from active and sometimes violent opposition to accommodation and acculturation, and nearly everything in between.

The essays in this part provide a variety of perspectives on the process of Native dispossession and Euro-American settlement in Kansas. Because the towns, farms, and homes of newcomers overlaid those of the previous and extant inhabitants, the process of non-Native migration to the region might better be seen as the resettlement of Kansas and the West. Each overlay of cultures marked a major transformation of land use, plant and animal communities, and types of human settlement.

Elliott West's essay is a wonderful overview of the various stages of settlement in Kansas. In "The Story of Three Families," we see how each succession of cultures not only brought something new to the region but also contained "ancient echoes of the ways of life before." In his unusual comparison of families over seven centuries, West makes the idea of resettlement clear. He examines three families in the middle valley of the Soloman River, one a thirteenth-century family that was part of the agricultural Central Plains culture, another a nineteenth-century hunting and trading Cheyenne family, and the last a Euro-American farm family in the second half of the nineteenth century.

West's approach emphasizes the significance of families in creating social and cultural structures. For thousands of years the family has been the economic and social center of life. Examining the past through the lens of the family illuminates not only day-to-day experiences but also how various cultures ensured survival, created identity, and developed meaning for the world around them. While there are significant differences in the lives of the region's peoples over seven centuries, there also are some remarkable similarities in their experiences on and adaptations to the Plains.

Richard White's essay on the Pawnees, the second in this part, also incorporates various elements of the new history and is an excellent example of how a specific culture adapted to changing conditions on the Plains. In particular, White examines the reciprocal relationship between the natural environment and Pawnee culture. He explores this relationship in the sacred meaning of the buffalo hunt, the relationship between the hunt and all Pawnee ceremonial life, the adoption of the horse, difficulties in adapting horse herds to the Central Plains, and Pawnee solutions to that problem. White provides insight into various aspects of Pawnee thinking and behavior not only by examining their own words and actions but also by contrasting them with missionaries' perspectives on Pawnee behavior and beliefs. In this way, White gives us a complex understanding of the changes in the cultural landscape of the Pawnee.

One of the most significant moments in Native American history came in 1830 with the passage of the Federal Indian Removal Act. Joseph Herring's essay examines one part of the history of Removal and how it affected the peoples of eastern Kansas. Herring discusses the experience of the Munsee and Chippewa, small bands of Native Americans who were forced to move to Kansas through the Removal program. In particular, he examines both their desire to remain in Kansas in the face of pressures to move them once again and the actions they took to achieve that goal. Both the Munsee and the Chippewa accommodated some of the demands of the missionaries and government agents, including cultivating farms, converting to Christianity (though some continued Native religious beliefs and practices), dressing in Euro-American-style clothing, and sending their children to missionary schools. However, many refused to discard tribal ways, accept citizenship, sell their land, or move south to Indian Territory. The Munsees and Chippewa were not initially unified in their responses to missionary attempts to "civilize" and Christianize them. Factions developed within the two bands over how to react. In the end they chose to acculturate, thereby securing their lands, but in the process surrendering much of their identity and their separate social and political organizations.

For many tribes the Dawes Act was the final step in their dispossession. Congress intended the new law, passed in 1887, to push Native Americans down the road toward civilization by making them individualistic, property-owning farmers and by eliminating tribes as political groups. Reformers saw the law as a way to simultaneously civilize and protect native people. The law also created "surplus" lands from the remaining reservation lands that were to be sold to white settlers. Some saw the lands given up as a great boon to white settlement and economic development. Certainly it was a major step in the ongoing conquest of Kansas. We know a great deal about the way the legislation was fashioned and passed in 1887. Yet historians have told us little about the way particular Native groups saw the Dawes Act, whether they lobbied against it, and whether they accepted the inevitable land distribution or resisted it.

The fourth essay in this part, written anonymously, gives a surprising and graphic picture of how the Prairie Band of Potawatomi in Kansas fought to stop the implementation of land allotment. When the Prairie Band were originally forced to relocate to Kansas, they worked to retain their lands and to perpetuate communal ways. After resettlement in Kansas, they were again faced with an effort to take their lands and destroy their way of life. In response, they used the weapons of the larger society to protect their communal lands, political system, and economy. Here we see a people who understood the opposing society well enough to fashion their defense with the opponents' weapons, ultimately securing the right to live by alternative values and systems. This is an important case study of Native goals and methods in resisting Euro-American expansion. That the Prairie Band failed to prevail does not blunt the power and meaning of their attempts.

Just as Native Americans sought to perpetuate their cultural and social fabric in the face of Removal and westward expansion, the Euro-Americans who relocated to Kansas also attempted to maintain some semblance of continuity with the societies they left behind. Migrants to Kansas and farther west were not a homogenous group but represented a conglomeration of various ethnicities. Until recently historians focused on the idea of the "melting pot" and the ways in which various ethnic groups assimilated into the larger American society. This approach generally ignored the ways immigrants perpetuated their own culture through maintaining familiar values, practices, and institutions once they arrived in their new homes. It also precluded the exploration of the extent to which immigrants influenced the character of Kansas or western culture and society. Rather than simply 'melting' into American culture, immigrants typically clustered together and worked to form communities of people with shared backgrounds, values, and languages. These groups built their own churches, conducted schools in their own languages, created voluntary associations, and printed their own newspapers. Although they maintained some social isolation, immigrants also participated in the larger political and social systems of their adopted homes. Eleanor Turk's study describes this process as she examines the efforts of German immigrants to create both their own subcommunity in Atchison, Kansas, and make significant contributions to the history of Kansas as a whole.

As we have seen, resettlement in Kansas entailed not only the moving of people from one place to another but also the transplantation of cultural, economic, and social structures and traditions. One of the primary and most significant places this transplantation occurred was in the home. Nineteenth-century constructions of gender identified the home and family as a woman's domain. Thus, examining the material culture in the homes of newly arrived Kansans sheds light on the ways in which settlers attempted to remake their society in a new place and also reveals important insight into gender relations in Victorian America. Angel Kwolek-Folland gives us a unique view into women's attempts to establish domesticity in a new, seemingly wild, environment. Re-creating the visible symbols of home and "civilization," whether in a rude sod house or a more finished frame building, was an important aspect to women's settlement experiences. Kwolek-Folland focuses on the creation, organization, and utilization of physical domestic space, drawing important conclusions about what those activities meant.

Examination of the daily lives of women who attempted to re-create civilization in a new environment and exploration of the ways Native Americans fought and adapted to the pressures of westward expansion provide us with a greater understanding of our past and ourselves. The old history was inadequate to the task, and the new history has just begun to remedy its faults. In endeavoring toward an inclusive history, we gain a better view of the quilt of cultures that is Kansas.

The Story of Three Families

Elliott West

It's a typical summer day on the family farm along the Solomon River. The mother is working in the garden, looking up occasionally to see if her husband is bringing home a deer from his hunt. While the older children do their chores, the grandmother is looking after the younger ones, who are running and squealing as they play along the riverbank. Not far downstream is a similar scene among neighbors, cousins of the first family, and beyond them other homesteads of earthen houses and green gardens that dot the whole valley at regular intervals, like stitching along a seam.

This description might be from the Kansas frontier of the 1870s, but it's not. The scene I've just sketched for you is from eight hundred years ago, fully six and a half centuries before the first freesoilers arrived in Kansas. That family's story is a healthy reminder of some basic but often forgotten points about this remarkable state and its past. We've met today in this marvelous new facility to help recognize—to celebrate, really—Kansas history. There is plenty to celebrate. Anyone standing where I am today would have to choose from thousands of topics and dozens of themes to talk about. What I would like to do is to choose just two items from that generous menu, two themes that I think are often overlooked but are also fundamental to appreciating what it means to be Kansan.

The first theme is the antiquity of this place, the fact that this beautiful new history center sits on a very, very old meeting ground. It is a strange American notion that our East is old and our West represents the new. In our collective vernacular, going back to pioneer days, the West typically is called the "new country." But that way of looking at things has got it exactly backwards. In terms of human history, Bob Dole's Kansas is far older than Thomas Jefferson's Virginia or John Winthrop's Massachusetts. Where we sit and stand today, in fact, may well have been some of the first American soil ever touched by human beings—something that Kansans might take both interest and pride in.

My second theme is the crucial significance of family. As the small army of genealogists using the Kansas History Center perhaps is trying to tell us, families are absolutely essential to understanding Kansans present and past—their day to day lives and survival, their societies, their sense of who they are, even the meaning they have found in the world around them. Kansas history without families is a contradiction in terms.

One way to consider these two themes is to take one spot in Kansas—the middle valley of the Solomon River, a hundred and twenty or so miles west of Topeka—and look at three families who made their lives there, not during the recent past but throughout eight hundred years of plains history.

The first family is the one I described briefly a few minutes ago. In the early 1200s, Genghis Khan (recently chosen by a major newspaper as the "man of the millennium") was at the peak of his power, King John signed the Magna Carta, leprosy first appeared in Europe, and Londoners were installing the first tile roofs to replace the traditional thatch. And along the Solomon and Republican Rivers, our family lived amid thousands of others in a flourishing and prosperous farming culture. They were part of what archaeologists call the Central Plains tradition. It began about 1000 AD and was over by about 1400.[1]

Even then the human presence in western Kansas was many millennia old. The earliest confirmed occupation of the High Plains was about twelve thousand years ago, near the end of the last Ice Age. Those first plainsmen were part of the Clovis complex of master hunters who preyed on an almost unimaginable bounty of game roaming over the grasslands during those wetter, cooler times. Clovis peoples were followed by a series of other hunting cultures that worked within the long swings in climatic change on the Plains. The peoples of the Central Plains tradition, however, were the first to farm this region.

It could only have happened because, once again, the weather changed. A thousand or so years ago, the climate where we meet today and well to the West of us turned warmer and wetter. Suddenly it was raining as much in what are today Clay, Osborn, and Russell Counties as it does now in western Missouri. People living along the Missouri River and to the east in the Ohio Valley had been cultivating maize for at least a couple of hundred years, but the drier climate to the west, on the Plains proper, had prohibited agriculture there. Now, with the shift in climate, it was possible to farm in country where growing crops had been unthinkable a few generations before.[2] From somewhere to the south, new groups migrated into the valleys of the Solomon, Smoky Hill, and Republican Rivers and began to plant gardens.

Our first family lived in a squarish house with rounded corners and about seven hundred square feet of living area. It was dug slightly into the ground, with walls of standing logs probably plastered with mud. Four posts held up the roof, with a fire pit in the middle for cooking and warmth. This substantial, reasonably comfortable dwelling spoke of security and stability.

If we could have flown over the region then, we could have seen hundreds of dwellings like this one, strung out along creeks that fed into the larger rivers, clustering loosely into hamlets of fifty or seventy-five people each. Nine or ten centuries ago this country experienced something of a prolonged land rush. Archaeologists today have found that by 1200 or 1300 more Native Americans were living in the Kansas plains than at any time before or since then.

As with all peoples long gone, we know this family best by its garbage. They and their neighbors left behind heaps of trash containing round-shouldered pots, bone fish hooks, chipped stone knives and choppers, pendants made of animal teeth, and at least one cup shaped crudely from the top of a human skull. There were also amulets made from conch shells, as well as other items that could only have come from the Ohio Valley, middle Atlantic Coast, and the Gulf of Mexico. Eight hundred years ago Kansas was connected by a webbing of vigorous trade to the Appalachians, to towns in New Mexico, and to cities along the Mississippi, like Cahokia (today just outside St. Louis), where as many as twenty-five thousand persons lived, more than in New York City at the time of the American Revolution. But there was nothing new in that. A gravesite not far to the north, dating from nearly fifteen hundred years earlier (ca. 230 BC), shows that natives from that time were plugged into a trading system stretching from British Columbia to Florida, from New England to Baja California.[3]

Mostly, of course, these people sustained themselves by what they secured on their own from the land around them. They were accomplished farmers. Unlike later pioneers of the 1800s, they did not try to break and turn the tough sod thick with grassroots. Instead they made their gardens along the softer banks of streams, protected from the blistering winds of late summer and periodically enriched by the silt of floods. They worked the moist soil with simple digging sticks of wood and deer antlers and hoes made from the shoulder blades of bison. In their gardens they planted the three plants that were grown across North America—maize (or corn), beans and squash—as well as marshelder, or sumpweed, and that most familiar Kansas plant, the sunflower. Dozens of other plants were gathered wild, many for food, but many others for making and processing clothing, for bedding and other household needs, for decoration, and for medicine.

Away from the fields they hunted an equally wide array of animals, not only bison but deer, elk, pronghorn antelope, and bear, not to mention an impressive buffet of small game. The remains of at least thirty-six kinds of mammals have been found in excavated villages, from voles and pocket gophers and kangaroo rats to wolves, minks, woodchucks, cougars, jackrabbits, raccoons, wolverines, and skunks. There were feathers from game birds, the bones of bullheads and channel catfish, and the shells of snapping turtles.[4]

All those leavings, unfortunately, cannot tell us much about the daily life of these remarkable early Kansans. Probably, however, they were not too different from others in the tribes that Europeans first found in villages along rivers to the east—the Pawnees, who probably were descendants of these thirteenth-century plains farmers. Family labor likely was divided by sex. Men hunted and if necessary fought. Women did a lot more—planting, working and harvesting crops, making meals from plants and game, overseeing all domestic work. Their heavy work load brought with it power. Women held authority over lodges and their contents; they controlled all that came from the gardens, and may have been in charge of one of the family's most important assets—its dogs, which padded and sniffed around the lodges in great numbers, serving two important roles: they could be beasts of burden or dinner.

Although children probably were left to play much of the time, they probably had their duties too. Not long past infancy they would ease into helping with a few tasks, and as the years unrolled they gradually observed and learned the many hundreds of complex and subtle skills expected of any full member, woman or man, in that society.

What more can we know about the texture—the dailiness—of this family's life? Not much. But there's room for guessing. A few scholars have tried to look into the spiritual world of these Kansans, with some fascinating results. On a bluff overlooking the junction of the Smoky Hill and Republican Rivers, there is an excavated lodge, built around 1300. There is reason to believe it was home to a Native American priest. It was built precisely on an east-to-west axis, aligned so that on one morning each year, exactly at the spring equinox, the rising sun would have come through its doorway and illuminated a spot at the rear of the lodge that seems to have been an altar. Its four support poles are positioned at the four sacred semicardinal points of the compass.

Most intriguing is what was found in a storage pit next to the altar— the remains of an eagle, a bluejay, a woodpecker, a long-eared owl, and four bobwhite quail. For the Pawnees, some of these were divine messengers and protectors; the eagle gave power in battle, the bluejay and owl flew back and forth between humans and Tirawahat, the ultimate power above who created all gods, and the woodpecker looked after the welfare of men and women.

But what about the bobwhites? Some archaeologists think that those ancient farmers may have looked on these birds as their closest kin. Their quail's nests in the grass resembled the people's saucer-shaped earthlodges dug into the ground. The bird's annual cycle ran parallel to the one probably followed by the Plains hunter-farmers. Most of all, there was the quail's human-like qualities. Our own folklore, of course, recognizes the social traits of this familiar bird—the banding together in coveys, the springtime chicks following the mother as both parents keep close watch over their brood. Anyone who has watched these birds has seen what seems to be all sorts of human-like behavior, such as the elders' patient teaching of the young in the fundamentals of being bobwhite. A covey of quail was a natural model for people well nested in this open country.

Were these plainsmen from centuries ago bird-worshippers? Did they take pride in themselves as the Quail People? Maybe. We can speculate about that, and a lot more, but some things are certain. More than thirty generations before today—six or seven centuries before Lewis and Clark, four hundred years before Coronado—a vibrant society of successful farmers was settled and at home to the west of us, and even they were only the latest in the much longer history of being and living Kansan. By all the evidence, their knowledge and appreciation of their homeland ran broad and deep. They managed to maintain a productive, self-supporting way of life for close to four hundred years. If our modern farmers hope to match that record, they are going to have to keep at it well into the twenty-third century. These earlier Kansans survived by understanding their country's many parts and where they fit among them, and I, for one, am pretty impressed.

But in the end, it was not enough. These Kansans were driven away, toward the east, when once more the weather changed. In the thirteenth and fourteenth centuries devastating droughts struck this region, and the Plains became much more like the place we know today. Rainfall was skimpier and chancier. Those ancient Plains farmers did not adjust to this change—whether they could have is a slippery question—but instead they migrated to the area along the Platte and Loup Rivers where enough rain fell to support their gardens. Instead of adapting to a changed climate, they simply followed the climate they knew as it moved east. And with that, the population on the Central Plains took a dramatic dip.

During the next three centuries, native peoples continued to use the High Plains, and some lived there. But the population stayed pretty thin until the middle of the 1700s. Then the region experienced a new boom time. This was a changed America. By then the invasion and spread of Euro-Americans was well underway. Euro-Americans had begun to transform the continent and had set in motion hundreds of native societies. Most Indian people were driven ahead of the Europeans, colliding with other tribes, and careening off on new courses, sometimes into oblivion.

But Europeans also brought with them an astonishing array of opportunities for Indian peoples—new technologies, new goods to trade, new sources of power. Tribes quickly saw new possibilities that accompanied the grimmest results of the frontier invasion. Early in the 1700s Cheyennes were farming along the Missouri River, but late in that century they began moving westward into the Dakotas. By 1800 they were near the Black Hills, and from there they drifted south to around the Platte River, with some moving even farther south to the Arkansas River.[5]

The Cheyennes were being shoved westward by whites and other Indians, but they also were chasing opportunities—wondrously alluring opportunities—when they moved onto the Plains. Those opportunities had appeared, more than from any other single source, because of one of the hundreds of new items brought by the European invasion—the horse.

The horse persuaded the Cheyennes to give up agriculture and turn to a more nomadic way of life. On horseback they became more formidable warriors and far more efficient hunters of what suddenly was the main item on the Plains buffet—the bison. Cheyennes also became master traders, first shuttling European goods as well as—what else?—horses among tribes from North Dakota to New Mexico and then hunting more and more bison for trade, turning their skins into robes that were funneled through St. Louis to an eager market back east.[6] A few centuries after the first family was driven off the Plains by slackening rainfall, the region suddenly became highly attractive once again as these new migrants learned how to use horses to forge a new relationship with the country.

Our second family resided among these Cheyennes who were living and hunting in eastern Colorado and western Kansas, including the Solomon Valley, by the 1830s. This was a very different country from that of 1200 AD, and this family, like the farmers who had moved there eight hundred years before them, had to find their own distinctive answers to the puzzles of this place. This family negotiated its own bargains with the land.

It was a truly remarkable performance. We are used to admiring European-American and African-American pioneers for fashioning new ways of life on the Plains. But think for a moment of the perception and imagination demanded from this Cheyenne family in its tribe's westward expansion, as it made that great leap from one place and means of living into a radically different one. When we look back on the frontier, maybe we should save some of our admiration for these—surely some of the West's all-time champions of adaptability.

This Cheyenne family lived most of the year with others, related by blood through the women's line, in groups of forty or fifty persons. They kept as many as ten horses for every man, woman, and child. To survive in the demanding Plains environment, these families learned to live by a shrewd annual cycle. In the spring they could be found living along the Plains rivers, fattening their horses on lush grasses that sprouted there soon after the snowmelt. In summer they shifted to the highlands, where they hunted bison on this immense pasture of short-grasses, then they drifted in the fall back into protected, wooded enclaves along rivers and streams where they hunkered down and waited out the worst during the treacherous winter months.

They hunted vigorously the huge populations of game found on this American Serengeti. According to a government report in 1855, the Southern Cheyennes, with a population just over three thousand, every year were killing twenty-five thousand deer, three thousand elk, two thousand bears, and forty thousand bison.[7] The last creature, the bison, was of course the most important. This family used its meat for food, its hide for housing and bedding, its sinews and bones to help make weapons and tools. The bison is the largest lifeform in North or South America, and parents and children, grandparents, aunts and uncles found nearly a hundred purposes for it, including a flyswatter, made from its tail, and a comb, fashioned from its rough, dried tongue.

Bison hides, made into robes, could be traded for all sorts of other things this Cheyenne family could not provide for themselves—bed ticking to line their tipi, colorful material for clothes, blankets, knives and metal scrapers, pots and needles, coffee and the sugar to sweeten it, clay pipes and the tobacco to smoke in them. Measured simply in material goods, our family's wealth increased because of their move onto the plains, which meant the family members needed a bigger tipi; that was possible because, with horses, they now had the muscle power to pull around that larger lodge and everything that went in it.

These Kansans quickly learned to use the wondrous abundance of wild goods available to them. A recent study catalogued 121 edible forbs, woody shrubs, and grasses on the Plains.[8] Some, like sarvisberries and haws, were familiar to white settlers, but the native menu was far greater. It included prairie turnip, beebalm, and buffalo gourd, rice-grass, pussy toes, and much more. The long and slender bulbs of *Calocortus gunisonii* (the Cheyennes called it "war bonnet") were gathered and dried, then ground into meal and boiled for sweet winter mush. There was one type of red currant, *Ribes inebrians,* that was sometimes pounded and dried into small round cakes and eaten straight and sometimes stewed with the inner scrapings from buffalo hides. Dozens of plants were used to cure ailments from dyspepsia to lung hemorrhages. If pounded into a powder, the leaves and stems of *Lithospermum lineari-folium* (the whites would call it "goldie") were said to revive a paralyzed limb; when brewed into tea and rubbed on the face and head, it relieved temporary irrationality. Plants were used as well in the making of shelter and weapons and much more. Young men chewed the leaves of *Monarda menthoefolia* (or bitter perfume) and blew them onto their favorite horses to give a pleasant scent to the manes and tails.

The key to this masterful adaptation to Plains life was the family. Its members worked together with a netting of interlocking, essential tasks. Men hunted and fought; women put the slain animals to their different uses, saw to domestic jobs, bore and reared babies, cared for the sick. Children helped their elders, gathered plants, cared for younger brothers and sisters. This is not to say that the Cheyennes' way of life had anything resembling equality. The balance of work, in fact, was in some ways grotesquely out of whack. One effect of the horse was to enable men to kill bison far more quickly than women could skin them, process their meat, and perform the gruelling, backbreaking job of turning a green, bloody hide into a pliant, comfortable robe. Women also seem to have lost much of the power they used to have in their communities and families before Cheyennes moved onto the Plains.[9] But however imbalanced this way of life was between male and female, every member of the family knew he or she ultimately depended on all the others; without that meshing system of mutual support, survival was unthinkable.

In countless other ways this family learned about the Plains and made them home, not only in their material life but in spirit as well. During their journey west, as they trekked out of the Missouri Valley toward the Black Hills, the Cheyennes came upon a mountain shaped like a bear. This became their sacred mountain, Noaha-vose. A great door opened and the Cheyenne prophet, Sweet Medicine, was called inside by Maheo, the Supreme Being. There he lived for four years, learning of this new world of the Plains from Maheo and the four sacred powers. Then Sweet Medicine stepped back out of the mountain and returned to his people with four sacred arrows that gave them power over their enemies and the herds of animals.[10]

The Cheyennes were setting down their spiritual roots. Our family could not perceive itself apart from this Plains home. Around it were landmarks of identity. Above was the Near Sky Space of breath and birds, above that the Blue Sky Space of cosmic power. Below was Deep Earth with its great cavern where the bison lived before coming out every year in the annual renewal of the herds.[11]

In this spiritual universe, the family was preeminently important.

Plains peoples conceived of natural forces as living in households and having family squabbles. Human relations with other lifeforms were (and are) pictured and explained through kinship. The Cheyennes' right to hunt bison and other animals, for instance, was earned in part by a man who formed a household with a bison cow and calf, who helped him in a series of contests against other animals. The world of the Cheyennes is an intricate, enveloping web of familial bonds.

But by the middle of the nineteenth century, this was a troubled family household. The Cheyennes found themselves suddenly desperately short of the essentials of life. By the mid-1850s the bison herds were shrinking. The thick groves of timber that sheltered them in winter were disappearing from along the streams. Even the Plains grasses, the most vital resources of all, seemed to be evaporating. One culprit, once again, was the weather. At mid-century a series of withering droughts scorched the Central Plains. Part of the problem were the Cheyennes themselves, who despite all they had learned about their new homes, still pushed too hard, stripping away thousands of cottonwoods, probably overhunting the bison, using up too quickly what they had to have to survive.[12]

But a third cause of the Cheyennes' troubles compounded the first two—a massive immigration into Kansas of yet another wave of newcomers, this time families of white pioneers who were arriving in numbers that dwarfed anything the Plains had ever seen. These new arrivals were the prime force that undermined the lifeways of plains Indians. They also had their own story, their own variation on what by then was a very old tradition of becoming Kansan.

On the face of it, these newcomers might seem vastly different from the Indians who had come before them. Certainly they described themselves as everything Indians were not. Newspapers were filled with phrases of dramatic contrast. The pioneers were said to be "bringing civilization to the land of the untaught savage"; they were "making productive the empty land that has lay useless until now"; editors wrote that church spires soon would rise above the prairie, announcing that God's word now was spoken into what they saw as a spiritual void.

White frontier settlers certainly were setting in motion changes far greater than anything that had come before. But the delicious irony here was that these pioneers, who saw themselves as the vanguard of a new age, also found themselves living out patterns and learning lessons familiar for centuries to Plains life. A white pioneer homestead was full of ancient echoes from dozens of generations of earlier Kansans.

For one thing, these settlers, as much as any who had come before them, understood the value of families. Of the many misconceptions about the frontier, one of the greatest is that the typical pioneer was the stalwart individual, standing isolated and alone, nose-to-nose with the wilderness. In fact, the frontier was always a family enterprise. When that new army of farmers pushed beyond Topeka and into the valleys of the Solomon and Republican, they came as collections of family households.

Often whole interlocking family systems picked up from Missouri or Ohio or New York and came west as a whole. Take for instance, the Warners, who homesteaded in Osborne County (near present-day Downs) in 1871. This bunch was strung together in relations so complicated that you need a roster to keep the players straight. At the core were three brothers who were married to three sisters. These three households had nine children among them, including two from one brother's deceased first wife, who also had been a sister to the three current wives. A widowed brother to the four sisters came along with his daughter, as well as his deceased wife's brother. Also present was Alpheus Cleveland, described only as a "distant relative."[13]

There were good reasons for moving as a group. At a time when there was so much work to do and so many new situations to face, relatives were known quantities. The Warner clan didn't necessarily like each other, of course, but each knew what each of the others could be counted on to do; each household knew the peculiar combination of strengths and foibles in every other. In all work that was easier done collectively—housebuilding, breaking ground, harvesting, fighting prairie fires—these families arrived with tested relationships intact and ready to use. In dozens of other ways their intimacy and their depth of shared knowledge and seasoned intuition allowed the Warners to respond to each others' needs. When the alcoholic "Uncle Howard" suffered *delirium tremens*, for instance, a collection of relatives took turns nursing him through, just as they helped with the plowing and chores for one of the handicapped brothers who did his part by bringing in cash as a clockmaker in a nearby town.

If this sounds vaguely familiar, it should. The Warners—and many other white settlers—lived in clusters of interlocking, mutually reliant families similar to those of the Cheyennes they were helping push aside, and not so different from the much earlier native farmers. In fact, if the Warners had dug deeper into the soil they had cut into bricks for their sod houses, they probably would have found the remains of those saucer-shaped earth and wood lodges, strung out along the Solomon in small communities that had almost certainly been composed of related households, which six hundred years earlier we likely could have seen helping one another through their labors and infirmities (as well as squabbling and sniping at each other, as the Warners were doing too).

Also like their native predecessors, these newest Kansans were getting by, especially in their early years, by a mixed economy that drew on everyone's help. Women, as always, carried a heavy burden—the whole range of domestic chores, gardening, child rearing, and caring for the sick. During the first couple of years of a homestead, they usually brought in virtually all the precious cash needed to buy goods from the outside (just as those Cheyenne women had produced bison robes for that vital trade). Men did the heavy grunt work—busting sod, building houses. Just as Indian males had left on long summer hunts and raids, white fathers would take off for weeks in July and August to find temporary jobs that helped the family over rough spots. Children were real wild cards, filling in wherever needed. As one of their most important tasks, one or more echos from the Plains past, they gathered scores of wild plants from the fields and streams around their houses—wild plums, purslane and pigweed, prairie haws and a dozen kinds of berries. Whenever one boy found himself hungry, he would pull a barrel over to his sod house, stand on it, and graze directly from the greenery along the edges of the roof.

Survival was a collective enterprise, a joint effort that included work you might not expect. Luna Warner, teenaged daughter of one of the three brothers, told in her diary of a family group coming on a small herd of bison while out in their wagon. When they spotted a lone animal about a mile away, they quickly moved into action:

Pa took Arabella's [her young cousin's] horse and went after it. I went afoot, got there long before Pa did. . . . As soon as the horse saw the buffalo she snorted and stopped. Pa got off. He handed me the bridle while he went for the buffalo, revolver in hand. The buffalo saw him and went up the ravine out of sight. Pa went to the top of the hill and back on the other side, but saw nothing of him till at last he happened to spy him. He fired and then they came right toward us. The horse sprang and snorted and whirled around me, but

I kept fast hold and talked to her and she arched her neck. Patty [a young friend] had just come from chasing the other buffaloes, then she went for him and worried him until Pa had shot four times. Then he [no relative, just the buffalo] fell dead in the ravine. . . . [We] hitched the oxen to the buffalo and dragged him up where they could skin him . . . [and] they all went to skinning the buffalo with pocket knives. After it was dressed I went and drove up the oxen.[14]

Here was a traditional plains way of life trimmed down to a scale that we can visualize and understand more easily: male and female, older and younger working together in an essential job. It might be a metaphor for what had been happening for dozens of generations along the Solomon, Smoky Hill, and Republican.

No one should overemphasize the similarities between these white newcomers and the native peoples who had come before them. The differences were both obvious and profound, starting with numbers. The population in the Warners' home county, Osborne, went from 33 in 1870 to 12,517 in 1880. That second number was far greater than that of all Cheyennes at the height of their power. With a new technology the newcomers transformed the land more quickly and radically than anyone had in the millennia before them. These newest Kansans were deeply enmeshed in an international market economy. They looked at the land and its creatures and saw goods—wheat and cattle, corn and the skins and bones of bison—to be grabbed and shipped and sold. Deer and coyotes and little bluestem were important mainly for what they were worth. Take, for instance, quails—the bobwhites that those ancient farmers may have looked on as first cousins. By the 1870s Kansans were arguing vigorously about quail hunting. Some spoke out of affection for the birds, but the fight hinged mostly on money. Quails were good, some said, because they ate countless grasshoppers and other insects that otherwise would be gobbling up the crops. But no, others answered. Bobwhites also ate grain. One man figured that if hunters declared a moratorium on quails, after five years half a million quail would breed their way into four billion birds that would eat fifteen million bushels of grain every day. For settlers like this one, animals and plants had little value in themselves; they were digits in an intricate mathematics of profit and loss.[15]

That said, we should be just as sure not to miss another obvious point: those white pioneers, as different as they were from their Indian predecessors, also were living out an experience fundamental to all who had found homes on the Plains. Even as they were trying to shape the land to their will, they were drawing close to it, first with curiosity, then with affection, eventually with something deeper.

It was clearest in children, the natural explorers of any society. For these youngest pioneers Kansas became not an exotic destination but an intimate acquaintance. Luna Warner, she of the bison hunt previously described, first wrote in her diary about hating her new home. But within a week she was pressing out into the country with her brother, Louie, chasing rabbits, finding arrowheads, sniffing out adventures. She seemed driven to discover and name everything in her new world. She caught lizards and snakes, poked around every draw and buffalo wallow. She began collecting plants and cataloguing them, listing and describing 117 different specimens in four months.[16]

Luna Warner was living out a story repeated thousands of times with thousands of variations among the settlers of her generation. Setting out to subdue this country, they found they were taken in by it, too. They were changed by the same land they were working to make over. This latest wave of Warners and Sandholms, Smiths, and Oscarsons, Calabashes, and Sloans believed they were something wholly new in this country, and they were, but as Luna shot jackrabbits and roasted them over fires beside the frosty river grasses, as she studied prairie dogs and named wildflowers, she was helping to complete a very old cycle. The Warners were becoming part of the river valley where a few years before Cheyennes had hunted antelope and bison and camped in the groves of cottonwoods, where they had killed and been killed by Pawnees who came from the east to fight in the same country where their ancestors had farmed and reared twenty generations of children who grew up, like Luna and Louie, learning the land and themselves in a simultaneous exploration, Kansans who looked on the creeks and grasses as family and held conversations with God through owls and bluejays.

Luna Warner would live all her life on the Solomon homestead. She would marry Frank Lewis there, would bear and rear several children of her own. In the years that followed many of her descendants and those of her neighbors would be driven away, partly by chance (the Warner homestead now is at the bottom of the Glen Elder reservoir), partly by old, recurring turns of the weather, partly by changes in the land brought on by their own mistakes. Osborne County today has less than half as many people as it did when Luna was a girl. As its children have left, central Kansas today has become the oldest part of America, demographically speaking, with a higher percentage of persons over eighty-five years old than anywhere else in the nation.[17] That old story of coming into and leaving the country, of seeing it fresh and settling in, of conquering and being conquered continues to roll.

This magnificent Kansas History Center is a fine place for Kansans to remember what these three families have to teach us. We are meeting today in country with some of the continent's most ancient history. This land is layered deep in human experience, stories, and lessons that are still being laid down.

This old legacy should be a source of pride for Kansans and their children. But if you will allow a gratuitous comment from a visitor from a neighboring state, let me suggest that pride always brings with it obligations. Kansans whose lives are woven into this country through old stories and webs of kinship might learn to look on this place itself as one of the family. As we treat those closest to us around the Thanksgiving table, so we should treat the places that over time have become our close relations.

If we love and respect our grandparents and our children, we invite them into our lives, we listen to what they have to tell us, we recognize who they are and accept what they're not, and we never ask them for more than we can rightfully expect. The exhibits and the thousands of artifacts and documents in this history center remind us that these same principles of decent behavior should govern our treatment of where we live—places that, like our elders, tell us where we have come from, and like our children hold out the promise of where we still hope to go.

NOTES

1. The two best sources on this period and these people are Waldo R. Wedel, *Central Plains Prehistory: Holocene Environments and Culture Change in the Republican River Basin* (Lincoln: University of Nebraska Press, 1986), and Jeffrey L. Eighmy, "The Central High Plains: A Cultural Historical Summary," in *Plains Indians, A.D. 500–1500: The Archaeological Past of Historic Groups,* ed. Karl H. Schlesier (Norman: University of Oklahoma Press, 1994), 224–38.

2. Wedel, *Central Plains Prehistory,* chapter 3, brings together the best research attempting to reconstruct long-term climatic changes on the Plains.

3. Gayle F. Carlson, "Long Distance Trade," *Nebraska History* 75 (Spring 1994): 98.

4. Patricia J. O'Brien, "Prehistoric Evidence for Pawnee Cosmology," *American Anthropologist* 88 (December 1986): 939–46; Patricia J. O'Brien and Diane M. Post, "Speculations About Bobwhite Quail and Pawnee Religion," *Plains Anthropologist* 33 (November 1988): 489–504.

5. For useful overviews of Cheyenne history and ethnology during this period, see John H. Moore, *The Cheyenne Nation: A Social and Demographic History* (Lincoln: University of Nebraska Press, 1987); E. Adamson Hoebel, *The Cheyennes: Indians of the Great Plains,* 2d ed. (Fort Worth: Harcourt Brace Jovanovich, 1988); Donald Berthrong, *The Southern Cheyennes* (Norman: University of Oklahoma Press, 1963).

6. Joseph Jablow, *The Cheyenne in Plains Indian Trade Relations, 1795–1840,* Monographs of the American Ethnological Society 19 (New York: J. J. Augustin, 1951).

7. J. W. Whitfield to Superintendent of Indian Affairs, January 5, 1856, Letters Received, Office of Indian Affairs, Upper Arkansas Agency, Naitonal Archives, Washington, D.C.

8. James B. Hamm, "Plains Indian Plant Usage," in *The Prairie: Roots of Our Culture; Foundations of Our Economy. Proceedings of the Tenth North American Prairie Conference* (Dallas: Native Prairies Association of Texas, 1988); Kelly Kindscher, "The Ethno-botanical Use of Native Prairie Plants," ibid.

9. For a spirited argument of this point, see Margot Liberty, "Hell Came with Horses: Plains Indian Women in the Equestrian Era," *Montana: The Magazine of Western History* 32 (Summer 1982): 10–19.

10. John Peter Powell, *People of the Sacred Mountain: A History of the Northern Cheyenne Chiefs and Warrier Societies* (San Francisco: Harper and Row, 1981).

11. For a fascinating look at Cheyenne cosmology, see Karl H. Schlesier, *The Wolves of Heaven: Cheyenne Shamanism, Ceremonies, and Prehistoric Origins* (Norman: University of Oklahoma Press, 1987), especially 3–18.

12. The ecological and economic crises of the Cheyennes are considered in Elliott West, *The Way to the West: Essays on the Central Plains* (Albuquerque: University of New Mexico Press, 1995), especially chapters 1, 2.

13. Venola Lewis Bivans, ed., "The Diary of Luna E. Warner, a Kansas Teenager of the Early 1870s," *Kansas Historical Quarterly* 35 (Autumn 1969): 276–77.

14. Ibid. (Winter 1969): 420.

15. Eugene D. Fleharty, *Wild Animals and Settlers on the Great Plains* (Norman: University of Oklahoma Press, 1995), 135–36.

16. Bivans, "Diary of Luna Warner" (Autumn 1969): 283, 288.

17. "Where Many Elders Live, Signs of the Future," *New York Times,* March 7, 1993.

The Cultural Landscape of the Pawnees

Richard White

In June of 1871, at the Pawnee village on the Loupe River, the chiefs and soldiers of the four tribes of the Pawnee Nation met in council with their Quaker agent and superintendent. The council convened in the midst of the spring ceremonies; the women had already planted the fields and the priests had performed the Young Mother Corn ritual that ended the planting cycle. As it had for centuries, the attention of the Pawnees shifted to the mixed-grass plains hundreds of miles to the west where, in the first of their semiannual hunts, they would soon seek simultaneously to find the buffalo herds and to avoid contact with the Sioux. The chiefs who met with the Quakers would, in a week or two, hold a second, far more significant ritual council in which they, personifying Tirawahat, the primal power of the universe, would acknowledge their responsibility to lead the people in search of the buffalo. Then, after the Great Cleansing Ceremony, thousands of Pawnees with their thousands of horses and dogs would trail away from the earthlodge village and fields to live as nomads for the summer. Although this council with the Quakers was not directly concerned with the hunt, the approaching summer journey was what concerned Peta-la-sharo, the head chief of the Chaui Pawnee, as the meeting opened.

The Quakers had often spoken against these seasonal forays onto the Great Plains. This was natural enough for persons who wanted to transform the Pawnee men from hunters and raiders into farmers. But the Quakers were primarily concerned about the safety of the Pawnees. For almost forty years, the Sioux and their allies had been constricting the Pawnee buffalo-hunting range. They had repeatedly mauled the Pawnees while on the hunt; meanwhile other Sioux bands and some of the small, desperately poor tribes burned and looted the unoccupied Pawnee villages to the east. Americans added to the turmoil. Having first driven the buffalo away from the Platte River, they were now rapidly destroying the herds. The hunt, the Quakers argued, promised few rewards. The Pawnees should be sensible; they should confine themselves to their earth-lodge villages and trust to agriculture alone.

Peta-la-sharo knew the history of the last forty years well enough— the pistol he kept beside him every night was a constant reminder of conditions on the plains—but what the Quakers recommended was impossible. During the council he tried once more to explain to white men the deeper logic of the hunt. His speech survives only in a single sketchy (and almost certainly distorted) note taken by the Quaker agent Jacob Troth. "We want to go on Buffaloe hunt so long as there are any buffaloe—am afraid when we have no meat to offer Great Spirit he will be angry & punish us." The reply of Samuel Janney, the Quaker superintendent, was both condescending and uninformed; it was at once practical and irrelevant. "You must look forward," he replied, "to the time when there will be no buffaloe. We don't give the Great Spirit meat yet he favors us—what he requires is a good heart."[1]

The brief exchange between Peta-la-sharo and Janney led nowhere. The two men talked past each other; but, ironically, their conversation is revealing for precisely that reason. It allows us to glimpse, if only fleetingly, the difference culture makes and the crucial distinction it creates between landscape and environment. Although Peta-la-sharo and Samuel Janney both recognized an environmental crisis on the plains—the destruction of the buffalo herds—they fundamentally disagreed on what it meant and what constituted an appropriate response to it. They could not agree because what *buffalo* meant to each was not an obvious and immediate corollary of the animal's physical existence. Instead, meaning was the work of culture, and since the cultures of Janney and Peta-la-sharo differed substantially, so did the meaning they attached to the buffalo. Culture, as used here, is best defined as a plan or program for behavior. It is a symbolic ordering of the world, and actions and objects take on meaning only within such symbolic systems.[2] Culture translates environment into landscapes. A landscape is an environment imbued with specific cultural meaning. To understand Pawnee actions, then, one must understand the Pawnee landscape as well as the plains and prairie environments. But how does one distinguish the Pawnee landscape from both the natural environment and other landscapes, such as that of the Americans? What was the historical relationship between the plains environment and the Pawnee landscape and what kind of influences did they exert on each other? It is these questions that are at issue here.

PAWNEE AND AMERICAN LANDSCAPES

Peta-la-sharo's and Janney's worlds encompassed more than the physical world their senses revealed to them. They both saw Americans, Pawnees, and Sioux; grass, cornfields, cottonwoods, and willows; rivers and streams; horses and buffalo. They could even equate Tirawahat and the Christian God. Culturally, however, each man ordered these elements in distinctive ways and gave them different meanings. Out of the same environment, they constructed different landscapes. As accurately as Samuel Janney saw the components of the Pawnee landscape, its order and meaning escaped him.

To an outside observer like Janney, the Pawnee world was not a single landscape, but a series of physical environments: the terraces along the Loup, Platte, and Republican rivers where they built, or had built, their earth lodges and planted their crops; the tall-grass prairies surrounding their villages; and the mixed-grass plains where they traveled twice a year to hunt the buffalo. Ecologically, each landscape was distinct; materially, each seemed to produce a distinctive way of life. The eastern lands—the tall-grass prairies and the lands along the rivers— were among the richest agricultural areas of the world. The western lands—the mixed-grass plains beyond the one-hundredth meridian— were the lands of the buffalo nomads. In their semiannual travels from village to buffalo grounds the Pawnees seemingly transformed themselves. Part-time sedentary farmers, part-time horse nomads, they were losing their world to specialists—the Sioux hunters and their allies in the west and the American farmers in the east.

In Peta-la-sharo's view, by contrast, the Pawnee world was a single, coherent whole. Buffalo hunting was not an alternative to agriculture; nor was agriculture possible without buffalo hunting. Each existed because of the other and was necessary to the other's existence. This was what Peta-la-sharo tried to explain to the council. If there was no buffalo meat to be offered at the ceremonies, the ceremonies would fail; if the ceremonies failed, the crops would not grow. The Pawnees alone mediated between heaven and earth. Their ceremonies alone secured life-giving contact with Tirawahat. The buffalo, its meat pledged to all the ceremonies, was holy. The hunt "signified the entire ceremonial life."[3] Not to hunt the buffalo was to guarantee the failure of agriculture. The Quaker suggestion that they give up the buffalo hunt to increase the yields and security of their agriculture made no sense to the Pawnees. The Quakers did not understand Peta-la-sharo's explanation; they thought that the Pawnees feared punishment by a vindictive God.

In the Pawnee landscape the practical and the sacred merged, giving their natural world a meaning and ambience that whites could not perceive. In the Hako Ceremony the coming of the Father's party to the village of the Son became a complex and awesome journey through time, space, and social boundaries, in which the natural world served simultaneously as sustenance, symbol, and mediator between humans and Tirawahat. The ceremony made clear that the most common natural events were also sacred events.

> Mother Earth hears the call; she moves, she awakes, she arises, she feels the breath of the new-born Dawn. The leaves and the grass stir; all things move with the breath of the new day; everywhere life is renewed.
>
> This is very mysterious; we are speaking of something very sacred, although it happens every day.[4]

The distinction whites made between practical and sacred activities thus was far less clear to a Pawnee. Pawnees recognized that their arrows killed buffalo, but they also believed that hunters must secure the consent of the buffalo and all animals before they could be killed. Similarly, in the fields both hoeing the corn and plucking and dressing a corn plant as Young Mother Corn in the ceremony of the same name were equally necessary if the corn was to grow. Both were utilitarian acts, if by that is meant acts necessary to procure food. To a modern agronomist, however, the ceremony of Young Mother Corn appears irrelevant to the physical growth of the corn plant. A study of the ceremony would not yield much information on why and how corn grows. But for scholars who wish to understand the Pawnees, for those who wish to consider not only the physical existence of ecological systems but also their ordering into a meaningful cultural world, into a landscape, the Young Mother Corn Ceremony and the rest of the symbolic culture does matter.[5] Janney and Peta-la-sharo drew very different meanings from the same set of physical objects because, in a sense, neither experienced the physical world directly. For both of them culture mediated between themselves and the natural world.

Culture, of course, cannot control the natural world. For example, it does not prevent starvation when crops fail repeatedly. Just as clearly, however, history is not the automatic consequence of physical events such as crop failures. People who survive famines must interpret the meaning of their experience and act accordingly, and they do this only within a given cultural context.

Describing the significance of culture and distinguishing landscape from environment does not eliminate other possible distortions of meaning. Culture and nature—landscape and environment—may be distinct, but they are not unconnected. Clearly many possibilities exist (at least theoretically) in the cultural order that would prove disastrous if acted on in the natural world. If nature does not dictate, it certainly limits.

Culture and nature are neither insulated from each other nor static. Both not only develop according to their own internal dynamics but they are also subject to reciprocal influences. The range of connections between the Pawnee landscape and the plains and prairie environments is too vast to discuss in toto here. But an idea of the reciprocal influences at work, and a glimpse of the processes of change involved, can be obtained by looking at the adjustment the Pawnees made to a new element of their physical world that appeared among them in the early eighteenth century: the horse.

PAWNEES AND THE HORSE

Both the Pawnee ceremonial cycle and their seasonal cycle, which combined agriculture and the semiannual journey to the buffalo plains, antedate the horse. Indeed, the Pawnee eagerness for the horse appears to have arisen from the demands of this seasonal cycle. In 1724 the chief of the Skidi Pawnees informed the French that his people wanted peace with the Apaches to secure a steady supply of horses "which will help us to carry our belongings when we move to our winter grounds."[6] Initially, the horse simply replaced the dog as a burden bearer. Indeed, the Pawnee name for the horse translates as *superdog*.[7] The Pawnees soon discovered that the horse could do more than carry baggage. Horses quickly became critical to the buffalo hunt. Horses carried the villagers, their equipment and supplies to the plains; men rode on horses during the hunt; and horses transported the meat and hides back to the villages. By the eighteenth century participation in the buffalo hunt required horses; by the early nineteenth century the Pawnees, through gift exchanges and raiding, had increased their herds to at least six thousand, and possibly as many as eight thousand, animals.

The horse thus moved into the Pawnee landscape along available cultural avenues. The hunt, the gift exchange, and the raid were not invented because of it. The apparent ease of the animal's introduction into the landscape is, however, deceptive. The horse also created an undeniable series of stress points in the society. Each stress point, in a sense, represented friction between the social and cultural organization of the Pawnees and the material demands or consequences of the horse. Horses, for instance, helped to individualize the communal hunt. Older methods of impounding and driving on foot gave way to the "surround" on horseback, in which those hunters with the best horses killed the most buffalo. Families without horses either had to remain at home or else play peripheral and less rewarding roles in the hunt.[8] Since horses were unevenly distributed among the Pawnees—a rich family might have twenty or more while a poor family had two, one, or none—the horse threatened to introduce a deep and basic inequality into Pawnee society, inextricably dividing it into the rich and prosperous and the poor and marginal.

But because the Pawnee landscape was by its very nature cultural as well as material, no such drastic economic divisions seem to have emerged. The Pawnees' redistributive system, based on their symbolic organization of the world, checked many of the consequences of the uneven ownership of horses. Pawnees gave away horses at ceremonials to seek good fortune or to celebrate their own or their family's accomplishments. Horses became part of the bride price, and the Pawnees gave horses (usually mediocre ones) away at the begging dance. Commoners also gave animals as gifts to the chiefs and priests for the ceremonial knowledge and blessings that the Pawnees regarded as essential for success. This channeled the new wealth to existing elites who already had cultural obligations to validate their own status through generosity. Even more significant than this cultural exchange of horses were the Pawnee practices that ensured that individual gains from the hunt would be redistributed. Pawnee hunters, for instance, pledged much of their buffalo meat to the ceremonies, thereby ensuring redistribution. And on the hunt itself a Pawnee who butchered an animal received half the meat while the man who killed it got the other half and the hide. This last practice may well postdate the introduction of the horse, but the larger redistributive system and ceremonial cycle were created much earlier. The symbolic order, as part of the cultural landscape, controlled the impact the horse had on Pawnee society.[9]

ENVIRONMENTAL PROBLEMS

Not all the material consequence of the introduction of the horse could be absorbed so easily along existing cultural channels. The simple necessity of feeding and protecting the herds created two other stress points. One was to reconcile the horses with the existing agricultural order at the village sites. The other concerned the feeding of the horses during the winter hunt.

Within the Pawnee villages the horses were a source of friction because the women saw them as a threat to their horticultural plots. The horses could not be allowed to graze freely in the vicinity of villages partly because they would then invite attacks by raiding parties of Sioux and other tribes, but also because the horses, if unrestrained, would wreak havoc on the basic resource of the women's domain—cultivated crops.[10] This was made worse by the insistence of the men that the women and boys take care of the horses. The result was the conflict that Samuel Allis, a missionary, described: "There are more broils, jealousy, and family quarrels caused by horses than all other troubles combined. The horse frequently causes separation between man and wife, sometimes for life."[11]

The problems of feeding the horses around the villages only compounded the animals' economic and social liabilities. The Pawnees lived in a country of seemingly limitless grass, and a scarcity of feed might seem inconceivable to visitors in late spring or early summer, when the grasses of the valleys were waist- and chest-high. After early fall, however, especially during droughts, the lack of feed was acute. Missionaries reported that during the winter the lands around the earth-lodge villages simply could not support the horse herds. Even if tall-grass species remained abundant after the Pawnee herds had grazed, by the fall they had dried in the summer sun and lost most of their nutrients. The difference between the nutritive qualities of dry tall grass on the prairies and dry buffalo grass on the plains, which retained most of its nutrients year round, was so marked that John Charles Fremont noticed that his animals "began sensibly to fail as soon as we quitted the buffalo grass" and entered the tall-grass prairies.[12]

Because of the nature of the tall-grass prairies the difficult times for the Pawnee horse herds ranged from fall until mid-spring. During this period the grasses of the prairies had little food value since the plants stored their nutrients underground in the rhizomes for the winter. Cutting the grass in mid- or late summer and storing it as hay seemed the obvious solution to contemporary whites, and even as astute an ethnologist as Gene Weltfish expresses some surprise that the Pawnees did not begin to do so until the 1860s. But to harvest hay the Pawnees would have had to disrupt their whole economy and seasonal cycle. The tribe was absent on its summer hunts until early September and on returning both men and women labored in the fields for several weeks. There was no opportunity to cut hay while it still had value as feed unless they abridged their summer hunt, and this hunt was, after all, the economic rationale for the horse and central to the Pawnee symbolic order.[13] At the earth-lodge villages integration of the horse thus faced serious social and ecological problems.

Another stress point was reached during and immediately following the winter buffalo hunt. This was the most dangerous time for the horses. The Pawnees worked their horses hard in the late fall during the tribal hunt, and if storms during November and December were severe, losses to the herd could be serious. When William Ashley and Jedediah Smith visited the Pawnees in winter quarters in 1824, for example, early snows had seriously diminished the Skidi horse herds.[14] Moreover, if the number of horses increased, so did the danger of losses. Without larger supplies of well-cured, nutritious hay (which were impossible to obtain) there was simply no way to maintain thousands of horses at one location during an entire winter.

The end of the winter led to another challenge for the Pawnees. They had to return to the earth-lodge villages before the time when tall grasses had normally begun their spring growth. To wait for the grasses would mean late planting for the crops, an alteration in the ceremonial cycle believed necessary for their growth, and an increased danger of crop loss. But to leave too early could mean the loss of many horses.

PAWNEE SOLUTIONS

The Pawnee solutions to the environmental and cultural problems that feeding the horses presented were complex and varied. They demonstrate the reciprocal influences of landscape and environment, of culture and the material world. During the fall the Pawnees compensated for the poor feed around the villages by removing their horse herds to Grand Island in the Platte River, where feed was more abundant. When the horses returned to the villages, the women fed them on nubbin ears of corn and hand-carried fresh grass from lowlands and swales. As Allis indicated, the women did not bear this increased labor without complaint. Environmental limits were culturally extended at the cost of increased social and domestic tensions.

During the winter hunt itself environmental limits forced a pronounced cultural change. The Pawnees and other plains tribes quickly discovered that cottonwood bark and small branches made excellent substitutes for hay. The horses ate cottonwood readily, even in preference to grass, but repeated winterings in a single site rapidly depleted the trees. Among the Sioux, who wintered in much smaller bands, this is what happened around their regularly used winter campgrounds. Out of necessity, the Pawnees had to move repeatedly during the winter, until by the nineteenth century white observers regarded the winter buffalo hunt as an adjustment to the needs of the horse herds as well as a search for meat. On the western streams the Pawnees could cut cottonwood bark and boughs, and on the uplands, when the ground was clear of snow, the horses could eat the nutritious buffalo and grama grasses.[15] Almost certainly the winter patterns of the nation changed with the acquisition of the horse. They had to adjust to new environmental limits.

In early spring the Pawnees faced a final seasonal dilemma brought by the problem of feeding their herds of horses. In this case, instead of modifying their social patterns, they modified the environment itself. Already weakened by an arduous winter, the horses had to move the tribe back to the permanent villages during March or early April, when the grasses had as yet shown little growth. Obviously any way in which the Pawnees could encourage the early growth of prairie grasses would have significant benefits for the tribe and its horse herds.

For the Pawnees and other prairie tribes, fire provided the means for securing feed for their horses in early spring, the time of critical need. Much of the large body of writing concerning the fires Indians set on the plains assumes that the plains and prairie peoples, like the woodland peoples, were trying to maintain open land and increase the population of deer and elk in the already open woodlands of the Pawnee country. Indeed, by destroying trees and shrubs and encouraging grasses, the browsers would lose sources of food and probably decline in numbers. Nor would burning help the buffalo, since these animals generally inhabited the short-grass plains rather than the tall-grass prairies most often burned by the Pawnees. Occasional fires would be set by hunters to trap or control game, but the systematic burning of the tall grasslands carried out by historic tribes would seem to have little relation to the needs of local game animals.[16]

The prairie fires were instead directly related to the needs of the horse herds. A series of ecological studies carried out in Kansas and Nebraska have demonstrated that burning has a marked effect on the initial growth of prairie grasses. By eliminating the previous year's growth and excessive ground mulch, fire allows the sun to warm the earth more quickly, resulting not only in spring growth that comes weeks earlier but also in significantly higher yields from March to July—exactly the period when the Pawnees needed the grasses. In one experiment burned lands had by June yielded twice as much grass as unburned, excessively mulched land had.[17]

Early travelers in the Pawnee country noted the difference in the rate of growth on burned and unburned land. According to Lorenzo Sawyer, who journeyed through the Platte Valley in mid-May, 1850, "Those portions of the valley which have been burnt over, are covered with fresh, though short grass, giving them the appearance of smooth shaven lawns, while the portions still covered with old grass resemble thick fields of ripe grain waving in the breeze and just ready for harvest." Visitors realized that travel in the spring through unburned prairies would result in scarcity of feed, and it is not surprising that the more knowledgeable observers, such as George Catlin, understood that the purpose of these set fires was to ensure feed for the Indian horses.[18]

The Pawnees appear to have burned the prairies regularly in the fall, with less frequent burning in the early spring. They set these fires both in the vicinity of their earth-lodge villages and along the routes—the Platte, Republican, Blue, and Smoky Hill valleys—to their hunting grounds. The area covered by these fires could take in hundreds of square miles, since they could burn for days at a time if no rain fell. While the Long Expedition was camped at Council Bluffs in 1819, Edwin James witnessed a fire that burned from October 24 to November 10, and Captain Howard Stansbury reported that in 1850 a three-hundred-mile-long region on the Platte had been completely burned over by autumn fires. The kind of total destruction Stansbury reported was unusual, however. Winds and topography usually influenced the course of fires so that irregularly shaped patches of various sizes escaped burning in any given year. From contemporary descriptions it appears that although the Pawnees did not burn all of their territory every year, few tall-grass areas escaped at least one burning in any two- or three-year period.[19]

Necessary as these annual fires became for the maintenance of the horse herds, they also had less desirable ecological repercussions. Although the Indians might carefully protect trees in the immediate vicinity of the villages, the fires exacted their price in the more distant groves. During the early nineteenth century missionaries and explorers reported that large numbers of trees were destroyed each fall in prairie fires. Later, the first white settlers in the region complained vehemently about the loss of scarce timber. When the Americans won control of portions of the old Pawnee territory, a resurgence of tree growth along the streams and ravines often marked the change in sovereignty.[20]

CULTURE AND THE LANDSCAPE

Cultural integration of the horse thus was part of a complex process. It forced social and ecological adjustment, but only within the context of the existing culture. The Pawnee world did not begin anew with the horse. Horses did not, for instance, somehow cause nomadism. Except for the Crows and Cheyennes, who appear to have been forced initially into nomadism by the Sioux, no horticultural group of the western prairies became buffalo nomads when they acquired the horse. The idea of Indians adapting to the horse as if culture is a series of Pavlovian responses confuses the question of cultural and social change and, more to the point here, distorts the relationship between landscape and environment. The changes in Pawnee life that the horse brought are not a case of environment determining culture. Instead cultural mechanisms operated within certain environmental limits, and at times altered the nature of those limits. Manipulation of the physical world was not, after all, restricted to whites.

Specifically, the horse took on meaning within Pawnee culture, and the consequences of its adoption were dealt with in this context. If the horse encouraged unequal access to subsistence, this did not mean that the rich prospered and the poor starved. Instead, existing cultural elements—dedication of meat to the ceremonies, feasting, and, above all, redistribution—counteracted unequal access to the buffalo.[21] Although the spring growth of grasses did not begin early enough to maintain the horses at the villages where the Pawnees planted their crops, the Pawnees were not forced to choose between horses and corn. Instead they resorted to burning the prairies, which resulted in a change in the pattern of the growth of the grasses. Fire, however, also diminished the number of trees along streams and rivers, hurting other aspects of the Pawnee economy and introducing tensions into their dealings with whites. The influences between culture and nature, landscape and environment were, in short, complex and reciprocal. Without some appreciation of this complexity, human history can become either as incomprehensible to us as Peta-la-sharo's speech was to Samuel Janney, or, even worse, as simple as some current determinisms make it.

NOTES

1. "Minutes of Councils between Pawnee and Their Agents," vol. 18 (transcription), Nebraska State Historical Society, Lincoln; originals in Division of Indian Archives, Oklahoma State Historical Society, Oklahoma City. For ceremonial and seasonal cycles, see Gene Weltfish, *The Lost Universe* (New York: Ballantine Books, 1971). The standard, though biased and flawed, history of the Pawnees is George Hyde, *The Pawnee Indians* (Norman: University of Oklahoma Press, 1974). For the prehistoric plains and the early historical period, Waldo Wedel's *Prehistoric Man on the Great Plains* (Norman: University of Oklahoma Press, 1961) and his *The Direct Historical Approach in Pawnee Archeology*, Smithsonian Miscellaneous Collections, vol. 97, no. 7 (Washington, D.C., 1938), are still good, but Robert Grange's *Pawnee and*

Lower Loup Pottery, Nebraska State Historical Society, Publications in Anthropology no. 3 (Lincoln, 1968), should also be consulted.

2. Clifford Geertz, *The Interpretation of Cultures* (New York: Basic Books, 1973), p. 23.

3. Weltfish, *Lost Universe*, pp. 157–58.

4. Alice C. Fletcher, "The Hako: A Pawnee Ceremony," *Twenty-Second Annual Report of the Bureau of American Ethnology to the Secretary of the Smithsonian Institution, 1900–01* (Washington, D.C.: GPO, 1904), pp. 80, 99, 106, 136, 220, 302, 331.

5. Weltfish, *Lost Universe*, pp. 333, 150–56.

6. Henri Folmer, "French Expansion Toward New Mexico in the Eighteenth Century" (M.A. thesis, University of Denver, 1939), pp. 173–74.

7. Weltfish, *Lost Universe*, pp. 168–72.

8. Ibid., pp. 168–73; Charles A. Murray, *Travels in North America During the Years 1834, 1835, 1836*, 2 vols. (London: R. Bentley, 1839), 1:291–92.

9. John Dunbar, "The Pawnee Indians: Their History and Ethnology," *Magazine of American History* 4 (1880): 252, 265–66; John Dunbar, "The Pawnee Indians: Their Habits and Customs," *Magazine of American History* 8 (1882): 738; Weltfish, *Lost Universe*, pp. 169–72; Murray, *Travels*, 1:291–92; Samuel Allis, "Forty Years among the Indians and on the Eastern Borders of Nebraska," *Proceedings and Collections of the Nebraska State Historical Society* 2 (1887): 159.

10. Wm. Clark to James Barbour, December 8, 1825, Office of Indian Affairs, Letters Received, St. Louis, Microfilm 234, National Archives, Washington, D.C. (hereafer OIA, LR . . . M 234 NA); T. Harvey to L. Crawford, July 25, 1845, OIA, LR, Council Bluffs, M 234; John Henry Carleton, *The Prairie Logbooks: Dragoon Campaigns to the Pawnee Villages in 1844* (Chicago: Caxton Club, 1943), pp. 70, 75, 196; Harlan Fuller and LeRoy Hafen, eds., *The Journal of Captain John R. Bell: Official Jounalist for the Stephen Long Expedition . . . 1820* (Glendale, Ill.: Arthur Clark, 1957), p. 122; Lt. J. C. Fremont, "A Report on an Exploration of the Country Lying Between the Missouri River and the Rocky Mountains," *Senate Document* 243, 27th Cong., 3d sess., ser. 416, p. 16; Gottlieb F. Oehler and David Z. Smith, *Description of a Journey and Visit to the Pawnee Indians . . . April 22–May 18, 1851*, reprinted from the Moravian Church Miscellany of 1851–52 (New York, 1914), p. 29.

11. Allis, "Forty Years," p. 140.

12. J. E. Weaver and F. W. Albertson, *Grasslands of the Great Plains* (Lincoln: University of Nebraska Press, 1956), pp. 36–38; J. C. Fremont, "A Report of an Exploration of the Country Lying Between the Missouri River and the Rocky Mountains," *House Document* 166, 28th Cong., 2d sess., ser. 467, p. 289; J. E. Weaver, *Native Vegetation of Nebraska* (Lincoln: University of Nebraska Press, 1968), p. 63; John Dunbar, "Missionary Life Among the Pawnee," *Nebraska State Historical Society Collections* 16 (Lincoln, 1911): 281.

13. Weaver, *Native Vegetation*, p. 63; Weltfish, *Lost Universe*, p. 495. It appears that in the early 1870s the smaller tribes such as the Omahas, who were frequently driven

from the plains by the Sioux, grew proportionately more hay and oats than the neighboring Pawnees. The Pawnees, by this time under severe pressure from the Sioux, also had begun growing hay. *Annual Report of the Commissioner of Indian Affairs for 1871* (Washington, D.C.: GPO, 1871), pp. 445–47, 622; *Annual Report of the Commissioner of Indian Affairs for 1874* (Washington, D.C.: GPO, 1874), pp. 115–202.

14. Harrison Dale, ed., *The Ashley-Smith Explorations and the Discovery of a Central Route to the Pacific, 1822–1829* (Cleveland: A. H. Clark Co., 1918), p. 122.

15. Dunbar, "Pawnee Habits and Customs," p. 332; R. G. Thwaites, ed., "Edwin James' Account of S. H. Long's Expedition," *Early Western Travels*, 2 vols. (Cleveland: A. H. Clark Co., 1904–1907), 15:215–16; Dunbar, "Missionary Life Among the Pawnees," p. 281; Rufus Sage, *Scenes in the Rocky Mountains* (Philadelphia: Carey and Hart, 1846), p. 97; Lt. G. K. Warren, "Report of Lt. G. K. Warren . . . of the Sioux Expedition of Explorations in the Dakota Country, 1855," *Senate Executive Document* 76, 34th Cong., 1st sess., ser. 822, p. 17.

16. Conrad Moore, "Man and Fire in the Central North American Grassland, 1585–1890: A Documentary History" (Ph.D. diss., UCLA, 1974). Moore found that the majority of fires set by Indians occurred in the tall-grass areas.

17. J. E. Weaver and N. W. Rowland, "Effects of Excessive Natural Mulch on Development, Yield, and Structure of Native Grassland," *Botanical Gazette* 114 (1952); 1–19; T. L. Steiger, "Structure of Prairie Vegetation," *Ecology* 11 (1930): 217; R. L. Hensel, "Effects of Burning on Vegetation in Kansas Pastures," *Journal of Agricultural Research* 23 (1923): 631–43.

18. Lorenzo Sawyer, *Way Sketches: Containing Incidents of Travel Across the Plains* (New York: Edward Eberstadt, 1926), pp. 32–33; George Catlin, *Letters and Notes on the Manners, Customs, and Conditions of the North American Indians*, 2 vols. (London: Tosswell and Myers, 1841), 2:16.

19. Howard Stansbury, "Exploration and Survey of the Valley of the Great Salt Lake Including a Reconnaissance of a New Route Through the Rocky Mountains," *Senate Executive Document* 3, special session, ser. 608, p. 32; R. G. Thwaites, ed., "James' Account of Long's Expedition," 14:263, 15:139.

20. R. G. Thwaites, ed., "Maximillian, Prince of Wied's Travels in the Interior of North America," *Early Western Travels* 22:268; Sage, *Scenes in the Rocky Mountains*, 36–37; J. Dunbar to J. Hamilton, October 1839, OIA, LR, Council Bluffs, M 234, NA; R. Ricky to G. Manypenny, December 1, 1856, OIA, LR, Otoe Agency, M 234, NA; Petition for Removal of Pawnee, January 16, 1869, Inquiry of Specie and North, December 4, 1875, OIA, LR, Pawnee Agency, M 234, NA; Lt. G. Warren, "Explorations in Nebraska," *Senate Executive Document* 1, 35th Cong., 2d sess., ser. 975, p. 658; *Explorations and Surveys for a Railroad Route from the Mississippi River to the Pacific Ocean*, vol. 2 (Washington D.C.: GPO, 1855), pp. 12–13; Moore, "Man and Fire," p. 121.

21. Preston Holder, *The Hoe and the Horse on the Plains: A Study of Cultural Development among North American Indians* (Lincoln: University of Nebraska Press, 1970), pp. 54, 60–65; Weltfish, *Lost Universe,* p. 119.

The Chippewa and Munsee Indians: Acculturation and Survival in Kansas, 1850s–1870

Joseph B. Herring

In 1853 and 1854 Commissioner of Indian Affairs George Manypenny negotiated a series of land cessions with the tribes of eastern Kansas. At first he encountered opposition from many Indians who reminded him that the government had guaranteed them their lands for "as long as grass grew or water run." While Manypenny listened sympathetically to their arguments, he knew he had to act quickly or these Indians could lose all of their holdings. By promising the tribes a portion of their lands as a permanent home, he induced them to part with thirteen million acres.[1] The commissioner sincerely believed that the diminished reserves would serve as their permanent residences.

While he engaged in treaty negotiations. Manypenny had good reason to worry about the Indians' future in Kansas. To defraud tribesmen of their lands, politicians and Fort Leavenworth military officers had allied with scheming speculators and Indians willing to betray their people for a bribe. Men like former Missouri Sen. Thomas Hart Benton saw opportunity for profit in Kansas, and they used the slavery issue, then a topic of heated debate in Congress, to champion territorial expansion. Manypenny's efforts to defend Indian rights incurred the wrath of those intent on evicting all natives from Kansas and although the commissioner managed to delay Indian removal for a while, his opponents would quickly have their way. Within a few years white men would own the land and Indian Kansas would be but a memory.[2]

In May 1854, shortly after Manypenny and other federal officials concluded treaty negotiations with the tribes, Congress passed the Kansas-Nebraska bill. While legislators organized Kansas into a territory, speculators, claim makers, squatters, and other opportunists rushed into the area. Even before surveyors could carefully map out new Indian reserves, fights erupted among whites over conflicting claims.[3] Amid this scramble for land, Indians were hard pressed to protect their remaining possessions.

The tiny Chippewa and Munsee tribes appeared to be the least likely of all to retain their lands in Kansas. Indeed, with approximately forty members in each band, these Indians must have seemed most vulnerable to those interested in taking their territory. But in the years after 1854, while the Delawares, the Iowas, the Citizen Band Pottawatomies, and other larger tribes succumbed to sales talks by wily speculators and railroad agents and moved from their homes, the Chippewas and Munsees successfully retained their holdings. Beginning in July 1859, when the two tribes agreed by treaty to become allies,[4] through the early 1870s, they resisted all attempts to evict them from the state. Of the thousands of Indians living in the area when Kansas became a territory, the Chippewas and Munsees were among the few hundred remaining just twenty years later.

Holding on to their lands was not an easy task. By the time the Chippewas and Munsees were merged by treaty on July 16, 1859, settlers had flooded into Kansas and civil war loomed on the horizon. Meanwhile, they faced both mounting pressure from squatters and land speculators and internal dissension and turmoil among tribe members. Because they were two very disparate groups, disputes over tribal policy were frequent. Indian agents often complained that handling their affairs was difficult because "each tribe was jealous of the other and ready to oppose any measure because the other originated or favored it."[5]

The forces underlying these intertribal tensions were many. Since the mid–eighteenth century, the Munsees had endeavored to pattern their lives after the maxims of the Moravian church. They worshiped the Christian God, observed the Sabbath, shunned liquor, and took but one wife. They denounced sin and refused to participate in native dances, religious ceremonies, and other "heathenish festivals."[6] This tiny group of about forty souls had lost their lands in a questionable transaction in 1858,[7] necessitating their resettlement on the Chippewa reservation near Ottawa, Kansas.

The Munsees were headed by Henry Donohoe, a white man who had married into the band. As was typical of many tribes which had formerly resided in the East, Munsee leadership rested on a man with a thorough knowledge of both Indian and white world views. Able to understand the intricacies of racial interaction, so-called mixed-bloods like John Ross of the Cherokees and whites adopted into a tribe like Donohoe found many followers among Indians struggling to make a living in an ever-changing environment. Although Donohoe claimed that he would cease to act as an Indian as soon as the Moravians were established on the reservation, he enjoyed his role as chief and would never voluntarily relinquish that position. He would continue to work to assure that the Munsee remained true to the tenets of the Moravian religion.[8]

The Chippewas, in contrast, still observed the Algonquin religious practices which they had brought with them from Michigan in 1839. While they had modified their traditional Indian customs and had taken on many aspects of the white man's civilization, they continually resisted attempts by missionaries to convert them to Christianity. Their government agent in 1858 described them as a quiet, "industrious and domestic" people, who "have good farms and cultivate them well," but who insisted on following the religious precepts set forth by Chief Eshtonoquot, whom the agent called "a worthy good man and by nature very intelligent."[9]

Such accolades were rare after 1859 as Eshtonoquot, known to the whites as Francis McCoonse, often found himself at odds with those endeavoring to transform his people into imitation white men. The Chippewa chief believed that missionaries, government officials, and other advocates of white civilization were interlopers, more interested in expanding personal wealth than in promoting native welfare. He knew that most whites agreed with the sentiment expressed by the *Leavenworth Times* that "honest settlers" should replace the "few worthless redskins [who] are permitted to hold the finest acres in Kansas."[10]

Trusting neither agents nor missionaries, Eshtonoquot warned fellow tribesmen against listening to these champions of Indian social change. He scorned white customs and religion, quipping that while it took the "white man seven years to learn theology; Indians learn [it] . . . in one hour." Indians should adhere to their traditional beliefs, he warned. Any tribesman who walked down the "crookety" path "falls into deep gulf, water carries him away. Bad Indian lost."[11]

Eshtonoquot's leadership was severely challenged on August 19, 1862, when Moravian missionary Joseph Romig opened a school and mission on the reservation at the invitation of the Munsees. The mission included forty acres of prime, fenced land with a small grove of trees and ample water for livestock. A solidly built schoolhouse was furnished with modern supplies, desks, and a blackboard and could seat one hundred people for church services. Romig had come to Indian country to "Christianize and civilize," optimistically expecting Indians to cast off their ancient habits and customs because of his powers of persuasion. Although his church would not receive money from the federal civilization fund, Romig had reason to believe that Donohoe could eventually convince both bands to assist the Moravians financially. In the meantime, Romig advised church superiors to operate the school at their expense because it would facilitate his conversion efforts and would give the Moravians control of the lands surrounding the mission.[12]

Evangelists like Romig typically set up schools to educate Indian children, instruct women in the proper homemaking skills, and show men the benefits of adopting white farming techniques. Thus, Romig and his wife opened elementary and Sunday schools, taught sewing and singing, and "labored to advance Indians in their farming." The enthusiastic Moravian held high hopes for his new charges, for he was convinced that they appreciated his efforts. Deeply imbued with the ethnocentrism of the day, Romig predicted to church superiors that much could be done to uplift these "half-civilized" peoples who were "not heathen" and who seemed eager to learn the ways of the white man. Somewhat blinded by his pious fervor, he was unable to foresee the immense obstacles to achieving his goals.[13]

Following Romig's arrival, Eshtonoquot advised his Chippewa followers to ignore those urging the tribe to accept American citizenship. Referring to neighboring Kansas tribes who had adopted at least some of the trappings of white civilization and were rapidly losing their lands, he added, "we see those that has gone on to be citizens, they are not able to take care of themselves." Resenting Romig's involvement in tribal affairs, he continually accused the Moravian of siding against the Chippewas in inter-tribal disputes, and he charged that the missionary's influence had enabled the Munsees to reap most of the financial benefits of the 1859 treaty.[14]

When Eshtonoquot attempted to exercise this control over both tribes by uniting them against the missionary and the civilization program, Romig and government agents connived to undermine his authority. In late 1863, after agent Clinton C. Hutchinson ordered tribesmen to reject Eshtonoquot's leadership, he and Romig agreed to deal only with those Indians who accepted the view that they should "become citizens, pay taxes, and be subject to the laws of the country." While most Munsees already subscribed to these principles, many Chippewas were reluctant to reject the advice of their chief. By combining a strategy of threats, cajolery, offers of political favors, and bribery, however, the white men managed to persuade a number of Chippewas to betray their traditional leader. Romig attempted to justify these actions by reasoning that if the "silly complaints" of the chief could "prejudice his people against me, he may destroy much of my usefulness here." Taking his cue from the Moravian, agent Henry W. Martin, alleging that Eshtonoquot was "old and childish, and totally unfit . . . and incapable of doing the business of the tribe," ordered the natives to restructure tribal government by forming a council of four men—two from each band—to administer tribal affairs.[15]

Romig wholeheartedly supported Martin's actions. The missionary had wearied of Eshtonoquot's interference in the religious affairs of the reserve. He complained that the chief had instigated constant turmoil among the Indians, "interfered with the school, and maligned myself, not withstanding my utmost efforts to please him." He lamented that "some of the Chippewa houses are holding dances and most of the young people are attending," and the "noisy music [is] sounding in my ears all night, for it is within hearing and seeing distance." Holding Eshtonoquot responsible for such activities, Romig denigrated the chief's character, called him infirm in body and mind, and argued that the Indians suffered under the rule of an old man who was "very illiterate or ignorant, and a bigotted [*sic*] Catholic." If Eshtonoquot continued to hold sway, Romig would lose "all hope of doing good or seeing the Indians prosper." He considered it fortunate that "agents have been led to discard him as chief in order to put an end to troubles."[16]

The new four-man council proved more to Romig's liking. In November 1863, headmen Henry Donohoe and Ignatius Caleb, representing the Munsees, and Louis Godey and Edward McCoonse of the Chippewas decided that rejection of tribal ways and the acceptance of American citizenship constituted the prudent course to follow. McCoonse, who was the son of deposed chief Eshtonoquot, evidently valued his new leadership role over loyalty to his father. He may, however, have been convinced that following the white man's road was the only hope for his people's survival. He joined with the other councilmen in denouncing Eshtonoquot who was, they avowed, "against improvement and encourages degradation and ignorance." On November 30, Donohoe and McCoonse left for Washington to petition for their people's citizenship.[17]

Such news delighted Romig, who now believed a majority of the reservation Indians desired to travel the road to civilized respectability. He felt secure that his word carried weight with the new leaders. "I had an interesting time with my councilmen," Romig wrote church elders. They "receive all I say with the simplicity of children and ask questions with familiarity. They are like Job, they wish to be Christians." Romig believed the tribesmen would easily part with profits from future land sales to help expand and improve mission buildings. Without Eshtonoquot's effective opposition the bands seemed amenable to selling their possessions, and Romig encouraged eastern Moravians to act quickly to buy Indian lands at a bargain. "If any of the brethren of the Moravian Church wish to emigrate to Kansas I could not recommend any better place," he wrote.[18] It is not clear whether Romig intended from the outset to persuade the Indians to sell their lands or whether he decided to do so after his arrival. At any rate, he was determined to induce them to sell and move to the Indian Territory.

In late January 1864, Donohoe and McCoonse arrived in Washington to negotiate a treaty with government officials. Representing the Moravians, Donohoe sought an agreement that would solidify the church's influence on the reservation and permanently nullify Eshtonoquot's power. His plan included donating forty acres of tribal lands to the Moravian church. For the scheme to succeed Donohoe needed the support of McCoonse who was demanding $800 for his corroboration. So Donohoe wrote to the church elders at Bethlehem, Pennsylvania,

81

advising that they pay "some compensation" to the Chippewa delegate. The Moravians agreed to pay a bribe of $128, and although this was considerably less money than he had asked for, McCoonse agreed to the deal. In February, he and Donohoe signed a treaty that, pending Senate ratification, gave the two tribes citizenship and assigned land to the church provided the Moravians continued to educate the tribes' children.[19]

Despite being deposed as official leader, Eshtonoquot still commanded a considerable following among the Chippewas who, when they learned of the treaty, threatened violence and revenge. Opposed to the citizenship treaty, Eshtonoquot and his supporters accused the Washington emissaries of holding secret councils with the missionary and the agent and then sneaking off to the capital without informing either tribe. Insisting that he alone was chief, and denying the agent's right to intervene in tribal politics, Eshtonoquot called on authorities to permit an open council to discuss these matters.[20]

Eshtonoquot recognized Romig's role in disrupting tribal cohesiveness. Distrusting the missionary, who he thought was more interested in enhancing his own financial position than in helping Indians, Eshtonoquot told all who would listen that he intended to drive the Moravian off the reserve. Throughout 1864 and into 1865, the chief challenged Romig's every move. Using his traditional religious powers to counteract missionary influence, he ordered the Chippewas to shun Moravian services and to keep their children from attending school. Advising them to reject white civilization and to return to traditional ways, he threatened to unleash his shamanistic powers against all who failed to heed his word. When many Chippewas obeyed, Donohoe and McCoonse angrily complained to the agent. "This old man encourages dancing, evil, and ignorance," they declared. Parents were afraid to send children to school because they thought Eshtonoquot was "an old witch" and feared that he could bring death to those who disobeyed him. "He makes them believe that by drawing a picture of a man, woman, or child on a walk or any other place, and placing a heart in the left side and naming the individual to be witched—death or something terrible will follow," Donohoe and McCoonse lamented. The council leaders asked the government to issue "a reproval and final condemnation" of Eshtonoquot's "meddlesome disposition [that] would have the effect of quieting and forever silencing this old troublesome Indian."[21]

By the middle of 1865, Eshtonoquot's opponents had gained the ascendancy. In defiance of the chief, and despite fear of retaliation, most children attended Romig's school at least part of the time.[22] The tribal council, ignoring Eshtonoquot's wishes, asked for government approval to sell their "surplus" lands. Since Washington official believed that breaking up the reservations and reducing Indian holdings to the forty to eighty acres needed by individuals were major factors in the civilization program, they agreed to the council's request, and in June of that year soldiers from Fort Leavenworth began a survey of the reservation. By late fall, after the soldiers had mapped out 1,428 acres to be made available at public auction, Romig's contention that Eshtonoquot had "no more influence in tribal business than the most ragged Indian on the reserve" seemed accurate. The Moravian, nevertheless, continued to worry that the chief would prove a future source of "ferment" and "difficulty." After all, Romig reminded his eastern superiors, this was Kansas, and anything was possible "on the borders of civilization and heathenism."[23]

While the army surveyed their reservation, the Chippewas and Munsees faced a difficult future in Kansas. Neighboring tribes such as the Delaware fell deeper in debt and, after selling their homes to meet their obligations, moved to Indian Territory. Yet except for Eshtonoquot and his followers, most Indians on the reserve seemed oblivious to the fact that other natives were being removed from the state. Eshtonoquot argued, meanwhile, that the government's civilization program and white men's land schemes were the major forces responsible for Indian dispersal, and he took every opportunity to denounce the citizenship treaty still pending in the U.S. Senate. Agent Martin reported, nevertheless, that most of the "respectable" tribesmen favored accepting citizenship and ending their tribal status. He regretted, however, that a small minority, "zealously opposed" to the treaty, could hold up Senate ratification.[24]

Events during the winter months of 1866–67 demonstrated the tribes' ability to withstand pressure and proved crucial to the defense of their homeland. The agent reported that "one of the severest winters we ever had" killed much of the livestock and caused suffering and "great privations" among the Chippewas and Munsees. Compounding the Indians' difficulties was an 1866 government agreement with the Kansa tribes which stipulated that they either must become citizens immediately or move from the state.[25] Since the Senate had yet to ratify their proposed treaty, the two bands found themselves in a dilemma. Although they were adopting white customs, they were not technically citizens. Romig and the agent, seeing an opportunity to acquire more land for white interests, pressured the Indians to sell their homes.

Faced with such momentous problems, the two tribes might have engaged in their usual disputes and factionalism, but in fact the Chippewas and Munsees cooperated as never before. On January 11, 1867, the McCoonse-led council informed Romig and Martin that the Indians would not sell their remaining lands. Council members still desired citizenship, but they were determined to retain their homes in Kansas. Eight days later, Eshtonoquot joined with the council to petition against removal. Still opposed to citizenship but not wanting to lose his home, Eshtonoquot rallied to the side of his erstwhile detractors in this battle. He argued that because his people were hardworking, quiet, and peaceful neighbors to the whites, they should not have to leave. The old Chippewa denounced the removal advocates who "never had the good of the tribe at heart."[26] Fortunately, a favorable summer growing season allowed the Indians to raise an abundant crop, which alleviated suffering and enabled them to face future challenges on a better footing. As 1867 drew to a close, they appeared ready to resist all efforts to expel them from the state.[27]

On January 29, 1868, misfortune struck the Indians and jeopardized their struggle to save their homeland when Eshtonoquot, the most vocal opponent of removal, died. The Moravian missionary reported with some satisfaction that his adversary, "who was so long a source of trouble to his people and to the church here," had passed away. "He died as he lived," wrote Romig, "an ignorant heathen and a Catholic." With Eshtonoquot gone, Romig stepped up his campaign to force the tribes to move. He was confident that most would be willing to leave Kansas as soon as favorable terms with the government could be arranged.[28]

By late spring 1868, most of the neighboring tribes had agreed to emigrate to Indian Territory. Romig pointed out that the Delawares had deserted their reservation, the Ottawas were moving "as fast as they can sell out," and the Sacs and Foxes would go as soon as Congress ratified their treaty. The missionary wished that some settlement could be worked out soon, before his Indians were left alone. His hopes apparently were realized on June 1, when federal officials signed a new agreement with the Chippewas and Munsees. The treaty stipulated that individual Indians would receive patents in fee simple, or titles, to their own allotments of land. Each person could sell his holding without consulting the tribe and could move from Kansas whenever he wished.[29] Similar agreements had proven disastrous to other tribes which gave up authority over individual members. Those tribes were not able to prevent individuals from selling their farms under pressure from unscrupulous whites.

Certain that his charges would leave the state soon, a delighted Romig informed Moravian officials that some of the Munsees had made arrangements to settle among the Cherokees in Indian Territory. But while the Senate delayed consideration of their latest treaty, the Indians found themselves in a difficult position. After Eshtonoquot died, leadership of the tribes rested in the hands of the less capable council members. The positions on removal taken by men like Edward Mc-Coonse wavered between loyalty to their people and considerations of personal financial gain. Believing they might be forced to move soon, Indians saw little reason to make repairs on their homes and farms. The confusing state of affairs demoralized some and angered many. A few resorted to alcohol, others to violence. Romig noted with regret "the growing evil of intemperance among our own and other Indians, threatening to destroy their soul and body." When some young men persisted in disturbing the peace and terrorizing law-abiding families, Romig spoke out. He denounced the government annuity system, arguing that "the sooner all Indians are removed and compelled by necessity to labor for their daily bread, the better it will be for them temporally and spiritually."[30] Frustration evidently caused Romig to lose sight of the fact that both Indian bands had labored long and hard to make a living in Kansas. The annuity system had nothing to do with their current situation.

When neighboring Sacs and Foxes emigrated south in November 1869, the tiny group of Chippewas and Munsees stood virtually alone amid a sea of white faces. With the exception of a few hundred Kickapoos and Pottawatomies to the north, some Kansa Indians to the west, and a scattering of other natives elsewhere, they were the only resident Indians left in eastern Kansas. Pressures on those remaining grew intense as citizens, politicians, and the press all clamored to have them expelled. But by late 1869, most Chippewas and Munsees had made individual commitments to hold on to their homes at all costs. While members of both bands now saw acceptance of citizenship as the key to success, a majority would no longer heed the advice of councilmen, missionaries, or agents, but would make decisions as individuals either to move or to stay in Kansas. Their feelings were stated best by Commissioner of Indian Affairs Ely Parker, himself an acculturated Seneca, when he reported that the tribes were "well advanced in civilization, cultivating small farms, dwelling in good houses, and interested in the education of their children. They have no desire to remove, and will, no doubt, soon become citizens."[31]

For the Chippewas and Munsees, however, their unstable situation extended into the 1870s. Although Romig continued to urge them to sell out and move, fewer and fewer Indians listened to his advice. Blaming the "unsettled state of minds relative to their anticipated removal" for the loss of adherents, Romig alleged that "certain enemies of the church" had created an atmosphere of "prejudice" against him. While many Chippewas had always resented Romig, many Munsees now sided against him as well. Realizing that his influence among the Indians waned, Romig railed against laziness and alcohol for making a shambles of his mission efforts. "When we look for grapes behold sour grapes," Romig lamented, "some who promised fair and walked well are trapped by the monster intemperance."[32]

Indeed the rapidly changing circumstances which demanded constant readjustment demoralized some tribesmen over the years. A few had "yielded to evil influences and temptations thrown in their way," and missionary reports of the late 1860s mentioned more alcohol abuse than previously. Disease took a toll as well. In 1870, Romig noted that "fifty or more" had died since his arrival in the state. While that may have been an exaggeration, the combined membership of the two bands did drop from eighty-four in 1867 to sixty-three just three years later. Some may have moved to Indian Territory, but a physician examining health conditions among the natives in the area noted that the two bands were "diminishing in part from the remains of a syphilitic disease." The doctor warned that unless they were relocated closer to other tribes, they would soon die out. "Constant intermarriage in so narrow a circle," he reasoned, "tends to a constant physical deterioration."[33]

Against such odds, the Chippewas and Munsees remained in Kansas. After 1870 they cast off native habits, traveled the white man's road, and at the time of Romig's departure early in the decade, most had begun to profess Christianity. Frequent intermarriage with whites enlarged the genetic pool and reduced disease. Indians of both bands traded their native garments for trousers and shirts, dresses and petti-coats. "The women are as neatly attired as the same number of white women collected in the country," noted one admiring visitor.[34] Like their white neighbors, individuals owned and tended small farms. As individuals outside of tribal authority they could sell their land if they pleased,[35] but most steadfastly refused to part with their holdings. Of the thousands of Indians subjected to the government's 1850s treaties with Kansas Indians, they were among the few remaining in 1870. Among those who voluntarily surrendered their tribal status, they alone managed to stand their ground. At the beginning of the twenti-eth century these acculturated peoples assumed full responsibility for themselves as members of the community at large and severed all legal ties with the federal government. The little Chippewa and Munsee bands had merged into the mainstream of American society.[36] The irony was not lost on those hardy individuals—they had retained their lands, but had lost themselves as Indians.

NOTES

1. George W. Manypenny, *Our Indian Wards* (Cincinnati: Robert Clarke and Co., 1880), 121–22.

2. H. Craig Miner and William E. Unrau discuss Manypenny's treaties and the efforts by opportunists to defraud Indians of their lands in *The End of Indian Kansas: A Study of Cultural Revolution, 1854–1871* (Lawrence: Regents Press of Kansas, 1978), 1–24.

3. For excellent discussions of the land situation in Kansas and its bearing on In-dians see Paul Wallace Gates, *Fifty Million Acres: Conflicts over Kansas Land Policy, 1854–1890* (Ithaca: Cornell University Press, 1954), 16–48, and Miner and Unrau, *The End of Indian Kansas*, 1–141.

4. A treaty uniting the Chippewas and Munsees was concluded on July 16, 1859; see Charles J. Kappler, ed., *Indian Affairs: Laws and Treaties* (Washington, D.C.: Gov-ernment Printing Office, 1904), 2:792–96.

5. Henry W. Martin to Commissioner of Indian Affairs D. N. Cooley, June 26, 1866. Letters Received, Sac and Fox Agency, Bureau of Indian Affairs, Record Group 75, National Archives, Washington, D.C. (Microcopy 234, Roll 736). Here-inafter cited as Letters Received, Sac and Fox Agency, with microcopy and roll numbers.

6. For discussions of the interaction between Indians and Moravian missionar-ies see Kenneth G. Hamilton, "Cultural Contributions of Moravian Missions

Among the Indians," *Pennsylvania History* 18 (January 1951): 1–15; Marcie J. Kohnova, "The Moravians and Their Missionaries: A Problem in Americanization," *Mississippi Valley Historical Review* 19 (December 1932): 349–54; and Paul A. W. Wallace, "The Moravian Records," *Indiana Magazine of History* 48 (June 1952): 143–44.

7. For an excellent analysis of this transaction see Paul Wallace Gates, "A Fragment of Kansas Land History: The Disposal of the Christian Indian Tract," *Kansas Historical Quarterly* 6 (August 1937): 227–40.

8. Henry Donohoe to Brother G. Oehler, February 27, 1862, Moravian Mission Records, Kansas Mission, Box 185, Folder 1, Item 2, Moravian Church Archives, Bethlehem, Pa. (Microfilm Roll 23). Hereinafter cited as Moravian Records, with folder and item numbers.

9. Francis Tymoney to Central Superintendent of Indian Affairs Alexander M. Robinson, September 1, 1858. *Report of the Commissioner of Indian Affairs,* 35th Cong., 2d sess., 1858–59, H. Ex. Doc. 2, 472–74 (Serial 997).

10. *Leavenworth Times,* August 27, 1859.

11. Quoted in Ida M. Ferris, "The Sauks and Foxes in Franklin and Osage Counties, Kansas," *Kansas Historical Collections, 1909–1910* 11 (1910): 362.

12. One reason federal officials permitted the Moravians to establish a mission among the tribes was because church elders agreed to finance the entire venture themselves. Even before Romig arrived on the reservation, however, Donohoe informed Moravian elders that the Indians might ask the government to give the Moravians permanent status on the reservation and allow the church to acquire tribal monies to support the school and mission. See Donohoe to Oehler, February 27, 1862, and Joseph Romig to Brother S. Wolle, March 24, 1862, Moravian Records, Folder 1, Items 2 and 3.

13. Romig to Wolle, March 24, 1862, Romig to Oehler, April 24, 1862, Romig to Wolle, June 23, 1862, Romig to Brother John Jacobsen, March 9, 1863, Moravian Records, Folder 1, Items 4, 5, and 6, and Folder 2, Item 1; Clinton C. Hutchinson to Central Superintendent of Indian Affairs Harrison B. Branch, September 17, 1862, *Report of the Commissioner of Indian Affairs,* 37th Cong., 3d sess., 1862–63, H. Ex. Doc. 1, 253–54 (Serial 1157). Robert F. Berkhofer discusses the typical missionary civilization plan for Indians in *Salvation and the Savage: An Analysis of Protestant Missions and American Indian Response, 1787–1862* (New York: Atheneum, 1976), 1–15.

14. Francis McCoonse (Eshtonoquot) and others to Commissioner of Indian Affairs William P. Dole, February 15, 1864, Letters Received, Ottawa Agency, Bureau of Indian Affairs, Record Group 75, National Archives, Washington, D.C. (Microcopy 234, Roll 656). Hereinafter cited as Letters Received, Ottawa Agency, with microcopy and roll numbers. Francis McCoonse and others to Dole, December 6, 1864, Francis McCoonse to the Commissioner, April 10, 1866, Letters Received, Sac and Fox Agency, M234, R735 and 736.

15. Romig to Jacobsen, March 9, 1863, Moravian Records, Folder 2, Item 1;

Hutchinson to Dole, February 20, 1864, Letters Received, Ottawa Agency, M234, R656; Martin to Dole, January 2, 1865, Letters Received, Sac and Fox Agency M234, R735.

16. Romig to Jacobsen, August 4, 1863, Moravian Records, Folder 2, Item 2; Romig to Dole, February 13, 1865, Letters Received, Sac and Fox Agency, M234, R735.

17. Hutchinson to Dole, December 1, 1863, Letters Received, Ottawa Agency, M234, R656, "Council of the Chippewa and Christian Indians," report signed by Henry Donohoe, Edward McCoonse, and others, January 18, 1865. Martin to Dole, March 15, 1865. Letters Received, Sac and Fox Agency, M234, R735; Report of Commissioner D. N. Cooley, October 31, 1865, *Report of the Commissioner of Indian Affairs,* 39th Cong., 1st sess., 1865–66, H. Ex. Doc. 1, 212–13 (Serial 1248).

18. Romig to Wolle, April 4, 1866, Moravian Records, Folder 5, Item 2; Romig to Martin, August 6, 1866, Letters Received. Sac and Fox Agency, M234, R736.

19. Donohoe to Jacobsen, January 29, 1864, Hutchinson to Wolle, January 30, 1864. Romig to Wolle, February 12, 1864, Donohoe to Jacobsen, April 15, 1864, Oehler to Jacobsen, May 5, 1864, Moravian Records, Folder 3, Items 2, 3, 4, 6, and 8.

20. Francis McCoonse and others to Dole, February 15, 1864, Letters Received, Ottawa Agency, M234, R656; Donohoe to Jacobsen, April 15, 1864, Romig to Wolle, April 27, 1864, Moravian Records, Folder 3, Items 6 and 7.

21. Romig to Jacobsen, December 13, 1864, Moravian Records, Folder 3, Item 13; "Council of the Chippewa and Christian Indians," January 18, 1865, Romig to Dole, February 13, 1865, Letters Received, Sac and Fox Agency, M234, R735.

22. The June 1865 census listed thirty-eight children; Romig reported twenty-nine attending his school. See "Statement of the number of Indians belonging to the Sac and Fox Agency, Kansas, June 30, 1865," Letters Received, Sac and Fox Agency, M234, R735; Romig to Martin, August 8, 1865, *Report of the Commissioner of Indian Affairs,* 39th Cong., 1st sess., H. Ex. Doc. 1, 565 (Serial 1248).

23. Martin to Dole, March 17, 1865, Martin to Dole, June 26, 1865, Letters Received, Sac and Fox Agency, M234, R735; Report of Commissioner Cooley, October 31, 1865, *Report of the Commissioner of Indian Affairs,* 39th Cong., 1st sess., H. Ex. Doc. 1, 213 (Serial 1248); Anna Heloise Abel, "Indian Reservations in Kansas and the Extinguishment of Their Title," *Kansas Historical Collections, 1903–1904* 8 (1904): 99; Romig to Wolle, May 1, 1865, Romig to Jacobsen, August 3, 1865, Moravian Records, Folder 4, Items 5 and 2.

24. Francis McCoonse to the Secretary of Interior, June 29, 1866, Donohoe and others to Martin, June 24, 1866, Martin to Cooley, June 26, 1866, Letters Received, Sac and Fox Agency, M234, R736.

25. Albert Wiley to the Commissioner of Indian Affairs, June 6, 1867, Letters Received, Sac and Fox Agency, M234, R737; Wiley to Central Superintendent of Indian Affairs Thomas Murphy, July 30, 1867, *Annual Report on Indian Affairs by the Acting Commissioner,* 40th Cong., 2d sess., 1867–68, H. Ex. Doc. 1, pt. 2, 300 (Ser-

ial 1362); Report of Acting Commissioner Charles E. Mix, November 15, 1867, ibid., 17.

26. Edward McCoonse and others to Martin, January 11, 1867, "Petition opposing removal from Kansas," signed by Francis McCoonse and members of the council, January 19, 1867, Eshtonoquot (Francis McCoonse) to the Commissioner of Indian Affairs, February 8, 1867, Letters Received, Sac and Fox Agency, M234, R737.

27. For crop reports see Wiley to Murphy, July 30, 1867, Romig to Wiley, July 31, 1867, *Annual Report on Indian Affairs by the Acting Commissioner,* 40th Cong., 2d sess., H. Ex. Doc. 1, pt. 2, 300, 302–3 (Serial 1326).

28. Romig to Wolle, February 16, 1868, Romig to Wolle, March 10, 1868, Moravian Records, Folder 7, Items 3 and 4.

29. Romig to Wolle, April 1, 1868, Romig to Wolle, June 2, 1868, Moravian Records, Folder 7, Items 5 and 6; Murphy to the Commissioner of Indian Affairs, June 1, 1868, Letters Received, Sac and Fox Agency, M234, R737.

30. Romig to Wolle, August 25, 1868, Romig to Wolle, October 12, 1869, Moravian Records, Folder 7, Item 10, and Folder 8, Item 1.

31. Report of Commissioner Ely S. Parker, December 23, 1869, *Report of the Commissioner of Indian Affairs,* 41st Cong., 2d sess., 1869–70, H. Ex. Doc. 1, 474 (Serial 1414).

32. Romig to Brother Kampman, January 7, 1870, Romig to Wolle, August 9, 1870, Moravian Records, Folder 9, Items 1 and 4.

33. Romig to Wiley, July 7, 1869, *Report of the Commissioner of Indian Affairs,* 41st Cong., 2d sess., H. Ex. Doc. 1, 806 (Serial 1414); Romig to Wolle, August 9, 1870, Moravian Records, Folder 9, Item 3; William Nicholson, "A Tour of Indian Agencies in Kansas and the Indian Territory in 1870," *Kansas Historical Quarterly* 3 (August 1934): 309.

34. Nicholson, "A Tour of Indian Agencies," 308.

35. Although the Indians did not receive patents in fee simple until 1900, individuals could sell their land before that time if declared competent by a court. During the 1850s and 1860s there was much fraud connected with this process and many individuals from other tribes lost their holdings. See Grant Foreman, *The Last Trek of the Indians* (Chicago: University of Chicago Press, 1946), 228 n. 3.

36. C. A. Weslager, "Enrollment List of Chippewa and Delaware-Munsies Living in Franklin County, Kansas, May 31, 1900," *Kansas Historical Quarterly* 40 (Summer 1974): 234–35.

The Prairie Potawatomie: Resistance to Allotment

Anonymous

Few of the American Government's attempts to create a workable Indian policy offer a more vivid record of failure than the Dawes Allotment Act of 1887. The Dawes Act sought to resolve the Indian "problem" by persuading, or forcing if necessary, Indians to abandon their traditional tribal-communal way of life for the life of independent, individualistic yeoman farmers. In order to pave the way for the elimination of tribes as distinct social, political, and legal entities, the Dawes Act provided for the division of communally-held reservation lands into individual 160 acre holdings. "Surplus" lands were then to be made available for the benefit of the ever-mounting wave of white settlers.

The Dawes Act wreaked substantial mischief without accomplishing any of its major goals except that of making Indian lands accessible to white settlement. Between 1887 and 1934, when the Act was finally abrogated, the land holdings of Native Americans diminished from 130,000,000 to 50,000,000 acres. Much of the remaining acreage was too poor to interest encroachers. In spite of their increasing impoverishment, however, Native Americans clung with unwavering tenacity to

"The Prairie Potawatomie: Resistance to Allotment," by Anonymous, *The Indian Historian* 9 (1976): 27–31.

their traditional ways. Thus not only did the Dawes Act fail to protect the property rights of Native Americans, but it also failed to destroy their centuries-old patterns of life.

Allotment had been used in various forms since the Eighteenth Century, and in 1887 many Tribes already knew that the primary accomplishment of that policy had been to deprive them of their lands without any meaningful compensation. Not surprisingly, then, many Tribes opposed the Dawes Act. Such resistance on the part of Native Americans to the United States Government was nothing new; American history is replete with bloody, tragic examples of that resistance. Resistance to the Dawes Act, however, took a different form from traditional Native American resistance. Instead of fighting or fleeing, Native Americans sought to counter the Dawes Act by standing their ground within the dominant society. Such resistance anticipated several of the major themes of Twentieth Century struggles for Native American and indeed all minority rights—passive resistance, nonviolence, resort to the legal system, and in general attempts by Native Americans to manipulate the institutional dynamics of the dominant society to their advantage. This article focuses upon such resistance by the Prairie Band Potawatomie of northeastern Kansas.

The Potawatomie were no strangers to allotment even before 1887. After migrating to Kansas from the Great Lakes region in the late 1830s and early 1840s, the Potawatomie agreed in 1846 to a treaty which created a Reservation of 576,000 acres. In 1861 the Forest and Christian Bands agreed to another treaty which provided for individual allotments of their part of the Reservation. Only the Prairie Band chose to retain its Tribal status and communal land system. The diminished Prairie Band holding consisted of 77,357 acres in Jackson County, Kansas. By 1887 the Forest and Christian Bands had lost most of their 500,000 acres, 340,000 of which had been sold as surplus lands to the Atchison, Topeka and Santa Fe Railroad.[1] After losing their lands, many Forest and Christian Band members sought refuge on the lands of the Prairie Band. This experience fostered well-deserved skepticism in the Prairie Band about the efficacy of the allotment policy.[2]

Such skepticism was all the more pronounced because the Prairie Band, in stark contrast to the impoverished condition of its Forest Christian Band neighbors, had fared well using the traditional communal methods. The fertile lands of northeastern Kansas provided the Prairie Band a comfortable existence as agriculturalists. In 1886

Potawatomie Agent I. W. Patrick described the Prairie Band as a prosperous people, possessors of well-cultivated farms, large herds of cattle, and ample supplies of hay.[3] In external appearances the Prairie Band led a life not unlike that of their white neighbors except that they held their land in common instead of as individuals. Protestant and Catholic missions had numerous Prairie Band adherents, and Potawatomie children attended Reservation schools regularly.[4]

This did not mean, however, that the Prairie Band slavishly imitated its white neighbors. Some members of the Prairie Band chose a different way of life, as is indicated by this description by Agent C. H. Grover, who replaced Patrick in 1887:

> It is difficult to convey a correct idea of the social condition of these tribes. There are members of each who are educated, refined in their manners, prosperous in business, and living in homes of elegance and luxury. There are other members of each tribe occupying the other extreme . . . , speaking the Indian language only, dressing in the Indian fashion, and living in bark houses.[5]

In short, the Prairie Band way of life allowed for diversity.

Grover's arrival as new Potawatomie Agent coincided with the enactment of the Dawes Act. He and his successors devoted a major portion of their time and energy to efforts to implement the Act in spite of an unwilling and uncooperative constituency. The presence of disinherited members of the Forest and Christian Bands on Prairie Band lands dampened whatever sentiment there was for allotment. Indeed some members of the Prairie Band decided to take up the fight against allotment even before it was to be implemented on their lands.

The first signs of serious Prairie Band resistance to allotment appeared in January 1888. The Office of Indian Affairs had worked out a staggered schedule for introducing allotments. Under this schedule the Prairie Band's Kickapoo neighbors were among the first in line. Thus some members of the Prairie Band decided to make the Kickapoo both a test case and the first line of the Prairie Band defense. Wah Quoh Bosh Kuk of the Prairie Band entered the Kickapoo domain and urged the Tribe to follow a policy of non-cooperation with the allotment Agents from the Office of Indian Affairs. His advice apparently took hold, because Agent Grover soon complained to Washington that the Kickapoo were causing trouble over the matter of allotments.[6]

The Kickapoo eventually succumbed, however, and the Prairie Band opponents of allotment found themselves facing the threat on their home grounds. In early 1889 President Grover Cleveland appointed three commissioners to negotiate an allotment agreement with the Prairie Band. All three were from the vicinity around the Reservation, and none of the three appeared to be completely disinterested parties—one was a lawyer, one a prominent businessman from a nearby white community which had always pushed for the break-up of the Reservation, and the third was a real estate agent.[7] The commissioners were warned to expect widespread Prairie Band opposition. That warning was underscored when Agent Grover resigned and in his letter of resignation implied that Prairie Band resistance to allotment might even be justified since many Kickapoo allotments had found their way into the hands of whites in a matter of weeks. Thus it came as no surprise to the allotment commissioners when they arrived at the Prairie Band Reservation and found not a single member of the Prairie Band willing to discuss allotment.[8]

Again Wah Quoh Bosh Kuk, the Prairie Band member who had gone to the Kickapoo Reservation to urge a policy of resistance, led his people in the fight against allotment. By fostering a variety of anti-allotment activities, Wah Quoh Bosh Kuk gradually consolidated a firm position as leader of the Prairie Band. His tactics varied, but his objective remained constant—turn back allotment by mounting a non-violent campaign of passive resistance.

In June 1890, the Prairie Band leader initiated a petition to Washington which was signed by eighty-eight adult Prairie Band males.[9] But despite the cool reception given the allotment agents and despite indications of Prairie Band resistance such as the petition, the Indian Office proceeded at full speed with its plans for allotment. On September 1, 1890, President Benjamin Harrison issued an order to proceed with allotment, and on March 3, 1891, Congress ratified that order.[10]

Meanwhile, Agent Grover, who had apparently become at least somewhat sympathetic to Prairie Band opposition to allotment, was replaced by J. A. Scott. Scott was a "company man," prepared to enforce the allotment policy by whatever means proved necessary. His immediate solution to the problem of Prairie Band resistance was to remove the leaders of dissent from the Reservation.

As has already been indicated, many members of the Forest and Christian Bands had moved to the Prairie Band Reservation after losing their own lands. This had been a source of minor misery to the Office of Indian Affairs for a number of years. In 1884 and again in 1886 that Office ordered Forest and Christian Band members removed from Prairie Band lands but took no action to enforce that order. Almost immediately after his arrival, however, Agent Scott revived the removal issue as a pretext for getting rid of troublemakers. Even though Wah Quoh Bosh Kuk was a Prairie Band member, Scott recommended that he be removed along with Forest and Christian Band interlopers. The Agent's dispatches on the removal issue described Wah Quoh Bosh Kuk and his followers as "insolent, restless, vicious, and dangerous." It is significant that despite all of Scott's attempts to discredit the anti-allotment faction, he never charged a single violent act. There is little doubt that if he had even the slightest pretext for making such a charge he would have done so. Nevertheless, Scott recommended that Wah Quoh Bosh Kuk and his followers be removed to a military prison so that allotment could proceed peacefully.[11]

Scott's pleas persuaded local military authorities, and in August 1891 a detachment of the Seventh Cavalry entered the Prairie Band Reservation and removed Wah Quoh Bosh Kuk and several of his followers to Ft. Riley.[12]

Once he had succeeded in securing Wah Quoh Bosh Kuk's imprisonment, Scott launched a concerted campaign to keep his Prairie Band adversary out of circulation until the allotment process could be completed. The agent maneuvered continuously in an effort to manipulate the levers of power against his foe. He implored the central office of the Office of Indian Affairs to support him on Wah Quoh Bosh Kuk's imprisonment because the Indian's release would "upset the precarious balance of Potawatomie opinion" on allotment.[13] In January 1892 Scott paid a personal visit to the Assistant U.S. District Attorney to try to convince him to resist efforts to free the Prairie Band leader.[14] In every way possible, Scott did his best to discredit the entire anti-allotment faction, describing its adherents as "the most trifling [elements] on the reservation [who] . . . have never missed an opportunity to create contention."[15]

Throughout the affair Scott schemed and maneuvered to discredit and defeat his Prairie Band foe. He did not hesitate to use the power of his office to ride roughshod over legitimate Prairie Band opposition to allotment—the Dawes Act itself had stipulated that allotment could not be undertaken without the approval of the Tribes. This time, however, Scott had miscalculated the guile of his opponent, for despite his best efforts, Wah Quoh Bosh Kuk soon had his freedom. Demonstrating his grasp of the forces with which he was vying, the Prairie Band leader had already retained the services of not one but two attornies—J. C. Tillotson of Topeka and J. V. Bottineau of Minneapolis.[16] Thus armed, Wah Quoh Bosh Kuk secured his freedom by successfully instituting *habeus corpus* proceedings. By April 1892 he was back on the Reservation agitating against allotment. Not only did the Prairie Band leader return to carry on the fight, but he also instituted legal action against Scott and the Seventh Cavalry, alleging illegal confinement.[17]

With the Prairie Band leader out of prison, the struggle over allotment reached an impasse. Only ten Prairie Band families had agreed to allotment in more than two years of negotiations, and the prospects for further agreements seemed dim.[18] Agent Scott showed no sign of relenting on his insistence that allotment would proceed no matter what the obstacles; Wah Quoh Bosh Kuk and his followers were equally determined. Indeed they redoubled their efforts. Anti-allotment forces persuaded the Prairie Band Council to take a formal stand against allotment, and in early June the Council issued a direct appeal to the Office of Indian Affairs in Washington.[19] This was only one of many times that Prairie Band opponents of allotment sought help directly from Washington under the mistaken assumption that they would find a sympathetic ear by going over Agent Scott's head. Several Prairie Band members left the Reservation secretly to lobby in Washington; Wah Quoh Bosh Kuk made the journey twice. Indeed, the faith with which Prairie Band opponents of allotment undertook that long and costly journey is striking considering their singular lack of success.

Retaining legal help and direct lobbying were just two of the tactics used by opponents of allotment. To strengthen their numbers, they persuaded a number of their Potawatomie brethren from Wisconsin to make the trek to Kansas.[20] This early example of Native American nationalism was supplemented by other evidence of an ability to muster resources for the anti-allotment cause that impressed even Agent Scott. He marveled, for instance, at Wah Quoh Bosh Kuk's ability to solicit contributions from the "oldest, poorest, and most needy Indians of the tribe." The Prairie Band leader raised more than $2,500 to finance his legal expenses and his travel.[21]

It should by now be apparent that Wah Quoh Bosh Kuk and other

Prairie Band opponents of allotment used sophisticated and in a sense modern tactics and organization to try to carry their point. They attempted to manipulate the "system" to their advantage by using some of the tactics and instruments whites used to manipulate that system, particularly direct lobbying and skilled legal counsel.

Prairie Band resistance took another path, however, a path that paid homage to traditional Potawatomie ways. Prairie Band opposition to allotment featured an overt affirmation of traditional Potawatomie ways and a distinct throwing-off of white men's ways which had been gradually adopted through the years.

Opponents of allotment discovered that one of the most effective means of rallying support was to sponsor traditional religious ceremonies and dances.[22] Agent Scott likened these ceremonies to the Ghost Dances which were at that time increasingly popular among the Plains Indians. The Agent was deeply disturbed by the revival of traditional ceremonies—the Ghost Dance had after all been involved in events leading up to the notorious Wounded Knee massacre on the Oglala Sioux Reservation in 1890.[23] Again, however, even in his agitated state of mind Scott did not claim that Prairie Band religious ceremonies and dances fostered violence. As with most manifestations of the Ghost Dance among Plains Indians, Prairie Band ceremonies were peaceful. While they may have hoped that performing the Dance would help sweep white men away and lead to the return of game and dead Indians, Prairie Band dancers did nothing overt to make that dream into reality.

If the traditional dances and religious ceremonies did not lead to overt violence, they were in Agent Scott's mind a serious threat nevertheless because they contributed to an equally distressing turn of events. According to Scott, the stalemate over allotment and particularly the efforts of the anti-allotment faction had virtually paralyzed the Reservation. Instead of working their farms, sending their children to the Agency school, and attending services at the mission churches, Prairie Band people were increasingly reverting to their old ways or else doing nothing at all. Scott predicted that as many as 100 Prairie Band families would leave the Reservation rather than submit to allotment.[24]

Scott complained bitterly that the widespread return to Tribal religious practices had "driven all practical ideas from the minds of men who had heretofore made considerable progress." The Agent concluded that because of "romantic barbarism under the guise of religion," the Potawatomie march toward a civilized way of life had been halted indefinitely.[25] To Scott the evidence of that arrested march was obvious. Since the dispute over allotment had reached a stalemate, Potawatomie agricultural production had declined markedly, and the once well-tilled fields had often been left unattended. The Protestant and Catholic missions on the Reservation also felt the impact of the deadlock as Prairie Band members returned in increasing numbers to their traditional religious forms. Many Prairie Band parents signalled both their despair and their hostility toward the allotment policy by removing their children from the Agency-operated schools.[26]

By the summer of 1893, the battle lines were clearly drawn. Although an occasional Prairie Band member caved in to the pressure to accept allotment, it was clear that a substantial portion of the Band's membership would never yield voluntarily. The anti-allotment faction continued to press its campaign of passive resistance with considerable success. This solid wall of Prairie Band resistance held together with barely a crack for another year before the Indian Office finally decided to resolve the conflict by resorting to its arbitrary power. In 1894 the Commissioner of the Office of Indian Affairs, Daniel Browning, instructed Prairie Band allotment agent H. W. Aten to notify the Band that because of the "unsatisfactory" progress in securing a voluntary agreement on allotments, the three allotment agents would be empowered to make arbitrary allotments after September 30, 1894.[27] Thus the Indian Office dropped all pretense that allotment was a voluntary and cooperative venture. Browning's edict effectively obliterated Prairie Band opposition, although fully half of the Prairie Bands heads of family remained firmly opposed to allotment and refused to cooperate with the allotment commissioners until the menacing shadow of the September 30 deadline was virtually upon them.[28] Then and only then did the obdurate anti-allotment faction submit and apply for individual allotments.

By the end of 1895 allotments had been made to all members of the Prairie Band including Wah Quoh Bosh Kuk. Subsequent events did little to lessen Prairie Band apprehension about the course they had been forced to follow. In less than a year after the process had been completed, nearly a quarter (177 out of 812) of all Prairie Band allotments had been either sold or leased to whites.[29] Once the proceeds from these sales were gone, a number of dispossessed Prairie Band members joined the landless members of the Christian and Forest Bands in crowding onto the diminished holdings of their Prairie Band brethren who had been fortunate enough to retain their allotments. This experience left the Prairie Band more determined than ever not to sell their "surplus" lands.[30] Even though only a few thousand acres remained unallotted, the Prairie Band was determined to hang onto the remnants of its land base. Thus the Band refused to talk to Government Agents assigned to negotiate the possible sale of surplus lands. The tactic of passive resistance was again used to frustrate the desires of the Agents.

The Prairie Band struggle against allotment, even though it eventually proved futile, demonstrated some telling points about the strong current of continuity in the reactions of Native Americans to claims of hegemony on the part of the dominant society. The primary theme of the struggle was the willingness of the Prairie Band to change and adapt in order to hold onto what the Band perceived as the essential elements of the Prairie Band way of life. The Prairie Band resisted the threat posed by the allotment policy by using tactics significantly different from traditional Prairie Bands ways. Hiring lawyers, raising funds for legal fees, lobbying in Washington, mobilizing what were in effect non-violent protest tactics—these were not the traditional Prairie Band way. Yet the ends these means were intended to serve were most definitely traditional—communal land holding and social structure.

In contrast to the common perception of Native American societies as static and unchanging, the picture that emerges from the story of Prairie Band resistance to allotment is that of a flexible and creative effort to preserve a highly valued way of life. The Prairie Band in the 1890s proved that they were more than ready to move into the twentieth century by borrowing what was needed from the dominant society to preserve traditional ways. Even though they eventually lost the battle, the Prairie Band demonstrated the resilience of their way of life in the face of increasing impoverishment. Far from destroying the Prairie Band way of life, the struggle over allotment only served to demonstrate its underlying strength.

NOTES

1. Potawotamie Letterbooks, Outgoing Letters, Book 15, August 27, 1893, U.S. Federal Records Center, Kansas City, Missouri.

2. William E. Connelly, "The Prairie Band of Potawatomie Indians," *Kansas History Collections,* XIV (1915–1918), 533.

3. U.S. Department of the Interior, *Annual Report of the Commissioner of Indian Affairs* (1886), 162.

4. Ibid.

5. Ibid. (1887), 121.

6. Letterbooks, Outgoing, Book 11, January 26, 1888.

7. Ibid., Incoming, Book 20, May 8, 1889.

8. Ibid., Outgoing, Book 11, January 6, 1889; Connelley, "Prairie Band," *Kansas Collections,* 531.

9. Letterbooks, Incoming, Book 20, June 9, 1890.

10. Connelley, "Prairie Band," *Kansas Collections,* 531.

11. Letterbooks, Outgoing, Book 13, August 24, 1891.

12. Connelley, "Prairie Band," *Kansas Collections,* 534.

13. Letterbooks, Outgoing, Book 13, December 17, 1891.

14. Ibid., January 14, 1892.

15. Ibid., December 3, 1892.

16. Ibid., Book 14, April 29, 1892; Book 15, February 14, 1893.

17. Ibid., Book 14, April 29, 1892.

18. Ibid., August 29, 1892.

19. Ibid., June 10, 1892.

20. Ibid., August 27, 1892.

21. Ibid., July 15, 1893.

22. Ibid., October 7, 1892.

23. Ibid., Book 15, August 27, 1893; Murray L. Wax, *Indian Americans. Unity and Diversity* (Englewood Cliffs, New Jersey: Prentice-Hall, 1971), 139–41.

24. Letterbooks, Outgoing, Book 15, November 1, 1892.

25. Ibid., August 27, 1893.

26. Ibid., Book 16, October 16, 1893; Connelley, "The Prairie Band," *Kansas Collections,* 535–36.

27. *Annual Report of the Commissioner of Indian Affairs* (1894), 20–21.

28. Connelley, "Prairie Band," *Kansas Collections,* 537.

29. Ibid., 555–70.

30. *Annual Report of the Commissioner of Indian Affairs* (1895), 100.

The Germans of Atchison, 1854–1859: Development of an Ethnic Community

Eleanor Turk

In 1854 the Kansas territory was opened for settlement by American emigrants, marking a significant leap forward in the American Western frontier. The year 1854 was also a peak year of German immigration to the United States, symbolic of a major shift in the European population movement. In the 1850's Germany replaced Ireland as the primary European source of immigrants, and for the next four decades Germans predominated in the movement of peoples from the old world to the new. Understandably, Germans have always comprised the largest foreign ethnic component in the state of Kansas, and because Kansas was opened to settlers in a systematic way, its history allows us to observe the development of the immigrant community on the frontier.[1]

There are still questions to be answered about this development. Frederick Jackson Turner theorized that the frontier was the crucible, blending foreign and American-born alike into a "composite nationality." Yet John Hawgood, the foremost historian of this era of German immigration, insisted that "a determined and conscious resistance against assimilation or Americanization was a significant 'German' peculiarity." Milton Gordon, who laid much of the groundwork for our

"The Germans of Atchison, 1854–1859: Development of an Ethnic Community," by Eleanor Turk, *Kansas History* 2, 3 (1979): 146–156. Copyright Kansas State Historical Society. Reprinted by permission.

current understanding of assimilation, offered a compromise position. According to Gordon, new entrants into an established society may accommodate themselves to the cultural patterns of the dominant group, but they retain the structural characteristics of their native society, such as marriage patterns and religious affiliations. The resultant society is therefore not an amalgamation, but a collection of subcultures, separate in structural forms, but interacting in areas of mutual concern, such as economic and political interests. An examination of the German immigrants in Kansas affords an opportunity to observe more closely the initial contacts along the frontier, and to understand what actually occurred there.[2]

Germans came to America with high expectations. Generally, they had received a better basic education than most other immigrants and many Americans. Those who could afford the trip to America were usually professionals, skilled artisans, or independent peasants proficient in village trades and hungry for the low-cost lands of the American West. They also looked forward to a more compatible political climate. This outlook was summarized by Rev. W. F. Bogen, writing an immigrant's guidebook for his German countrymen in 1851:

> A great blessing meets the German emigrant the moment he steps upon these shores. He comes to a free country; free from the oppression of despotism, free from privileged orders and monopolies, free from the pressure of intolerable taxes and inposts, free from constraint in matters of belief and conscience.
>
> Everyone can travel, free and untrammelled, whither he will, and settle where he pleases. . . . Before him lies the country, exhaustless in its resources, with its fruitful soil, its productive mines, its immense products, . . . its countless cities, and villages, where flourish industry, commerce, and wealth.
>
> The industrious farmer is invited by the "Far West," even by the whole country, to furrow its bosom and reap its treasures. The skillful and active craftsman readily finds a livelihood in the country and the cities, with but little effort. The scholar is welcomed with his attainments. . . .
>
> "Help yourself," is the American proverb, and God will help you.[3]

Yet even while seeking this new opportunity in America, Germans were reluctant to abandon entirely their continental past. Reassuring customs and cultural traditions gave them security and a sense of identity in the new world, and they sought out the earlier settlements of their countrymen and communicated with each other through a burgeoning German-language press. Although most immigrants, including the earlier multitudes of Irish, had sought similar contacts, the Germans were the first nationality group sufficiently large and differentiated by language to endow this natural practice with a somewhat negative cast. Americans disliked this exclusivity and expected the newcomers to adjust. Thus Bogen warned his countrymen that they must avoid "an obstinate reliance on . . . *German habits and customs*":

> It is true, we can enjoy many happy hours in associating with estimable German brethren; we can derive instruction and entertainment from German books and newspapers; but are we in Germany, and are Germans the only people in whom we are now interested? . . . That man alone can enjoy, to their full extent, the rights of an American citizen, who understands and speaks English; and as long as we do not accomplish this, so long we neither appreciate nor enjoy the whole freedom and independence which this land has in store for us. We are *half Germans* and half Americans, but no real Germans any more.[4]

Many aspects of this cross-cultural conflict were present to affect the Germans of Atchison county during the territorial period, 1854–1861. However, in order to understand them we cannot rely solely on the traditional demographic records which reflect the group patterns in established communities. The period under study is too brief, and the population too fluid for these records to give us real insight. Instead, we will pay particular attention to the contemporary press. Although newspapers are frequently used as an historical source for events and editorial opinions, they can also provide the social historian with other, less authoritive, but equally valuable data. For an examination of the cross-cultural relations between ethnic groups, it is also rewarding to look at the secondary materials of the press, the column fillers, witticisms, and commercial puffery which fleshed out the pages of these journals. In particular, we can observe expressions which reveal the expectations of each group about the other, as well as their reaction to the events of daily life together. In this regard the press functions as an actor in society, reflecting and influencing latent attitudes which could either facilitate group interaction or contribute to the formation of stereotypes and prejudices. Availability of the English-language *Squatter Sovereign/Freedom's Champion*, and the German-language *Kansas Zeitung*, all published in Atchison during the territorial period, facilitates the examination of the initial German experience in Kansas.[5]

The opening of the Kansas territory was not marked by a land scramble which might have set group against group on the frontier. There was ample government land to go around in Kansas, and under the terms of the Preemption act of 1841, settlers could purchase up to 160 acres at the rate of $1.25 per acre before the land went for public auction. However, the Kansas frontier was the setting for an intense political struggle which frequently erupted into violence and earned the territory the epithet of "Bleeding Kansas." Under the terms of the Kansas-Nebraska act of 1854, residents of these two prospective states would exercise "popular sovereignty" to determine whether they would enter the Union as free or slave states. It must never be forgotten that this controversy was as much a part of the frontier life as any physical obstacles of the rugged and unfamiliar territory. All immigrants to Kansas, American or foreign-born alike, were forced to take a stand on this issue and to deal with the events caused by that struggle.

The first Kansas residents came mainly from Missouri. They were proponents of slavery and people who were generally accustomed to the rigors of the undeveloped frontier. . . . But Eastern abolitionists also wished to control the future state, and were urging Antislavery settlers to develop the territory. . . .[6]

The main tide of immigration into Kansas came from New England, the Ohio valley and the upper Midwest. These emigrants were mainly white Americans, generally opposed to slavery, moving west to increase their economic opportunities. They came overwhelmingly from settled areas already fully integrated into the dominant political processes and social patterns of America. Because these areas also coincided geographically with the so-called "German Belt of settlement," these emigrants would bring with them attitudes determined by previous experiences with Germans. These Americans held generally positive views of Germans, although they disapproved of the German's fondness for beer.[7]

John Hawgood maintained that "the German was not a pioneer except in isolated cases or in exceptional circumstances," and it is true that there were not many Germans in Kansas at first. The territorial census of 1855 identifies only 115 individuals of German birth. There were 94 males, 21 females, and only 18 family units among this initial group. Almost half, or 55, of these immigrants had already been naturalized, however, a sign not only of familiarity with the American system, but of a desire to become active in it. Another 13 had declared their intention to become citizens. The largest contingent had gone to Leavenworth, an established settlement and military outpost on the Missouri river. Tiny Atchison was a mere hamlet, and only three Germans and one Swiss-German were recorded in its vicinity.[8]

Despite the town's small size, the city fathers inaugurated its first newspaper, the *Squatter Sovereign,* in February, 1855, as an outspoken advocate for slavery. Its major concern was to win adherents to its political viewpoint, and it addressed itself primarily to the American emigrant. Nevertheless, there was a definite awareness of Germans from the beginning, and five of the first seven issues referred to the immigrants. There were factual tidbits, such as the item noting that seven of the 13 foreign-language newspapers in New York City were German. Another item reported admiringly that, "The New York Board of Emigration estimate that $20,000,000 in money have been brought into this country, in the last year, by German emigrants." But more common were the ethnic jokes at the expense of the foreigners. The following are typical examples:

A Dutchman thus describes the New Yorkers: Fine peebles; dey go about der sthreets all day, cheating each oder, and day call dat pizziness.

An honest Dutchman, on being asked how often he shaved; replied—Dree dimes a week effery other tay put Sunday—den I shafe effery day. [The paper liked this one so much it repeated it two years later.]

When a German stops flute-playing, he is either out of wind or drinking a large beer.[9]

The elements of these column fillers are worth analyzing. The "Dutchman," on the one hand, is successful in making money, neat, and apparently well educated. Yet, withall, as the careful reconstruction of the accent indicates, he is comical in his speech, and incapable of grasping the subtleties of the language. Moreover, he drinks beer! There was, despite a grudging recognition for these foreigners, no real basis for friendly communication or social interaction. It was preferable to find them amusing and slightly simple. Yet these five items also reflect an ambivalence not seen in the paper's attitudes toward other nationality groups. For each of them, there was a consistent stereotype. For example, the French were portrayed as sophisticated but supercilious:

> What a strange thing it is remarked a Frenchman, after making a tour of the United States, that you should have two hundred different religions and only one gravy.

Like the Irish, the French were frequently viewed with negative humor:

> An Irishman and a Frenchman were to be hanged together. Monsieur was considerably troubled about it, while Paddy took the matter quite coolly, telling his companion to "be aisy, for sure it is nothing to be hanged at all, at all." To which poor Francaise replied, "Ah, be gar, de grand deeference is, dat you Irishmen are used to it!"

The Irish were also funny in their superstitions:

> A dying Irishman was asked by his confessor if he was ready to renounce the devil and all his works. "Oh your honor," says Pat, "don't ask me to do that; I'm going into a strange country, and I don't want to make myself enemies."

Other jokes alluded to the Irishman's fondness for drink and for fighting. These well-formulated images are not surprising, given the long interaction of Irishmen and Frenchmen with Americans over the years. It is also significant to notice here that in almost every instance the stereotype was personified with a name, as if to complete a familiar portrait. There was a certain degree of familiarity in calling the Irishman Pat or Paddy, the Frenchman, Francois. The black was also named, usually either Sambo or Julius. But the Germans were treated differently. In only two stories did the *Sovereign* attach a name to an individual portrayed in a German joke, and one involved a father calling to his son. The German, therefore, appeared more remote than the others, alien, and identified mainly by his comical language.[10]

The *Sovereign* did not appear to consider the Germans a significant political force on the frontier and made only an occasional effort to convert them to the Proslavery side. In one instance it tried to link the abolitionists to the Know-Nothing party which was beginning to emerge in the East. Epitomizing anti-Catholic and anti-foreign bigotry, in 1855 the Know-Nothings had successfully passed a law in Massachusetts requiring naturalized immigrants to spend an additional two years in residence before they could exercise their rights as citizens of the state. In an article entitled, "A 'Nigger' Better Than an Irishman or Dutchman," the *Sovereign* marveled that the abolitionist state would refuse to enforce the Fugitive Slave law, on the one hand, yet also reject the constitutional rights of naturalized citizens on the other. "Such is 'law and order' practiced by Abolitionists in Massachusetts," it censured; "What think Irishmen and Dutchmen of 'law and order men' here?" On another occasion the *Sovereign* reprinted a brief item from the *Michigan Expositor,* reporting that the "Border Ruffians" (the epithet for Missouri raiders in Kansas) were "shooting all the Germans they can get sight at in Kansas, because the Germans are in favor of freedom." The *Sovereign* replied:

> Such are the low and despicable means resorted to in the Eastern States to prejudice the foreign population against the nominees of the Democratic party. Although there are many Germans in Kansas, we have yet to learn of the first one who has been harmed in the least, by the "Border Ruffian." They are here, as in the States, a peaceable, law-abiding people, and are not only willing to submit to the laws, but actually have assisted in enforcing them. If supporting the law and order party in Kansas favors "freedom," then can all the Germans be placed on the list.[11]

However, the *Sovereign* soon returned to drawing comical characterizations of Germans. The following item was typical of its subsequent references:

> Vonce, a long vile ago, I vent out in my apple orchard and climbed a pear tree to get some peaches to make my vrow a plum paddin' mit, and when I got to the toppermost branch, I fell from the lowermost limb, with one leg on both sides of the fence, and like to stove my outsides in.[12]

From 1854 to 1857, Atchison was dominated by the proponents of slavery. However, the tides of both sentiment and emigration were running against them, and abolitionist forces were growing consistently stronger. The Emigrant Aid Company, in its ongoing effort to develop the territory, took the significant step of founding a German-language abolitionist newspaper in Atchison in order to draw German settlers to Kansas. As editor it hired Dr. Charles F. Kob, born and trained as a surgeon in Germany. Emigrating from Massachusetts, Kob inaugurated the *Kansas Zeitung* in July, 1857. The early issues set a high standard of journalism, leading off with a serial critique of the social system which included discussions of the major philosophical schools. The regular content included news from Europe, mixed news items from the United States, and a serialized novel. The objectives of the paper were spelled out in English and German. To his English readers Kob proclaimed:

> The main object of this paper is, (besides helping build up Kansas a Free State, to diffuse knowledge and political news among the German settlers, mechanics and businessmen throughout the territory) to give the millions of German citizens in the States, and the emigrants who come to our shores from Europe, a vivid and true picture of our land so blessed by nature, to show them that there is a broad field and a speedy reward for their labor, and that they will find all conditions for future happiness, which a congenial and healthy climate, a fertile soil, and an energetic, intelligent, and industrious population under a new and liberal government can afford.

However, his German readers were reassured that they would not be lost out on the frontier, because Kob would promote:

> . . . *German* spirit, *German* customs, *German* culture, affording them their honorable recognition and preservation, so that out of the heterogeneous elements which will form this state, a viable and strong character will be developed in which the German element will be one of the major components.[13]

Kob pursued his goals vigorously. Besides being outspokenly in the Free-State camp, the *Kansas Zeitung* published numerous articles boosting Kansas as an ideal place for settlement and refuting its detractors. In addition to preparing a guidebook for emigrants, Kob wrote articles explaining the voting system, clarifying land sale procedures, and making suggestions on how to farm in this new terrain. Noting progress toward the recognition of the German element in the territory, he reported that the Free-State committee had voted to distribute 30,000 copies of its proposed constitution in English, and 5,000 copies in German.[14]

Like the *Squatter Sovereign*, the *Kansas Zeitung* was intensely political; it did, however, reflect some of the other attitudes and actions of the Germans throughout the territory. In so doing it served as a means for their mutual communication and thus helped to integrate them into a recognizable ethnic community. It increasingly bore witness to the German presence. Kob himself ran for county coroner, although he lost the election. A German Free-State Club was formed in nearby Wyandotte, and local Germans were urged to follow suit. Germans and Americans joined to form a city choral society in Atchison, while in Leavenworth the *Turnverein,* a typical German social and sport club, formed a militia unit and managed to capture several cannon from the Border Ruffians. In February, 1858, the Germans formed a cooperative insurance society. In April the Turners from neighboring Sumner and Leavenworth joined for a gala day of music and sport, topped off by a grand ball. Meanwhile, Kob helped promote new German settlements in Humboldt and Bunker Hill, and soon moved to Leavenworth to further his developing business interests.[15]

The *Kansas Zeitung* was also aware of the American community, however, and before long began to give evidence that the Germans were not impressed with all the facets of the dominant culture. In September, 1857, it voiced strong criticism of American family life. Americans tended to ignore the basic institutions such as the family, it complained. By overstressing individualism, Americans made marriage simply a contractual arrangement, characterized by laxness in child-rearing and easy divorce. European marriages were far sounder, being sanctified by church, state, family, and custom. The *Zeitung* reprinted this article from another German-language paper, indicating that the attitude was probably widely held among the Germans in America. There were other indications as well. The Germans tended to look down on less educated Americans, and in one item the *Zeitung* pointed out that 10 American students were now at the University of Berlin, ". . . yet another sign," it concluded, "of how intelligent Americans value German Culture."[16]

Social interaction with Americans was judged unpleasant. In February, 1858, the paper complained:

On Monday the insurance association held a ball for its members in the Melodeon Hall. The intention appeared to be to make money, not to entertain the guests, or at least the German guests, because not one of the Germans had so much fun there as they had had at their *exclusive* socials during the winter. Germans and Americans have such different ideas of what is enjoyable, that any attempt to entertain them together inevitably ends with boredom for both.

One major source of friction was the difference of opinion over the consumption of alcohol. In the spring, 1858, the *Zeitung* complained:

> As a result of the new Sunday Laws, almost all of the German population of the city and surrounding areas met at the Missouri River, in part to enjoy the beauties of nature, but also to enjoy a rest after six days of hard work without being smothered by the puritanical sabbath laws.
>
> A considerable amount of money is spent away from this city for relaxation and recreation, and sooner or later the local tavern owners are going to feel the pinch, especially since they have to pay $100 for a license to serve beer, and they are prohibited from operating on their best day.

These laws restricting the Sunday sale of beer were branded pointless and anti-progressive, and Germans were urged to unite in proposing candidates for the local election so that *"we* can elect whom *we* want." However, on this issue a compromise was reached. A German petition to modify the Sunday law was approved in May, 1858, and henceforth beer could be dispensed on Sundays except when church services were being held. The *Zeitung* vigorously applauded this successful exercise of political influence.[17]
Early in 1858 the conversion of Atchison to the Free-State cause was completed when the Emigrant Aid Company acquired the majority stock in the town company and placed an abolitionist editor in charge of the *Squatter Sovereign*. As a result of this more congenial political atmosphere, immigrants came in greater numbers to Atchison, and the city's population grew rapidly. Symbolically, the *Squatter Sovereign* was renamed the *Freedom's Champion* in February, 1858. Its new editor, Johnathan Martin, also initiated a positive editorial attitude toward the Germans. Although the humorous jabs at all ethnic groups continued, ethnic jokes involving Germans declined, and those which did appear

placed Germans in more positive situations. Martin promoted the sale of the *Zeitung* and spoke positively to his English-language readers about German contributions to the Free-State cause. His outlook is epitomized by the paper's lead editorial on April 24, 1858. Entitled "The Germans of Kansas," this statement was repeated in various forms in a number of subsequent issues of the paper:

It is estimated that there are now over ten thousand Germans in Kansas, and of this very large number there are not, we venture to say, over one hundred pro-slavery men. The Free State Germans are among the most zealous, ardent and earnest anti-slavery men in the Territory, and to their devotion to the good cause—to their courage and their steadfast faith in the principles of Freedom, more than to any other, do we owe the Liberty of Kansas. Had it not been for their emigration in such vast numbers, Kansas would long ago have been lost to Freedom, and her soil groaning beneath the curse of slavery. We honor the Free State Germans of Kansas. . . . They have felt the galling yoke of tyranny in the Old World, and they bring with them to the New a warm, enthusiastic love of Liberty, which the darkest night of trouble cannot extinguish.[18]

As Martin's appraisal recognizes, the German community was growing prosperous, and becoming increasingly stable in its new environment. The 1860 federal census identified 379 Germans in Atchison county, almost evenly divided between the city and the rural townships. In the city they listed 29 occupations, in which merchants, carpenters, laborers, saloon-keepers, and domestics predominated. In the rural townships Germans worked mainly in the areas of agriculture and construction as farmers, laborers, masons, smiths, and carpenters, although 17 other occupations are also mentioned. Of the total German population, nearly 52 percent listed gainful employment, and 78.5 percent of those worked in occupations which required either skilled training or initial capital investment. Roughly 70 percent had immigrated in family units. The growing German population attracted the Benedictine Order of the Roman Catholic Church to the city, and a German-language Protestant service was conducted every second Sunday by the Episcopal Reverend Staudenmeyer. In July, 1859, the men in the community established a *Turnverein,* a characteristic social center of German-American activities.[19]

Even this brief glimpse of territorial Atchison through the eyes of its press provides valuable insight into the immigrant experience. For one thing, it demonstrates that Hawgood underrated the ability of the Germans to adapt to the rigors of the American frontier. By their skills and stability, pioneering Germans managed to prosper economically, to survive the hostility and ridicule of the Proslavery factions, and to win the support, and even admiration, of Republican abolitionists. They were able to establish their presence politically, and used their influence to win certain social goals, as in the case of the beer petition. Together with the Free-State Americans, Germans helped to determine the political future of the territory and, to a certain extent, fulfilled Editor Kob's wish that German interests form one of the major building blocks of the state.

But it is evident that while these experiences may have assured the survival of Atchison as a viable community, they did little to reduce the immigrants' self-awareness as Germans, or to develop fully the "composite nationality" which Turner concluded was a major product of frontier life. The resistance which Hawgood identified is demonstrated by the attitudes expressed in the *Kansas Zeitung*, the development of the strongly German Roman Catholic churches and schools, and the ultimate foundation of the *Turnverein* as a separate and culturally unifying social center. All of these cultural structures developed into permanent institutions which prospered and survived well into the 20th century. They prove the long-term existence of a thriving German-American subculture within the greater Atchison community. Not until the identity crisis [created] by World War I was this desire for separation relinquished.[20]

Moreover, although Hawgood said that cultural resistance was a peculiarly German trait, it is apparent from the American comments that there was resistance on both sides. Neither ethnic community felt it had much in common with the other, except in their political outlook and economic cooperation. Thus, although we can accept Turner's premise of the "composite nationality" on a strictly political basis, at the more sensitive cultural and social levels we must recognize with Gordon that the two communities functioned as separate subcultures. Both sets of immigrants carried with them to the frontier attitudes that were not overcome by their mutual experiences. It is clear that from their earliest contacts, Germans and Americans in Kansas wished to keep a certain distance, establishing a firm basis for cultural pluralism and the tradition of the hyphenated American.

A few final examples serve as epilogue. In 1858, in Leavenworth and

Sumner, the two biggest towns in the area, the Turners played prominent roles in the July 4 Independence Day celebrations. In Sumner they
marched down the main avenue, demonstrating their athletic prowess,
and carrying a new flag donated by local merchants and seamstresses.
"God Bless the Germans," wrote the editor of the local paper. "They are
true to freedom." Germans participated enthusiastically in these patriotic celebrations thereafter. On the other hand, in November, 1859, the
German communities everywhere gathered for a major celebration of
the centennial anniversary of the birthday of their great German poet,
Schiller. In Atchison a magnificent banquet and ball were held at
Holthaus Hall, "the finest and largest then in the city," owned by baker
and *Turnverein* president Julius Holthaus. Well into this glorious
evening, the festivities were interrupted by some American soldiers, out
on the town, who tried to crash the party. The German doorkeeper resisted, and his fellows came to his aid. There were fist fights and shots
fired, and one of the guests was wounded in the shoulder before order
was restored. The Germans made no complaint, and nothing came of
the incident. Nevertheless, Martin, of the *Freedom's Champion*, scolded his
readers and tried to explain to them the importance of Schiller to the
Germans. The disturbance illustrates the differing outlooks of the two
subcultures. To the pragmatic Americans, geared for the stress and excitement of the frontier, it was probably inconceivable that anyone could
seriously celebrate the birth of a poet. Yet, for the immigrant Germans,
the birthday commemoration demonstrated that even in the foreign
wilderness their spirit and tradition would survive and flourish.[21]

NOTES

1. United States Department of Commerce, Bureau of the Census, *Historical Statistics of the United States, 1798–1945* (Washington, D.C., 1949), pp. 33–34. German
immigration in 1852 was 145,818; in 1853 it was 141,946, and in 1854 it reached
215,009. In 1856 it fell off sharply to 71,918. It reached peaks of 205,630 in 1883,
and 119,168 in 1892. During the 1850's Germans comprised 35 percent of the persons immigrating from abroad, and took the lead away from the previously dominant Irish. Although other immigrant groups cut into the German numerical lead
in subsequent years, Germans continued to immigrate in larger numbers than any
other nationality until the wave of "new immigration" from southeastern Europe at
the turn of the century—Carrol D. Clark and Roy L. Roberts, *People of Kansas: A Demographic and Sociological Study* (Topeka, 1936), p. 51.

2. Frederick J. Turner, "The Significance of the Frontier in American History," *Annual Report of the American Historical Association* (1893), pp. 199–227; see especially pp. 215–216; John A. Hawgood, *The Tragedy of German Americans* (New York, 1940), pp. 55–67; Milton M. Gordon, *Assimilation in American Life: The Role of Race, Religion and National Origins* (New York, 1964), pp. 117–121. See also, David F. Bowers, ed., *Foreign Influences in American Life: Essays and Critical Bibliographies* (Princeton, N.J., 1944), and Richard Hofstadter and Seymour Martin Lipset, eds., *Turner and the Sociology of the Frontier* (New York, 1968).

3. F. W. Bogen, *The German in America: or Advice and Instruction for German Emigrants in the United States of America; Also, a Reader for Beginners in the English and German Languages* (2d ed., Boston, 1851), pp. 7–9, 33 (emphasis original). This interesting handbook serves two purposes. By providing its introduction to America in both German and English, it also serves as a reader with which immigrants can begin to learn the English language.

For an examination of the educational practices in 19th century Germany, see Peter Lundgreen, "Industrialization and the Educational Formation of Manpower in Germany," *Journal of Social History,* v. 9, no. 1 (Fall 1975), pp. 64–80. For an excellent history of German emigration see Mark Walker, *Germany and the Emigration, 1816–1885* (Cambridge, Mass., 1964). A penetrating analysis of the many factors which stimulated German emigration in midcentury is provided in Theodore S. Hamerow, *Restoration, Revolution, Reaction: Economics and Politics in Germany 1815–1871* (Princeton, N.J., 1958), especially pp. 75–93, and 199–237.

4. Bogen, *The German in America,* p. 17 (emphasis original). In 1764 German settlers in Philadelphia founded the German Society of Pennsylvania in order to help their countrymen deal with the hardships of immigration. It was successful in effecting the passage on ships docking in Pennsylvania. Similar organizations were founded in Charleston, S.C., Baltimore, and New York City before the revolution. In the following century German organizations of this type were established in Boston, Cincinnati, Birmingham, Ala., Hartford and New Haven, Conn., Rochester, N.Y., Allentown, Pa., Pittsburgh, Chicago, Milwaukee, St. Paul, Minneapolis, St. Louis, Kansas City, New Orleans, San Francisco, Portland, Ore., Spokane, and Seattle.—Rudolf Cronau, *Denkschrift zum 150. Jahrestag der Deutschen Gesellschaft der Stadt New York 1784–1934* (1934), pp. 70–71. For information on the German-language press, see Karl J. R. Arndt and May E. Olson, *German-American Newspapers and Periodicals 1732–1955* (Heidelberg, 1961); and Carl Wittke, *The German-Language Press in America* (Kentucky, 1957).

5. This study was made possible through the support of the University of Kansas General Research Fund, and greatly assisted by the cooperation of the Kansas State Historical Society, which retains extensive holdings of Kansas newspapers.

Leavenworth, another Missouri river city, attracted more Germans than Atchison. It did not begin publishing a German-language newspaper until after the inauguration of the *Kansas Zeitung*, however, and in any event too few issues of the Leavenworth paper have been preserved to afford a systematic study.

6. Samuel A. Johnson, "The Emigrant Aid Company in the Kansas Conflict," *The Kansas Historical Quarterly*, v. 6, no. 1 (February, 1937), p. 25. In an examination of the first six parties brought to Kansas by the Emigrant Aid Company, Louise Barry includes only nine individuals of probable German origins.—Louise Barry, "The Emigrant Aid Company Parties of 1854," ibid., v. 12, no. 2 (May, 1943), pp. 115–155.

7. In a special study of state or territory of birth of the native population of Kansas in 1860, it is indicated that 55,002 residents came from New England, New York, New Jersey, Pennsylvania, and the upper Midwest, 27,472 from the confederate states, including 11,356 from Missouri, and that 10,997 had been born in the Kansas territory.—Clark and Roberts, *People of Kansas,* p. 208. Hawgood discusses the "German Belt" on pp. 80–90.

8. Hawgood, *The Tragedy of German America,* p. 26; Territory of Kansas, Census of 1855. Hawgood observed that Germans preferred to settle on developed land, near established markets and navigable rivers (p. 23). Carman's study of Europeans in rural Kansas during the territorial period tends to refute this in part. He identified 26 German settlements reaching well into the interior sections of the territory. It is true, however, that with only five exceptions, all were located on rivers.—J. Neale Carman, "Continental Europeans in Rural Kansas, 1854–1861," *Territorial Kansas: Studies Commemorating the Centennial* (Lawrence, 1954), pp. 164–196.

Atchison's early days are described in Peter Beckman, "Overland Trade and Atchison's Beginnings," ibid., pp. 148–163. Beckman places the town's population at 40 in 1858, with an increase to 2,616 by 1860 (p. 154). A. T. Andreas and W. G. Cutler, *History of the State of Kansas* (Chicago, 1883), v. 1, p. 373, placed Atchison city's population at about 500 in 1859.

9. *Squatter Sovereign,* February 20, 1855 (and January 13, 1857), March 6, 13, 20, 27, 1855.

10. Ibid., February 26, July 1, 29, 1856, February 17, 1857.

11. Ibid., June 26, 1855, October 14, 1856; Alice Felt Tyler, *Freedom's Ferment: Phases of American Social History from the Colonial Period to the Outbreak of the Civil War* (New York, 1962), pp. 374–396, describes the development of the Know-Nothing movement.

12. *Squatter Sovereign,* February 17, 1857.

13. Russell K. Hickman, "Speculative Activities of the Emigrant Aid Society," *The Kansas Historical Quarterly,* v. 4, no. 3 (August, 1935), p. 238n; *Kansas Zeitung,* July 22, 1857.

14. *Kansas Zeitung,* July 29, August 19, 26, September 2, 30, October 7, 1857.

15. Ibid., September 2, 16, 30, 1857, January 20, February 24, April 10, 17, 1858.

16. Ibid., September 30, 1857.

17. Ibid., August 26, 1857, February 24, May 1, 8, 1858 (emphasis original).

18. *Freedom's Champion*, February 20, March 6, April 24, 1858; Frank A. Root, "Early Reminiscences in Atchison in 1859," Atchison *Daily Champion*, February 20, 1880.

19. Kansas Territorial Census, 1860, v. 1, Atchison and Doniphan counties, pp. 1–200; *Freedom's Champion*, August 21, 1858. For details of the establishment of the German-influenced Catholic church see Peter Beckman, *Kansas Monks: A History of St. Benedict's Abbey* (Atchison, 1957), pp. 44–50. Reverend Staudenmeyer was "a German of middlelife, florid, unmarried, who had come to Atchison in the spring or summer of 1857. . . ." He resigned in 1860 to go to Carolina, being one of the few Germans with Pro-slavery inclinations.—See Francis S. White, *The Story of a Kansas Parish* (Atchison, n.d.), pp. 5–6. Information on the role of the Turnverein in German-American society is provided in Heinrich Metzner, *A Brief History of the North American Gymnastic Union*, transl. by Theor. Stempfer (Indianapolis, 1911).

20. Although the *Kansas Zeitung* apparently ceased publication in 1859, it was followed by a number of other German-language newspapers in Atchison, including: *Die Fackel* (1866–1868); Der Atchison *Courier* (1874–1881).—Arndt and Olson, *German-American Newspapers*, pp. 151–152.

See Beckman, *Kansas Monks*, for the development of the Benedictine church and schools.

The Freedom's Champion, July 2, 1859, announced the foundation of the *Turnverein*. The records of the Atchison *Turnverein* are in the collection of the Kansas State Historical Society and include lists of active members through 1903.

The impact of World War I on the German-Americans is summarized in Frederick C. Luebke, *Bonds of Loyalty: German Americans and the World War I* (DeKalb, Ill., 1974). See Herbert Pankratz, "The Suppression of Alleged Disloyalty in Kansas During World War I," *The Kansas Historical Quarterly*, v. 42, no. 3 (Autumn 1976), pp. 277–307; and James C. Juhnke, "Mob Violence and Kansas Mennonites in 1918," ibid., v. 43, no. 3 (Autumn, 1977), pp. 334–350, for evidence of this crisis in Kansas.

21. Cora Dolbee, "The Fourth of July in Early Kansas (1858–1861)," ibid., v. 11, no. 2 (May, 1942), p. 138; Root, "Early Reminiscences."

The Elegant Dugout: Domesticity and Moveable Culture in the United States, 1870–1900

Angel Kwolek-Folland

Most middle-class American women of the late nineteenth century lived out their lives within the domestic realm, performing tasks that had come to be identified as intrinsically female: caring for small children, tending the ill or aged and managing the daily operations of the household. These things have been so closely identified with Victorian American womanhood that it has been possible to overlook the existence of the physical home as an autonomous cultural creation. Historians frequently have focused on the emotional or political content of the set of beliefs and activities called "domesticity" without analyzing the personal or cultural significance of domestic physical space. Yet for the average late Victorian woman who accepted the conventional wisdom of her time—who was neither a reformer nor a reactionary—the home was a constant physical presence, the arena wherein the behavior of day-to-day life helped to define domesticity.[1] In addition to these personal meanings, the material home was a vital symbol within the context of late Victorian culture, and its continuance as a significant part of American life seemed to hinge on whether or not it would adapt to the rapidly-changing society of the late nineteenth century.

Late Victorian definitions of what it meant to be an American derived from a profound awareness of cultural and physical change and the perceived need to stabilize or standardize American social institutions. Although mobility always had been a contributing factor to the reality of American political and social institutions, after the Civil War it became a part of the cultural awareness of Americans. The United States Census Bureau, in its documentation of the 1880 census, concentrated almost exclusively on the fact that Americans frequently changed their residence. The attention given by the Bureau to this one aspect of American life at the expense of others illustrates that, perhaps for the first time in American experience, the fact of mobility became a conscious part of national self-definition.[2]

Historians writing about the period 1870 to 1900 have discussed this awareness of change as manifested in areas such as the family, business, religion and politics. Of all these, however, the least-explored is the family and, especially, that construct of feminine experience called "domesticity." The primary purpose of this article is to explore several insistent questions raised by this gap in our knowledge about the late Victorian family. How was domesticity, an essentially conservative construct, reconciled with the virtues of a mobile society? What was the relationship between women themselves and the mobile physical home? Was personal as well as cultural womanhood bound up with the objects and spaces of the domestic environment? In order to illuminate these questions, I will discuss the behavior of individual women as they created living spaces in both settled and frontier areas of Kansas between 1870 and 1900. Since settlement on the frontier confronted the experience of mobility head on, it magnified phenomena characteristic of the settled life of those who did not choose to become pioneers. Thus, while the pioneer experience was in a certain way unique, in another sense it serves to shed light upon common cultural circumstances.

In addition, this article will augment a relatively new area of historiography by focusing on the experience of women settlers on the frontier. The recent work of Julie Roy Jeffrey and Glenda Riley suggests the crucial importance of the female contribution to settlement of the American West. Both these scholars reconstruct women's experience; and, in so doing, they have challenged the notion that frontier hardship demoralized women or, in the alternative, that the breakdown of prescribed roles on the frontier created a climate of equality for women. Rather, Jeffrey and Riley have given us a powerful image of the complexity of women's contributions to settlement, as well as the great variety of ways in which women dealt with that experience. However, neither have addressed the question of women's *cultural* role on the frontier in relation to *the physical domestic space* which women occupied and the objects with which they surrounded themselves. The belief in the power of the physical home to transform individual character was an underlying aspect of woman's ideal role in the late nineteenth century. In addition, her ability to create a satisfying domestic environment through the manipulation and placement of domestic objects was an essential part of the late Victorian woman's sense of herself, as well as her awareness of what it meant to be "civilized." The secondary purpose of this article, then, is to explore the cultural role of women on the frontier in relation to the physical arena of domesticity.[3]

I

The settlers of the Kansas frontier of the 1870s and 1880s strove to accommodate rough, make-do living arrangements with ideals of comfort and coziness. The Kansas frontier was not so much conquered as it was domesticated, and women played a leading role in this transformation. The promoters of Kansas settlement expressed their awareness of woman's cultural role when they urged male settlers to cultivate the minds and hearts of the inhabitants by establishing tasteful homes in the new land. "The neat calico dresses and sunshade hats of the ladies, and the cheap but durable raiment of the gentlemen," remarked Evan Jenkins, "were in harmony with the times, and with the plain domestic spirit that prevailed in the homestead region."[4]

Kansas women, whether in rural, frontier or urban areas, attempted to reproduce the visible symbols of home that were an important part of the late Victorian notion of civilization. Frontierswomen brought with them the furniture and books, the pianos and pans, that would recreate the stable family home wherever they went. Julia Hand was in a prairie schooner on the way to Kansas from Illinois when she presented her husband with "a volume of Shakespeare" for his thirtieth birthday. Some women compared frontier accommodations favorably to their Eastern background. When Carrie Robbins moved with her husband to Kansas from Quincy, Illinois, soon after their marriage in 1887, they lived in a sod house in the sagebrush and cactus flats west of Dodge City. At a dinner with some neighbors, she commented on the delicious meal which was "well cooked and well served. [The] table was really elegant with nice linen and silverware." Despite the fact that Carrie Robbins found herself on the vast open spaces of western Kansas, with their nearest neighbor a prairie dog colony, she applied her Illinois standards to Kansas homemaking and did not find it wanting.[5]

To understand the significance of the domestic environment for these women we must first turn to the physical artifacts of the frontier home. The photo shows the interior of a dugout in Ford County, Kansas. Despite the crowding, it is evident that the homemaker has found a place for everything. Since the photograph was taken as a permanent record of their living arrangements, she probably set out her best items for the benefit of the family history or to show relatives or friends "back East" the cultured style of dugout living. The photograph bore witness to the similarity between her present environment and that she had left behind. She propped the massive family Bible on the hutch, and on the cloth-covered table in the foreground set an impressive fancy tea service. Pictures and a calendar hang on the already-loaded walls near the stove, and a birdcage and books are prominently displayed. A doll even sits in the infant's chair, in place of a child who would not have remained still for the length of time it took to expose the photograph, but whose presence would help to define a family's rather than an individual's dwelling.

In *The Northern Tier* (1880), Evan J. Jenkins described a Kansas scene that could have taken place in any parlor in the nation: "In one of those dug-outs which I visited on a certain rainy day, an organ stood near the window and the settler's wife was playing 'Home! Sweet Home!'" Jenkins, a surveyor for the Federal Land Office, noted the ability of Kansas women on the western frontier to transmit culture through the objects and arrangement of domestic interiors. He praised the urbane quality of even the most modest Kansas homes and acknowledged that credit for this condition went to women:

Many of those "dug-outs" . . . gave evidence of the refinement and culture of the inmates. . . . The wife had been reared in the older states, as shown by the neat and tastefully-arranged fixtures around the otherwise gloomy earth walls.

Interior of dugout in Ford County, Kansas (Kansas State Historical Society, Topeka)

Jenkins' reference to the presence of culture focused on the woman's ability to turn sod walls and a dirt floor into the equivalent of an Eastern parlor. "A neatly polished shelf, supported by pins driven into the wall, contained the holiday gift books, album, and that indispensable household treasure, the family Bible."[6] The woman who displayed objects which had cultural significance—birdcages, Bibles, tea sets—was able to give her relatives and neighbors visual proof of her lack of privation, and of the identity of her living arrangements to those she had left behind.

The apparent "sloppiness" of the clothing and other objects hanging on the walls of the Ford County dugout is less aberrant when compared with the calculated casualness of other interior scenes . . . , suggesting that the crowded interior was not caused solely by a lack of space. Studied casualness was intended to communicate comfort, and an expression of comfort was closely tied to the visual impact of material objects. In an 1871 article for *The Ladies' Repository*. Mrs. Willing explained to her readers that one homemaker "had wrought miracles of comfort—a ten cent paper on the wall, fresh and cheery, a bright rag carpet, a white bed spread, groups of engravings from the Repository and some pencil sketches . . . ," when she decorated the family home.[7] In other words, actual comfort in the form of soft chairs, warm blankets or heated rooms was not as necessary in home decoration as the appearance of comfort communicated through physical objects. Some objects themselves expressed relaxation such as the shawls draped over pictures or the mantle, and the "throw" pillows on chairs or divans. Comfort also could be expressed via a carefully-planned jumble, as though the rooms were "lived-in." In the dugout, where space was at a premium and the items were "arranged" for the picture, there is the same sense of studied casualness as in the other rooms. The owner of the dugout expressed the ideal of comfortable, inexpensive, pleasant home surroundings by carefully positioning her visual clues to achieve order in a tight space.

Many photographs of architectural interiors focus on the same imagery as the illustrations in popular magazines and books; others represent a type of iconography that is related to traditional domestic genre scenes. They illustrate the transference of at least some portions of the ideal home to the trans-Mississippi West. For example, we can make a further comparison of the intent and content of the Ford County dugout photograph by looking at [three other dugouts with tables] . . . set for a meal. . . . [One] probably shows a lower-middle-class dining room since the chairs do not match one another and the table service largely is inexpensive ceramic or glass. [Another] . . . shows a middle-class home where all the chairs match and the service is silver or silver-plate, as well as ceramic. [Last there] . . . is an upper-class home in San Francisco. In each one, however, the intent of the record was identical: to exhibit the abundance of the family and to illustrate the skills of the homemaker who provided these examples of the transitory domestic art of table arranging. The preparation of a table for holidays or parties was a "high art" form within the aesthetics of the household; correct positioning in the placement of dishes, silver and glassware expressed a refined, educated sensibility. While acting as housekeeper of her father's sod house in Rice County, Kansas, Emily Combes prepared an elaborate meal with four kinds of meat, three vegetables, jelly and relishes, dessert and coffee. She "added to the table that 'charm of civilization' napkins and a white table cloth using for

View of kitchen in unidentified residence (Kansas State Historical Society, Topeka)

decoration a bowl of wildflowers and green leaves. . . . I was quite proud of myself," she admitted. Even in the upper-class or upper-middle-class household, where the work of setting a holiday or party table might go to a servant, the homemaker received the credit since this function expressed the homemaker's skill in beautifying the home.[8] By executing this function in small town or frontier areas, homemakers linked themselves to other women across the nation.

In addition to their practical uses, certain objects possessed symbolic meanings. Their presence in a home testified that a cultured sensibility pervaded the household. . . . [A number of pictures] document a middle-class genre piece of the late nineteenth century: a piano, carefully draped by a shawl, with one or more people in attendance. Women appeared most often in such photographs, but occasionally males were present as spectators or vocalists. Mrs. Sweet, who lived on a farm near Baldwin, Kansas, took piano lessons from a Miss Doyle, who came out once a week to give music lessons and usually stayed for dinner. Small, collapsible pump organs were available in the late nineteenth century, and it probably was this type of instrument which Mr.

Interior of a Kansas residence, location and date unknown (Kansas State Historical Society, Topeka)

Jenkins heard in the dugout he visited. A piano or organ was one of the signals which communicated culture and refinement, whether one lived in a dugout, a frame house, or like Mrs. Bishop . . . , in a rented room in Junction City.

Books were another signal intended to communicate the degree of a family's culture. Domestic decoration manuals and magazines pictured shelves laden with reading material, as well as vases, plates and pictures. This juxtaposition of items partially transformed the status of the book to that of a decorative object. . . . [In a comparison of] illustrations from Clarence Cook's *The House Beautiful* (1881 edition), . . . [and] interiors of Kansas homes [one can see that] the objects displayed are essentially the same. [A]n interior view of the living room of the Rob Roy ranch house in Kansas has nearly the same arrangement as [a room of another Kansas home], with a center plate hung over the mantle and statuary and feathers or shells. Photographs and diaries indicate that the emblems of cultivated life transferred to the frontier, although the substance of currently fashionable taste was not perfectly reproduced. Emily Combes had to settle for wildflowers instead of cultivated blooms, and the dugout dweller could fit a collapsible organ but not a full-sized piano into the small space.[9]

This necessity for a certain amount of make-shift in the accommodations of Kansas rural and town dwellings was seen by Kansans as both a virtue and a liability. An almost schizophrenic mingling of attitudes appeared in most public and some private statements about the quality of Kansas life. Kansas boosters somewhat defensively claimed that the rough prairie state was healthier than other areas, as they simultaneously averred that all the advantages of civilization were present in Kansas. This seems to have been a general rural phenomenon rather than a regional one. Sociologist Harry Braverman points out that in the late nineteenth century there were far fewer differences among the lives of people in rural areas around the country than between those in urban and those in rural areas. Despite their distance from the more populous East, the women of late nineteenth century Kansas or Nebraska, for example, lived much the same sort of life they would have lived in rural or small-town areas of Ohio, New York or Pennsylvania. Braverman notes the persistence of semi-rural and rural areas only a few miles from New York City even as late as 1890.[10]

Newspapers such as *The Rural New Yorker* (which had a large circulation in all farming areas of the country) carried articles or letters to the editor protesting against an image of rural isolation or small-town cultural backwardness. In "A Country Housekeeper's Ideal," Annie L. Jack claimed that it was as easy to lead a "refined" life in the country as in the city. "There need not be any roughness in our amusements; there is every facility for a beautiful and cultivated life, if one can have flowers and books, even if the other surroundings are simple and inexpensive." Emily Combes wrote to her fiancé in April 1871 from Manhattan, Kansas, that "The houses are neat and pretty, many being built of stone and furnished nicely—plenty of books, carpets, pictures, piano. . . . One meets some very cultured people."[11] Other people claimed that being rough around the edges was a positive quality. An article in the Manhattan (Kansas) *Nationalist* on 13 January 1871 claimed that Kansas women were not ignorant of fashion in house furnishings, but that the family and its needs took precedence over the whims of outsiders.

Therefore excuse my prefering the comfort of my family to the entertainment of my acquaintances. And, society, if you choose to look in upon us, you must just take us as we are without pretence of any kind; or you must shut the door and say good-bye![12]

This defensiveness reflects the transition women were experiencing as they went from producers within the home economic system to consumers of mass-produced goods in the marketplace. In this respect, the tenor of the articles directed to women in *The Rural New Yorker* changed dramatically over the last thirty years of the nineteenth century, from an emphasis on frugality to information on fashion trends. In the 1870s, the magazine contained two types of articles addressed to women. One concentrated on recipes, gardening tips and prescriptive articles on how to make a home more comfortable and attractive with very little money. Down-playing the importance of objects, these articles urged women to concentrate on the inner spirit of the home: on music, books and good feelings among the family members in order to create a congenial home. The second type of article claimed that rural women did not need to follow fashion since that was too expensive. By the 1890s, however, there was only one focus in articles aimed at the female reader. These articles suggest that rural women no longer were identifying themselves as "farmers' wives" or "farm mothers" but as something economically different from a frugal helpmeet. The women's section advised on the latest clothing styles and contained articles against woman's suffrage and information on tenement reform. The articles still evidenced concern with economy, but now in the form of guidelines on current clothing and furniture styles rather than the virtues of home-made rugs. By 1899, the newspaper no longer separated rural women from the urban ideals which appeared so strongly in magazines that were not oriented specifically to a rural audience.[13]

Prior to this change, women maintained that frugality should be balanced with beauty, and that adaptability and practicality were more important than following the dictates of prescribed fashion. Historian David P. Handlin refers to this preoccupation with the cost-effective selection of objects as the "beauty of economy," which continued to be the dominant aesthetic ideal in many homes until well into the twentieth century. The task of balancing tasteful, comfortable surroundings and inexpensive purchases fell to women, who took this aspect of consumption very seriously. A woman's ability to economize was as important as her creativity in home decoration. Mrs. French asked her brother in April 1891 whether Solomon was keeping the family farm at the same time that he had opened a store. "Is his wife any help to him at all, in using economy?" she inquired anxiously.[14]

Kansas women generally evidenced great concern for their role as women responsible for maintaining a congenial and civilized home environment, within the constraints of economy. Contrary to the dictates of magazines, however, their attention to home spaces frequently was as much for themselves as for their families. Mrs. Bingham regretted the move from Junction City to a small farm outside town. Her first experience of the tiny farm dwelling, and her realization of its distance from the tree-lined streets of Junction City, shocked and frightened her. "When I went into the little one-room place, with a loft reached by ladder, the tears came to my eyes, thinking of the contrast with the neat new home we had left." Nevertheless, Mrs. Bingham reconciled herself to her new home once her furniture and fixtures were in place. "We finally got things in shape to live. A bed in one corner, the cupboard in another, the stove in another, with chairs and tables between and around." For Mrs. Bingham, the division and distribution of the interior spaces and objects of the home was an important part of creating a livable situation. Her first thought was for the interior of her home, and she carefully arranged her furniture to create a sense of orderliness even in the small space. Mrs. Sweet, who moved to a farm near Ottawa, Kansas, in 1890, spent her first days in her new home freshening and arranging the fixtures and furniture. Her diary carefully notes each object, and possessively refers to all of them: "I worked at arranging things and unpacking my white dishes . . . I fixed my safe and unpacked my glass dishes." She put down carpet, hung pictures, put up curtains, papered the walls and painted some of her furniture. With these tasks accomplished, she felt she had transformed a house into her home.[15] Home, in this sense, could be anywhere as long as one had the things which made anywhere into one's special place. Home was transportable, in other words, by transporting objects. The essential ideal of home as a domestic ambiance created by women could be physically moved in the form of household articles or interior arrangements. Thus, the homemaker provided stability for the family not by her person but by her ability to obtain and arrange objects.

The western frontier of the 1870s challenged women's capacity to maintain the quality of the home environment. Carrie Robbins noted in her journal that she was not pleased with her first impressions of frontier dwellings but she remained undiscouraged. ". . . I had my first look at a sod house, rather low, dark and gloomy looking on the outside yet with floors windows, and the walls plastered. They are pleasant and comfortable upon the inside. I think I can make ours seem homelike." The situation frequently was not much better in the towns, where housing was short and women often had to make do with what was available. "I cant [*sic*] bear the idea of living in the Preston house it is so banged up and there are no conveniences either," lamented Emma Denison in 1873. "It is nothing but a dreary house, pretty enough on the outside but ugly enough inside."[16] Carrie Robbins and Emma Denison mentioned the exteriors of their dwellings, but focused sharply on the interiors. For many women, the inside of their homes mattered more to them than the exterior. It is evident that domestic space had a particular significance for these women.

The arrangement of the objects in the domestic interior occurred within a time frame that set women's domestic life apart from a clock-regimented society. In the first place, it was tied to the seasonal changes for the household and marked the transitional points of the year in the spring and fall. These changes were the same whether the woman kept house in the city or on a farm, and would not have varied much from New York to Kansas to Oregon. Taking down heavy winter drapes to replace them with lighter summer shades or removing wool carpets in favor of mats or light rag-rugs were seasonal chores that varied little from year to year, but which were always special events in the usual household routine. Susan B. Dimond moved to a farm near Cawker City, Kansas, in 1872. Entry after entry in her diary, beginning when she was in eastern Pennsylvania and continuing while she was in Kansas, simply stated, "Done my usual work," or "Done my housework." Then, in the seasons of change her entries became more detailed, with such comments as "varnished a bedstead" or "commenced to cover our lounge in the evening," "worked on my counterpain, & papered some up stairs and fixed up the chamber."[17]

As further evidence of the importance of this domestic ritual, even women who had regular servants usually reserved the largest part of this seasonal activity for themselves. Mrs. James Horton of Lawrence, Kansas, whose diary almost never mentions her attention to the details of housework unless her servant was ill, noted in April 1874 that she "took up North-chamber carpet & cleaned room." During the course of the month she installed wallpaper in the hall, put down carpets in the bedrooms and on the stairs, removed the blinds so they could be painted, and "arranged Books." Such entries received the same weight as her trips to Leavenworth, her social and literary meetings and her reading habits, which dominate her diary during other months.[18]

For newly married women, the formation of a home was important as the symbol of conjugal happiness. "Ella and Harry are just as cozy as they can be," Emma Denison commented during her own betrothal. "It made us just a little bit homesick for our cozy little home that is to be." Martha Farnsworth, whose alcoholic and tubercular husband once threatened her life with a shotgun, lived what she described as a "dreary, lonely life in tears." Nevertheless, her home symbolized the happiness they were unable to achieve in their personal relations. When her husband died, she gave away or "burned up" the silverware, blankets, bedstead and other household items in order not to be re-minded of how unhappy she had been. Ridding herself of the physical artifacts of her marriage seemed a way to rid herself of its unpleasant memories. Her second marriage, to Fred Farnsworth, gave her all of the happiness she had missed in the first. While living with his parents, she remarked excitedly that she and Fred purchased a "new Gasoline Stove," their *first purchase . . .* in household furnishing." They later pur-chased a small home of their own in Topeka.[19] With virtually no funds, Mrs. Farnsworth set about to create a pleasant ambiance by decorating the rooms.

> I have one pretty Wolf rug, which I placed in front of a Bench, I made myself and covered, then I have a box, covered and two chairs. I got at [the] grocery, common, manila wrapping paper and made window shades, and we have our Piano, and we have music in our home and are happy. . . .

In late summer she put the final touches on the interior of their home by selecting and installing wallpaper. "Got a lovely Terra Cotta Ingrain, with 18 inch border, for the Parlor; a beautiful pink flowered, gilt for the diningroom and Leavender [*sic*] flowers for the bed-room and we will have a dear 'little nest' when once we get settled."[20] By combining found objects such as grocery wrapping paper, hoarded treasures such as the Wolf rug and the piano, various purchased wallpapers, a rocker and a home-made bench, Martha Farnsworth created a personal fam-ily space to give physical manifestation of her happy marriage. Simi-larly, in the damp cellar under the Dimond home, where they lived during a particularly cold winter, Susan Dimond assured her family's material and spiritual comfort as well as her own. "We moved our stove and bed down into the basement this afternoon," she noted in her diary on 28 November 1872. "We were over to Dyton['s] to dinner . . . brought some pictures home to hang in our basement." Lacking funds for commercial wallpaper, she used newspapers to cover the earth walls.[21]

In their diaries and letters, homemakers frequently made allusion to themselves as aristocrats or "queens." This may have indicated an awareness on their part that the home could symbolize economic status. Ella Whitney wrote to her cousin Hattie Parkerson in 1872, "How do you like keeping house on your own responsibility. I expect you feel as grand as a queen and step about." Mrs. Bingham felt the crowning touch in the cottonwood shack was two carpets which she had brought with her from New York. When these were down on the floor, she felt "quite aristocratic." It is also possible that the use of words such as these referred to the contemporary cultural metaphor of the home as a castle. Either way, the central position of the physical home is evident. For Mrs. Bingham, her New York carpets provided links with other homes she had lived in as well as a sense of personal completeness and pride.[22] The objects within the home were inextricably tied to women's concept of self as well as to their cultural role.

II

The vital soul of an ideal Victorian home was the wife and homemaker who transformed an architectural shell into a "Home" by the selection and arrangement of domestic spaces and objects. Most women were committed to the reality of this ideal to the extent that they seemed unable to separate their self-image from the physical domestic environment. When Eva Moll wanted to bring her absent friend Hattie Parkerson to mind in 1898, she conjured up an image of Hattie in her home in Kansas, where "everything impressed itself so deeply upon my memory that if you have made any changes in furnishings or the arrangement of the furniture, I believe I could put everything where it was when I was there." Eva used the image of an unchanged domestic environment to tell Hattie that their friendship endured in spite of distance. Belle Litchfield, in 1899, sent Hattie a photograph of the exterior of her new home in Southbridge, Massachusetts, and then took careful pains to describe the interior: "The room where the corner Bay Window is, is our library. . . . [she then put herself into the picture] where I now sit writing. The chamber above it is my chamber, and the bay window over that is my studio."[23] Her description would not have satisfied an architect, but that was not Belle's intent. She hoped to recreate for her friend a sense of a home—not of a building—where people lived and moved within the various rooms, where the dramas and comedies of the domestic world played on their own timeless stage.

By locating a part of the home's significance in the presence of particular types of objects, Americans attested to the essentially mobile nature of the physical and spiritual home. In addition, the pianos, pictures and tables set with napkins in the "wilderness," told the world that a cultivated woman was present, one who understood and could communicate her cultural womanhood. Whatever else their ultimate role may have been in providing the institutional marks of culture such as schools and churches, women first "domesticated" the frontier, and linked it to other areas of the nation, by their awareness and use in the home of commonly accepted cultural symbols. Rather than consider a dugout, a rented room or a damp cellar as temporary living arrangements, and thus not worth improving, they created a stable home by their attention to the domestic interior and the objects which filled it regardless of the size or condition of the dwelling. Like Julia Hand, who began moving her household goods into her sod house before it was finished, the arrangement of domestic space was one of a woman's first considerations in the frontier environment.[24] No doubt a portion of this concern stemmed from the fact that home was a woman's place of work, and organized quarters simplified household tasks. Then too, the objects a woman brought to her new home provided a sense of continuity whether she moved across the nation or across town. Neither of these assumptions, however, explains why Dimond troubled to get pictures to hang in a temporary shelter, or Farnsworth's proud, detailed description of her new wallpaper, or why the anonymous decorator of the Ford County dugout wanted her fancy tea service at center-front for a photograph. In addition to the personal meanings associated with objects, the homemaker also was aware of the cultural significance of domesticity. The domestic environment, in other words, provided an essential link between personal and cultural womanhood.

NOTES

1. Two works that deal with domestic material culture have informed this study. See Bonnie G. Smith, *Ladies of the Leisure Class: The Bourgeoises of Northern France in the Nineteenth Century* (Princeton, 1981); and Lizabeth A. Cohen, "Embellishing a Life of Labor: An Interpretation of the Material Culture of American Working-Class Homes, 1885–1915," *Journal of American Culture* 3 (Winter, 1980), 752–775. The women whose diaries and letters formed the basis of this study can be termed "middle-class" based on their husbands' occupations (postman, butcher, etc.), their level of literacy and the apparent amount of their family's wealth. There is no reason to believe, however, that only middle-class women shared the cultural awareness described in this article. Lizabeth Cohen's article suggests the importance of certain objects (such as religious icons) in working-class homes.

2. For discussions of the place of mobility in American culture and of the attempt to "nationalize" or "standardize" the American character, see Robert H. Wiebe, *The Search for Order, 1877–1920* (New York, 1967); Henry Nash Smith, *Virgin Land: The American West as Symbol and Myth* (New York, 1950); Howard Mumford Jones, *The Age of Energy: Varieties of American Experience, 1865–1915* (New York, 1971). *Statistics of the Population of the United States* (Tenth Census of the United States, 1880), vol. 1 (Washington, D.C., 1883).

3. See Julie Roy Jeffrey, *Frontier Women: The Trans-Mississippi West, 1840–1880* (New York, 1979); Glenda Riley, *Frontierswomen, the Iowa Experience* (Ames, Iowa, 1981). For an analysis of the belief in the moral impact of interior decoration, and women's role as domestic decorators, see Angel Kwolek-Folland, "The Useful What-Not and the Ideal of Domestic Decoration," *Helicon Nine* 8 (Spring, 1983), 72–83.

4. Evan J. Jenkins, *The Northern Tier: or, Life Among the Homestead Settlers* (Topeka, 1880), 150.

5. Julia Hand, Diary, 24 November 1872, Kansas State Historical Society, Manuscript Department, Topeka, Kansas. Mrs. Carrie Robbins, Journal, 4 March 1887, Kansas State Historical Society, Manuscript Department, Topeka, Kansas.

6. Jenkins, *Northern Tier,* 150, 154.

7. Mrs. Jennie F. Willing, "Helpmeets," *The Ladies Repository* 31 (January, 1871), 2.

8. Emily Combes to her fiancé, 27 August 1881, Kansas State Historical Society, Manuscript Department, Topeka, Kansas. See Smith, *Ladies of the Leisure Class,* 67, for her analysis of the symbolic significance of table arrangements. I have assumed that the photographs used in this article as evidence of material culture were taken as historical records or as objects to be shared with contemporaries. Thus, photographs act both as diaries and as letters.

9. Mrs. Sweet, Diary 5 and 12 May 1891, Kansas State Historical Society, Manuscript Department, Topeka, Kansas.

10. This quality is analyzed by Karl Menninger in "Bleeding Kansas," *A Psychia-*

trist's World: The Selected Papers of Karl Menninger, M.D., ed. Bernard H. Hall (New York, 1959), 16–22. Harry Braverman, *Labor and Monopoly Capital: The Degradation of Work in the Twentieth Century* (New York, 1974), 293.

11. Annie L. Jack, "A Country Housekeeper's Ideal," *The Rural New Yorker* (March 22, 1884), 190. Combes, letter of 25 May 1871.

12. Manhattan (Kansas) *Nationalist* (January 18, 1871), 1.

13. This information was gleaned from a general survey conducted by this author in April 1982 of thirty years of issues of *The Rural New Yorker*. Sophia Bennett Crowe mentioned subscribing to the newspaper in her Diary on 14 April 1874, Kansas State Historical Society, Manuscript Department, Topeka, Kansas. Susan Dimond recorded her paid subscription to the newspaper in her budget for 1870, Diary, Kansas State Historical Society, Manuscript Department, Topeka, Kansas.

14. David P. Handlin, *The American Home: Architecture and Society, 1815–1915* (Boston, 1979), 429. Mrs. French to her brother, 5 April 1891, Domestic Science Club Papers, Kansas State University Archives, Manhattan, Kansas.

15. Anne E. Bingham, "Sixteen Years on a Kansas Farm, 1870–1886," unpub. ms., Topeka, Kansas, 1921, 9–10. Mrs. Sweet, Diary, March 1890.

16. For a discussion of the impact of frontier conditions on women's work place in the home, see Riley, *Frontierswomen*, 29–54. Robbins, Diary, 4 March 1887. Emma Denison to Hattie Parkerson, 5 January 1873, Domestic Science Club Papers, Kansas State University Archives, Manhattan, Kansas.

17. Dimond, Diary, August, October, November, 1870; March and April 1872.

18. Mrs. James Horton, Diary, April 1874, Kansas State Historical Society, Manuscript Department, Topeka, Kansas.

19. Emma Denison to Hattie Parkerson, 5 February 1873, Domestic Science Club Papers. Martha Farnsworth, Diaries, 18 November 1893, Kansas State Historical Society, Manuscript Department, Topeka, Kansas.

20. Farnsworth, Diaries, 16 May 1894, 6 March 1890, 2 December 1890, 9 May and 28 July 1896.

21. Dimond, Diaries, 25 and 28 November 1872.

22. Ella J. Whitney to Hattie Parkerson, 28 July 1872, Domestic Science Club Papers. Bingham, "Sixteen Years," 9–10. "Belle" [Isabelle W. Litchfield] to Hattie Parkerson, 19 March 1898 and 27 February 1899, Domestic Science Club Papers.

23. Eva Moll to Hattie Parkerson, 18 February 1898, Domestic Science Club Papers; [Isabelle] W. Litchfield to Hattie Parkerson, 27 February 1899, Domestic Science Club Papers.

24. Hand, Diary, 7 November 1872.

Kansas in the Nineteenth Century: From "Bleeding Kansas" to Modernity

Dispossession and resettlement were only part of the extensive changes to the cultural and physical landscapes of Kansas in the nineteenth century. The convergence of cultures brought conflict, at times violent, but it also evoked cooperation and reform. Kansans in the nineteenth century increasingly faced the questions and pressures of modernization, both social and technological. The midpoint of that century witnessed the area's most violent period, "Bleeding Kansas." This episode was but a prelude to the even bloodier Civil War, which ravaged the nation from 1861 to 1865. The war itself has been called the first of the modern wars and effectively ushered in the beginnings of modern America. Starting with the question of slavery and its place in Kansas statehood, moving through reforms in the social and political systems of the newly admitted state, and ending with questions of how to accommodate and incorporate two of the most important technological innovations into Kansas society, this section introduces some of the most important themes that define this tumultuous period.

The issue of whether slavery should be allowed to spread to the newly opened territories had a long history in the region. Beginning with the Missouri Compromise (1820), through the Compromise of 1850, and culminating in the Kansas-Nebraska Act (1854), the debate over slavery's future in the Great Plains ended in violence. Before the Civil War, there was "Bleeding Kansas," five years of partisan conflict involving antislavery activists from the North and pro-slavery sympathizers from the South. Rhetoric on both sides was vitriolic and incendiary, and the actions of both parties were no less vituperative. History tends to favor the victors, however, and our understanding of the pro-slavery faction is less than complete.

Whether due to the lack of primary sources voicing pro-slavery sentiment or to the bias of historians in favoring the free-state position, the history of slavery's advocates has been largely ignored. Bill Cecil-Fronsman seeks to redress this weakness in his essay "'Death to All Yankees and Traitors in Kansas.'" The most extensive extant records of the pro-slavery opinion are the newspapers from towns such as Atchison and Leavenworth, hotbeds of the pro-slavery faction. Cecil-Fronsman's analysis of the *Atchison Squatter Sovereign* provides us with an excellent view of the fundamental ideas of the pro-slavery leadership, as well as the propaganda these leaders used to attract settlers sympathetic to their point of view.

If the history of the pro-slavery faction in Kansas has been largely understudied, so has the experience of the African-Americans who lived in the area. Although the symbolic importance of Kansas in the African-American struggle for equal rights inspired a number of studies on race prior to the development of the "new history," the early works seldom produced information on African-Americans themselves. Part of the reason for this gap in scholarship is the lack of primary sources left behind by those whose stories we wish to tell. In order to uncover this past, historians must be creative in searching for and analyzing available evidence. By examining a variety of sources, including archaeological findings, newspapers, biographies, and census records, Richard Sheridan sheds light on an important period in the history of African-Americans in Kansas.

In "From Slavery in Missouri to Freedom in Kansas," Sheridan narrates the story of the migration of African-Americans into Kansas from 1854 to 1865. Most had escaped slavery through the Underground Railroad or had been "jayhawked" from neighboring Missouri. Freedom did not necessarily mean an end to discrimination and prejudice, however. Sheridan's study demonstrates that the creation of a free state in 1861 did not solve racial problems in Kansas. He notes how the influx of former slaves elicited divergent responses from the white populace of the state; some greeted the freedmen and women with equanimity, while others responded with increased racism. In fact, according to Sheridan, the end of the war brought increased racial separation and feelings of betrayal.

We are only beginning to understand the reaches of racism and the fight against it in the West. Race was a pervasive issue in Kansas, particularly in the more urban areas where a majority of African-Americans lived. Because the state legislature created a permissive approach to segregation, most of the towns and cities had segregated schools at some level. Despite widespread racism, there was a general belief that African-American children should be educated. James C. Carper's essay, "The Popular Ideology of Segregated Schooling," examines the rhetoric behind both the education of African-American children and the segregation of schools. Carper's analysis of African-American views of education, their debates over integration, and their development of newspapers to publicly express their views marks an important contribution to our understanding of race relations in nineteenth-century Kansas.

Education was not the only quarter for reform. Concerns over unfair labor practices, workplace safety, pollution, social equality, and political representation also captured the attention of reformers in the last part of the nineteenth century. At the base of these reforms was the question of power: who had it and who should have it. As has already been seen, throughout the nineteenth century (and into the twentieth), women's power rested primarily in the home. The notion of domesticity, integral to the ideology of "separate spheres," limited women's participation to the home and family. However, following the Civil War, women began expanding the definition of home, exerting their influence on a broader scale. Women justified their increased participation in the public sphere on the basis of their moral superiority, a key tenet of the "separate spheres" ideology. Women reformers thus co-opted a seemingly limiting construction of gender in order to increase their political power. The Woman Movement declared that women, as moral beings, should have the power to vote and participate in America's political culture.

Like any political movement or organization, the Woman Movement was a cooperative effort between disparate individuals. Michael Goldberg's essay on woman suffrage in Kansas illustrates this fact very well. Goldberg shows that the women who participated in the movement were not an undifferentiated bloc. Rural and urban divisions were particularly important; middle-class urban women who fought for suffrage did not understand the position of farm women, nor did they recognize the need to incorporate them fully into the movement. There were fissures along party lines as well, despite a public concordance between Republican and Populist women to rise above party for a common cause. Ultimately, the accord proved tenuous, and factionalism undermined women's bid for political power. But more tellingly, the Woman Movement failed to overturn the most powerful obstacle in its path: a gender ideology that assumed that politics was man's domain.

Women were not the only group in American society that sought greater participation in the political process. As America moved toward a modern society, farmers, too, felt disfranchised and often blamed modern technology for their problems. The technologies of a modern industrial society tended to differentiate Americans along economic lines and rural and urban divides. Although most people saw promise in the new age of telegraphs, railroads, and gas and electrical lights, they were less certain about the power of the corporations that monopolized their production. Populism developed as an alternative to the political and economic domination of urban industrial magnates and argued specifically for the democratization of the railroad.

According to Thomas Frank, Populists in Kansas viewed monopolies, especially the railroads, as perversions of capitalism that corrupted the economic system. The Populists offered the concept of the public utility as a corrective, arguing that railroads were communal property created by public subsidies and brought into being by legislative charters. Moreover, they were essential to the welfare of all in a market economy. As a public necessity, railroads and other public utilities needed to be operated for common benefit, not the profit of a few individuals.

Like the railroad, automobiles caused conflict between the rural and urban populations of Kansas. The automobile, a symbol of modern America, generated a great deal of concern almost from its inception. One part of the issue centered around building and maintaining roads, because autos, of course, necessitated roads on which to drive them. In Kansas the discussion took the form of a debate over rural improvement, and the sides split almost entirely along rural-urban lines. According to Paul Sutter in his essay, "Paved with Good Intentions," urban Kansans saw new technology and expertise as a necessary factor of modernization that would produce economic growth, a higher standard of living, and a new aesthetic. Town and city dwellers argued for the use of professional engineers to construct and maintain roads and painted farmers as backward hayseeds who were unwilling to spend money on road improvement. Farmers, on the other hand, feared increased taxes in a time of a depressed economy. They recognized that greater costs would require more cash, which they could acquire only by producing more for the market. Their experience with a boom and bust economy, the high cost of modern technology, and mortgages and loss of farms told them that such a course was fraught with danger. Rural Kansans recognized that cars and trucks made marketing cash crops easier, but they also understood that the costs for doing so were high. In the face of pressures to raise taxes and build better roads, caution seemed the better strategy.

Modernization took many forms in Kansas, ranging from reform movements in education and women's rights to technologies such as the railroad and the automobile. Questions of race, class, and gender permeated the debates that accompanied the modernization process. Who would benefit from the new technologies and the new opportunities afforded by a modern society? Who should be allowed to participate in the decision-making process? What rights do individuals have, and will modern society enhance or undermine those rights? These are just a few of the questions Kansans asked themselves as the nineteenth century closed. The following six essays begin to tell the story of how those questions were answered.

"Death to All Yankees and Traitors in Kansas": The Squatter Sovereign and the Defense of Slavery in Kansas

Bill Cecil-Fronsman

When Kansas bled during its tumultuous territorial years, no newspaper defended slavery or condemned free-soil settlers with more force or more venom than the *Squatter Sovereign*. Published out of Atchison, the *Squatter Sovereign* never minced words as it led proslavery forces in their struggle for Kansas: "Let us begin to purge ourselves of all Abolition emissaries who occupy our dominion, and give distinct notice that all who do not leave immediately, for the East, WILL LEAVE FOR ETERNITY!"[1]

Free-state contemporaries were quick to condemn the paper. In 1855 Julia Louisa Lovejoy wrote back to her New Hampshire readers that the paper was "one of the vilest pro-slavery sheets that have ever disgraced the American press." Historians, who generally have been sympathetic with the free-state cause, have not dissented from that assessment. The most thorough historian of territorial newspapers, Herbert Flint, called the *Squatter Sovereign* "the real red-blooded, murder-seeking, Abolitionist-hanging, murder-condoning, blood-thirsty pro-slavery paper of all Kansas journalism." Flint went on to

"'Death to All Yankees and Traitors in Kansas': The *Squatter Sovereign* and the Defense of Slavery in Kansas," by Bill Cecil-Fronsman, *Kansas History* 16, 1 (1993): 22–33. Copyright Kansas State Historical Society. Reprinted by permission.

charge that "this paper was a vicious accomplice if not an instigator of crime and violence as perhaps few papers have ever been."[2]

Even those relatively few historians who have been sympathetic with the Southern cause have blanched at the paper's reckless utterances. Elmer Craik called it "the most outspoken and enthusiastic champion of southern institutions. Perhaps it did more than any other agency to stir up enmity between the two sections." Floyd Shoemaker described its senior editor as "perhaps the most virulent proslavery writer and speaker in Kansas."[3]

Kansas proslavery newspapers did not acquire a reputation for even-handed discussions of the controversial issues of the day. But among them was a wide variety of opinions and approaches. The *Squatter Sovereign* stood out for its vitriolic rhetoric. The tone was incendiary: "The abolitionists shoot down our men without provocation, whenever they meet them. LET US RETALIATE IN THE SAME MANNER—A FREE FIGHT IS ALL WE DESIRE. . . . DEATH TO ALL YANKEES / AND TRAITORS IN KANSAS." For those needing more specific guidance, it suggested: "Scourge the country of abolitionism, free soilism, and every other damnable ism that exists. Destroy their property, crops and every article that would conduce to the support of any or every person who is known or suspected of acting, co-operating or sympathizing with abolitionism."[4]

But there is a great deal more to the issue. Merely knowing that the *Squatter Sovereign* was a virulently proslavery newspaper does not explain *why* it was a proslavery newspaper. The *Squatter Sovereign* was the leading voice of Kansans who were willing to kill (although perhaps somewhat less willing to die) to make Kansas a slave state. Too often historians have been content to chronicle the incidents of violence and vote fraud that the proslavery group perpetrated. But if we are to understand why the proslavery group battled the Yankees so vigorously, we need to go beyond the hyperbole and start to understand how they viewed their free-state opponents and how they viewed themselves. Only then can we begin to comprehend why Kansas bled.

Too often historians' sympathies have interfered with their abilities to understand the proslavery group. Free-staters had the twin advantages of being both the winners and the good guys. No large body of losers survived and remained in the state to create a Kansas version of the cult of the lost cause. Not surprisingly, it would take a Missourian to note that the Bleeding Kansas episode "is one of the few examples I know of of one side being simon-pure and the other side being simply poor, of one side having all the proof and the other side getting all the punishment, of one side receiving the bravos and the other side, the Bronx cheers."[5] It is certainly not the intention here to rehabilitate the proslavery cause. It is rather the intention here to try to understand it.

This article will explore the *Squatter Sovereign*, the shrillest, most widely-read voice of Kansas proslavery opinion.[6] In a fundamental sense, its defense of slavery was an attack on life as its contributors imagined it was lived in the North. The *Squatter Sovereign* did not defend slavery as the institution of the planter elite. Rather, the paper portrayed itself defending the common man against an aggressive, demoralizing industrial capitalism. The proslavery faction's Northern opponents were not free, independent men of the land, but hirelings, manipulated by their moneyed masters in the East. Such men had no legitimate rights in Kansas. By protecting slavery in Kansas against men like these, the *Squatter Sovereign* sought to preserve the territory as a new home for an independent, autonomous yeomanry that lived side-by-side with slaves and slaveholders.

The *Squatter Sovereign* began as a company paper. The Atchison Town Company, composed of "Southern pro-slavery people," awarded its editors $400 to establish the paper.[7] The editors in turn regularly boosted the area as a place with an unbridled future: "A number of large farms are being made in the vicinity of Atchison. Some of our farmers are putting in from forty to eighty acres of prairie. The crops in this region never looked more promising."[8]

The senior editor was Dr. John H. Stringfellow. Born in Culpepper County, Virginia, Stringfellow was a graduate of the University of Pennsylvania Medical School. His fortunes took him to Missouri where his brother Benjamin F. Stringfellow served as attorney general. He married Ophelia J. Simmons, niece of Gov. John C. Edwards, a connection that encouraged him to set up his practice in Missouri. He practiced medicine in Brunswick and Carrolton before moving to Platte City in 1852. When Kansas was opened, he helped to form a town company, encouraged it to name the town after Missouri's proslavery senator, David Rice Atchison, and selected a town lot for himself.[9]

Robert S. Kelley, born in Fredericksburg, Virginia, was the junior editor. Herbert Flint, who apparently interviewed him, wrote that as a boy Kelley ran away to Boston where he learned the printer's trade and "where he has said, he also learned to hate the Yankees." When a rumor surfaced that he was born in Massachusetts, Kelley responded,

"We can stand anything but being called a Yankee and brand the author a coward, a base calumniator, and a willful liar." Prior to coming to Kansas, Kelley ran the *Democratic Platform,* a St. Joseph, Missouri, newspaper that regularly blasted slavery's opponents. In November of 1856 Stringfellow and Kelley sold a half interest in the paper to Peter H. Larey who joined the staff as coeditor. A native of South Carolina and "an uncompromising States Rights Democrat," Larey brought no changes in editorial policy or outlook.[10]

One can understand the *Squatter Sovereign* only within the context of the emerging national debate on slavery. Although several decades of abolitionist critics had condemned slavery as an institution that cruelly abused slaves, these assaults had not generated a broad political consensus among a racist Northern population. Rather, Northerners were far more likely to condemn slavery as a retrogressive institution that created a backward and stagnant society. Whatever sympathy Northerners may have felt for slaves was overshadowed by their revulsion with the effects of slavery on whites. As Eric Foner wrote, "The Republican critique of southern society thus focused upon the degradation of labor—the slave's ignorance and lack of incentive, and the laboring white's poverty, degradation, and lack of social mobility." The result was a two-class society: "the slaveholding aristocracy and the very poor."[11]

The Southern response to Northern criticism likewise emphasized a variety of points. Some defenders directly responded to abolitionist charges that slavery cruelly abused slaves by claiming that the slaves were more humanely treated than their working-class counterparts in the free states. Others directly took on abolitionist charges that slavery was incompatible with Christianity by searching for biblical justifications for that peculiar institution. These lines of defense appeared in the pages of the *Squatter Sovereign.* Quoting an observer of slave life in Louisiana, it asserted that the slaves' "appearance contrasts brightly with the doleful accounts we daily recieve [*sic*] from Northern towns and cities of the distress and forlorn condition of the poor miserable white slaves who drag out a wretched existence there."[12]

During the summer of 1855 the paper printed "A Brief Examination of Scripture Testimony on the Institution of Slavery" written by editor Stringfellow's kinsman, Thornton Stringfellow of Culpepper County, Virginia. Anything but brief, the examination covered several columns on the front pages of two months' worth of issues and rehearsed the standard defenses: slavery was a part of the Hebrew civilizations; St.

Paul recognized slavery and told runaways to return to their masters; slaves owed obedience to their masters who in turn would treat them kindly. In another context, the paper suggested that it was abolitionists who were irreligious. It was they who wished to see Kansas "patterned after Massachusetts where . . . the Bible [is] denounced as humbug."[13]

The bulk of the paper's proslavery argument, however, focused on other issues. The *Squatter Sovereign* attempted to stand the free labor argument on its head. Rather than producing a society dominated by a plutocratic planter class, slavery created a uniquely egalitarian social order, a social order that was the prerequisite for a republican society. It was Northern capitalism that created an exploitative elite class and a degraded working class.

This type of reasoning was scarcely the exclusive property of the *Squatter Sovereign*. Many proponents of slavery maintained that equality among whites depended on a subordinated black population. Gov. Henry A. Wise of Virginia argued, "Break down slavery and you would with the same blow destroy the great democratic principle of equality among men." Georgia's Thomas R. R. Cobb advanced a similar position:

> The mass of laborers not being recognized among citizens, every citizen feels that he belongs to an elevated class. It matters not that he is not slaveholder, he is not the inferior race; he is a freeborn citizen; he engages in no menial occupation. The poorest meets the richest as an equal; sits at his table with him; salutes him as neighbor; meets him in every public assembly, and stands on the same social platform. Hence, there is no war of classes. There is truthfully republican equality in the ruling class.[14]

The editors of the *Squatter Sovereign* surely shared these sentiments. In a slave society, the paper proclaimed, "color, not money marks the class: black is the badge of slavery; white the color of the free man and the white man, however poor [and] whatever his occupation, feels himself a sovereign." Like Cobb, the paper contended that this made slavery the basis for republican equality. The white man in a slave society "looks upon liberty as the privilege of his color, the government peculiarly his own, himself its sovereign. He watches it with the jealous eye of a monarch." The free white man is "proud of his freedom" and "jealous of his privilege." Such a man "will resist every attempt to rob him of his dominion."[15]

Appeals like these resonated with the *Squatter Sovereign*'s readership.

The paper regularly boosted Kansas as a slaveholders' paradise, claiming in March of 1856 that over one thousand slaves were in the territory.[16] But wishful thinking would not make Kansas a slave state. Proslavery partisans needed the active support of nonslaveholding Southern whites. Missouri, the most likely source of proslavery Kansas emigrants, was dominated by small farmers. These common whites were the heirs to an egalitarian ethos that looked with suspicion upon any claims of social superiority over themselves. Racist in outlook, they had worked out a series of accommodations with their slaveholding neighbors. Slavery ensured that their status would be protected by an unbridgeable gulf between them and the degraded slaves. The *Squatter Sovereign* had to mobilize its supporters by appealing to their values, not the values of the planter class.[17]

The *Squatter Sovereign*'s constituency translated its egalitarian values into political thought through the medium of republicanism. Emerging as a political ideology in the last quarter of the eighteenth century, republicanism warned of what Harry Watson called the constant conflict between personal liberty and the power of the state. Liberty, Watson explained, "implied that no white man would be subject to the arbitrary rule of another and that the community of white men might rule themselves by means of majority rule." Power, in contrast, "was the threat of control by others." The delicate balance between the two could be preserved only by a virtuous citizenry that would safeguard its own interests without threatening the liberty of others. But to be truly virtuous, the citizenry had to be independent, a condition that required possession of productive property. "Control over their own property," wrote William L. Barney of eighteenth-century white Americans, "enabled them to withstand economic coercion and left them independent and fiercely self-assertive." It was this material basis that the *Squatter Sovereign* saw itself preserving.[18]

Juxtaposed against the image of the South as a white man's democracy came the image of the North as a land of class oppression. The *Squatter Sovereign* drew upon traditional republican suspicions to make its point. Quoting Thomas Jefferson, the paper declared that towns were "sores on the body politic." In the towns one finds "great wealth gathered in the hands of the few, the toiling millions struggling for bread; the one class is corrupted by luxury, the other debased by destitution." This was life in the North as the *Squatter Sovereign* imagined it. In the country, however, (and here the paper really meant in the rural

South) "there be no excessive wealth, there is no poverty." This was vital for the survival of a virtuous republic. Excessive wealth "creates an improper distinction, corrupts the morals of the people." For a republic to survive, wealth must be "fairly distributed so that each of its members, easy and independent in his property, shall feel himself practically equal to his fellows." In the absence of the kind of equality found among whites in a slave society, "of necessity money must distinguish the classes—mark the master, separate the servant."[19]

The *Squatter Sovereign*'s outlook required that it distinguish between Northerners. The paper periodically claimed that it did not hate *all* persons from the free states. It suggested that unlike their opponents, proslavery men did not seek to exclude anyone. The victory of the proslavery side would mean that anyone could make a home in Kansas: "The Southerner with his slaves, the industrious yankee with his mechanic arts can side by side, with good will and kindly feeling push on our bright destiny." Some Northerners clearly were welcome: "If Kansas could be peopled by honest citizens of the free States, who desired to transfer their own, and children's property, and if it were made a free State by such people, who were always willing to protect the rights of their neighbors, the Country, would have nothing to fear."[20]

Statements suggesting peaceful coexistence between proslavery forces and free-staters were rare. At times the *Squatter Sovereign* imagined a large mass of proslavery Northerners and contended that they "frankly admit they have their prejudice against negro slavery, but that experience has demonstrated to them that slaveholders and negro slaves suit them better than abolitionists." Naturally, to such men the editors "bid a hearty welcome to the shores of Kansas." In a column referring to the arrival of a group from Tennessee, the paper declared, "Companies coming from slave States will be heartily welcomed by our citizens, as well as those from free States who are all 'right on the goose.'" The editors knew well that many Northerners were from rural backgrounds similar to those of the Southern yeomanry. "There will be many a good citizen settle among us," the paper proclaimed, "from Illinois, Indian[a], and Ohio, whose notions of slavery are parallel with our own."[21]

The logic of the *Squatter Sovereign*'s proslavery defense dictated that it draw distinctions between Northerners. "There are two classes of people who come from the free States," a correspondent claimed, "the independent and dependent. The first have some means and intelligence. They are observant and practical as well as theoretic." This group, the correspondent maintained, would become proslavery men "If they find the country better suited to slave labor." But there were also dependent Northerners: "The other class are the subjects of the 'emigration Aid Society,' who come without means and with Utopian anticipations and are sadly disappointed and curse the men who sent them hither."[22]

At times the paper drew a harsh distinction between the honest midwesterner searching for a better place to farm and the eastern recruit of the New England Emigrant Aid Company. Established in 1854 by Eli Thayer, the company provided assistance to antislavery settlers. Although it supported only a relative handful of emigrants, its influence in the free-state movement went far beyond its numbers.[23] To the *Squatter Sovereign* the fact that settlers had received assistance made their presence fundamentally illegitimate. "We are not contending against the honest, but mistaken Free-Soiler, but with *the scum and filth of the Northern cities;* sent here as hired servants, to do the will of others; not to give their own free suffrage." The real enemies of slavery were not honest farmers seeking homes in a new territory. "No one can fail to distinguish between an honest, bona fide emigration, prompted by choice or necessity, and an organized colonization with offensive purpose upon the institutions of the country proposed to be settled."[24]

Although on one level the *Squatter Sovereign* recognized the midwesterners' existence, it generally ignored them when considering the situation or else assumed that they could be won over once the eastern influences were eliminated. Despite making an occasional reference to these honest men of the North, the paper took it as an article of faith that the true enemies of slavery "are not free men, but paupers, who have sold themselves to Eli Thayer & Co., to do their master's bidding." It mattered little to the paper that Southerners were organizing and subsidizing their countrymen's emigration to Kansas. It mattered little to the paper that many of the people helped by the New England Emigrant Aid Company were midwestern farmers. The paper made an implicit assumption that its opponents were "the hirelings of the Emigrant Aid Societies, the scruf[f] of the eastern cities."[25]

The image of white men, reduced to dependency, surely shocked the *Squatter Sovereign*'s constituency. Such men were not an independent group of free agents engaged in a legitimate dispute over the future of Kansas. They were "a Hessian band of mercenaries" who were presumably for sale to the highest bidder. Not only were they the slaves of Eli Thayer and company, but the free-state partisans were also subjects of other antislavery outsiders. A proslavery mob led by Robert Kelley put the abolition preacher Pardee Butler on a raft and set him adrift in the Missouri River. The *Squatter Sovereign* then asked its supporters, "Will they allow the Greel[e]ys and Sewards of the Northern States to inundate our broad territory with the scruf[f] and scum, collected from their prisons, brothels, and sink-holes of iniquity?"[26]

As men with no legitimate interest in Kansas, it is no surprise that this group would presumably be unwilling to engage in the hard work of transforming the territory into a land of prosperous farms. "They are not sent to cultivate the soil, to better their social condition, to add to their individual comforts, or the aggregate wealth of the nation," charged the paper. Instead, it viewed them as perpetually dependent on an outside force. "They are mostly ignorant of agriculture, picked up in cities and villages they, of course have no experience as farmers, and if left to their unaided resources—if not clothed and fed by the same power which has effected their transportation—they would starve."[27]

The Emigrant Aid men were inherently lazy! As Southern whites understood laziness, the concept meant refusing to do the work needed to maintain personal independence. Upon discovering that their benefactors were ready to abandon their New England hirelings, "As many as are able return. Those who are unable to do so, are obliged to labor—hard manual labor—such as they are unaccustomed to. They are not used to it, nor have they the physique, to handle the marl and wield the axe with the brawny sons of the west." In June of 1855 the paper published a letter during the territorial legislature making advocating abolition a felony. If passed, the author suggested, "We will soon rid ourselves of the most troublesome portion of the Emigrant Aid men. *They don[']t like work*, and if the legislature, will only make the penalty . . . a 6 or 12 month-service in a chain gang, these lazy meddlesome fellows will soon find their way back to some more congenial clime." Not only were the men lazy, so were the women. In that same issue the paper printed a joke that reported an alleged conversation between a father and son. "How could you marry an Irish girl?" the father asked. "Why father?" went the reply, "I am not able to keep two women—if I'd married a Yankee girl, I'd had to have hired an Irish girl to take care of her."[28]

The *Squatter Sovereign* portrayed its opponents as men without honor. Honor, as Southerners understood the concept, was sustained by the productive property required for republican virtue. Men without an independent position could scarcely uphold any legitimate claim to honor. Bertram Wyatt-Brown reminded us how Southerners viewed "republicanism, property, and personal honor as mutually supportive." Honor required, moreover, regular demonstrations of personal courage. The paper contrasted the current crop of "Gallant New England Free-Soil Abolition Braves" with their fathers, "the defenders of Bunker Hill." "Hold, they were slaveholders, traffic[k]ers in human flesh, aye men stealers. But they were men. They wrote no sickly sentimental novels, but were men who could go *alone* into the den of the savage wolf and make him captive." But the current crop of New Englanders lacked the mettle of their ancestors. "Here is another instance of Northern Bravery! Forty-four men well armed with Rifles, Revolvers and Bowie-knives, were disarmed by about six Pro-Slavery men, and forced to return, *disgraced* to the State [of Massachusetts] that boasts so much of Northern chivalry and courage." During a clash with Jim Lane's free-state forces at Hickory Point, the paper alleged that a band of proslavery partisans "Charged with a yell that struck panic into the ranks of the white-livered Yankees" who "scattered like a flock of startled sheep without firing a gun." The coolness under fire demonstrated by the proslavery warriors proved to the Yankee commander that he "had met with men that were made of material he could not conquer."[29]

The Yankees' lack of honor was further demonstrated by their stinginess. An honorable man was supposed to be generous, free with his possessions, and above all, personally honest. The Yankees were none of the above. When the antislavery *Kansas Herald of Freedom* urged its readership to boycott the town of Parkville, Missouri, the *Squatter Sovereign* responded: "We predict that for every skin-flint yankee who may withdraw his patronage from Parkville, twenty liberal Missourians, who can buy without 'jewing' and pay without 'grumbling' will take his place." When a Lowell, Massachusetts, newspaper criticized the town of Atchison, the *Squatter Sovereign* assured its readership, "The more that is written to the disadvantage of our town in the land of Puritanism, the better we shall be pleased. We would have no inducements held out to the grasping, skin-flint nigger stealing Yankees to show their tallow-faced countenances in the beautiful region of country around Atchison." Not only were the Yankees cheap, they were dishonorable thieves. The *Squatter Sovereign* suggested that Atchison merchants "have plenty of honest men to buy their goods, and they well know if the abolitionists were permitted to come among us, they would steal more than they would spend in our town."[30]

Allegations like these called into question the New Englanders' antislavery commitments. "Abolition philanthropy is about the cheapest commodity the market affords," claimed an Illinois newspaper cited by the *Squatter Sovereign.* "An Abolitionist will be the most humane, benevolent kind hearted fellow in the world, if it isn't likely to cost him anything. But just ask him to fork over half a dollar to buy a beef-steak for one of the negroes he professes to pity so much, and he'll squeak out like a cart-wheel that hasn't seen tar for a month."[31]

The Yankees' miserliness made their support for abolition illegitimate. Early in the debate, the paper denied any interest in reopening the African slave trade, but added that "if this were done, abolitionists would give us no further troubles, they would as did their fathers, become slave-catchers, and thus being able to make a profit of slavery, would cease to hate slave-owners; would forget their mock love of the negro in their real love of money." The paper was of two minds when it came to evaluating abolitionist sincerity. Some were apparently sincere believers, which made them all the more dangerous. "It is useless to say that these people are crazy theorists or impracticable zealots. If they are not honest themselves, they have certain tens of thousands of honest adherents." But the paper also claimed that the whole drive for abolition was "kept up by a few fanatical leaders" who presumably had no direct financial interest in the outcomes. The rest of the followers were "the most despicable part of the population" who joined "for their own pecuniary benefit. Dollars and cents will at anytime and in any manner turn them as easily as a weathercock is turned by the gentle breeze."[32]

As the Yankees' parsimony invalidated their abolitionism, so did it invalidate their support for free-soil emigration. All of the claims that border ruffians were invading Kansas were allegedly stories "merely got up to hide the cold-blooded speculation of [former governor Andrew] Reeder's land company . . . or of the New England Settlement Company to which the Boston and New York Abolition papers are partners." In sum, a conspiracy had emerged among the moneyed interests of the North to deprive honorable men of their lands. "A few weeks since we announced that a conspiracy was on foot to force slavery and slaveholders out of Kansas. Day by day our mails arrive, evidences of this fact develop themselves." The battle in Kansas was not a struggle between competing ideologies or between two sets of men, each with legitimate claims on the land. It was a struggle to stop a takeover by a moneyed aristocracy at war with the hard-working, independent producers, "the bone and sinew" of the country.[33]

The conspiracy was attempting to turn Kansas over to a group that had no scruples about the way it treated white men. Benjamin Stringfellow charged in his brother's paper that "the necessity for labor demands that slavery be brought here, else the people may be driven to seek white labor, not being able to get negroes, and from necessity be forced to exclude negro slavery, that white slaves may be induced to come." Another correspondent claimed, "It makes my ears tingle, and my heart beat with shame to think that a swarm of lousy, lazy, stinking, poor, miserable, pusillanimous, contemptible, God-forsaken, man-despised, devil-rejected fanatics . . . were taken from the poorhouses and jails of Yankee land and transported by a company of speculators to further their own interests." By controlling these sorts, the paper's enemies could seize control of the territory. "The abolitionists of the north intend, during the coming month, to introduce large numbers of their hired hands to put their treasonable, pretended government into operation by force." A takeover by these hirelings had to be stopped—by any means necessary![34]

Men such as these had no fundamental rights in Kansas. "How much longer are we to suffer from the atrocities of these unprincipled cowardly murdering villains?" the paper asked. It suggested that these "pests" needed to be "taught a summary lesson." Southern white culture maintained that communities had a right to unite to drive out those who deviated from accepted codes of conduct. "We as a general thing, disapprove of lynch law, and are the last to justify people in taking the law into their own hands. . . . But there are certain cases in which a community are [*sic*] justifiable in resorting to *any means* to protect themselves and punish offenders—they are in cases where the law makes no provisions for such punishment." The paper suggested that the current invasion by these dishonorable men was a case in point.

> We proclaimed to the world that . . . although we preferred Kansas being made a Negro slave State, yet, we never dreamed is making it so by the aid of bowie-knives, revolvers, and Sharp's Rifles, until we were threatened to be driven out of the Territory, by a band of hired abolitionists, bought up and sent here to control our elections, and steal our slaves and those of our friends in adjoining States.[35]

Just as the paper's description of the roots of the Kansas conflict was disingenuous, so too was its account of the political situation by late 1856. Shortly after the 1856 elections, the *Squatter Sovereign* proclaimed that President-elect James Buchanan and the Democratic majority in Congress would ensure that Kansas would enter the Union as a slave state. It suggested in December of 1856 that Gov. John W. Geary should resign and be replaced by Missouri's proslavery senator David Rice Atchison. "Gen. Atchison would be, to-day, the choice of three-fourths of all the voters in the Territory for that office."[36]

But reality was forcing its way into the paper. In November of 1856 the paper published an invitation to "All honest, orderly, law-abiding people . . . regardless of their political or religious opinions" to come and settle in Atchison. The circular was issued by thirty-seven individuals including senior editor Stringfellow and new co-owner Peter Larey. By February a further concession to the inevitable had been made. "Let us make Kansas a slave State and Democratic if possible," the *Squatter Sovereign* broadcast, following its familiar political line. But it then made an unusual departure. "If not, then next best we can, which is to make it a National Democratic State should slavery be abolished."[37]

The last extant issue of the *Squatter Sovereign* under the editorship of Stringfellow, Kelley, and Larey was printed on March 3, 1857. Both Stringfellow and Kelley soon left the territory and eventually served in the Confederate army. The owners explained that they had no choice but to sell. They had "repeatedly called upon the South for aid, and the response has been a moneyless one." The paper did not die, however. The town fathers found someone to take it over. Clem Rohr, an early resident of Atchison, recalled that by 1857 the town was "a new straggling village with some promise for the future." Business demands took precedence over politics. "The town company was composed of Southern pro-slavery people, but soon saw that Eastern immigration was desirable and necessary. They looked around for someone to cast that pro-slavery odium from the town's name, and negotiated with Samuel C. Pomeroy, a staunch and well known Free State Yankee from Massachusetts."[38]

Pomeroy was a good deal more than that. An agent for the New England Emigrant Aid Company, Pomeroy went on to represent Kansas in the U.S. Senate as a Republican. Although Pomeroy sold the paper to John A. Martin in 1858, it did not abandon its newfound principles.

Martin served as publisher and editor for more than twenty years. During his tenure, Martin chose to rename the paper, reflecting both his own antislavery principles and the new political realities of Kansas. The *Squatter Sovereign,* the once proud defender of slavery, took as its new name *Freedom's Champion.*[39]

NOTES

1. *Squatter Sovereign,* Atchison, May 8, 1855.

2. Julia Louisa Lovejoy, "Letters from Kansas," *Kansas Historical Quarterly* 11 (February 1942): 43; Herbert Flint, "Journalism in Territorial Kansas" (Master's thesis, University of Kansas, 1916), 140, 142.

3. Elmer LeRoy Craik, "Southern Interest in Territorial Kansas, 1854–1858," *Kansas Historical Collections, 1919–1922* 15 (1922): 348; Floyd C. Shoemaker, "Missouri's Proslavery Fight for Kansas, 1854–1855," *Missouri Historical Review* 48 (April 1954): 231.

4. *Squatter Sovereign,* June 10, September 9, 1856. On other newspapers, see Flint, "Journalism in Territorial Kansas."

5. Shoemaker, "Missouri's Proslavery Flight," 221.

6. This was always the claim of the paper. The editor described the paper as "having the largest circulation of any Newspaper in Kansas," *Squatter Sovereign,* November 22, 1856. Allan Nevins called it "The proslavery organ in Kansas" in *Ordeal of the Union,* 2 vols. (New York: Charles Scribner's Sons, 1947), 2: 386. More recently, Kenneth Stampp called it "the leading proslavery newspaper" in Kansas in *America in 1857: A Nation on the Brink* (New York: Oxford University Press, 1990), 148. The paper's chief rival, Leavenworth's *Kansas Weekly Herald,* disputed the claim. See *Kansas Weekly Herald,* May 4, 1855.

7. The characterization of the town company was from Clem Rohr, "Early Recollections of Atchison and Its Business Men," *Atchison Daily Globe,* December 3, 1909. On the relationship of the paper and the town company, see *Atchison Daily Globe,* June 5, 1905.

8. *Squatter Sovereign,* June 5, 1855.

9. On Stringfellow, see "Biographical Sketch of Dr. J. H. Stringfellow, Speaker First Kansas Legislature," Misc. Stringfellow Papers, Library and Archives Division, Kansas State Historical Society. See also William H. Coffin, "Settlement of the Friends in Kansas," *Kansas Historical Collections, 1901–1902* 7 (1902): 331–32.

10. Flint, "Journalism in Territorial Kansas," 503; Kelley's comments are from the *Squatter Sovereign,* February 19, 1856. Kelley's career before coming to Kansas is discussed in James C. Malin, *The Nebraska Question, 1852–1854* (Ann Arbor: Edwards Brothers, 1953), 381–86; Larey is introduced in the *Squatter Sovereign,* November 22, 1856.

11. On Northern racial attitudes, see Leon F. Litwack, *North of Slavery: The Negro in the Free States 1790–1860* (Chicago: University of Chicago Press, 1961); James A. Rawley, *Race and Politics: "Bleeding Kansas" and the Coming of the Civil War* (Philadelphia: J. B. Lippincott Co., 1969); Eugene H. Berwanger, *The Frontier Against Slavery: Western Anti-Negro Prejudice and the Slavery Extension Controversy* (Urbana: University of Illinois Press, 1967). On the free labor ideal, see Eric Foner, *Free Soil, Free Labor, Free Men: The Ideology of the Republican Party Before the Civil War* (New York: Oxford University Press, 1970). Chapter 2 discusses the Republican critique of the South. The quotations are from pp. 50, 47.

12. *Squatter Sovereign,* March 6, 1855. The classic (and still useful) work on this subject is William Sumner Jenkins, *Pro-Slavery Thought in the Old South* (Chapel Hill: University of North Carolina Press, 1935). See also Larry E. Tise, *Proslavery: A History of the Defense of Slavery in America, 1701–1840* (Athens: University of Georgia Press, 1987); Eugene D. Genovese, *The World the Slaveholders Made: Two Essays in Interpretation* (New York: Pantheon Books, 1969).

13. *Squatter Sovereign,* June 5, 1855–July 24, 1855. The quotation is from ibid., June 12, 1855, and is part of a separate attack on abolitionists.

14. Wise is quoted in George M. Fredrickson, *The Black Image in the White Mind: The Debate on Afro-American Character and Destiny, 1817–1914* (New York: Harper and Row, 1971), 62. Cobb is quoted in James Oakes, *Slavery and Freedom: An Interpretation of the Old South* (New York: Pantheon Books, 1990), 132. Both works are essential to understanding the egalitarian racism found in the *Squatter Sovereign.*

15. *Squatter Sovereign,* February 20, 1855.

16. The claim was made in ibid., March 4, 1856. The editors added: "The climate and soil of Kansas is peculiarly adapted to slave labor, and hemp, corn, wheat, tobacco and other staples can be as profitably produced here as in Kentucky or other Southern States."

17. On the economic situation of Missouri, see Malin, *The Nebraska Question,* chapter 2. See also David Thelen, *Paths of Resistance: Tradition and Democracy in Industrializing Missouri* (New York: Oxford University Press, 1986), chapter 1. On common-white values, see Bill Cecil-Fronsman, *Common Whites: Class and Culture in Antebellum North Carolina* (Lexington: University Press of Kentucky, 1992), especially chapters 2 and 3.

18. The enormous literature on republican thought and its evolution includes Robert E. Shallope, "Toward a Republican Synthesis," *William and Mary Quarterly,* 3d ser., 29 (1972): 49–80; and Shallope, "Republicanism and Early American Historiography," *William and Mary Quarterly,* 3d ser., 39 (1982): 334–56; Harry L. Watson, *Liberty and Power: The Politics of Jacksonian America* (New York: Hill and Wang, 1990); William L. Barney, *The Passage of the Republic: An Interdisciplinary History of Nineteenth Century America* (Lexington, Mass.: D. C. Heath and Co., 1987). Watson's quotations are from pp. 43–44; Barney's quotation is from p. 122.

19. *Squatter Sovereign,* February 13, 20, 1855.

20. Ibid., April 17, June 19, 1855.

21. Ibid., June 19, September 4, April 10, 1855. The term "right on the goose" is a variation of the secret sign "Sound on the Goose" given by proslavery Missourians crossing the Kansas border to vote. See Alice Nichols, *Bleeding Kansas* (New York: Oxford University Press, 1954), 24.

22. *Squatter Sovereign,* May 29, 1855.

23. On Eli Thayer and the New England Emigrant Aid Company, see Samuel A. Johnson, *The Battle Cry of Freedom: The New England Emigrant Aid Company in the Kansas Crusade* (Lawrence: University of Kansas Press, 1954).

24. *Squatter Sovereign,* March 6, October 16, 1855.

25. Ibid., February 3, 1855. On Southern support for emigration, see Craik, "Southern Interest in Territorial Kansas." For the most celebrated proslavery emigration push, see Walter L. Fleming, "The Buford Expedition to Kansas," *American Historical Review* 6 (October 1900): 38–48. On the varieties of Northern recruits, see Johnson, *Battle Cry of Freedom.* The final comment from the *Squatter Sovereign* is from April 15, 1856.

26. *Squatter Sovereign,* October 16, August 21, 1855. The paper referred to Horace Greeley, antislavery editor of the *New York Tribune,* and to New York's Republican senator William Henry Seward. On Kelley's role in the incident, see Flint, "Journalism in Territorial Kansas," 500.

27. *Squatter Sovereign,* October 16, 1855.

28. Ibid., May 29, June 12, 1855. On Southern views of laziness, see Cecil-Fronsman, *Common Whites,* 107–10, and Allen Tullos, *Habits of Industry: White Culture and the Transformation of the Carolina Piedmont* (Chapel Hill: University of North Carolina Press, 1989), 72–73.

29. Betram Wyatt-Brown, *Southern Honor: Ethics and Behavior in the Old South* (New York: Oxford University Press, 1982) 72–73, discusses the relationship of landownership and honor. On the relationship of courage and honor, pp. 36, 37, 43, 154, 459–60; *Squatter Sovereign,* June 12, 1855, July 8, September 16, 1856.

30. See Wyatt-Brown, *Southern Honor,* 59, 60, 176, 327, 336, 434; *Squatter Sovereign,* May 1, April 10, 1855, February 5, 1856.

31. *Squatter Sovereign,* December 4, 1855.

32. Ibid., February 5, 1855, December 16, 1856, October 9, 1855.

33. Ibid., September 11, 1855, December 23, 1856. It should come as no surprise that a Democratic party paper like the *Squatter Sovereign* would use rhetoric like this. The notion of a struggle between a moneyed aristocracy and the independent producers is a common theme in Jacksonian rhetoric. See Marvin Meyers, *The Jacksonian Persuasion: Politics & Belief* (Stanford, Calif.: Stanford University Press, 1957), chapter 2. The phrase "bone and sinew" is from the *Squatter Sovereign,* April 3, 1855.

34. *Squatter Sovereign,* December 4, October 9, 1855, July 15, 1856.

35. Ibid., August 5, 1856, April 24, 1855, June 17, 1856. On Southern white culture's view of community authority, see Cecil-Fronsman, *Common Whites,* 156–58.

36. *Squatter Sovereign,* November 22, December 2, 1856.

37. Ibid., November 22, 1856, February 10, 1857. But note that Stringfellow continued to entertain hope for a revival of fortune. In the next issue he announced his candidacy for the office of delegate to Congress. See ibid., February 17, 1857.

38. The final edition of the paper under its original editors is no longer extant. The explanation for selling the paper was reprinted in Leavenworth's *Kansas Weekly Herald,* May 23, 1857. Rohr's comments are from "Early Recollections of Atchison and Its Business Men." On Stringfellow's career, see "Biographical Sketch of Dr. J. H. Stringfellow," Misc. Stringfellow Papers. On Kelley's career, see Flint, "Journalism in Territorial Kansas," 503.

39. G. Raymond Gaeddert, "First Newspapers in Kansas Counties," *Kansas Historical Quarterly* 10 (February 1941): 10.

From Slavery in Missouri to Freedom in Kansas: The Influx of Black Fugitives and Contrabands into Kansas, 1854–1865

Richard Sheridan

As is well known to students of American history, the passage of the Kansas-Nebraska bill in 1854 repealed the Missouri Compromise of 1820 and built upon the Compromise of 1850. It created two new territories, Nebraska and Kansas, in place of one. It led to the negotiation of cession treaties whereby some Native Americans, or portions thereof, were allowed to remain within Kansas, but the greater number were relocated in territories outside Kansas. Moreover, the principle of squatter sovereignty which had been established by the Compromise of 1850 was extended to both territories, in which the majority of white settlers were authorized to form and regulate their domestic institutions, especially the institution of chattel slavery.

Missourians first pushed across the border to claim choice lands under the terms of the Preemption Act of 1841. Their proslavery leaders perceived the necessity of flooding Kansas with slaves and establishing a slave state. Settlers from New England and the Ohio Valley followed, motivated by the same land hunger as the Missourians but

"From Slavery in Missouri to Freedom in Kansas: The Influx of Black Fugitives and Contrabands into Kansas, 1854–1865," by Richard Sheridan, *Kansas History* 12 (1989): 28–47. Copyright Kansas State Historical Society. Reprinted by permission.

determined to withstand slavery and found a free state. For a time the struggle resulted in victory of proslavery forces who waged guerrilla warfare throughout Kansas Territory and sacked free-soil Lawrence. Reprisals were led by John Brown, James Lane and others, whose forces plundered and killed proslavery settlers, running off their slaves to freedom in Canada. Kansas was born in a struggle for liberty and freedom, a struggle that raised the curtain on the Civil War and sounded the death knell of slavery.[1]

The contest for possession of the Territory of Kansas has been told many times from the standpoint of white Americans who were involved in the struggle. On the other hand, much less is known regarding the black people and their role in overturning slavery, both in the antebellum and Civil War years. This paper, in five parts, is concerned with the blacks of Missouri and Kansas. . . .

I

The slave economy of the western counties of Missouri, which was a small affair in the early decades of the nineteenth century, became of increasing importance in the years leading up to the Civil War. According to John G. Haskell, a resident of Lawrence, Kansas, who had seen military service in Missouri, the early western Missouri slaveholder was a poor man; his wealth at the time of settlement "consisted mainly in one small family of negro slaves, with limited equipment necessary to open up a farm in a new country." Owing to such factors as poor transportation facilities and limited market outlets, the typical farm was small when compared with the cotton plantations of the deep South, agricultural production was diversified, and almost all food, clothing, and shelter was of local production. Slavery in these circumstances was much more a domestic than a commercial institution. "The white owner, with his sons, labored in the same field with the negro, both old and young. The mistress guided the industries in the house in both colors. Both colors worshipped at the same time, in the same meeting-house, ministered to by the same pastor."[2]

From its near-subsistence stage, the farm economy of western Missouri grew slowly at first, but more rapidly as the Civil War approached. New markets were opened with the growth of steamboat traffic on the Missouri River, the relocation of Indian tribes from east of the Mississippi River to the territory west of Missouri, the establishment of new military posts, railroad construction, and the opening of Kansas to white settlement. Besides a variety of foodstuffs, Missouri farmers supplied these new markets with transport animals—oxen, horses, and mules. Rising farm profits led, in turn, to in-migration, land settlement, and lively markets for farming tools and implements and especially black slaves. By the eve of the Civil War there were a considerable number of medium to large slaveholdings. Hemp, which was used in ropemaking, came to be grown on slave plantations of some size, although its culture was mostly restricted to the Missouri River counties.[3]

The slave population of Missouri increased from 3,011 in 1810, to 9,797 in 1820, and to 25,091 in 1830. It then more than doubled to 57,891 in 1840, grew to 87,422 in 1850, and reached 114,931 in 1860. A disproportionate number of these slaves were concentrated in the Missouri River and western border counties is the finding of Harrison A. Trexler. . . . The total of the Missouri River and western border counties was 54,940 in 1850 and 75,107 in 1860, or 62.8 percent and 65.3 percent, respectively, of all slaves in the state.[4]

Slaves who planned to permanently abscond from their masters in Missouri had several modes and courses of escape. They might be aided by relatives or friends who had successfully escaped from slavery and returned to aid others. They might be aided by white people in Missouri and elsewhere who held strong views against slavery. Free coloreds are reported to have taken fugitives under their protection, written passes, given instructions and directions, and provided temporary board and lodging. The so-called Underground Railroad was a secret system to aid fugitives bent on flight to Canada, by transporting them from station to station along well-defined trails or routes. Some slaves managed successful flight solely by their wits and luck. Slaves escaped as stowaways on steamboats. Others stole small boats or built rafts to speed their flight to freedom. The coming of the railroad furnished a new means of escape. Prior to the passage of the Kansas-Nebraska Act, the runaway slaves from Missouri headed for the two contiguous free states of Iowa and Illinois, and thence northward to Canada.[5]

Much greater opportunities for escape came with the filling of Kansas with free-soil settlers. By 1857 the problem was so great that both the federal and state governments were appealed to for protection of slave property in Missouri. Bills were introduced into the Missouri General Assembly to provide special patrols in the counties on the Illinois, Iowa, and Kansas borders. After the Kansas struggle had resulted in a victory for the antislavery forces, writes Trexler,

> the golden age of slave absconding opened. Escapes apparently increased each year till the Civil War caused a general exodus of slave property from the State. The enterprising abolition fraternity of Kansas—Brown, Lane, Doy, and the rest—seemingly made it their religious duty to reduce the sins of the Missouri slaveholder by relieving him of all the slave property possible.

In 1855 one editorial writer asserted that "ten slaves are now stolen from Missouri to every one that was spirited off before the Douglas bill."[6]

The raids into Missouri to free slaves struck terror into the minds of slaveholders and contributed indirectly to black flight from bondage. John Brown is known to have made several such raids and to have escorted a group of fugitives from Kansas to Canada in 1859. Less well known are the guerrilla chieftains James Montgomery and Dr. Charles R. Jennison whose bands of "Jayhawkers" terrorized proslavery settlers in southern Kansas and made raids across the border into Missouri. . . .[7]

In the years immediately preceding the Civil War, the Underground Railroad was increasingly active in helping slaves escape from Missouri. The Rev. Richard Cordley, Congregational minister and historian of Lawrence, Kansas, said that the Underground Railroad line ran directly through Lawrence and Topeka, then on through Nebraska and Iowa. He had been told by people who ought to know "that not less than one hundred thousands dollars' worth of slaves passed through Lawrence on their way to liberty during the territorial period." Cordley, himself, together with his wife and members of his congregation, harbored a slave named "Lizzie," about whom he wrote an interesting account of their efforts to secrete her from a federal marshal and his deputies and see her safely on the road to Canada. . . .[8] [James B.] Abbott asserted that the slaves across the border were far from the least interested party in the Kansas conflict. Indeed, they were early taught "the places and men to shun, as well as the places and men to trust."[9]

The Underground Railroad intensified the Missouri slaveowners' resentment toward the free-state settlers of Kansas. Moreover, it carried a growing number of passengers through Lawrence and other stations in Kansas because of the fears of both masters and slaves. Indeed, it has been asserted by Wilbur H. Siebert "that the Underground Railroad was one of the greatest forces which brought on the Civil War, and thus destroyed slavery."[10]

II

Opportunities for blacks to escape slavery increased during the Civil War as Union armies invaded the South. Although some Union generals returned slaves when they escaped to Union camps, on grounds that the Fugitive Slave Law of 1850 required that the fugitives be returned to their masters, other commanders refused such surrender lest the slave property contribute to the armed rebellion. Declaring the slaves who escaped to his camp contraband and liable to confiscation by the laws of war, Gen. Benjamin F. Butler, whose forces occupied Confederate territory in Tidewater Virginia in 1861, established a precedent which was followed by other Union generals as the war expanded into the South. In March 1862 an act of the Union government "declared contraband slaves—those belonging to persons in rebellion—henceforth and forever free," and on January 1, 1863, President Abraham Lincoln issued his Emancipation Proclamation which declared forever free the slaves in the rebellious states.

Blacks who first escaped to the Federal lines were eagerly recruited for a variety of occupations. They built fortifications, served as teamsters, wheelwrights, blacksmiths, hospital attendants, officers' servants, and employees of the commissary and quartermaster departments. Many of those who had skills settled in cities as barbers, draymen, carpenters, blacksmiths, servants, seamstresses, nurses and cooks, of whom a large number conducted businesses of their own. In rural areas they became tenant farmers or were employed as farm laborers and woodchoppers.[11]

In Kansas, after years of political rivalry between proslavery and free-state factions, free-state delegates framed an antislavery constitution at the Wyandotte Convention. It was ratified by a large majority on October 4, 1859. After Lincoln's victory, Kansas entered the Union under the Wyandotte Constitution on January 29, 1861. Charles Robinson was elected governor, and Martin F. Conway congressman. On April 4 of the same year the Kansas legislature elected Samuel C. Pomeroy and James H. Lane to the U.S. Senate.[12]

161

James Henry Lane (1814–1866) was a remarkable leader whose actions as a military commander and politician were responsible for the influx of large numbers of slaves into Kansas and their recruitment into black regiments. . . . He was called the "Grim Chieftain," a tall, thin, stern-visaged man, who, like Cassius, bore "a lean and hungry look." It was said of Lane that no man ever had firmer friends or more bitter enemies. Lane was an ardent supporter of Abraham Lincoln for the presidency, and, as a U.S. senator, a close personal friend of the wartime President. He took his own life in 1866, in a fit of depression after losing political support in Kansas and being accused of involvement in fraudulent Indian contracts.[13]

Lane was appointed a brigadier general of volunteers by President Lincoln in June 1861. He proceeded from Washington, D.C., to Kansas to raise volunteer regiments under the authority of Congress, at a time when Confederate armies had won several important battles. . . . Lane marched with his hastily gathered troops to Fort Scott, Kansas, near the Missouri border, where Price was expected to attack. On September 2, Lane sent twelve hundred mounted men to Dry Wood Creek, twelve miles east of Fort Scott, where a brisk skirmish was fought with Price's advance-guard. Price decided to discontinue his advance into Kansas upon learning that Lane was waiting to give battle, and turned north toward Lexington, Missouri.[14]

"As Lane's 'Kansas brigade' marched through Missouri," writes Stephenson, "a 'black brigade' marched into Kansas." Two of Lane's chaplains wrote long accounts of the slaves who flocked to Lane's brigade and of their march into Kansas. In his *The Gun and the Gospel,* Chaplain Hugh Dunn Fisher tells of the trek of the black brigade. While the Kansas brigade rested at Springfield and on the march to Lamar, Lane's camp was "the center of attraction to multitudes of 'contrabands' and refugees." Lane sent for Fisher the second day out of Springfield, explaining the imminent danger of attack and the helpless condition of the great multitude of blacks. He asked Fisher, "Chaplain, what can we do to relieve the army of these contrabands, without exposing them to their enemies?" Whereupon, Fisher replied that "all the men were in the army, and the women and children in Kansas needed help to save the crop and provide fuel for winter, and I advised to send the negroes to Kansas to help the women and children." Lane's laconic reply was "I'll do it."[15]

When the Grim Chieftain's brigade arrived at Lamar, forty miles southeast of Fort Scott, he directed his three chaplains, Fisher, Moore,

162

and Fish, to take charge of the refugees and escort them to Fort Scott. . . . It was a nondescript emigration. They traveled day and night, eating only cold food until they came upon a small herd of cattle, of which three were killed and hastily broiled and eaten.

When they reached Kansas, Fisher halted the caravan and drew the refugees up in a line. He raised himself to his full height on his war horse, "commanded silence, and there under the open heavens, on the sacred soil of freedom, in the name of the Constitution of the United States, the Declaration of Independence, and by the authority of General James H. Lane, I proclaimed that they were 'forever free.'" Immediately the blacks "jumped, cried, sang and laughed for joy." Fisher claimed that they were the first slaves formally set free. He said it occurred in September 1861, long before Lincoln's Emancipation Proclamation was issued. . . .[16]

After he returned to Washington, Lane told the Senate of the success of his policies and actions in Missouri and Arkansas. In a speech of May 15, 1862, he claimed that 4,000 fugitive slaves from Missouri and Arkansas were then being fed in Kansas, and two months later he said the number had increased to 6,400. In a speech to the New York Emancipation League in June he said that he had himself "aided 2,500 slaves to emigrate" during the year, and a month later he told the Senate that at one time he had 1,200 blacks in his brigade.[17]

Later in the Civil War several groups of contrabands were brought from Arkansas to Leavenworth on steamboats. After the victory of the Federals at Helena, Arkansas, on July 4, 1863, the camps were overrun with blacks seeking freedom. Chaplain Fisher was ordered to take control of large numbers of contrabands, who left that port and neighboring ports in three steamboats, and scatter them "throughout Missouri, Illinois, Iowa and Kansas, sending some of them as far as Ohio." Fisher said he had intended to go in charge of the slaves on the *Sam Gaty,* but at the last minute decided to go by rail instead to prepare for their reception at Leavenworth. Unfortunately, the *Sam Gaty* was captured by a band of guerrillas or bushwhackers at Napoleon, Missouri. Nine black men were killed and seven black women were shot, but none killed. The guerrillas searched the boat for Chaplain Fisher and would not be satisfied that he was not on board until they had killed three white men in his stead. When the *Sam Gaty* arrived at Leavenworth, hundreds of people assembled on the levee to welcome the survivors. Fisher said that the whole party of contrabands was promptly provided with homes in good families.[18] Among other contrabands who arrived by boat, one Lieutenant Colonel Bassett is said to have returned to Kansas from a military campaign in Arkansas with over six hundred black refugees on board four steamboats.[19]

It would be misleading to leave the impression that all of the contrabands entered Kansas under the auspices of Union military units. Many of them, perhaps the greater number, came of their own volition, either crossing along the land border or the approximately seventy-five mile stretch of the Missouri River which separates Missouri from Kansas. Writing in February 1862, the editor of the Atchison *Freedom's Champion* adopted an attitude of mock sympathy for Missouri slaveowners whose property walked away, saying:

> The beloved darkies, the cherished possession of the secesh, are constantly arriving in Kansas from Missouri—they come singly, by pairs, and by dozens. . . . We acknowledge that it must be very trying to the feelings of our Missouri brethren to have those which they have brought up from infancy, or in whom they expended large sums of money, to thus forsake them at the first opportunity, and frequently not only take themselves away, but also a valuable horse or mule. We repeat that all this must be very trying, but all the consolation we can give them is that "such are the fortunes of war," and we trust that hereafter they will learn wisdom and not invest large sums of money in property of this description, for every day's experience only tends to convince us that it is a very uncertain species of riches, and although not taking "wings," nevertheless frequently takes "legs" and is lost forever.[20]

Slaves even walked across the Missouri River to freedom in Kansas when the ice was thick enough to support their weight, as was reported to be the case in February 1863 when contrabands in considerable numbers crossed over on the frozen river and enlisted in the Union army.[21] A few reportedly swam across the river at some peril to their lives, while others came on skiffs and ferries. One group that arrived by ferry at Wyandotte was said to consist of "poor, frightened half-starved negroes . . . men and women with little children clinging to them, and carrying all of their earthly possessions in little bags or bundles, sometimes in red bandana handkerchiefs."[22]

The exodus continued at a rapid pace until the end of hostilities.

Writing from Glasgow, Missouri, to Gov. Thomas Carney of Kansas, on August 24, 1863, B. W. Lewis said that hardly a night passed but what from two to a dozen slaves left their masters. Having incurred heavy costs in policing his own slaves, Lewis proposed "to sett [*sic*] all our Negroes free who may desire it and put them on a Boat and pay their way to some point in your State." Those who preferred to stay, he said, would be paid wages. Lewis asked the governor to advise him if there would be any objection to his sending the slaves to Kansas. Though Lewis' proposal was no doubt unique, it was symptomatic of the despair of Missouri slaveholders regarding the viability of the peculiar institution. That the slave population of Missouri was seriously eroded by the flight of blacks during the turmoil and destruction of the Civil War can be demonstrated by population statistics. In fact, only 73,811 slaves remained in the state in 1863, as compared with 114,931 in 1860, or a decline of thirty-five percent. The loss was probably greater in a qualitative sense than the statistics indicate, since the greater part of the fugitives were reportedly able-bodied males and females capable of performing heavy field labor.[23]

III

The influx of contrabands was significant from the standpoint of the numbers involved and their impact on the economy and society of wartime Kansas. Table 1 shows that the black population increased from 627 in 1860 to 12,527 in 1865, or from 0.6 percent to 8.8 percent of the Kansas population. The influx may have been as great as 15,000, since many black soldiers from Kansas were out of the state when the census of 1865 was taken. Although blacks came to Kansas in growing numbers after the Civil War, and especially in the late 1870s and early 1880s when the "Exodusters" arrived from the South, the white population increased even more rapidly. Thus, the blacks declined as a percentage of the total population—to 4.7 in 1870, 4.3 in 1880, and 3.5 in both 1890 and 1900. In the twentieth century the black population of Kansas increased from 3.5 percent of the total in 1900 to 5.4 percent in 1980. It is therefore noteworthy that the influx during the Civil War years raised the black population of Kansas to its highest level in relation to whites and Indians.

Not only did the blacks constitute a larger proportion of the total population of Kansas; they were also highly concentrated in certain

Table 1. Growth of Kansas Population, 1860–1900, Distinguishing Whites, Blacks, and Indians

Race	1860	1865	1870	1880	1890	1900
White	106,390	127,261	346,377	952,155	1,376,619	1,416,319
Black	627	12,527	17,108	43,107	49,710	52,003
Indian and other races	189	382	914	834	1,679	2,173
Total population	107,206	140,170	364,399	996,096	1,428,108	1,470,495
Percentage white	99.2	90.7	95.1	95.6	96.4	96.3
Percentage black	0.6	8.8	4.7	4.3	3.5	3.5

Source: U.S. Censuses, 1860, 1870, 1880, 1890, 1900; Kansas 1865 MS. Census, Vol. 10, Compendium of Statistics Reported to the Legislature, Archives Department, Kansas State Historical Society.

towns and counties, as shown in Table 2. Eight of the thirty-seven counties that were enumerated in 1865 contained 77.5 percent of the black population, and the three leading counties—Leavenworth, Douglas, and Wyandotte—contained 55.5 percent of the blacks. Although it lacked a town of any consequence, Wyandotte County had the third largest black population in 1865, with nearly half as many blacks as whites.[24] The Kansas census of 1865 shows that seven towns contained 37.6 percent of all blacks in the state, and that four towns—Leavenworth, Lawrence, Atchison, and Fort Scott—contained 33.4 percent. There was one black to every three whites in Fort Scott, a ratio of one to four in Osawatomie, one to five in Leavenworth, Lawrence, and Mound City, and one to seven in Atchison and Topeka. In the eight most populous counties, females accounted for 52.3 percent and males for 47.7 percent of all blacks in 1865. It is significant that four of the leading towns—Lawrence, Topeka, Mound City, and Osawatomie—had been stations on the Underground Railroad. More or less protection was afforded the contrabands who came to Kansas by the Missouri River, the Union military establishments at Fort Scott and Fort Leavenworth, and the antislavery and abolitionist sentiments of the townspeople and rural inhabitants.[25]

The "Black Brigade" was brought to Kansas chiefly to supply much

Table 2. Blacks in the Leading Kansas Towns and Counties, 1865, Compared with the Total Population

	Blacks in town population	All blacks in county	Total town population	Total county population
Leavenworth (Leavenworth County)	2,455	3,374	15,409	24,256
Lawrence and North Lawrence (Douglas County)	933	2,078	5,401	15,814
Wyandotte County	—	1,504	—	4,827
Atchison (Atchison County)	432	613	3,318	8,909
Fort Scott (Bourbon County)	359	787	1,382	7,961
Mound City (Linn County)	270	690	1,494	6,543
Osawatomie (Miami County)	138	409	750	6,151
Topeka (Shawnee County)	118	257	958	3,458
Totals	4,705	9,712	28,712	77,919

Source: Kansas 1865 MS. Census.

needed farm labor. As more and more contrabands arrived in the state, many were dispersed over the countryside and employed as rural wage laborers. After several wagons loaded with contrabands had passed through two of the border towns in January 1862, one editorial writer predicted that the coming crop season would find "Kansas better provided with free labor than any of the Western States." Later in the same year the editor of the *Fort Scott Bulletin* made a tour of the Neosho River valley. He observed that cultivated farms were springing up on all sides, and "almost every farm was supplied with labor in the shape of a good healthy thousand dollar Contraband, to do the work while the husbands, fathers and brothers are doing the fighting."[26] Another journalist noted that black labor, mostly that of fugitives from Missouri, was largely responsible for producing the bountiful Kansas harvest of 1863. He said that large quantities of labor were needed to harvest the wheat, since very little machinery was used on Kansas farms and the crop needed to be taken off quickly once it had ripened. Even Senator Lane was reported to have used contrabands to build a fence around his Douglas County farm and to experiment with the growing of cotton with free black labor.[27]

Whether or not the contrabands settled on farms or in the towns depended upon several circumstances. Relatively few arrived with sufficient wealth and experience to begin as farmers. The overwhelming majority depended upon wage employment, and as the demand for farm labor was to a large extent seasonal, the contrabands' chances of obtaining work was contingent upon their arrival in Kansas during the crop season. If they arrived in the winter months the towns were most likely to supply the means of subsistence.

"Contrabands in large numbers are fleeing from Missouri into Kansas and especially into Lawrence; 131 came into Lawrence in ten days, yesterday 27 had arrived by 2 P.M.," wrote John B. Wood of Lawrence to George L. Stearns in Boston on November 19, 1861. Continuing, he said, "thus far they have been taken care of, as the farmers needed help." He warned, however, that the hundreds, if not thousands, who were employed in harvesting the crops would soon be unemployed, and they would gather in Lawrence for the inhabitants to feed and clothe with the assistance of the "friends of humanity at the East." The contrabands came to Lawrence by the scores and hundreds, according to Richard Cordley. For a time their numbers and needs threatened to overwhelm the inhabitants. "But they were strong and industrious, and by a little effort work was found for them, and very few, if any, of them, became objects of charity," said Cordley. . . .[28]

Besides helping the contrabands secure a livelihood, Lawrence citizens made a concerted effort to teach the newcomers to read and write. While the children attended the public schools, adults were encouraged to join classes after working hours. S. N. Simpson, who started the first Sunday school in Lawrence in 1855, established a night school for contrabands which met five or six nights a week for two hours in the courthouse. Classes were taught by a corps of volunteer teachers who were described as women and men of culture, character, and consecration. About one hundred adults, entirely ignorant of their letters, applied themselves earnestly to the simple lessons given in the spelling books. Study and recitation were interspersed with the singing of familiar hymns. In the course of a few weeks several of the blacks were able to read with some fluency and were ready to commence with figures.[29]

The contrabands who came to Lawrence were a church-going people. Cordley said that a Sunday school was organized and Sunday evening services were conducted for them at the Congregational Church. They outgrew this facility, and, about one year after their arrival, the new Freedmen's Church was dedicated on September 28, 1862. It was described as "a fine comfortable brick Church," believed to be the first one ever erected in the United States for fugitive slaves. Cordley said the church was "filled with an attentive congregation of 'freedmen'—all lately from bondage, all neatly dressed as a result of their short experience of free labor."[30]

After the difficult period of first arrival when white paternalism was most conspicuous in the adjustment to freedom, the contrabands encountered racial hostility and reacted by drawing on their own latent but slender resources in an effort to build a viable black community. Agnes Emery recalled that the freedmen did their share in becoming good citizens. "They were kind to each other in times of illness and misfortune, their demands were few, they were strong, eager, and willing to work, and soon made themselves useful in the community." After meeting in white churches and then in the inter-denominational Freedmen's Church, the blacks "divided into various ecclesiastical camps" with their own preachers. They met together to celebrate such anniversaries as the Fourth of July, slave emancipation in the British West Indies, and, beginning in 1864, Lincoln's Emancipation Proclamation. In 1864 the black women of Lawrence organized the Ladies Refugee Aid Society to collect food, clothing, and money to assist freedmen who had fallen on hard times.[31]

The occupations of 624 blacks in Douglas County are shown in the 1865 census, of which 349 lived in Lawrence and North Lawrence, and 275 in rural parts of the county. Soldiering was the leading occupation of the blacks in Lawrence and North Lawrence, where 95 were so designated. Following behind the soldiers were 85 day laborers. Of the 92 female workers, 49 were domestics, 27 were employed at washing and ironing or as washerwomen, 7 worked as housekeepers, 6 as servants, and 3 as cooks. In all, some 270 blacks, or four-fifths of the town total, were unskilled laborers. The other one-fifth consisted of skilled and semi-skilled workers. There were 23 teamsters, 8 blacksmiths, 6 porters, 4 barbers, 3 hostlers, 3 woodcutters, 2 stonemasons, 2 draymen, 2 rock quarriers, and one each of distiller, saloonkeeper, miner, harnessmaker, brick moulder, coachman, carpenter, shoemaker, printer, and preacher.[32]

The high ratio of rural to urban black workers, or 44.0 percent of all workers, may possibly be explained by the fact that the census was taken on May 1, 1865, when much farm labor was needed. There were 145 blacks designated as farmers, 59 as laborers or day laborers, and 31 as farm laborers. Although these occupations are not defined clearly, it seems reasonable to assume that almost all of the blacks so designated performed agricultural wage labor. Thirteen other farmers and one other farm laborer were residents in Lawrence and North Lawrence. The remaining rural males consisted of 10 teamsters, 6 soldiers, 4 brickmakers, and one each of porter, blacksmith, and schoolteacher. The rural females consisted of 9 domestics, 5 servants, 1 washerwoman, and 1 employed at washing and ironing.[33]

As the oldest town in Kansas, Leavenworth and the nearby federal fort by the same name was the largest population center in Kansas in 1865. Its growth was largely a result of its steamboat and overland wagon transport facilities and its place as a mobilization and supply center. The towns of Atchison and Leavenworth were first settled primarily by Missourians whose sympathies were proslavery. By 1858, however, Leavenworth had a free-state majority and the town hosted a state convention that adopted a radical antislavery constitution, which, although nominally approved by a popular vote, was defeated by the U.S. Congress. Within months of the outbreak of the Civil War, Leavenworth had become a cosmopolitan town with inhabitants from all quarters of the Union and refugees and fugitives from the rebel states. A soldier from Wisconsin wrote home in February 1862, saying, "The city is full of 'contrabands,' alias runaway negroes from Missouri; of whom it is said there are a thousand in the neighborhood.—They are of all ages and characters, pious Uncle Toms and half-ape Topseys."[34] Five months later, in an editorial entitled "Our Colored Population," the black population of Leavenworth was estimated at fifteen hundred, almost all of whom were newcomers and the great majority fugitive slaves from Missouri. These people, with scarcely a single exception, had arrived at Leavenworth "wholly destitute of the means of living." As they came in large numbers, and many of them in mid-winter, suffering among them was inevitable.[35]

Compared with Lawrence, Leavenworth had a more formal and extensive organization to provide for the contrabands' welfare. On February 5, 1862, some of the town's white leaders met with their black counterparts at the First Colored Baptist Church to "take into consideration measures for the amelioration of the condition of the colored people of Kansas." Prominent white leaders in attendance were Col. Daniel R. Anthony, Dr. R. C. Anderson, and Richard J. Hinton. The black community was represented by the Rev. Robert Caldwell of the Baptist church, Lewis Overton, a teacher in a black school, and Capt. William D. Mathews, a free mulatto military officer. Several months later, Charles H. Langston, a free mulatto schoolteacher, became a prominent leader in the black community. Hinton, a prominent journalist and abolitionist, had interviewed John Brown and his chief aide, John Henrie Kagi, during their stay in Kansas in 1858. At the Leavenworth meeting Hinton presented a plan of organization for the Kansas Emancipation League, which was approved. Anthony was elected president, Dr. Anderson treasurer, Hinton, chief secretary, Overton and Caldwell, members of the executive committee, and Mathews superintendent of contrabands. Dr. Anderson told the audience of the origin of the scheme for sending an agent East to lay before the public the condition of the contrabands and to solicit aid. Before the meeting adjourned, a committee submitted a skeleton constitution and by-laws which were adopted.[36]

The Kansas Emancipation League's second meeting was held on February 10, 1862. After the minutes of the preceding meeting and the formal constitution and bylaws were read and approved, Richard Hinton "brought to the attention of the League the constant attempts at kidnapping which occur daily in this city." This matter was taken into consideration by a committee that was directed to work with police and military officials to provide protection to the black residents of Leavenworth and the state of Kansas. The object of the league, it was agreed, should be to "assist all efforts to destroy slavery, but more especially to take supervision and control of the contraband element so freely coming to our State." Furthermore, it was "the object of the League to encourage industry, education and morality among these people, to find them employment and thus make them a benefit and not a burden to the State which shelters them." As superintendent of contrabands, Captain Mathews was instructed "to take charge and provide for their temporary wants and in every way look after their interests."[37]

Beginning on February 13, 1862, and continuing for several months, the *Leavenworth Daily Conservative* ran an advertisement of the Labor Exchange and Intelligence Office established by the Kansas Emancipation League at the drugstore of Dr. R. C. Anderson on Shawnee Street. All persons in need of black workers, including hotel waiters, porters, cooks, and chambermaids, were asked to apply at this office. Furthermore, laborers were supplied for such jobs as woodsawing, whitewashing, teaming, etc., at the same office. About a month after the first advertisement was printed the Labor Exchange general agent reported that good work had already been accomplished, and that "over one hundred colored men have been sent from our city to labor on farms and that the demand for this kind of labor is still constant and pressing."[38]

Although the Labor Exchange and Intelligence Office helped to reduce the number of contrabands who were dependent upon the league, it by no means eliminated unemployment since many of the laboring men not only had large families but were unable to work as a result of sickness and exposure. For these people the league appealed for assistance in Leavenworth and elsewhere. Early in May 1862, Richard Hinton authorized a printed circular which stated the problems encountered by the league and appealed to "friends in other states" for material support. One copy of this circular at the Kansas State Historical Society has a handwritten note, probably appended by Hinton, that states that the first money contributed to the league came from George L. Stearns, the Boston merchant who supplied John Brown with money for his abolitionist crusade.[39]

IV

Soldiering was the chief occupation of able-bodied male contrabands in the war years from 1862 to 1865, and it was General Lane who led the campaign in Kansas to organize black regiments and recruit black soldiers. In a speech at Leavenworth in January 1862, Lane recalled that contrabands who came into his camps in Missouri had played at soldiering after their evening meal; he said they took to military drill as a child takes to its mother's milk. "They soon learn the step, soon learn the position of the soldier and the manual of arms." He urged the government to arm the blacks, citing as precedents the use of black soldiers in the armies of George Washington and Andrew Jackson.[40] At a time when President Lincoln was calling for 300,000 volunteers, Lane was appointed commissioner of recruitment for the Department of Kansas. He was authorized to appoint recruiting officers, arm and equip volunteers, establish camps of instruction, and arrange for the procurement and transportation of supplies. Lane assumed that his recruiting commission, issued by the War Department in July 1862, entitled him to enlist blacks as well as whites.[41]

Arriving at Leavenworth on the 3rd of August, Lane appointed recruiting agents and disposed of related matters. That he took speedy action is indicated by a *Leavenworth Daily Conservative* advertisement that appeared three days later. It announced that all able-bodied colored men between the ages of eighteen and forty-five had an opportunity to serve in the First Kansas Regiment of the "Liberating Army," and said that one thousand such men were wanted. It went on to say that "Ten Dollars Per Month will be paid, and good quarters, rations and clothing provided." A similar advertisement in an Atchison newspaper promised that, in addition to the pay and rations, a certificate of freedom would be issued to each black volunteer, as well as freedom for his mother, wife, and children.[42]

Recruiting and training proceeded at a fast pace in the weeks following Lane's initial appeal for black volunteers. An item in a Leavenworth newspaper on August 28 said the colored regiment had received one hundred recruits within the previous twenty-four hours. At Mound City some one hundred fifty black recruits were drilling daily, and more were reported to be on their way to the camp adjoining that town. North of the Kansas River approximately five hundred blacks had been enlisted within a short time. They were instructed to rendezvous by September 10 at Camp Jim Lane, near Wyandotte bridge. Capt. George J. Martin returned from Wyandotte to Atchison on September 12, and reported the regiment to be six hundred strong, with daily additions from Missouri. "The men learned their duties with great ease and rapidity," he said, "and are delighted with the prospect of fighting for their freedom, and give good earnest of making valiant soldiers." On October 17, 1862, the First Kansas Colored Infantry was organized near Fort Lincoln, in Bourbon Country.[43]

There is evidence that not all of the blacks recruited into the regiment entered voluntarily. One Missourian wrote to President Lincoln, complaining that a party of some fifteen Kansans had entered Missouri to "recruit Negroes for General Lane's Negro brigade." They forcibly took possession of some twenty-five blacks and about forty horses. However, a company of militia captured eight of the Jayhawkers and recovered all the blacks and horses. Another incident involved a recruiter for the contraband regiment at Hiawatha, in the northeast corner of Kansas. On August 21, 1862, he announced that he would pay "two dollars per head for buck niggers—that is, for every negro man brought over from Missouri, he will pay two dollars to the person bringing him across."[44]

That the black regiment's fighting qualities brought honor to Afro-Americans in Kansas and elsewhere is well documented. Writing from Fort Africa, Bates County, Missouri, on October 30, 1862, a *Leavenworth Daily Conservative* correspondent told of a campaign against a notorious band of bushwhackers. In a sharp engagement in which some two hundred thirty black troops were pitted against about six hundred bushwhackers, "The men fought like tigers, each and every one of them, and the main difficulty was to hold them well in hand. . . . We have the guerrillas hemmed in, and will clean them and the county out," said the correspondent. Gen. James G. Blunt wrote an account of the Battle of Honey Springs, near Fort Gibson in Indian Territory, on July 25, 1863. Soldiers of the First Colored Regiment "fought like veterans, with a coolness and valor that is unsurpassed," he wrote. "They preserved their line perfect throughout the whole engagement and, although in the hottest of the fight, they never once faltered. Too much praise can not be awarded them for their gallantry." The general, who was battle-hardened from long campaigns, judged the blacks to be "better soldiers in every respect than any troops I have ever had under my command." General Lane, who continued to support the enlistment of blacks, often paid tribute to their fighting ability.[45]

Beginning in June 1863, a second Kansas black regiment was recruited and molded into an effective fighting unit by Col. Samuel J. Crawford, afterwards governor of Kansas. Besides the Kansas regiments, a black brigade was recruited and sent into action. Altogether, a total of 2,083 black soldiers were recruited, or approximately one-sixth of the black population of Kansas in 1865. Kansas lived up to its radical tradition by recruiting the first black troops to engage in military action against Confederate forces.[46]

The black military achievement was even more remarkable when it is considered that the soldiers faced great obstacles in the form of race prejudice and bureaucratic procrastination and delay. General Lane received blacks into the First Kansas Colored Regiment under what he thought was congressional authority, only to be informed that such recruitment had to have presidential authority which was not forthcoming for several months. As a result, this regiment was not mustered into the service until January 13, 1863. Instead of soldiering, the troops were first put to work building fortifications and in fatigue duty. This led to anger, disillusionment, and, for a time, numerous desertions. Lane had promised his black recruiting officers that they would be commissioned as officers of the companies they recruited, but this was denied and white officers were appointed in their place. Even after the regiment was mustered in, payment of the troops was delayed until June 1863. Furthermore, the Union government defaulted on its pledge to pay black recruits at the same rate as whites—actually three dollars less per month than white soldiers and a deduction of three dollars for clothing. "Not until 1864," writes Dudley Taylor Cornish, "and then only after furious debate in the army, in the press and in congress, did Negro soldiers finally get what amounted to equal pay for equal work." Race prejudice raised its ugly head, as is indicated by the advice given by an editorial writer for the *Fort Scott Bulletin*. He advised that the black regiment be kept away from Kansas troops which were then in the field for "with one exception, there is not a Kansas regiment from which they would not have as much to fear as from the rebels."[47]

While the black soldiers felt insulted and betrayed by the government's delay and discrimination in matters of mustering into service and pay, the dependents they left behind in Kansas suffered real hardships. In Leavenworth, the public was urged to subscribe clothing, food, and money to the wives and children of the men in service. When it was discovered that a group of blacks planned to hold a bazaar to raise money for a charitable cause outside the town, a public meeting of colored citizens was called. It was resolved, that since the great majority of the black population was poor, and that many continued to arrive in Kansas "destitute of money, clothing and bedding," that the blacks should be urged *not* to send money out of town but "to do all within their power to relieve the poor and suffering among us, and urge our friends here and elsewhere to aid us in this good work."[48]

v

Kansas Territory attracted a small group of ardent abolitionists who, with moral and material support from the East, established stations and conducted "passengers" on the Underground Railroad to freedom. When the Civil War commenced, contrabands from Missouri made straight for these stations and other places of refuge and opportunity for employment. As the editorial writer of the *Leavenworth Daily Conservative* pointed out, "These freed men settled in various parts of the State, guided by their interests, inclination or supposed safety, our city and Lawrence being the principle [*sic*] points of location."[49]

Kansas became more Negrophilic during the Civil War when the contrabands supplied much needed labor to harvest crops and perform a variety of tasks in rural and urban areas. Most importantly, black men volunteered for military service and made a notable contribution. Unfortunately, race prejudice and bureaucratic delay and discrimination brought great hardships to the families of black servicemen and proved to be a serious obstacle to progress on the road toward racial integration.

Before the Civil War had ended, much of the cooperative effort that had characterized the Kansas Emancipation League and other organizations broke down and the black and white communities tended to go their separate ways. In Leavenworth, for example, the black community held public meetings to protest the treatment accorded black soldiers; the Suffrage Club was organized to agitate for an amendment to the Kansas Constitution which would extend the franchise to black males. Beginning in October 1863, the Kansas State Colored Convention met annually in the leading cities to debate and act upon such issues as equal suffrage, the right to serve in the state militia, the right of trial by a jury of political equals, and the abolition of discriminatory practices by the proprietors of stages, railroad cars, barber shops, hotels, saloons, and other public institutions.[50]

In the face of an overpowering Negrophobic white majority, the blacks of Kansas turned more and more to their own cultural heritage, to their schools, churches, lodges, mutual aid societies, and the celebration of anniversaries that marked their progress from slavery to freedom. One such celebration was the emancipation of the slaves in the British West Indies on August 1, 1834. On August 1, 1864, the black community of Leavenworth and vicinity began their celebration of West Indian emancipation with a procession headed by the Colored Battery of Capt. William D. Mathews, followed by the Sabbath schools, and the Suffrage Club. Not less than two thousand people met at Fackler's Grove where a fine dinner, interesting speeches, and splendid music were enjoyed.[51]

It is ironic that when the U.S. Supreme Court came to consider race discrimination a century after Kansas Territory had been a staging ground for civil war on the issue of chattel slavery, it was a case brought by a black Kansan against the school board in the state's capital city that overturned court-enforced segregation and ushered in the Civil Rights Movement.

NOTES

1. James A. Rawley, *Race and Politics: "Bleeding Kansas" and the Coming of the Civil War* (Philadelphia: J. B. Lippincott Co., 1969), vii–xvi, 1–99; Roy F. Nichols and Eugene H. Berwanger, *The Stakes of Power, Eighteen Forty-five—Eighteen Seventy-seven*, rev. ed. (New York: Hill and Wang, 1982), 47–59, 66–69; David M. Potter, *The Impending Crisis, 1848–1861* (New York: Harper and Row, 1976), 199–244, 297–327; Eugene H. Berwanger, *The Frontier Against Slavery: Western Anti-Negro Prejudice and the Slavery Extension Controversy* (Urbana: University of Illinois Press, 1967), 97–118; Benjamin Quarles, *The Negro in the Civil War* (Boston: Little, Brown and Co., 1953), 113–15, 120, 126–28; William E. Parrish, *Turbulent Partnership: Missouri and the Union, 1861–1865* (Columbia: University of Missouri Press, 1963); Albert Castel, *A Frontier State at War: Kansas, 1861–1865* (Ithaca, N.Y.: Cornell University Press, 1958); James C. Malin, "The Proslavery Background of the Kansas Struggle," *Mississippi Valley Historical Review* 10 (December 1923): 285–305; James C. Malin, *John Brown and the Legend of Fifty-Six* (Philadelphia: American Philosophical Society, 1942); G. Raymond Gaeddert, *The Birth of Kansas* (Lawrence: University of Kansas, 1940).

2. John G. Haskell, "The Passing of Slavery in Western Missouri," *Kansas Historical Collections, 1901–1902* 7 (Topeka: State Printer, 1902), 28–39.

3. Ibid., 32–33; Harrison Anthony Trexler, "Slavery in Missouri, 1804–1865," *Johns Hopkins University Studies in Historical and Political Science*, ser. 32, no. 2 (1914), 9–56.

4. Trexler, "Slavery in Missouri," 10–13.

5. Ibid., 178–79, 203–4.

6. Ibid., 202–4.

7. George M. Beebe, Acting Governor, to President James Buchanan, dated Lecompton, Kansas Territory, November 26, 1860, "Governor Medary's Administration," *Kansas Historical Collections, 1889–1896* 5 (Topeka: Kansas State Printing Co., 1896), 632.

8. Richard Cordley, *A History of Lawrence, Kansas: From the First Settlement to the Close of the Rebellion* (Lawrence: E. F. Caldwell, 1895), 162–64, 183; Richard Cordley, *Pioneer Days in Kansas* (New York: Pilgrim Press, 1903), 122–36.

9. James B. Abbott, "The Rescue of Dr. John W. Doy," *Kansas Historical Collections 1886–1888* 4 (Topeka: Kansas Publishing House, 1890), 312–13.

10. Ibid., 358. For a critical essay on the Underground Railroad legend, see Larry Gara, *The Liberty Line: The Legend of the Underground Railroad* (Lexington: University of Kentucky Press, 1961), 190–94.

11. Louis S. Gerteis, *From Contraband to Freedman: Federal Policy Toward Southern Blacks, 1861–1865* (Westport, Conn.: Greenwood Press, 1973), 3–7, 11–26, 31–40, 120–25.

12. Leverett W. Spring, *Kansas: The Prelude to the War for the Union,* rev. ed. (Boston: Houghton, Mifflin and Co., 1913), 257–67.

13. James Henry Lane's chief biographer is Wendell Holmes Stephenson, *Kansas Historical Publications: The Political Career of General James H. Lane* 3 (Topeka: Kansas State Printing Plant, 1930). Other biographies are: John Speer, *Life of Gen. James H. Lane, "The Liberator of Kansas"* (Garden City, Kan.: John Speer, 1897); William Elsey Connelley, *James Henry Lane, the "Grim Chieftain" of Kansas* (Topeka: Crane and Co., 1899); Albert Castel, "Jim Lane of Kansas," *Civil War Times Illustrated* 12 (April 1973): 22–29.

14. Stephenson, *Political Career of General James H. Lane,* 105–10; Thomas A. Belser, Jr., "Military Operations in Missouri and Arkansas, 1861–1865," 2 vols. (Ph.D. diss., Vanderbilt University, 1958), 1:177–79.

15. H. D. Fischer, *The Gun and the Gospel: Early Kansas and Chaplain Fischer* (Chicago: Kenwood Press, 1896), 42–43, 155–56; Stephenson, *Political Career of General James H. Lane,* 126.

16. Fischer, *Gun and Gospel,* 155–57.

17. *Congressional Globe,* 37th Cong., 2d sess., pt. 3, May 15, 1862, p. 2149, pt. 4, July 10, 1862, p. 3235; *Official Records of the War of the Rebellion,* ser. I (Washington: Government Printing Office, 1881), 3:742–43; for Lane's New York speech, see *Leavenworth Daily Conservative,* June 12, 1862; Stephenson, *Political Career of General James H. Lane,* 127.

18. Fischer, *Gun and Gospel,* 164–69; *Freedom's Champion,* Atchison, April 4, 1863.

19. [J. B. McAfee], *Official Military History of Kansas Regiments During the War for the Suppression of the Great Rebellion* (Leavenworth: W. S. Burke, 1870), 61–63.

20. *Freedom's Champion,* February 8, 1862.

21. W. M. Paxton, *Annals of Platte County, Missouri* (Kansas City: Hudson-Kimberly Publishing Co., 1897), 337–38.

22. Pearl W. Morgan, ed., *History of Wyandotte County, Kansas and Its People,* 2 vols. (Chicago: Lewis Publishing Co., 1911), 1:232.

23. Records of the Governor's Office, Correspondence Files, Administration of Gov. Thomas Carney, 1863–64, box 2.1, folder 14, Archives Department, Kansas State Historical Society [hereafter cited as KSHS]; Trexler, "Slavery in Missouri," 206–7.

24. Recent excavation by archeological consultant Larry Schmits and his firm, Environmental Systems Analysis, Inc., has revealed artifacts from Quindaro, an abolitionist river port on the Missouri River in Wyandotte County, Kansas. Founded in 1857 with help from the New England Emigrant Aid Society, the town served as a major port of entry for freed and escaped slaves and free-soil settlers. The town grew rapidly to a population of about two thousand, but by 1862 was a ghost town.

John Reynolds, assistant state archeologist with the Kansas State Historical Society, who toured the site, said that the findings were much more extensive and significant than most expected. *Kansas City Times,* July 16, 1987, p. 10A.

25. *Kansas 1865 M.S. Census,* vol. 10, Compendium of Statistics reported to the Legislature, Archives Department, KSHS. In a report of the Committee on Freedmen to the General Association of the Congregational Churches of Kansas in June 1865, two ministers wrote "that there are not less than fifteen thousand freedmen in Kansas. Most of them have become free since the commencement of the war. They are most numerous in the eastern part of the State, especially in and near the larger cities and villages." *The Congressional Record,* 7 (June 1865): 13.

26. *Osawatomie Herald,* reprinted in the *Conservative* (daily), Leavenworth, January 25, 1862; *The Fort Scott Bulletin,* November 29, 1862.

27. *Leavenworth Daily Conservative,* May 27, 1863; Stephenson, *Political Career of General James H. Lane,* 132–33.

28. John B. Wood to George L. Stearns, November 19, 1861, Papers of George Luther Stearns and Mary Elizabeth Stearns, Manuscript Department, KSHS; Cordley, *Pioneer Days in Kansas,* 137–38.

29. *Lawrence Republican,* January 2, 1862; Cordley, *Pioneer Days in Kansas,* 138–44; Cordley, *History of Lawrence,* 182–85.

30. *Lawrence Republican,* October 9, 1862; Cordley, *Pioneer Days in Kansas,* 144–49.

31. Emery, *Reminiscences of Early Lawrence,* 20; Cordley, *Pioneer Days in Kansas,* 145; *Lawrence Republican,* July 20, August 7, 1862; *Kansas Daily Tribune,* Lawrence, December 25, 1863; Kathe Schick, "Lawrence Black Community" (unpublished manuscript, Watkins Community Museum, Lawrence), Chapters 1 and 12, cited by Marilyn Dell Brady, "Kansas Federation of Colored Women's Clubs, 1900–1930," *Kansas History* 9 (Spring 1986): 19–30.

32. *Kansas 1865 MS. Census,* Vol. 3, Douglas County.

33. Ibid.

34. *Leavenworth Daily Conservative,* February 7, 1862.

35. Ibid., July 8, 1862. For the autobiography of Henry Clay Bruce, a slave who escaped from his master in Brunswick, Missouri, and, together with his intended wife, came to Leavenworth, Kansas, and lived there for some years, see H. C. Bruce, *The New Man: Twenty-nine Years a Slave. Twenty-nine Years a Free Man* (York, Pa.: P. Anstadt and Sons, 1895; reprinted New York, 1969); the author is indebted to William Lewin for calling his attention to this book.

36. *Leavenworth Daily Conservative,* February 8, 1862; Richard Warch and Jonathan F. Fanton, eds., *Great Lives Observed: John Brown* (Englewood Cliffs, N.J.: Prentice-Hall, 1973), 41, 53–56; Quarles, *The Negro in the Civil War,* 126–28.

37. *Leavenworth Daily Conservative,* February 12, 1862.

38. Ibid., February 13, 15, March 15, 1862.

39. Ibid., March 15, 1862; [Richard J. Hinton], *Kansas Emancipation League; To the Friends of Impartial Freedom* (Leavenworth: 1862).

40. *Conservative* (daily), January 29, 1862.

41. Ira Berlin, ed., *Freedom: A Documentary History of Emancipation 1861–1867; Series II, The Black Military Experience* (Cambridge: Cambridge University Press, 1982), 6, 9, 37, 67–71; Stephenson, *Political Career of General James H. Lane,* 127–32.

42. *Leavenworth Daily Conservative,* August 6, 1862; *Freedom's Champion,* August 16, 1862.

43. *Leavenworth Daily Conservative,* August 28, 1862; *Freedom's Champion,* September 13, 1862; Stephenson, *Political Career of General James H. Lane,* 129; Daniel W. Wilder, *The Annals of Kansas* (Topeka: Kansas Publishing House, 1875), 325.

44. Edward H. Samuel to President Lincoln, dated Liberty, Missouri, September 8, 1862, quoted in *Official Records of the War of the Rebellion,* ser. 1 (1885), 13:619; also quoted in Stephenson, *Political Career of General James H. Lane,* 130; *White Cloud Kansas Chief,* August 21, 1862, quoted in Grant W. Harrington, *Annals of Brown County, Kansas* (Hiawatha: Harrington Printing Co., 1903), 32.

45. *Leavenworth Daily Conservative,* quoted in *Lawrence Republican,* November 6, 1862; *Leavenworth Daily Conservative,* November 9, 1862, August 6, 1863; Stephenson, *Political Career of General James H. Lane,* 132; Dudley Taylor Cornish, "Kansas Negro Regiments in the Civil War," *Kansas Historical Quarterly* 20 (May 1953): 426; Dudley Taylor Cornish, *The Sable Arm: Black Troops in the Union Army, 1861–1865,* Foreword by Herman Hattaway (Lawrence: University Press of Kansas, 1987), 69–78.

46. Cornish, "Kansas Negro Regiments in the Civil War," 426–27; Wilder, *Annals of Kansas,* 422–23.

47. *Fort Scott Bulletin,* July 26, 1862; *Leavenworth Daily Conservative,* May 19, June 7, 1863; Berlin, *Freedom,* 37, 44, 68–73; Stephenson, *Political Career of General James H. Lane,* 127–32; Cornish, "Kansas Negro Regiments in the Civil War," 424.

48. *Leavenworth Daily Conservative,* September 4, 1862, December 24, 1863.

49. Ibid., July 8, 1862.

50. Ibid., July 10, 21, August 22, September 13, October 11, December 24, 1863, January 15, February 4, 10, 1864, October 20, 1866; Thomas C. Cox, *Blacks in Topeka, Kansas 1865–1915: A Social History* (Baton Rouge: Louisiana State University Press, 1982), 16–35.

51. *Leavenworth Daily Conservative,* July 31, August 2, 1864.

The Popular Ideology of Segregated Schooling: Attitudes Toward the Education of Blacks in Kansas, 1854–1900

James C. Carper

A number of recent books, monographs, and essays have explored the educational aspirations and experiences of black Americans. The vast majority of these studies focus on the education of blacks in either the northern urban areas or the South.[1] They have suggested that the extent to which black Americans could exercise their faith in schooling was to a significant extent determined by the attitudes of the white majority.

But what of the educational experience of blacks in other regions of the country? This essay explores the grass-roots attitudes toward the schooling of black Americans in Kansas, a Great Plains state which throughout the 19th century prided itself as a political entity dedicated to the principles of freedom and justice.

The "race problem" and its inevitable manifestation in the educational enterprise was rather insignificant in areas where the number of blacks was small. Such was the case in Kansas prior to the Civil War. Although there were blacks present in the territorial period, they were very few in number. In 1855 there were only 151 free blacks and 192

"The Popular Ideology of Segregated Schooling: Attitudes Toward the Education of Blacks in Kansas, 1854–1900," by James C. Carper, *Kansas History* 1 (winter 1978): 254–265. Copyright Kansas State Historical Society. Reprinted by permission.

slaves. At the outbreak of intersectional strife free blacks numbered only 625 and there were two slaves.[2] The war, however, brought about a change in the size of the black community in the state. By the mid-1860's refugees from the South began to stream into Kansas, and in the 1870's immigration reached near flood proportions. Between 1860 and 1870 the state's black population jumped from 627 to 17,108. By 1880 the figure had grown to 43,107, and by 1890 to 49,710.[3]

Some type of schooling for black children was accepted as desirable by the vast majority of white Kansans throughout the 19th century. Only a handful of citizens voiced opposition to the idea of educating them. In the early 1860's most Kansans seemed satisfied with privately financed evening schools, freedmen's schools, or contraband schools as a means of educating what few blacks there were in the state. However, concomitant with the increase in the black population between the mid-1860's and the early 1880's was a growing popular concern with the problem of race, particularly as it was focused in the public schools. Charity schools simply could not bear the burden of the increasing number of black students. The public schools would have to assume the responsibility for educating them.

Together with religion in the schools, the most widely discussed issue in the history of education in 19th century Kansas was how blacks would benefit from the state's growing commitment to public education. As had been the case in other parts of the nation, educational opportunity for blacks in Kansas was determined by the convictions of the white majority. Despite the protestations of blacks and some whites, particularly in the 1870's, black children were usually assigned to separate and for the most part substandard educational facilities. In Kansas, a state characterized by the rhetoric of freedom and equality, black students were seldom part of what historian David B. Tyack has called the "ideal of common learning under the common roof of the common school."[4] Though the belief that blacks should be educated in some fashion was widespread and the ideal of the common school advocated loudly, popular unwillingness to transcend racial distinctions limited black educational opportunities in Kansas. Race animus eventually contributed to black acceptance of segregated education, a circumstance which they naively hoped would be temporary.

Unlike some parts of the country, particularly in the South, Kansans gave scant attention to the question of whether or not blacks should be educated at all; most white Kansans believed they should receive some schooling.[5] The rationale for educating blacks was a familiar one. Viewing blacks as a potential hazard to the general welfare, some Kansans argued that schooling them would insure public safety. Others believed that education could elevate blacks to the dignity of manhood and mold them into good and useful citizens. In an editorial decrying "war on the Negro," William Blakely, editor of the *Smoky Hill and Republican Union,* emphasized this theme. "We want the School . . . thrown open to the Negro," he averred, "we want nothing forbidden him that will elevate him in the scale of humanity."[6] Writing to the Leavenworth *Conservative,* Lewis Overton also emphasized the need to "diffuse knowledge among the colored children" in order to lift them to a higher level of humanity.[7] In a letter to the Wyandotte *Gazette,* "C" offered a similar rationale for educating blacks. "We owe it to ourselves to give all aid and encouragement in our power to this work [education of black children]," he declared, "for in the proportion that blacks are enlightened will they become good and useful citizens."[8]

Arguments used frequently for compulsory schooling were also offered for the education of blacks. An unschooled person was often perceived as a potential threat to the public welfare. If he would not attend school voluntarily, then the state had the right and duty to compel attendance for its own self-protection. Considering the pervasive racism of the era, it is not surprising that uneducated blacks, more so than any other group, were believed to be a possible hazard to public safety. It was, therefore, imperative that they be "socialized" through schooling of some sort. D. W. Wilder, editor of the Leavenworth *Conservative,* stated succinctly this case for educating blacks: "A community cannot afford to allow any of its members to grow to maturity without education, and as a consequence, liable to fall into the vices and crimes which ignorance generates. It is a measure of self-preservation to see that they [blacks] have opportunities for instruction. . . ."[9]

In a similar fashion, Champion Vaughn of the Leavenworth *Times* argued that if blacks were allowed to "grow up in ignorance," then they would fill the "stationhouses and jails."[10] George T. Anthony shared Vaughn's sentiment. "There can be no *honest* disagreement as to the right of colored children to the spelling book and school instruction. There is no reason to question the duty and necessity of educating every child in the State, regardless of color or condition," he told his readers. "Public safety and State power depend too directly upon educated masses to allow any portion of a people to grow up in ignorance."[11] Echoing Anthony, Milton Reynolds, editor of the education-conscious *Kansas State Journal,* Lawrence, maintained that "the freedmen must be educated . . . the safety of society demands this much."[12]

Although most Kansans accepted, in some cases grudgingly, the principle that blacks should be educated in order to "civilize" them, a few citizens rejected the belief that they should receive any instruction in schools. This antagonism toward the education of blacks in any setting was expressed in several ways. In one instance, a teacher in Oskaloosa who started a "colored school" was threatened with bodily injury.[13] Writing to the *Brown County Sentinel,* Hiawatha, an anonymous woman conveyed the same feeling in a more polite manner when she claimed that "it won't hurt them [blacks] if they never go to school."[14] At times this antagonism toward educating blacks was demonstrated in a violent fashion. For example, a correspondent from Pleasant Ridge, a community which failed to live up to its name, reported that "the school house intended for the colored is burned down. . . . Dislike for the 'darkies' continues."[15]

Despite these occasional outbursts of hostility, black Kansans, like their counterparts elsewhere, zealously sought education. As one historian has noted, ". . . no other group in the United States had a greater faith in the equalizing power of schooling or a clearer understanding of the democratic promise of public education than did black Americans."[16] This unquestioning faith in the power of education was evident when the first State Mass Convention of the Colored People held at Leavenworth in 1869 resolved that "all adults, as well as children, use all means in their power to secure an education."[17]

To many blacks in Kansas education was the basis for their hopes and dreams. Schooling was touted frequently as a prerequisite for participating in the American dream. "Let no man or woman stand and fold his or her arms and dream of life, liberty and enjoyment, without tendering a helping hand towards educating their race . . . ," stated a correspondent to the *Colored Citizen,* one of the early black papers in the state.[18] Speaking to the colored state convention of 1880, H. C. Bruce also argued that if blacks were to enjoy the fruits of the American experience, such as freedom and prosperity, then they needed to stress the education of the race. "No race of people can prosper in this country or any country who do not cherish and foster education," he asserted, "and no uneducated people have ever prospered permanently."[19]

A number of blacks also believed that education was one of the most important means of dealing with racial prejudice. Through schooling some blacks in Kansas, as well as elsewhere, hoped to break down the barriers of discrimination.[20] As the Freedmen's Aid Association of Dunlap declared, "Education of the heart, mind, and hand will remove prejudice."[21] In a letter to the *American Citizen*, Fred Scott, a citizen of Osage City, proclaimed this belief in the power of education to reduce discrimination. "Education is the mightiest weapon you can use to fight your way through," he told his fellow blacks. "Nothing will free the colored race from all disabilities and cause their general recognition on an equal with whites so fast as education. . . ."[22] S. A. Havey agreed with Scott's pronouncement. In a letter to the same newspaper, he wrote that "the breaking down of prejudice is the great end to be attained; money, education, and morality are the means by which this end must be accomplished."[23]

Whether the goal was economic improvement or the dissolution of racial prejudice, many black Kansans believed that education was one of the most important means of attaining it. Without adequate schooling they saw little hope for achieving full participation in the American experience. S. O. Clayton of the Parsons *Blade* summed up the faith blacks had in education when he proclaimed that "we must educate or we must perish."[24]

In the early 1860's the opportunities for exercising this faith were rather limited. Most blacks who received any formal instruction at all attended privately supported freedmen's schools, evening schools, or contraband schools. Due to the small number of blacks in the state at that time and what appeared to many Kansans to be their "degraded" condition, these schools seemed sufficient to most Kansans and the possibility of educating them in the public common schools was seldom mentioned.[25]

Charity schools such as those in Lawrence, Leavenworth, Osawatomie, Topeka, Wyandotte, and other eastern Kansas towns were praised universally as beneficial to all concerned. According to Hovey E. Lowman of the *Kansas State Journal*, the founding of an evening school for the "benefit of the colored people in this city" was an "excellent idea."[26] John Speer, editor of the Lawrence *Republican*, shared Lowman's sentiment and called the contraband school one of the "most praiseworthy institutions" in the city.[27] Speaking of the contraband schools in Lawrence and Osawatomie, John Francis of the Olathe *Mirror* declared that "we doubt whether charity was ever more wisely bestowed than in these instances."[28] In a similar vein, D. W. Wilder of the widely circulated Leavenworth *Conservative* urged his readers to support the newly organized freedmen's school and defended the right of blacks to an education. "This movement is worthy of the encouragement and pecuniary aid of our citizens, and we believe it will receive it from all but traitors," he observed. "Education is the right of blacks as well as whites, and every effort they make in this direction should gain our most cordial co-operation."[29] R. B. Taylor of the Wyandotte *Gazette* also encouraged his readers to support the local school for black children, calling it a "step in the right direction."[30]

Charity schools for blacks may have been a step in the right direction, but with the influx of freedmen in the mid-1860's their facilities were simply overwhelmed. Since privately supported and staffed schools would no longer suffice, the public schools would have to shoulder the burden. Amidst racial animosity which seemed to grow as the black population in the state increased, Kansans voiced their opinions on how blacks should benefit from the state's growing commitment to public education.[31]

Public discourse relative to the explosive issue of race and the schools in the latter half of the 1860's suggested that while most Kansans accepted the principle that blacks should receive some form of instruction, many citizens wanted no part of what was often called "mixed education." Separate educational facilities would have to be provided for black students. The only major dissent from this belief came from the Kansas State Teachers Association. Meeting at Lawrence in July, 1866, the KSTA upheld the common school ideal and resolved that "we, as teachers, use our best endeavors to overcome the unreasonable prejudice existing in certain localities against the admission of colored children upon equal terms with white children. . . ."[32]

Most Kansans, however, did not agree with the teachers' advocacy of admitting blacks and whites to the same school. Their distaste for integrated education, a practice which to many people implied the social equality of the races, was expressed in several ways. During a public school meeting in Olathe, the board of directors was advised to "have a separate school provided for the colored children should any apply for admittance into the free schools."[33] At Junction City, a community plagued with racial discord throughout most of the 19th century, citizens at a public meeting resolved that "we are in favor of educating the white children at a school separate from negroes and that any attempt

... to compel our white children to associate with and become equals of negroes . . . will result disastrously to the interests of the school in this place. . . ."[34]

If a separate school for black scholars could not be afforded, other strategies were employed to avoid "mixing" the races. For example, in response to public pressure, the school board in Burlingame designated one school term for blacks, the next for whites, and so on.[35] Stretching the race issue to an even more absurd length, the residents of Seneca instructed the school board to provide a separate room and teacher for the only two black students in the district![36] Such practices prompted Peter McVicar, state superintendent of public instruction, to observe that "in some localities a very great prejudice against the co-education of the races still exists."[37]

Occasionally citizens revealed their attitudes toward integrated schooling in letters to local newspapers. In a lengthy letter to the Council Grove *Press,* G. M. Simcock, the owner of the local dry goods store and flour mill, objected to the possibility of having to send his children to the same school with black students. Conveying the feelings of many Kansans on the subject, he wrote:

Now I would like to see harmony in our school [but do not] feel disposed to send my children to school with negroes. I may have inherited this feeling by being born in Virginia and principally raised in Missouri; be that as it may, I did not inherit an exalted opinion of the institution of slavery, and am truly glad that we are rid of it. But I think I have seen enough of negroes to know that I cannot nor will treat them as my equal, and I know it unsafe for any community to elevate them too high. I am in favor of treating them well, but not as well or better than our own race.[38]

Employing less temperate language, "Sylvan Retreat," a citizen of Vienna, inveighed against "race mixing" in the schools and "social equality" in a letter to the *Kansas Valley.* Claiming that whites had descended from a "superior race," he warned that any policy which might result in a nation of "mongrels" or "hybrids" was as "loathsome to God as to mankind."[39]

These beliefs which Kansans voiced in the latter part of the 1860's were reflected in a state law passed in 1867. According to the statute, school districts were responsible for the "education of white and colored children, separately or otherwise, securing to them equal educational advantages." With the passage of this law the state legislature reaffirmed earlier commitments to the doctrine of separate but equal education.[40]

Although this doctrine had been practiced in most parts of the state prior to 1869 without substantial dissent, a significant minority of Kansans protested the practice in the 1870's. As is the case with most reform movements, reasons for the protest were varied. While some Kansans objected to separate schools on moral grounds, others based their complaints on economic considerations.

In an effort to eradicate separate schools for black children, a number of Kansans questioned the morality of the practice. They pointed out that racial prejudice was inimical to the American way and the common school ideal. L. B. Kellogg, editor of the *Kansas Educational Journal,* argued against what he termed "the last relic of the senseless prejudice against color which has disgraced the American people. Kansas has already taken the advanced position that colored children are entitled to as good educational advantages as white children," he maintained. "Let the State now say that they shall have the same educational advantages; that they shall be educated in the same school. . . . Let the public schools be public. . . ."[41]

Following the same line of argument as Kellogg, John A. Martin of the Atchison *Champion* asserted that separate schools were not equal schools and recommended that the schools should be truly common to all. "There is no just reason why the colored children should be compelled to attend separate schools. . . . Give the colored children equal school privileges with the whites, and a fair and equal chance in the battle of life," he told his readers. "Let the separate schools be abolished, and let us have one system, one school, for all children of the great human brotherhood."[42]

Jacob Winter, a state senator from Leavenworth, agreed that separate schools did not provide equal educational opportunity. Speaking in favor of the 1874 civil rights bill, a nearly unanimously supported statute which removed the word "white" from all Kansas laws but had little impact on educational policy, he charged that laws condoning separate educational facilities for blacks were designed to mollify those afflicted with "Negrophobia" and a distaste for the common school. "[These laws] are strictly class legislation by which the white population can always keep the colored population from rising in the scale of intelligence," he declared, "and eject the colored children from the common school edifices, and thrust them into dilapidated shanties."[43] Echoing Winter, Albert Griffin of Manhattan's *Nationalist* urged his readers to work against the "unreasoning prejudices" which prohibited "colored brethren and sisters" from obtaining an equal education.[44]

Some opponents of segregated schools employed economic arguments against the policy. Perhaps reacting to the economic crisis of the early 1870's, some Kansans asserted that maintaining separate schools for the races was an unjustifiable waste of money. F. P. Baker of the *Kansas State Record* believed that it was a "costly prejudice" which resulted in separate schools for white and black children.[45] Likewise, the editor of the Leavenworth *Commercial* maintained that it was simply "foolish" to spend money to build schools to accommodate a few black students.[46] George W. Martin of the Junction City *Union* shared this belief. After elaborating upon the cost of maintaining a separate school for blacks, he asked his readers if their prejudice was not costing more than it was worth.[47]

Organized black public opinion also played a significant role in the protest against separate but equal educational policies. Though blacks never comprised more than five percent of the population of Kansas at any time in the 19th century, their ardent pursuit of educational opportunity and desire to participate in society more than made up for their lack of numbers. This growing zeal was apparent throughout the 1870's as black organizations condemned separate and frequently inferior educational facilities. Typical of the protests was that of the State Convention of Colored Men which met at Lawrence in 1872 and demanded that the state repeal all laws "making distinction of race, nationality or color among its citizens in regard to among other things education."[48]

Several individuals also expressed their anger over the manner in which black children were treated in the public school system. After several black students were refused admittance to an all-white school in Leavenworth, T. W. Henderson wrote a letter to the Leavenworth *Times* lamenting the oppression of blacks and asking when the white population would "throw aside their hatred of us black citizens, because of color, and give our children a chance."[49] In a letter to the *Colored Radical*, H. C. B., a citizen of Atchison, also expressed dissatisfaction with the way in which blacks were treated in the schools and identified one pernicious outcome of segregated schooling. "The effect of separate schools will be that the colored child must learn that the white child is either his superior or inferior," he stated, ". . . [and] that when they grow up to manhood they will not regard each other as men and fellow-citizens."[50]

The nascent black press joined the crusade against separate educational facilities for black students. Despite a constant struggle for survival in an environment that was sometimes less than friendly, black papers criticized the white majority for its insistence on segregated education. In a lengthy critique of education in Kansas, the editor of the *Colored Radical* noted that while there was a significant amount of discussion relative to "mixing the races" in the public schools, racial prejudice consigned most black children to separate and inferior schools. He maintained that the only way to vitiate such prejudice was to destroy the separate schools which perpetuated it.[51] In a later editorial, he urged his readers to petition the legislature to outlaw all "negro schools."[52] W. L. Eagleson, editor of the *Colored Citizen,* shared the sentiment of the editor of the *Radical.* He asserted that segregated schooling had to be abolished because "nothing now in existence in this State does help so much towards keeping up the low mean prejudice against the colored man as these separate schools. . . ."[53] "Race difficulties will always exist in this country while race barriers are allowed to exist," he proclaimed in a later commentary. "We say down with every race institution in the land, and the sooner we learn that we are all Americans, the better for all concerned."[54]

Most white Kansans, however, did not subscribe to Eagleson's viewpoint. While they, like most white Americans, at least in the North, were willing to permit blacks a modicum of civil and political equality, social equality, an ideal inextricably intertwined with the American experience, was another matter.[55] Since integrated education smacked of the social equality of the races, the weight of public sentiment in the state during the 1870's, and for that matter throughout the remainder of the 19th century, supported separate schools for blacks and prohibited any widespread efforts to integrate the schools.[56] As one editor observed, separate schools for "Smoked Americans" seldom upset those who were "nervous on the subject of social equality."[57]

Indicative of the public's uneasiness with the concept of the social equality of the races, which was apparently implied by "mixed education," was the volume of letters to the local press objecting to the idea of integrating the schools. Writing to the Leavenworth *Commercial,* "X" objected to the efforts of "demented white men" to legislate "social equality." He claimed that the majority of Kansans were against allowing their children to "mingle together in the common schools . . . [with] the aromatic African."[58] In a letter to the same paper, Fanny West warned of the possible consequences of "mixing the races" in order to achieve equality. She proclaimed that it would lead to the "horrid practice of amalgamation" which would degrade the white race.[59] Similar racial thinking was evident in a letter from a subscriber to the *Nationalist*. He, like West, lamented that if whites were compelled to associate with blacks in the schools, whites would be mongrelized and eventually enslaved.[60]

The press also disapproved of attempts to elevate blacks to a level of social equality with whites by abolishing separate schools and adhering to the common school ideal. While papers which advocated integrated education were always Republican, Democratic as well as some Republican papers opposed the policy.

Perhaps one of the most detailed and blunt rejections of integrated schooling and the concept of social equality came from the staunchly Republican Wathena *Reporter*. Condemning the possibility of educating blacks and whites in the same school, the editor of the *Reporter* posited:

> This idea of social negro equality can never be engrafted in the American people. And why should it be? Has not the Maker of the universe placed an unmistakable mark on the two races, the nature of which is to forbid social alliances, and consequently social contact. The negro may be the superior of the two races, but admitting that he is, does not justify his malgamating with the white. We have fought for, and advocated equal rights for every human being under this government, but we are not yet ready to array ourselves in antagonism to the immutable laws of nature.[61]

Complaining about what he called "African subjugation," T. W. Peacock, editor of the *Kansas Democrat*, also deprecated efforts to promote racial integration in the schools and elsewhere. He went on to urge his readers to resist any attempt to force white children to associate with "depraved blacks."[62] Nelson Abbott of the militantly anti-black Atchison *Patriot*, the self-proclaimed "Democratic Organ of Kansas," shared this racist sentiment. He objected to any "indiscriminate commingling of the African and Caucasian" and warned his readers that some people would not be satisfied until everything was "speckled."[63] Likewise, Sol Miller of the *Kansas Chief*, a Republican paper in Doniphan county, claimed that it would be wrong to attempt to "crush out the natural prejudice of the races" by sending black and white students to the same school.[64] In a similar fashion, U. F. Sargent of the Democratic Fort Scott *Pioneer* asserted that attempts to mix the races in the schools would violate the will of the majority and degrade the educational enterprise. "We don't want social equality," he continued, "but we want decent schools."[65]

While abhorrence of the notion of the social equality of the races served as the primary barrier to making the schools common to all, the concern that integration would damage, if not destroy, the public school also prohibited the achievement of the common school ideal. As was the case in other sections of the country throughout the 19th century, some Kansans based their opposition to integrated education on the assumption that if such a policy was followed, then the so-called better classes would withdraw from the public schools thus rendering them pauper-like institutions. To sacrifice the public schools for the benefit of a small group that was often perceived as degraded and powerless seemed unwise. As George F. Prescott of the Leavenworth *Commercial* maintained, "by the enforcement of obnoxious measures [mixing the races in the schools] will our public school system become practically a failure, and the good of the many be sacrificed to the narrow prejudices and selfish purposes of the few."[66] The editor of the Atchison *Patriot* agreed with this assessment claiming that "if races are mixed, the better classes will withdraw."[67] J. Clarke Swayze, the outspoken, and later assassinated, editor of the Topeka *Blade,* also warned of the possible result of actions designed to integrate the schools. "If the legislature undertakes to mix the public schools," he asserted, "we shall not be disappointed to see the excellent system now in operation in Kansas left to the negroes . . . while independent institutions . . . will educate the whites."[68]

Integrated education was occasionally condemned on the grounds that blacks would make better progress in separate schools. For instance, the editor of the Troy *Republican* argued that putting the two classes together in school would cause the black children to suffer and "not half the good would be done than would be if left alone."[69] Writing to the *Saline County Journal,* D. B. Powers echoed this belief. He claimed that blacks were making the best progress in "separate schools, homogeneous in character, strict in discipline, and incensed by rivalry as a race, instead of individuals."[70]

The emotional and sometimes violent controversy concerning the education of blacks which raged throughout the 1870's resulted in only two significant legislative actions. In 1868 the state legislature had authorized school districts in first- and second-class cities to maintain either separate or integrated educational facilities. Eight years later, for reasons not revealed in any public debates, the legislature recodified the Kansas school laws and omitted all references to separate schools. Separate schooling for blacks no longer enjoyed legal sanction. In 1879, however, the legislature again gave segregated education legal status. Responding to public sentiment, the heavily Republican legislature passed a measure allowing school boards in first-class cities (those with populations of at least 15,000) to operate separate elementary schools for black children. Segregated secondary schools were prohibited.[71] In other areas school boards were not permitted, at least legally, to maintain separate schools for blacks and whites. Although the statute sanctioned segregation in first-class cities where the vast majority of blacks resided, it left the door open for integrated education in other areas. Most blacks living outside first-class cities remained, however, in segregated schools as a result of community pressure, violence, and, occasionally, choice.

Between the passage of this bill and the turn of the century, the issue of the education of blacks received markedly less attention among white Kansans than it did in either the 1860's or the 1870's. When opinions were expressed on the matter of educating blacks they differed little from those of the 1870's. A number of factors, both state and national in nature, contributed to the slackening of public discourse on the question of integrating the schools and therefore making them truly common. Without doubt, the 1879 statute lessened the anxiety of many white Kansans about the possibility of having to send their children to school with blacks and consequently reduced their concern with the issue. The slowdown of black migration to Kansas in the early 1880's also contributed to the decline of public debate on the subject of race and the schools as fears of being overrun by what some called "hordes of degraded blacks" were calmed. Furthermore, interest in other issues such as prohibition and agrarian unrest probably steered public attention away from the race issue.[72]

On the national level, the two decades following the end of Reconstruction were characterized by a steady hardening of racial prejudice which was aided and abetted by racist Social Darwinism and imperialist ideology. What allies the blacks had in their struggle for freedom and equality dwindled in the face of increasing racial intolerance not only in the South but in many areas of the North.[73] This national phenomenon diminished popular concern for assimilating blacks into the social order by way of integrated schooling. Lastly, the civil rights cases of 1883, the well-known Plessy *vs.* Ferguson case of 1896, and the Cumming *vs.* Richmond County Board of Education case of 1899 not only mirrored the white majority's attitude toward the place blacks should have in the social order by providing national legal sanction to racial segregation, but also reduced public debate on the issue of integrated education. As one editor said of one of the 1883 civil rights cases, "Doesn't it knock their case [for biracial schools] from under them, and leave them where they deserve to be [in segregated schools]?"[74]

Despite these obstacles, the black press in Kansas continued to campaign vigorously for the abolition of separate schools throughout the 1880's. As was the case in the 1870's, black editors believed that racially mixed schools would help break down the barriers of prejudice and result in equal educational opportunity.[75] By the 1890's, however, the crusade for integration weakened and separation was increasingly accepted, and at times advocated, by influential blacks.

Faced with increasing white intransigence on the matter of social equality in general and biracial education in particular, many blacks advocated a moderately separatist stance resembling that of Booker T. Washington, the most influential black leader of the late 19th and early 20th centuries. They advocated self-reliance and racial pride and accepted separate schools.[76] O. S. Fox of the *Afro-American Advocate* summarized this position when he said, "As a race let us support race enterprises. Educate the young, get prosperity, be economical and in this way the Race Problem may be successfully solved."[77]

Separation was not considered an end but rather a means by which blacks hoped to demonstrate to white society that they were industrious, reliable, and worthy of assimilation into the mainstream of American life. Illustrative of this hope that the conditions imposed on blacks by the white majority might be used to demonstrate their value to the society was a lengthy editorial by C. H. J. Taylor of the widely circulated *American Citizen.* He wrote:

> We have no confidence in the Negro, be he teacher, patron, or pupil who desires to always mix with white people. Let us not be mis-

194

understood, we do not believe that mixed schools would necessarily injure the races, but we do contend that a people who have been doing business for themselves for centuries can with plausible reason object to a people less than thirty years old mixing with them, Again we do not believe it good sense for us to cry about it. Instead of becoming angry and declaring that we will do nothing unless allowed to mingle with white folks, we ought to accept their decision, which denies us admission [to their schools], and go to work to prove to them, beyond question, that they are losing something of worth by not being with us. We can do this if we will. . . .[78]

Echoing Taylor, W. M. Pope of the *Call* argued that blacks should not force themselves into "places where they are not wanted and are constantly subjected to humiliation." Instead he urged his readers to make the schools for blacks as good as possible in order to win the respect of the white majority.[79] S. O. Clayton of the Parsons *Blade* shared this belief and maintained that most blacks in Kansas felt the same way.[80]

Like George A. Dudley of the *American Citizen,* an increasing number of blacks were rejecting the traditional belief that "the education of the races together obliterates prejudice and renders it more easy for colored persons to obtain employment."[81] By rejecting the notion that integrated education would erase prejudice and provide economic opportunity, many blacks were coming to grips with the unwillingness of the white majority to transcend race while pursuing the common school ideal. They did not, however, abandon their faith in formal education. Blacks were as zealous for schooling in the 1890's as they had been in the 1870's when they and a small number of white Kansans spurred by a momentary idealism sought to make the schools common to both races. But as allies in the white community dwindled and racial intolerance hardened, blacks in Kansas, like most of their brethren elsewhere, were left with little choice but to accept separate educational facilities and second-class citizenship. Many believed that the situation would be temporary. By demonstrating self-reliance, industriousness, and success in the schools set aside for them, blacks hoped to be accepted not only into the same school with other Americans but also the mainstream of society.

For the majority of blacks in Kansas the situation was not temporary. It was not until the 1950's that large numbers of segregated schools began to be legally abolished.[82] Regardless of their efforts in the 19th century, and for that matter the first half of the 20th, blacks were unable to realize their aspirations because in historian Selwyn Troen's words, ". . . the schools, although promising openness and equality, in fact closely mirrored the prejudices and limitations of the society they served and represented."[83] The attitudes of the majority of Kansans indeed not only stifled the blacks' ardent quest for full participation in the promise of the common school, but also contributed to the development of an ideology of segregated schooling which remained influential well into the 20th century.

NOTES

1. Henry Allen Bullock, *A History of Negro Education in the South from 1169 to the Present* (Cambridge, Mass., Harvard University Press, 1967); Roger A. Fischer, *The Segregation Struggle in Louisiana, 1862–77* (Urbana, University of Illinois Press, 1974); Vincent P. Franklin, "The Education of Minorities in Cities in the United States: Toward a Comparative Historical Perspective," paper presented at the History of Education Society meeting, October 16, 1977, Toronto, Canada; Louis R. Harlan, *Separate and Unequal: Public School Campaigns and Racism in the Southern Seaboard States, 1901–1915* (Chapel Hill, University of North Carolina Press, 1958); Leon F. Litwack, *North of Slavery: The Negro in the Free States, 1790–1860* (Chicago, University of Chicago Press, 1961), pp. 113–152; Stanley K. Schultz, *The Culture Factory: Boston Public Schools, 1789–1860* (New York, Oxford University Press, 1973), pp. 157–206; Selwyn K. Troen, *The Public and the Schools: Shaping the St. Louis System, 1838–1920* (Columbia, University of Missouri Press, 1975), pp. 79–98; David B. Tyack, *The One Best System: A History of American Urban Education* (Cambridge, Harvard University Press, 1974), pp. 109–125; William Preston Vaughn, *Schools for All: The Blacks & Public Education in the South, 1865–1877* (Lexington, The University Press of Kentucky, 1974); Charles M. Wollenberg, *All Deliberate Speed: Segregation and Exclusion in California Schools, 1855–1975* (Berkeley, University of California Press, 1977).

2. Robert W. Richmond, *Kansas: A Land of Contrasts* (Saint Charles, Mo., Forum Press, 1974), pp. 162–166; William Frank Zornow, *Kansas: A History of the Jayhawk State* (Norman, University of Oklahoma Press, 1957), pp. 186–187.

3. For a detailed, though somewhat flawed description of black migration to Kansas, see Nell Irvin Painter, *Exodusters: Black Migration to Kansas After Reconstruction* (New York, Alfred A. Knopf, 1976).

4. Tyack, *The One Best System*, p. 110.

5. Horace Mann Bond, *The Education of the Negro in the American Social Order* (New York, Prentice-Hall, 1934), passim; Bullock, *A History of Negro Education in the South*,

pp. 42–44, 74–76; R. Freeman Butts and Lawrence A. Cremin, *A History of Education in American Culture* (New York, Holt, Rinehart and Winston, 1953), pp. 358–360; Harlan, *Separate and Unequal*, pp. 3–44.

6. *Smoky Hill and Republican Union*, Junction City, May 2, 1863.

7. Leavenworth *Conservative*, July 22, 1863.

8. Wyandotte *Gazette*, January 23, April 2, 1864.

9. Leavenworth *Conservative*, February 7, 1863.

10. Leavenworth *Times*, December 6, 1863.

11. Leavenworth *Conservative*, May 3, 1868.

12. *Kansas State Journal*, Lawrence, October 22, 1868.

13. *Independent*, Oskaloosa, November 23, 1866.

14. *Brown County Sentinel*, Hiawatha, March 25, 1869.

15. *Leavenworth Times*, April 24, 1873.

16. Tyack, *The One Best System*, p. 110.

17. *Times and Conservative*, Leavenworth, January 28, 1869.

18. *Colored Citizen*, Topeka, October 4, 1879.

19. *Herald of Kansas*, Topeka, May 14, 1880.

20. Rush Welter, *Popular Education and Democratic Thought in America* (New York, Columbia University Press, 1962), pp. 141–159.

21. *Kansas State Journal*, Topeka, February 16, 1882.

22. *American Citizen*, Topeka and Kansas City, June 28, 1889.

23. Ibid., July 19, 1889.

24. Parsons *Blade*, August 25, 1893.

25. Although the first state legislature had provided for the establishment of separate schools for black children, most communities preferred to leave the education of blacks to charity schools.

26. *Kansas State Journal*, Lawrence, December 19, 1861.

27. Lawrence *Republican*, January 2, 1862.

28. Olathe *Mirror*, January 16, 1862.

29. Leavenworth *Conservative*, May 7, 1862.

30. Wyandotte *Gazette*, June 6, 1863.

31. Zornow, *Kansas*, p. 123.

32. *Kansas Educational Journal*, Grasshopper Falls and Topeka, August, 1866.

33. Olathe *Mirror*, August 3, 1865.

34. Junction City *Union*, January 20, 1866.

35. *Osage Chronicle*, Burlingame, November 3, 1866.

36. Leavenworth *Conservative*, April 21, 1867.

37. *Times and Conservative*, Leavenworth, March 21, 1869.

38. Council Grove *Press*, September 22, 1865.

39. *Kansas Valley*, Wamego, December 9, 1869.

40. Leavenworth *Conservative*, June 7, 1868; *The Laws of Kansas . . . 1867* (Leavenworth, 1867), p. 207. After the first state legislature provided for separate schools

for blacks, subsequent legislatures limited the power to establish separate schools to first-class cities. In 1868, however, the legislature extended this power to second-class cities.—Richard Kluger, *Simple Justice* (New York, Alfred A. Knopf, 1976), p. 371.

41. *Kansas Educational Journal,* Emporia, September, 1870.

42. Atchison *Champion,* August 9, 1873.

43. *Commonwealth,* Topeka, January 30, 1874.

44. *Nationalist,* Manhattan, February 12, 1875.

45. *Kansas State Record,* Topeka, September 13, 1871.

46. Leavenworth *Commercial,* January 20, 1876.

47. Junction City *Union,* March 25, 1876.

48. *Kansas State Record,* Topeka, March 27, 1872.

49. Leavenworth *Times,* February 7, 1876.

50. *Colored Radical,* Leavenworth, September 28, 1876.

51. Ibid., August 24, 1876.

52. Ibid., November 18, 1876.

53. *Colored Citizen,* Topeka, September 20, 1878.

54. Ibid., December 14, 1878.

55. Henry Steele Commager, *The American Mind: An Interpretation of American Thought and Character Since the 1880's* (New Haven, Yale University Press, 1950), pp. 13–30; Robert T. Handy, *A Christian America: Protestant Hopes and Historical Realities* (New York, Oxford University Press, 1971), p. 70.

56. There were integrated schools in several communities throughout the 19th century. In cities such as Emporia and Ottawa, black and white students attended the same school without major difficulties. In some small towns there were integrated schools because the community simply could not afford a separate school. In these areas racial strife was common. The vast majority of blacks were, however, educated in separate facilities.

57. *Kansas State Record,* Topeka, January 5, 1870.

58. Leavenworth *Commercial,* February 1, 1870.

59. Ibid., March 5, 1870.

60. *Nationalist,* Manhattan, February 26, 1875. For letters expressing similar attitudes, see Olathe *Mirror,* June 6, 1872, *Nationalist,* Manhattan, March 5, 1875.

61. Cited in Topeka *Blade,* October 8, 1873.

62. *Kansas Democrat,* Independence, July 31, 1874.

63. Atchison *Patriot,* February 6, 1875.

64. *Kansas Chief,* Troy, March 9, 1876.

65. Fort Scott *Pioneer,* September 27, 1877.

66. Leavenworth *Commercial,* November 2, 1870.

67. Atchison *Patriot,* April 25, 1874.

68. Topeka *Blade,* December 7, 1876.

69. Cited in ibid., September 24, 1873.

70. *Saline County Journal,* Salina, January 25, 1877.

71. Kluger notes that the 1879 statute "remained unchanged until 1905, when Kansas City was allowed to open a separate high school for Negroes."—Kluger, *Simple Justice*, pp. 371–372.

72. Richmond, *Kansas*, pp. 162–163, 169–181; Zornow, *Kansas*, pp. 190–208.

73. Ralph Henry Gabriel, *The Course of American Democratic Thought*, 2d ed. (New York, Ronald Press, 1956), pp. 141–144; John A. Garraty, *The New Commonwealth, 1877–1890* (New York, Harper and Row, 1968), pp. 5–6; Rayford W. Logan, *The Negro in American Life and Thought: The Nadir, 1877–1901* (New York, Dial Press, 1954), passim; August Meier, *Negro Thought in America, 1880–1915* (Ann Arbor, University of Michigan Press, 1963), pp. 19–25; C. Vann Woodward, *The Strange Career of Jim Crow*, 3d ed. (New York, Oxford University Press, 1974), pp. 67–109.

74. Independence *Star*, October 19, 1883.

75. For typical editorials on the matter, see *Herald of Kansas*, Topeka, April 9, 1980; Leavenworth *Advocate*, May 4, 1889.

76. John Hope Franklin, *From Slavery to Freedom: A History of Negro Americans*, 3d ed. (New York, Alfred A. Knopf, 1967; Vintage Books, 1969), pp. 390–397; Meier, *Negro Thought in America*, pp. 55–56, 100–118.

77. *Afro-American Advocate*, Coffeyville, April 15, 1892.

78. *American Citizen*, Kansas City, May 15, 1891. See, also, ibid., August 7, 1891.

79. *Call*, Topeka, October 18, 1891. See, also, ibid., August 3, 1893.

80. Parsons *Blade*, March 15, 1895.

81. *American Citizen*, Kansas City, August 2, 1895.

82. Franklin, *Up from Slavery*, pp. 549–557; Richmond, *Kansas*, pp. 297–298.

83. Troen, *The Public and the Schools*, p. 98.

Non-Partisan and All-Partisan: Rethinking Woman Suffrage and Party Politics in Gilded Age Kansas

Michael Goldberg

War was officially declared between Populists and Republicans in Kansas on 21 January 1893. Attempting to win contested legislative seats, both sides marshalled armed forces and surrounded the state-house. Inside the building, fist fights broke out on the floor of the House, and the Republican speaker battered down the doors of the chamber with a sledge hammer to gain entrance. Although the combatants eventually fashioned a truce of sorts, charges continued to fly back and forth. Mainstream newspapers across the country gave the "Legislative War" full play while depicting it as the natural outcome of Populist-inspired anarchy.[1]

Although the "war" had been mostly sound and fury, with no shots fired and no serious injuries, it signified the bitter passions loosed since the Populists' sudden victory over the Republicans in 1890. Across the South and West, Populist candidates had been waging electoral battles under the banner of a broad array of political and economic reforms. In Kansas, Republican Party leaders, unused to any serious challenge, had responded to the new party with a steady barrage of vitriol, character assassination, and outright fraud. The Populists, though generally more truthful, were no less impassioned. The Legislative War, though extreme, was in keeping with the tenor of relations between the two parties. With the cessation of armed threats, both sides renewed their oratorical and editorial attacks, and prepared for a showdown in 1894.[2]

How strange, then, that a Kansas Republican and a Populist not only shared the stage at a national convention later that year, but also praised each other warmly. The Populist was the associate editor of the state's leading reform paper; the Republican headed the state chapter of a national party organization. To their audience they pledged mutual harmony and respect. The scene is only strange, however, if we stay within the standard interpretation of Populism and party politics in the late nineteenth century. The prominent Populist and Republican were Annie Diggs and Laura Johns, two women who had played important roles in Kansas politics for the previous ten years. They were addressing the annual meeting of the National and American Woman Suffrage Association, hoping to drum up support for a state woman suffrage campaign in 1894.[3] Yet, while they pledged mutual cooperation, they would return to Kansas committed both to woman suffrage and partisan politics.

Diggs's and Johns's divided loyalties to women and to partisan politics were not unusual—many women activists who comprised the Kansas Woman Movement held these beliefs. Led by the Women's Christian Temperance Union (WCTU) and the Kansas Equal Suffrage Association (KESA), this loose affiliation of women's groups had developed a distinctive political language, ideology, and set of tactics. This alternative culture allowed women to develop political skills and discuss new ideas away from the intimidating or condescending attitudes of most men. It also provided women with a sense of solidarity against those who ridiculed the notion of women's participation in politics.[4] But many women also held political beliefs that could not adequately be expressed within the non-partisan Woman Movement organizations. Significant involvement in a political party required fierce loyalty to the policies and leadership of that party. Most women activists in Kansas believed they could balance their commitment to both party and gender politics. The campaign would prove just how tenuous that balance could be. . . .

This essay focuses on the peculiarities of Kansas, a peculiar state indeed. Instead of augmenting the debate about why western states embraced woman suffrage before other regions, this essay will argue that state borders matter—that the combination of the particular cultures that developed within Kansas and the individuals who enacted the state's history was unique in the West, and in the nation. Colorado, Kansas's neighbor to the west, passed woman suffrage in 1893, while Nebraska, to the north, did not accept it until the nineteenth amendment was passed. Kansas voters, for their part, failed twice to give women the vote before granting it in 1912. Each state provided a different context, and the suffragists who fought to win the franchise made particular decisions that shaped the outcome of their struggle.[5]

Kansas Woman Movement activists adopted partisan or non-partisan strategies to meet the needs of particular situations. For while a distinct women's political culture did exist in Kansas, it was not a static entity. Woman Movement activists' conception of their political culture was in many ways an idealized vision. Much like the nineteenth-century notion of domesticity, the Woman Movement's vision of their political culture was a framework within which participants fought over, appropriated, and interpreted the meaning of gender relations and politics.

Kansas had long been an arena for gender politics and middle-class reform, leading the *New York Times* in 1887 to dub it "the great experimental ground of the nation."[6] A series of firsts punctuated the state's history—the first coed university, the first state woman suffrage campaign, the first constitutional prohibition amendment, and the first municipal woman suffrage law. Although woman suffrage activists had failed to win the vote during Kansas's constitutional convention, they had gained concessions on school board suffrage and property rights, making Kansas an acknowledged leader in these areas. The Grange, a farmers' protest movement that strongly supported woman suffrage, flourished in Kansas during the 1870s. After a second agrarian revolt fifteen years later, Kansas became the first state to create a "People's Party," and its representatives were the leading force in the creation of a national Populist Party.[7] Kansas thus provides a rich context in which to explore suffragists' strategies, tactics, and beliefs in their quest to attain the franchise.

Despite the state's reputation as a hotbed for radicalism, Kansas initially lagged behind others in forming a suffrage society and WCTU. For while the 1867 woman suffrage campaign had been the first to be waged in the nation, it had also been the first to be defeated, and roundly defeated at that. Beyond the blow to suffragists' morale, the campaign alienated many Republican Party leaders from the suffrage cause. National suffrage leaders Susan B. Anthony and Elizabeth Cady Stanton, upset with the GOP's failure to support the cause in Kansas, allied themselves with George Train, a virulently racist and—more importantly for Kansas politics—rabidly anti-Republican Democrat. Not surprisingly, the Republicans were outraged at Stanton and Anthony's repudiation of the Grand Old Party. Since the GOP had dominated Kansas since statehood, and the Democrats openly opposed woman suffrage, such a legacy did the cause little good.[8] The campaign became suffragists' first lesson in the perils of arousing the wrath of the Republican Party.

Kansas in the 1870s provided an inhospitable environment in which to revive a suffrage movement. Drought, depression, and grasshopper invasions dominated the decade, interspersed with numerous other economic and environmental disasters. These conditions, along with the legislature's failure to respond to the crises, motivated the Grange and other reform groups to oust the Republicans—temporarily—from power. The 1880s, however, brought an economic boom that rolled into Kansas with a mass of hopeful immigrants close behind. Town populations doubled, then tripled, then doubled again, accompanied by endless talk of expansion and progress, the usual symptoms of boom fever. The population explosion gave many towns a large enough middle-class to provide the necessary raw material for suffrage and temperance societies. The concomitant social upheaval led many middle-class women to assert their claim to providing a "civilizing" influence. Further, many men saw such efforts as necessary to establishing a sober and stable business environment for the town. Unhindered by the political battles caused by the depression, the Republican leadership was now willing to deal with questions of social reform, and to use these issues to their advantage if at all possible.[9]

During the 1880s, Kansas Woman Movement activists established the political tactics, language, and ideology they would use until the early 1900s. They developed their political culture within the shared experiences of Anglo urban middle-class women, defined in large part by the ideal of domesticity.[10] Urban middle-class Kansans, like their counterparts in the East, held that women were morally superior to men, and that woman's proper sphere was the home, her noblest vocation, motherhood. Woman Movement activists transformed these assumptions into a justification—in fact a moral imperative—for women to enter politics. If a woman was morally superior, then she could purify the political mess Gilded Age American men had created. If a woman was to raise moral sons to become good citizens, then she must not do so simply to have them set adrift in a wicked world. She must bring the virtues of the home to the public sphere—"to make the world HOME-LIKE," in national WCTU president Frances Willard's memorable phrase—a mission that fitted perfectly the evangelical Christianity of many of the Woman Movement's members.

Middle-class women, confronted with a proscribed sphere limited to domesticity and religion, turned these restrictions to their advantage. By creating "free social spaces" within the church and the tea parlor, they could organize a range of clubs and societies free from the domineering presence of men and learn the basic skills required for active political participation. Urban Christian men, for their part, had abandoned church-going, though not their religious-cultural identity. Thus, while mainstream men's politics appropriated business metaphors during the Gilded Age, Woman Movement activists embraced the language of evangelical Christianity and the Golden Rule.[11]

In the eyes of Kansas Woman Movement activists, men as a class were morally adrift, unable to tell right from wrong. Men, explained Laura Johns to the 1890 KESA convention, had a very different perspective than women. Men tolerated corrupt government because of

> the[ir] absorption . . . in business and professions, making them apathetic to other matters; . . . the fact that there's money for the corruptionists who form the ring, and none for the honest advocates of good government. What a pity that work for a principle hasn't money in it! If there were "boodle" on the side of fair play, decency and good order, would not these have more support?

By contrast, argued Johns, women

> had a higher standard of administrative efficiency . . . sincerity [and] character in candidates [because they had an] enthusiasm and . . . spirit of helpfulness, a thoughtfulness and knowledge . . . born of faith in the right and ultimate triumph.[12]

For Woman Movement activists, this conception of Woman as a naturally moral creature had several useful corollaries. First, all "respectable" women agreed about morally-based "women's issues," such as prohibition and the age of consent. The Woman Movement, in supporting these causes, was thus representing all "true women." Those who actively rejected these beliefs were "fallen" women, who had been toppled from their state of grace by a man's deeds.[13] Following this logic, Woman Movement activists could enable fallen women to regain their rightful, exalted position in society by driving male-created sin from the land.

This "politics of domesticity" drew on the culturally sanctioned assumptions about gender roles, enabling Woman Movement activists to attract middle-class women and men to their "respectable" cause. But this ideology also excluded those who did not or could not live up to the Woman Movement's definition of respectability, whether in terms of values, dress, manners, or language. Since the great majority of Kansas legislators were middle- and upper-class Anglos, the Woman Movement's exclusionism guaranteed that their credentials as members of the ruling class were in order.[14]

While the Woman Movement's elitism helped organize middle-class women and influence legislators, it proved less successful in garnering popular support among the Kansas electorate. For while most Kansans were Anglo-Americans, urban middle-class Anglos were not in the majority—Anglo farm people were. Although Anglo farm and town people shared an ethnic identity, their ways of life were different. The distance between farm women and Woman Movement activists was both cultural and geographical. Farm women lacked the "town ways"—including manners, language, and clothes—that would allow them to feel comfortable amidst KESA or WCTU meetings. Further, most farm women would have to travel significant distances to reach town for the meetings, taking up time that might be spent on the multitude of tasks they performed.

While Woman Movement activists were aware that farm women represented an untapped resource, few did anything to close the cultural chasm between farm and town. Indeed, farm people—men as well as women—had shown a far greater support for both woman suffrage and prohibition in Kansas than did townspeople.[15] Yet even after the establishment of the Farmers' Alliance and Populist Party, with its large contingent of politically active and organized women, the Woman Movement's activities remained outside the experience of most farm women.

The Woman Movement's policies worked well during the 1880s, largely because they focused most of their efforts on municipal politics and the state legislature. Women had played an important, though not dominant role in organizing popular support for the prohibition amendment, which was ratified by voters in 1879. However, the WCTU soon eclipsed the male-dominated Kansas State Temperance Union as the primary force behind the struggle for prohibition enforcement and against liquor-related graft, that inevitable side-effect of prohibition. With women leading the charge to prosecute liquor peddlers, the WCTU gained a central role in municipal and state politics by the mid-1880s. After the KESA was formed in 1884, the WCTU joined with suffrage activists to petition the Kansas legislature for municipal franchise, claiming that women needed the vote to ensure proper enforcement—and thus "the protection of our homes."[16]

Republican legislators waited several years until the political moment was right, and then passed the municipal woman suffrage bill in 1887, in response to ever-increasing pressure from suffrage lobbyists.[17] The Republican leadership, sensing a useful campaign issue against the "wet"—and hence "lawless"—Democrats, had grown supportive of prohibition. Republican politicians, who voted overwhelmingly for municipal woman suffrage, were convinced that the measure would increase their party's already powerful hold on local politics. At the same time, the measure did not grant too much power to women or endanger the status quo of state politics. For Republican leaders, municipal woman suffrage seemed a convenient arrangement. For suffrage activists, their legislative victory appeared to be a powerful lesson in the possibilities of Republican support.[18]

Republicans reasoned that Democratic-affiliated women would be less likely to vote, while those women who did vote would feel indebted to the GOP. A number of local Republican officials, however, were outraged to discover that Woman Movement activists intended to stand by their non-partisan approach to politics. For these women, the central issues were prohibition enforcement and "good government." Because the GOP dominated local offices—and because liquor-related graft had become a common feature of municipal governance—more than a few Republican politicians became the target of women reformers.

Woman Movement activists chose to concentrate on prohibition and eschew party affiliation in municipal elections in part because the liquor and graft threat was real, immediate, and an affront to their sense of morality. But it also made good political sense. Women saw that they could make an impact by organizing non-partisan slates. Women activists' dedication to local non-partisanship represented a political decision made within a specific context.

Following passage of the municipal suffrage bill, many Kansans believed that full suffrage was inevitable, a matter of a few years and a couple more petition drives. But 1887 was also the last year of the wave of economic prosperity that had fueled optimism for the future. Municipal suffrage passed on the crest of the boom; when the economy crashed the following year, talk of state suffrage was buried.[19] For most male politicians, the issue of woman suffrage was a luxury too politically risky in which to indulge during hard times.

But if the economic collapse forced woman suffrage off the mainstream political agenda, it also caused a reaction that would eventually help propel the issue to prominence. For in 1890, everything changed—politics in Kansas went topsy-turvy. In response to the economic disaster and the inequalities it exposed, the Farmers' Alliance and other reform groups organized the Populist Party to challenge Republican power. In a campaign that has aptly been compared to a prairie fire, the Populists swept to power in the state's legislature. Although the Populists failed to win the governor's office, the new party did elect five of seven congressmen, as well as a U.S. Senator.[20]

The Populist uprising of 1890 seemed momentarily to transcend the constraints of Gilded Age politics. People who had felt beaten by the environment and the economic system suddenly found a reason to believe. Thus inspired, they began to educate themselves about political issues, and to demand a part in the political process. In the oft-quoted words of Elizabeth Barr, the 1890 campaign was "a religious revival, a crusade, a pentecost of politics. . . . The meetings grew bigger and bigger, till no buildings could be found to house the crowd which drove for miles and miles to hear the speakers who were fast gaining national fame. All day picnics were held and people by the thousands came . . . to hear the tiding of great joy."[21] In that first summer of political innocence and passion, all that seemed necessary to regain the democratic ideal of the mythologized past was to listen, to learn, to speak, to act—and to vote. The political millennium appeared to be at hand.

But if passion and faith fueled the movement to victory, it could also speed it to defeat. Faith, after all, could be a fragile thing. Populists put supreme faith in the abilities of the people's representatives to reform the system once in office. But the system proved more resistant to change than the insurgents had imagined. Further, many of the Populist politicians and party functionaries, once in office, developed the occupational disease of self-preservation.

Some Populist leaders, choosing practical politics over principle, attempted to "fuse" their efforts with the by-then desperate Democrats. In 1892, Democrats ran almost no candidates, instead supporting Populists with the implicit understanding that the Democrats would share the patronage of the new administration. This arrangement generated resentment among rank-and-filers, particularly ex-Republicans, whose new loyalty to Populism had not lessened their hatred of Democrats. Further, the patronage arrangement led to numerous graft scandals in Populist Governor Lewelling's administration. By 1894, Populism was beginning to look disturbingly like political business as usual, even as the state sank into economic depression. As a result, many of the crusaders grew restless, then disturbed, and finally disillusioned with their crusade.[22] This shattered faith would take its toll on both Populism and the woman suffrage amendment. . . .

In early 1893, Populists and Republicans stopped their wrangling long enough to pass a bill authorizing an election for a state woman suffrage constitutional amendment. Republican support for the bill was largely the product of a coup by the reform wing of the party. These "Young Republicans," who had wrested control of the state machine from party regulars, believed the party needed to respond to the apparent popular appeal of reform issues. As a sign of their intent, the Republicans placed a pro-woman suffrage amendment in their platform. Since most Populist legislators had already expressed support for woman suffrage, the bill became one of the few reform efforts of either party to survive the War.[23]

The Alliance's political culture was based on the farm family, and all members of the family were encouraged to take part. The urban middle-class had created numerous separate gender institutions, thus establishing the foundation for distinctive women's and men's political cultures. Kansas farm people, especially those in isolated homesteads on the Plains, tended toward heterosocial events and institutions. This included church-going, which was still a family occasion in the Kansas countryside. Thus, the sites for Alliance meetings—the schoolhouse, church, and picnic grove—were mixed-gender spaces where women and men had met together in the past. And because both women and men attended church together, both were drawn to the Alliance's evangelistic oratory. Unlike most urban women and men, rural women and men spoke the same political language.[24]

While the Farmers' Alliance was a cross-gender political culture, it was not a completely egalitarian one. The farm family, like its counterparts in the city, was still a patriarchal institution where men expected to have the final word. Much that went on in the alliance between women and men was a negotiation between societal expectations and immediate realities. With the establishment of the Populist Party, these negotiations immediately tipped heavily against women, as Populist writers turned away from the non-voting members of the family and focused almost exclusively on men.[25]

The creation of the Populist Party made clear to Alliance women that despite the rhetoric of equality within the Alliance, they would remain in a supporting role with the vote. Yet even as farm women's involvement in the Alliance and Populist Party sharpened their appreciation for the power of the ballot, their immediate commitment remained with the broader struggle for economic and social change.

Had Woman Movement activists reached out to these farm women at this time, they might have been able to establish "Country Suffrage Clubs," a project Johns had spoken of but never implemented. Instead, men's support for woman suffrage in the Alliance and the Populist Party remained widespread, but nebulous and informal. Ironically, a number of Populist Woman Movement activists gained both notoriety and influence in Kansas politics, but almost all of these lived "in town." These women, the best known of whom were Annie Diggs and Mary ("Raise less corn and more Hell") Lease, published the *Farmer's Wife,* a newspaper which had little to do with farm women, but which bridged the concerns of the Populist Party and the Woman Movement.[26]

Although the urban women Populists were great favorites at Alliance and Populist rallies, they never used their unique position to organize suffrage clubs among farm people. Indeed, the *Farmer's Wife* urged suffragists to "give your attention almost wholly to the city people. The country is all right," assured the writer, "and when we say that we make no idle boast. The *Farmer's Wife* is in close communication with these sisters and knows how their men will vote." Despite these claims, almost no Kansas farm women appeared as correspondents in the pages of the *Farmer's Wife.* Instead of connecting with Alliance women, urban Populist women used the ascendancy of Populism to gain influence in the

KESA, and some, like Annie Diggs, maintained positions of power in both organizations. In 1893, Diggs was both vice president of the KESA and associate editor of the state Populist paper.

Republican women in the KESA were initially hostile to the influx of Populists into the suffrage movement, but Laura Johns, president of the KESA, was able to placate the different factions. At the same time, Johns channeled Republican women's partisan energies into the Kansas Republican Women's Association (RWA). Populist women, however, enjoyed far more prominence and respect from their party's leadership than the RWA received from the Republicans. In 1892, Kansas Populist women formed the Women's Progressive Political League, using the *Farmer's Wife* as its official newspaper. Because the membership contained a number of well-connected Populist women, it received much attention and a certain amount of influence within the party. The political turmoil amongst the parties thus served as a catalyst for a growing Woman Movement. By 1893, with the state suffrage amendment as an organizing tool, the number of women's organizations supporting suffrage was at an all-time high.[27]

In September 1893, the woman suffrage forces assembled in Kansas City to recount past successes and to plan their strategy for the coming campaign. The "Great Suffrage Convention" was a remarkable event, with more than twice the number of participants than any previous year. It was a boisterous celebration, replete with colorful streamers, exuberant speakers, and joyous song. Delegate after delegate from a wide variety of organizations—from the State Teachers Association to the Social Science Association, from the Women's Relief Corps to the Adult Sorority PEO—marched to the podium and read their resolutions. All proclaimed support for the amendment, and most reported on the growing activity by suffragists throughout the state. The Woman Movement appeared ready for its own "pentecost of politics."[28]

The convention passed a number of resolutions declaring that the amendment campaign would be non-partisan and ecumenical and that the KESA would "confine the work for the amendment strictly to argument and propaganda for the enfranchisement of women." The delegates also acknowledged that women could work for their respective parties while not "under the auspices of the amendment campaign committee." As Laura Johns described the committee, "it is non partisan in its work, although ALL PARTISAN in its make up. . . . Not for one instant will these women be disloyal to their respective political or religious affiliations." Another resolution called on the various state and local party conventions to endorse the amendment. All the resolutions apparently passed with little debate and much enthusiasm.[29] No one mentioned that being simultaneously non-partisan and all-partisan might be trickier than it appeared.

Throughout the winter and into the spring, suffrage activists worked hard to translate the energy and enthusiasm of the convention into an ever-expanding network of grass roots support. Several papers committed solely to woman suffrage were started, and joined the already established *Farmer's Wife* and the WCTU's *Our Messenger* in spreading the "good word" of suffrage.[30] The spirit of unity, forged at Kansas City, appeared to be withstanding the test of time. A *Farmer's Wife* editorial summed up the mood of suffrage activists when it proclaimed, "the Democrats will howl resubmissions [of prohibition] and oppose the suffrage amendment. The Republicans will stake their issue on the late legislative unpleasantness and the downfall of the state under Populist rule. The Populists will hold to the issue of land, money, and transportation. They will all be drowned . . . by the vast army of women."[31] With this inexorable tide of support, how would anything but complete victory be possible, whether men willed it or not?

But within this inspiring image of a politically transcendent woman's crusade lay potential disaster. The editor of the *Farmer's Wife* may have dismissed men's partisanship with a rhetorical flourish, but Populist women could less easily ignore their own partisan interests. What if their two causes—Populism and woman suffrage—came into conflict? And beyond the internal fractures that might occur, how in fact was this "women's army" going to overwhelm the mainstream parties when the ground troops lacked the most important weapon in an electoral battle—the vote. The franchise would usher in a woman's political millennium, its supporters argued, but this could only be achieved if men bestowed the vote on women. What then would overwhelm men to such a degree as to ignore partisan concerns? The suffrage activists had what to them was an irrefutable answer—the unassailable power of moral force. In the words of one KESA member, "Our cause represents what is right. It represents moral progress, the forward movement of civilization. It cannot be denied."[32] Like the Populists, suffragists had a nearly religious faith and evangelical zeal in the possibilities of their movement.

Suffrage activists were soon confronting numerous obstacles on that very bumpy road of moral progress. The first signs of trouble occurred in May 1894, just before the parties held their nominating conventions. As suffrage leaders began organizing their lobbying efforts, some women activists made it clear that they wanted no part of men's political culture. In the suffrage paper *Woman's Friend,* a local KESA officer named E. A. Templins launched a scathing attack against the plan to influence the party platforms. Referring to the Kansas City resolutions, Templins charged, "The whole scheme of going to the parties was hatched under a political trickster, and the claim that it is non-partisan is as false as the trick is gauzy." Claiming that all the political parties were run by "bosses," she encouraged women to boycott the upcoming conventions. Templins's view was supported by a number of other important suffrage activists, including one who wrote, "if we owe our success to any party we are *honor bound* to support that party, no matter how obnoxious its leaders . . . may be to us." The Yates County ESA passed a resolution rejecting all party platform endorsements, stating, "We all know that when partisan blood stirs in men's veins, their instincts of justice and fairness are often swept aside by the passion of the hour."[33]

Laura Johns, the obvious focus of Templins's attack, took exception to both the tone and the content of the criticism. In her response, Johns urged a more temperate approach, while generally ignoring the moral thrust of Templins's argument. Instead, she reiterated that no particular party dominated the KESA, and that by necessity suffrage activists were forced to do "whatever must be done." In fact, she carried this utilitarian argument to the extreme, noting that "the platform will induce the men to vote for suffrage who will do anything his party tells him," thus substantiating the claims of the radical non-partisans.[34] It is telling that Johns, a product of the Woman Movement, chose to delegitimize the basic assumptions of the movement. Rather than admit the difficulty of being both "non-partisan and all-partisan," she stressed the need to gain victory on men's terms. While Johns's position displayed political savvy in addressing those who held power, she also demonstrated considerable naivete in not considering the possible dangers to her own organization.

Several weeks later, Johns got a hint of the consequences of her position when the Kansas Republican Women's Association attempted to gain their party's support for a suffrage amendment plank in the platform. Party bosses, who had regained control of the state committee from the "Young Republicans," were the undisputed masters of the convention. They made clear that the convention would address just one "legitimate" issue: the "redeeming" of Kansas from the "anarchistic" Populists. Yet Republican women activists were optimistic: they had many long-time allies in the powerful editors of the leading Republican dailies, and they had secured the services of a number of nationally-known suffragists.[35]

Their first conflict, however, came not from the party bosses—at least not directly—but from within their own ranks at the RWA's pre-convention meeting. The RWA's Resolutions Committee, chaired by Minnie D. Morgan, had prepared a resolution to present to the Republican convention. Tiptoeing gingerly around the issue of woman suffrage, the resolution read, "While disclaiming any desire to make it a test of party fealty, we recognize the justice of the pending suffrage amendment and ask in every Republican its just and earnest consideration."[36] It was the perfect statement for a party wishing to avoid any hint of controversy or disunity among the delegates.

However this strategy might have gone over with the Republican leadership, it did not sit well with the more prominent women suffragists at the RWA meeting. The resolution, which some claimed was written by Morgan's husband, a well-connected Republican, caused an immediate and emotional reaction. Laura Johns insisted, "It is unthinkable for women to adhere to the Republican party and not demand suffrage. I doubt if I can ever lift my head again if this resolution is adopted." Susan B. Anthony, as usual, was even more forceful, and declared that the resolution was "an insult to the women who came to Kansas in the interest of suffrage. . . . If you adopt such a resolution my work is ended in this state." J. Ellen Foster, president of the national RWA, argued for a resolution with some type of request for suffrage but then pointedly noted, "I care more for [R]epublican principles than woman suffrage." In the end, Anthony's reputation and Johns's influence won out, and the RWA's Resolutions Committee retreated to hammer out a rather tortuous resolution. Anthony was little more pleased with this second attempt; she labeled the new resolution "the veriest spaniel-like position imaginable," and accused Foster of being "the hired emissary of Republican politicians who have determined to silence the women on this question," an accusation probably close to the truth.[37]

Anthony carried her gloomy assessment of Republican policy to the GOP convention. In a short speech uncomplicated by political tact, she warned the delegates, "If you leave [the amendment] out you are dead." Johns was more willing to address the concerns of the delegates, but was no less unrelenting in her demands than Anthony. After presenting a petition with "yards and yards" of signatures supporting the amendment, she asked for and received unlimited time for the women to present their case. She concluded by referring to the potential importance of the Republican women's partisan efforts, declaring, "Refuse to recognize us, treat our petitions with contempt, then tell us that you can expect us to rally to the party's support." Whether pitched hard or soft, however, none of the women's demands had any effect on the Republican delegates. Their unanimity was complete, and they rejected the woman suffrage resolution without debate and without dissent. The pro-suffrage editors did show some remorse at having to sacrifice the women's cause, but offered only paternalistic platitudes about patience and priorities. As for the Republican suffrage activists, "their amazement and grief was beyond expression."[38]

However traumatic their defeat, Republican women activists did nothing to reassess their strategy following the GOP convention. Instead, they pushed on to the Populist convention, in order to support the Populist women's bid for a pro-amendment plank. Conditions for Populist suffragists were much more favorable than those experienced by their Republican "sisters." Across the state, those Populists opposed to fusion with the Democrats—the "anti-fusionists"—had been reasserting control of the county conventions. Many of these local conventions had passed resolutions supporting woman suffrage while condemning cooperation with the Democrats. However, Populist Party Chairman John Briedenthal and Governor Lewelling still hoped to accomplish fusion by taking command of the state convention. In order to steer the Populists clear of any resolutions likely to anger the Democrats, Briedenthal stacked the resolutions committee with anti-suffragists and pro-fusionists. Populist woman suffrage activists, most of whom were anti-fusionists, and anti-fusionist men, many of whom supported woman suffrage, were aware of these maneuvers, and came prepared for a fight.[39]

Besides having active and influential male allies, Populist suffrage activists had another advantage over their Republican counterparts. Republican leaders spoke a business-oriented political language—when they talked of "Redeeming Kansas," they were referring to the state's business credit and reputation, not its moral redemption. The Populists, however, used a moral, religious-political language; pleas for "doing what was right" held particular force. It was, in fact, a language much like that of the Woman Movement.[40]

Populist pro-suffragists put this language to good use during the convention debate, painting the opposition as political opportunists willing to abandon their principles to gain office. If the delegates who spoke are to be taken at their word, it would appear that over 80 percent of them favored suffrage, as one paper reported. Being in favor of suffrage did not necessarily mean supporting the resolution, however, because many delegates voiced the opinion that Populist support of suffrage would mean sure defeat for the party in November. Susan B. Anthony, in an attempt to counter this argument, electrified the crowd by promising that she would campaign for the Populists if they supported a suffrage plank. Other pro-suffrage speakers attacked the "cowardly expediency" of their opponents, and countered with moral arguments, usually referring to the Populist motto of "Equal rights for all, special privileges for none." Judge Frank Doster, a Christian Socialist and long-time suffrage supporter, proclaimed "I do not want a platform . . . made for the express purpose of catching votes. I want a platform with God Almighty in it."[41]

Delegates responded enthusiastically to such appeals for moral purity but many delegates were no doubt still concerned with the practical political ramifications of the plank. The fate of the resolution was ultimately in the able hands of Annie Diggs who had been chosen to present the pro-suffragists' closing argument. Of all the members of the Kansas Woman Movement Diggs was perhaps most comfortable with the mainstream political culture. Her short speech revealed her knowledge of the people she addressed. Adroitly combining expediency with moral arguments she demanded of the delegates:

> Don't you want to have the leverage of having the gratitude of the women of the state? If you take a noble, manly, and courageous stand, as I am sure you will, then every cowardly republican candidate will be forced to go upon the rostrum and plead the record of his party in its defense. My friends, the thing for you now to do, from a people's party perspective, is to have the courage of your convictions.[42]

Diggs was essentially telling the Populist delegates, "you can have it all—morality, manliness, and victory." Whatever the truth of this claim, it struck a responsive chord in her audience. Her speech was followed by several minutes of applause and cheering. When Diggs's opponent failed miserably in his response, the audience exploded in a spontaneous, cacophonous demonstration, and the resolution passed, 333–269. . . .[43]

Thus, while the Populist convention seemed to be an exuberant kickoff for the amendment campaign, it also brought suffragists' basic disagreements about partisanship into the open. Here the Populists had the advantage, for they could support both party principles and the amendment. Some Populists even suggested that women who worked against the Populist Party were helping defeat the suffrage amendment. Just one week after the convention, a Populist woman wrote that Republican suffragists, "being under the despotic rule of their lords and masters, may strive to undermine the foundation of the stately structure the *real* women of Kansas are now erecting. . . . Their puny efforts to destroy will only create discord in their own hearts and homes."[44]

In October, the *Farmer's Wife* declared that the "campaign made by the KESA is of small importance compared with that of the People's Party for the suffrage amendment." Several times during the campaign, Populists accused Johns of favoring Republican speakers over Populists. During the winter lull in party politics, the *Farmer's Wife* could wholeheartedly declare for a non-partisan "army of women." With the inception of the summer campaigns, however, the two parties were now engaged in the struggle to control the state's political future. Both Republican and Populist women found themselves caught up in the heat of the battle, often staring at each other from opposite sides of the line.[45]

Such divisions, however, were not completely of men's makings. Partisan women suffragists were no doubt aware that if the suffrage amendment became law, several hundred thousand women voters would be looking to affiliate with an organization. Populist women hoped to win over new members by positioning their party as the deliverers of woman suffrage. As the *Farmer's Wife* pointedly noted, "You may talk about equal suffrage being a non-partisan movement, but if the amendment carries, which it is almost sure to do, some party will take credit for the victory. This is as sure as the sun rises and sets."[46] Thus within the "vast army of women" were several camps hoping to take charge of the battle. By declaring themselves the "real" women of Kansas, Populist suffragists hoped to become the obvious choice to lead the women's crusade in post-amendment Kansas. If such a maneuver were successful, they would also gain enormous influence in state and party politics. Yet for such a scenario to occur, the amendment would have to pass; for the amendment to pass, woman suffragists would have to present a united front. Thus, the *Farmer's Wife* constantly tempered their partisan thrusts by declaring their allegiance to a unified political sisterhood.

Just as Populist women had conflicting agendas, so too did national figures like Susan B. Anthony. Anthony sincerely hoped Kansas would pass the amendment, yet she also remained committed to a long-term, national focus. Further, she was not one to forget old scores. Following the conventions, Anthony proceeded to fulfill her pledge to the Populists with a vengeance. No doubt still stung by the rebuffs to her cause and her reputation—and perhaps not unmindful of the Republicans' actions in 1867—Anthony lashed out at the GOP all along the campaign trail. Referring to the Republicans' convention, she declared, "I have read your platform thoroughly and can find nothing in it but irrigation. You seem to offer no redemption of Kansas except water, and I hope there will be enough of that to wash your dirty selves clean." But while the Populist crowds greatly enjoyed Anthony's anti-Republican potshots, Republican women were horrified that the leading national suffrage activist was attacking their party. As in 1867, however, Anthony had no regrets about her actions.[47]

Given the animosity that marked Kansas politics at the time, it is remarkable that despite the sporadic bickering among suffrage activists, they were able to manage such a well-organized campaign. Besides the myriad parlor meetings, assemblies, speaking contests, and rallies throughout the state, Laura Johns organized an exhaustive speaking tour, utilizing local speakers as well as teams of "notables"; whenever possible, she combined representatives of different factions on the same platform. The speakers usually maintained the delicate balancing act between gender and party loyalties during these tours, but it was no easy task. As Populist journalist Frances Butler related to her readers in one of her columns, while Mrs. Denton, the first district president of the KESA, proved to be an agreeable traveling companion, "I cannot help but feel that each of us had some real practical experience in human toleration as our . . . opinions were so widely at variance. Mrs. Denton being as radical a [R]epublican as I am a [P]opulist (and you all know what that means), while each tried to convert the other we parted unchanged as to our political views yet good friends."[48]

Butler's account makes it clear that suffragists' adherence to particular economic and political policies was just as central to their ideological makeup as were their opinions on woman suffrage. Many Woman Movement activists, especially Populists, were as involved with their party's activities as they were with their suffrage tasks. That such passionate partisans could maintain civility—even friendship—toward one another attested to the strength of the Woman Movement's vision of a political sisterhood. Their relationship was particularly notable given the partisan war raging throughout the state, and the probable lack of any such relationships between male Populist and Republican politicians.

By 1894, Republican politicians and editors had pulled out all the stops in their effort to redeem Kansas, committing nearly every kind of fraud and dirty trick. These tactics included inventing damaging "interviews" with prominent Populists, paying Populists to declare publicly for the Republicans and/or denounce the Populists, and secretly financing an "anti-fusionist" reform ticket to challenge the Populists. To some extent, the suffrage amendment was a victim of the poisoned political atmosphere. Many Republican editors declared they would vote against it because it had become "a Populist measure." The Register (Great Bend) intoned darkly, "when a lot of old women get together and resolve to make the question a political one and swear . . . that they will work for the election of a certain political party that saw fit to endorse suffrage, then we quit trying to solve the matter. . . . Since they foolishly sold the suffragists to the pops we desire to not be considered in that deal."[49]

Clearly, Anthony's barbs found their targets. But the editor's comments also display antagonisms toward suffrage activists beyond the partisan issues. As in 1867, Anthony's attacks on the GOP had given those Republicans already ambivalent or hostile to woman suffrage the excuse—in fact the imperative—to attack it.

During the campaign, most Republican editors, including some of the staunchest supporters of woman suffrage, enforced a ban on anything concerning the amendment. Given the Republicans' ruthless slash-and-burn campaign strategy, this is not surprising. More startling is that Populist newspapers soon became little more attentive toward the issue than their Republican counterparts. The only suffrage pieces that appeared in Populist papers were submitted by women; relegated to "Women's Columns," they were kept discreetly away from the din and roar of the "real" war. As the *Liberator* (Norton) explained, "Probably we editors will be too much engaged in the work of the campaign to pay attention to Woman's Rights the subject deserves, the attention of the Populist editors being directed to the maintenance of what few rights we now have."[50] Thus, with all the deep divisions between Populist and Republican editors, they had at last found common ground: the shared assumption that the cause of woman suffrage must be sacrificed to the demands of partisan politics.

For most Republican politicians, such a conclusion was in keeping with their basic political ideology. The GOP leadership believed that without economic progress, moral progress was impossible. Thus, before issues such as woman suffrage could be considered, the Populists had to be defeated and the state returned to sound business principles. The Populist leadership, however, had a much more difficult ideological tightrope to maneuver than their Republican counterparts. As the *Liberator*'s editorial suggested, Populist newspapers had a duty to support the suffrage cause, both because it was part of the platform and because the Populists were supposedly a party that eschewed the amoralist politics of the GOP. Further, Populist leaders had long acknowledged their debt to farm women in the Alliance for playing such an important part in the formation of the movement.

Yet, as the *Liberator* explained, the Populist Party was principally concerned with issues of economic justice. Slighting social issues—even ones that a majority of the membership supported—was nothing new for Populists. In 1890, the party had resisted Republican efforts to bait them with the prohibition issue, despite farm people's overwhelming support for the cause. Similarly, the national Populist Party convention, with its large Kansas contingent, had suppressed an effort to place woman suffrage in its platform. By 1894, in fact, many Populist leaders had become committed to "practical politics," arguing that it was more important to capture the statehouse than to maintain the ideological high ground. Further, the Populist Party—unlike the Alliance—was concerned primarily with the (male) voter. Populist editors probably reasoned that woman suffrage was not the issue that would bring swing voters into the Populist camp. They thus stuck to the issues of "land, money, and transportation," leaving woman suffrage to such speakers as Annie Diggs.

Despite the many obstacles suffrage activists faced during the campaign, their optimism seemed to strengthen as 6 November—Election Day—approached. With no opinion polls available, the women could only rely on the impressions they received while organizing and campaigning. All the suffrage newspapers seemed confident of victory, and looked forward to celebrating at what was expected to be the second Great Suffrage Convention in December. On 7 November, suffrage activists learned that the amendment had been overwhelmingly defeated, 130,000 to 95,000. These women would have had to search their newspapers to find this information among the masses of stories concerning the party elections—few papers even recorded the results.[51]

The Populists joined the suffrage amendment in defeat—although not as overwhelmingly—and lost control of every state office, as well as the Senate and the Assembly. Some historians have claimed that Populist support of suffrage contributed heavily to their loss. However, Peter Argersinger seems persuasive in his argument that the Populist defeat was caused by voter disillusionment due to past fusion efforts, legislative ineffectiveness, the ever-worsening depression, and administrative corruption, aided by the additional Republican smears.[52] Kansas voters, like the newspapers, were more concerned with these issues than with suffrage. In fact, one quarter of the electorate ignored the amendment question entirely. One newspaper suggested that voters had failed to notice the amendment because of its position at the bottom of the ballot, although this had never caused problems before. More to the point, the amendment's place at the bottom of the ticket represented many voters' priorities in the election.

Suffrage activists pointed to "party endorsements" as the primary reason for the amendment's overwhelming defeat.[53] However, the endorsement strategy might have worked if both parties had voted in a suffrage plank. The suffrage activists' mistake was not in appealing to the parties, but in attempting to gain the support of one party after failing with the other. The tensions between the movement's nonpartisan local and partisan state strategy, between its vision of political sisterhood and quest for political power and legitimacy, had at last been laid bare.

Had the Kansas suffrage campaign taken place in 1892 instead of two years later, perhaps the outcome would have been different. Sarah A. Thurston, an influential WCTU and KESA officer, was able to tabulate the returns from 71 to 105 counties. Her figures, while not official, do suggest some intriguing conclusions concerning voting behavior and partisan concerns. Thurston calculated that 14 percent of the Democrats, 38.5 percent of the Republicans, 54 percent of the Populists, and 80 percent of the Prohibitionists supported the amendment.[54] Apparently, the numerous Republican editors and politicians who had renounced the amendment as a "Populist measure" had demonstrated their influence at the polling booth. In part, Republican leaders feared that if the amendment passed, Woman Movement activists would display their gratitude for the Populists at the next state election. Had the Republican Party endorsed woman suffrage, and had the Democrats at least refrained from denouncing it, the amendment would have gained considerable support.

Yet, the partisan issue does not explain away the lopsided vote on the amendment. The average Kansas voter in 1894 did not hold a particularly optimistic opinion about promises to purify politics. That type of talk had been discredited by the legislative war and the Populists' fusion experiments. Each party, when in power, had proven itself capable of corruption and incompetence. Little wonder, then, that not a few Kansas men decided that woman suffrage was simply not worth the risk of upsetting the status quo. Municipal woman suffrage had been passed when change meant economic progress, moral reform, expansion, and optimism. State suffrage was defeated when change meant economic depression, Populist disillusionment, and political anarchy. At a time when everything seemed uncertain, such a leap into the unknown probably did not appeal to a number of men. Add to this group those men who never really liked the idea of woman suffrage in the first place, and the suffragists' formidable task becomes clear.

Woman Movement activists added to their troubles by concentrating their campaign on the urban Anglo middle-class. Perhaps the suffragists' greatest mistake was to ignore farm women and men. The relatively low Populist vote for the amendment belies the *Farmer's Wife's* assumption that "the country is all right." The country was in fact in need of active organizing. Had suffragists made the effort, they could have connected with the many Alliance women who had demonstrated their passion for political participation. When one includes the other groups of women and men left out of the suffragists' strategy—Blacks, Catholic immigrants, and the working class—then the Grand Suffrage Campaign, impressive as it was in miles covered, appears narrow in its scope.

However the suffrage activists' endorsement strategy may have influenced the vote on the amendment, it had a devastating effect on their movement. Following the November election, the *Farmer's Wife* folded without so much as a parting message. In December, the second "Great Suffrage Convention" was transformed into a bitter, vicious struggle. The *Kansas City Times* gleefully proclaimed, "The women KNOW IT ALL— Kansas Equal Suffragists Lobby Like Old Politicians," and in many ways the convention did resemble those of the male political culture.[55] There were bitter floor fights, parliamentary maneuvers, and free-swinging accusations. At one point, a faction bolted from the assembly hall and re-caucused elsewhere. The main struggle was over renominating Johns, who was opposed by an alliance of certain Populists and non-partisan radicals. The delegates also battled over whether the KESA should work for resubmission of the amendment, which Johns opposed.

Johns was eventually re-elected, but by then the damage was done. Almost all the women who attended the convention were demoralized and angry with some other faction. The 1895 convention drew only a fraction of the previous year's delegates, and the number continued to decrease steadily for the next fifteen years.[56] Rather than having women overwhelming the dominant male political culture, as the *Farmer's Wife* had suggested, the women themselves had become caught up in mainstream politics, and had been overwhelmed by it.

Ultimately, suffragists were unable to develop a method of address-ing male political power effectively without being subsumed by it. They wanted simultaneously to be in the trenches and above the fray—to gain access to the political power of the parties while maintaining an autonomous movement with priorities, tactics, and a language differ-ent from most men. Yet Populist and Republican women, whose loyal-ties were particularly conflicted, seemed unaware of the great contradictions inherent in their position.

Balancing between the ideal of political sisterhood and the reality of partisan politics was the only real option women activists had. As Johns realized in her response to Templins, the vote—potential political power—could only be won on men's terms. It was men, after all, who had to agree to share that power. Further, women could no more ig-nore their party-based ideology than they could reject their gender-based beliefs. And there was no questions of abandoning their own political culture, for it was their raison d'etre, as well as their means to organize and inspire other middle-class women. They could as well turn their backs on their Christianity. . . .

NOTES

1. O. Gene Clanton, *Kansas Populism: Ideas and Men* (Lawrence, 1969), 131–35.
2. Histories of Kansas Populism include Clanton, *Kansas Populism;* Peter H. Arg-ersinger, *Populism and Politics: William Alfred Peffer and the People's Party* (Lexington, KY, 1974); Walter T. K. Nugent, *The Tolerant Populists: Kansas Populism and Nativism*

(Chicago, 1963); Scott G. McNall, *Road to Rebellion: Class Formation and Kansas Populism, 1865–1900* (Chicago, 1988). For a helpful review of the historiography of the national movement, see Martin Ridge, "Populism Redux: John D. Hicks and *The Populist Revolt*," *Reviews in American History* 13 (March 1985).

3. Susan B. Anthony and Ida Husted Harper, eds., *The History of Woman Suffrage*, vol. 4 (1902; reprint, New York, 1969), 221–22. Other accounts of the Kansas suffrage campaigns may be found in Wilda M. Smith, "A Half Century of Struggle: Gaining Woman Suffrage in Kansas," *Kansas History* 4 (Summer 1981); MaryJo Wagner, "Farms, Families and Reform: Women in the Farmers' Alliance and Populist Party" (Ph.D. diss, University of Oregon, 1986).

4. Numerous historians have studied the role of a separate middle-class women's political culture in developing women's political skills. For an overview of this literature, see Paula Baker, "The Domestication of Politics: Women and American Political Society, 1780–1920," *American Historical Review* 89 (June 1984).

5. On the historiography of western women and politics, see Elizabeth Jameson, "Women as Workers, Women as Civilizers: True Womanhood in the American West," in *The Women's West*, ed. Susan Armitage and Elizabeth Jameson (Norman, 1987), 154–61. For a recent overview of western politics, See Richard White, *"It's Your Misfortune and None of My Own": A New History of the American West* (Norman, 1991), 353–87. Regarding woman suffrage, White writes, "the West's willingness to grant women the vote still ends up as something of a mystery." As White argues, while one can find some possible explanations for this regional trend, the real story lies in the variations between the states.

6. McNall, *Road to Rebellion*, 63.

7. Robert W. Richmond, *Kansas: A Land of Contrasts* (St. Louis, 1974), 83–84; Edward T. James, ed., *Notable American Women, 1607–1950*, vol. 2 (Cambridge, MA, 1971), 625–26; *Kansas City Star,* 30 January 1927, University of Kansas clippings, Kansas State Historical Society, Topeka (hereafter KSHS); Argersinger, *Populism and Politics,* 87–89.

8. As Ellen Carol DuBois has argued, the Kansas campaign enabled Stanton and Anthony to envision the possibility of an autonomous woman suffrage movement. Because of their national strategy and their indifference to political parties beyond the suffrage question, however, Stanton and Anthony displayed little sensitivity to local politics. Ellen Carol DuBois, *Feminism and Suffrage: The Emergence of an Independent Women's Movement in America, 1848–1869* (Ithaca, NY, 1978), 84–103; see also Bettina Aptheker, *Women's Legacy: Essays on Race, Sex, and Class in American History* (Amherst, MA, 1982), 47–49.

9. On Kansas in the 1870s and 1880s, see Craig Miner, *West of Wichita: Settling the High Plains of Kansas, 1865–1890* (Lawrence, 1986), 53–66, 118–31, 201–11. On middle-class women's approaches to "civilizing" frontier towns, see June O. Underwood, "Civilizing Kansas: Women's Organizations, 1880–1920," *Kansas History* 7 (Winter 1984/85); Robert L. Griswold, "Anglo Women and Domestic Ideology in

the American West in the Nineteenth and Early Twentieth Centuries," in *Western Women: Their Land, Their Lives,* ed. Lillian Schlissel, Vicki L. Ruiz, and Janice Monk (Albuquerque, 1988), 15–33.

10. By using the term "Anglo," I am referring to the British-stock Americans who made up the majority of Kansas's population.

11. Sara M. Evans and Harry C. Boyet, "Schools for Action: Radical Uses for Social Space," *Democracy* 3 (Fall 1982): 60–61. For the roots of this middle-class women's political culture, see Nancy F. Cott, *The Bonds of Womanhood: "Woman's Sphere" in New England, 1780–1835* (New Haven, 1977), 200–204; Minutes to the Annual Meeting of the Kansas WCTU, 1885, 41, KSHS; Minutes to the Annual Meeting of the KESA, 1888, 32, KSHS. On the importance of business metaphors for mainstream men's politicians, see Richard Slotkin, *The Fatal Environment: The Myth of the Frontier in the Age of Industrialization, 1800–1890* (New York, 1985), 281–85.

12. Minutes of the KESA, 1890, 11.

13. See, for example, *Kansas Suffrage,* August 1893; Minutes of the WCTU, 1887, 41.

14. Barbara Leslie Epstein, *The Politics of Domesticity: Women, Evangelism, and Temperance in Nineteenth-Century America* (Middletown, CT, 1981), 125–37. It is important to note that Woman Movement activists based their exclusionism on notions of respectability, rather than on explicit barriers based on race, ethnicity, or class. Thus, middle-class black women, whose values and manners resembled those of the Anglo middle-class, were accepted into the Woman Movement, particularly the WCTU, though not necessarily on equal terms. On Kansas Woman Movement attitudes toward non-Anglos, see Minutes of the KESA, 1890, 13; *Our Messenger,* February 1892, December 1981, and January 1886. The WCTU tended to be more accepting of middle-class blacks than the KESA. Woman Movement activists were very successful in forwarding their legislative agenda during the 1880s. Robert Smith Bader, *Prohibition in Kansas: A History* (Lawrence, 1986), 99–102.

15. On the cultural differences and tensions between farm and town, see Everett Dick, *The Sod House Frontier, 1845–1890: A Social History of the Northern Plains from the Creation of Kansas and Nebraska to the Admission of the Dakotas* (New York, 1937), 234–36. For economic, cultural, and political differences between farm and town on the Plains, see Stanley B. Parsons, *The Populist Context: Rural Versus Urban Power on a Great Plains Frontier* (Westport, CT, 1973). On the Woman Movement's realization of lack of connection to farm women, see Minutes of the KESA, 1887, 56; *Our Messenger,* April 1887.

16. Bader, *Prohibition in Kansas,* 95–103; *Our Messenger,* June 1887; Minutes of the WCTU, 1886, 41.

17. The fight for municipal woman suffrage is detailed in Minutes of the KESA, 1884–1887.

18. Minutes of the KESA, vol. 1 (1884–1887), 116–18; Bader, *Prohibition in Kansas,* 103–5. Among the Republican legislators were a number of committed

woman suffragists, who supported the cause even when it was not politically expedient. The great majority, however, were motivated by more practical concerns, as evidenced by the GOP's maneuvers concerning the bill between 1885–1887.

19. Minutes of the KESA, vol. 1 (1884–1887), 119; Franklin G. Adams and W. H. Carruth, *Woman Suffrage in Kansas* (Topeka, 1888), 35, 47. For a discussion of the boom and bust in 1880s Kansas, see McNall, *Road to Rebellion*, 74–83; Raymond Curtis Miller, "The Background of Populism in Kansas," *Mississippi Valley Historical Review* 11 (March 1925): 469–89; Miner, *West of Wichita*, 203–29.

20. Argersinger, *Populism and Politics*, 46–48.

21. Elizabeth Barr, "The Populist Uprising," in *History of Kansas: State and People*, vol. 2, ed. William E. Connelly (New York, 1928), 1128. On the 1890 campaign, see Peter H. Argersinger, "Road to a Republican Waterloo: The Farmers' Alliance and the Election of 1890 in Kansas," *Kansas Historical Quarterly* 33 (Winter 1967): 443–69. On Populist demands and the economic context, see Argersinger, *Populism and Politics*, 58–79.

22. Argersinger, *Populism and Politics*, 162–63.

23. Argersinger, *Populism and Politics*, 146–47; Clanton, *Kansas Populism*, 122; Republican State Central Committee, "Proceedings of the Republican State Convention" (1892), KSHS.

24. On the cultural divide between Alliance and urban Populist women, see Marilyn Dell Brady, "Populism and Feminism in a Newspaper by and for Women of the Kansas Farmers' Alliance, 1891–1894," *Kansas History* 7 (Winter 1984/85): 276–77. On Kansas rural people's religious practices, see Peter H. Argersinger, "Pentecostal Politics in Kansas: Religion, the Farmers' Alliance, and the Gospel of Populism," *Kansas Quarterly* 1 (Fall 1969): 24–35. For a study of southern women in the Farmers' Alliance, see Julie Roy Jeffrey, "Women in the Southern Alliance: A Reconsideration of the Role and Status of Women in the Late Nineteenth-Century South," *Feminist Studies* 3 (Fall 1975). Jeffrey does not distinguish between town and farm women.

25. Wagner, "Farms, Families, and Reform," 364–65, discusses the shifting role of women from the Alliance to the Populist Party.

26. Brady, "Populism and Feminism," 288.

27. At a KESA meeting in 1891, several speakers excoriated the Populist "calamity howlers," but Johns was able to avoid open war within the ranks. Smith, "A Half Century of Struggle," 78. A number of important Republicans, such as U.S. Senator J. J. Ingalls and party "boss" Sol Miller, were strongly opposed to woman suffrage and resisted any attempts at what they called "petticoat politics." Bader, *Prohibition in Kansas*, 116. Although they hoped the new organization would prove to be a springboard for a national movement, the WPPL remained confined to Kansas. *Advocate*, 26 April 1893, 4 October 1893. An overview of the WPPL's activities may be found in Wagner, "Farms, Families, and Reform," 320–33; *Farmer's Wife*, December 1893.

28. Accounts of the suffrage convention from the *Advocate*, 6 September 1893.

29. *Kansas Suffrage*, November 1893; *Advocate*, 6 July 1893.

30. These newspapers included *Kansas Suffrage, Kansas Sunflower,* and *Woman's Friend*. For more details of the campaign, see Anthony and Harper, eds., *History of Woman Suffrage*, vol. 4, 646; *Kansas Suffrage*, March 1894; *Our Messenger,* May 1894.

31. *Farmer's Wife,* December 1893.

32. *Woman Suffrage Clippings,* vol. 1 (n.p., n.d.), KSHS.

33. *Woman's Friend,* May 1894; *Journal and Triumph,* 19 May 1894 in *Woman Suffrage Clippings,* vol. 1; *Woman's Friend,* May 1894.

34. *Woman's Friend,* June 1894.

35. Clanton, *Kansas Populism,* 151, *Kansas Suffrage,* May 1894.

36. *State Journal,* 6 June 1894 in *Woman Suffrage Clippings,* vol. 1. All quotes in this paragraph are from this source.

37. The compromise resolution read, "That we, the Republican women of Kansas, having worked for the best interests of the state, using the ballot with judgment in school and municipal elections, demonstrating the benefits to be obtained, ask the Republicans in Kansas state convention assembled to testify and advocate an equal ballot and a fair count to all citizens."

38. *Republican Party Clippings,* vol. 1 (n.p., n.d.), 45, KSHS; Anthony and Harper, eds., *History of Woman Suffrage*, vol. 4, 645.

39. Argersinger, *Populism and Politics,* 166–73.

40. On the business-oriented language of Republican Party leaders, see McNall, *Road to Rebellion,* 164–67.

41. *Journal and Triumph,* 21 June 1894.

42. Ibid.

43. Ibid.

44. *Woman Suffrage Clippings,* vol. 1, 7.

45. *Farmer's Wife,* October 1894. A comprehensive, though somewhat confusing account of tensions between Populist and Republican suffragists may be found in Wagner, "Farms, Families, and Reform," 338–41.

46. *Farmer's Wife,* December 1893.

47. *Barton County Beacon,* 28 June 1894; Smith, "A Half Century of Struggle," 90–92.

48. *Barton County Beacon,* 23 August 1894.

49. Clanton, *Kansas Populism,* 166–67; *Register,* 7 July 1894.

50. These observations are based on surveying fifteen Populist papers, including the *Barton County Beacon,* the *Opinion,* the *Liberator,* the *Advocate,* the *Industrial Advocate,* the *Kansas Agitator,* and the *Industrial Free Press; Liberator,* 22 June 1894.

51. Clanton, *Kansas Populism,* 167–68. In addition to the Populist papers cited in note 50, I also surveyed a number of Republican papers, including the *Daily Capitol,* the *Register,* and the *Republican-Plaindealer.*

52. McNall, *Road to Rebellion,* 284, argues that "the key to the Populist loss was

their position on suffrage." (Clanton also makes this claim in *Kansas Populism.*) But McNall's figures prove that Democrats who voted Populist in 1892 (the year that Democrats ran no candidates and endorsed the Populists) voted their own party in 1894, after the Populists had rejected fusion and the Democrats had run their own slate. Further, McNall does not factor in lost votes due to the issues raised by Argersinger, nor in this instance does he even consider his own analysis of why Populism failed: organizational weakness, ideological fuzziness, and estrangement from the working class. The first of these points is especially important to understanding Populism, and needs to be integrated into Argersinger's electoral and legislative focus. Argersinger, *Populism and Politics,* 151–91.

53. See, for example, "Women's Column" in the *Industrial Advocate,* 11 December 1894; Laura Johns to Lucy Johnston, 11 November 1894, Lucy Browne Johnston collection, KSHS.

54. Thurstan, secretary for the amendment campaign committee, was able to gain access in the ballots after the election, and then "carefully tabulated" the results. Anthony and Harper, eds., *History of Woman Suffrage,* vol. 4, 647. For the vote count of the amendment, see Clanton, *Kansas Populism,* 168–69.

55. *Kansas City Times,* 6 December 1894 in *Woman Suffrage Clippings,* vol. 1.

56. Ibid., 7 December 1894; Smith, "A Half Century of Struggle," 93.

The Leviathan with Tentacles of Steel: Railroads in the Minds of Kansas Populists

Thomas Frank

Among the most important technological transformations to alter western society was the invention of the steam locomotive. From the inception of the diminutive Baltimore and Ohio Railroad in 1828 to the days of the Twentieth Century Limited, the phenomenon of the railroad fascinated the American people. Leo Marx recounts the vast significance of the new device in *The Machine in the Garden,* his influential study of the reactions of American literati to the coming of industrialism: "In the 1830s the locomotive . . . is becoming a kind of national obsession. It is the embodiment of the age, an instrument of power, speed, noise, fire, iron, smoke. . . . The 'industrial revolution incarnate' one economic historian has called it."[1] Symbolizing the forces which were to revise the rural agrarian orientation of American society, railroads evoked a variety of public reactions.

In the Midwest, where the existence of a railroad led to extensive economic development, the iron horse met with both enthusiasm and opposition. The People's—or Populist—Party, which was to offer the nineteenth century's most determined challenge to railroad expan-

"The Leviathan with Tentacles of Steel: Railroads in the Minds of Kansas Populists," by Thomas Frank, *Western Historical Quarterly* 20, 1 (1989): 37–54. Copyright Western History Association. Reprinted with permission.

sion, ironically enjoyed its greatest popularity in regions where the railroad constituted the sole effective mode of transportation to agricultural markets. The railroad issue was, of course, one of overwhelming importance for Populists: they believed that the practices of railway corporations were among the primary factors making agriculture profitless in the 1890s.

Thus, in Kansas, a state where railroad technology was essential to the sustenance of a large population, the railroad issue became the paramount populist concern. As Hallie Farmer explained in a 1925 article in the *Mississippi Valley Historical Review,* "The Farmer who was living and suffering in Kansas, Nebraska, or the Dakotas through the decade following 1887 . . . saw the cause of all his troubles in the capitalists; and chief among his capitalistic enemies he ranked the men who owned western railroads."[2] Indeed, the railroad problem was of such magnitude that it produced an enormous body of literature by reform leaders, who enumerated complaints, proposed solutions, and composed memorable passages vilifying the "great Railway Bogieman."[3]

While historians agree that antagonism existed between farmers and railroaders, almost none have evaluated the theoretical concepts behind the facade of the Populists' complaints. For Kansas Populists, the panoply of railroad offenses—excessive charges for freight, mistreatment of employees, stock-watering, and so on—were intrinsically linked to the notion of public utility. The railroad was rightfully a publicly-owned and community-oriented enterprise, they contended, and its problems stemmed not from steam locomotives, but from the fact that they were privately owned and were operated for the profit of a small group of individuals rather than for the community.

The grievances and solutions articulated by the People's Party have been the source of much historiographical conflict. In the 1950s Richard Hofstadter portrayed the Populists as an assortment of angry, reactionary rustics, dreaming of preindustrial times rather than facing the permanence of recent changes. Others found the Populists a far-sighted group of reformers concerned with America's industrial future. But in the most influential work on Populism in recent years, *Democratic Promise* and *The Populist Moment,* Lawrence Goodwyn transcends prior debate and asserts that Populism grew from a working class subculture that was alien to most Americans. The Populists' movement culture and analytical approach, Goodwyn argues, were unique and their language remains incomprehensible to mainstream individuals.[4] Of the historians who deal specifically with the issue of Populism and railroads, most (such as John Hicks) have examined the empirical validity of Populist complaints about freight rates. Others have characterized Populist dissatisfaction with the railroads as simple frustration with an insuperable obstacle. Echoing the analysis of Hofstadter, adherents of this school of thought believe that Populist demands for nationalization of the railways constituted a visceral reaction to the farmer's difficult financial position.[5] According to these writers, Populist criticism of railroads was shallow, lacking intellectual depth or empirical validity.

The actual accusations by Kansas Populists against railway corporations provide the student of history with ample material to assess these conflicting views. Evaluating statements made by Kansas reformers about railroads leads one to reject the Hofstadter thesis, but this sort of evaluation also challenges Goodwyn's ideas of cultural autonomy. Far from being a homegrown concept unfamiliar to other Americans, the Populists' notion of public utility was rooted in railroad history and was patterned after recommendations by prominent economic thinkers. A brief study of these statements also undermines other historians' efforts to verify or invalidate Populist complaints about the railroad by comparing rhetoric to economic facts. The Populist critique of railroads was a theoretical one; while its outward manifestations entailed such concrete charges as excessive freight rates, its heart was philosophical. Populists demanded government ownership or control of railroads not simply because of the hardships afflicting farmers, but because they felt the society as a whole should operate railroads.[6]

In *Railroads and the Character of America,* James A. Ward catalogs the expectations placed upon railroads by the public and how these expectations were met by railroad promoters. He divides the nineteenth century into two periods during which, he claims, the American "image" of railroads changed. Until the 1850s, according to Ward, the construction of railroads was approved by the public under the assumption that these new highways would serve the common good rather than particular interests.[7] Above all, the invention was to be a servant of the national will, developing and uplifting the United States. As Peter Lyon explains in *To Hell in a Day Coach:* "From the outset it was quite clear, at least in charter and law, that the railroads were public thoroughfares, like turnpikes or canals; . . . that the railroad corporations were quasi-public in nature, having been formed to serve the public convenience and necessity. . . ."[8] It was this attitude, reverberating through the railroad literature of the early nineteenth century cited by Ward, which induced government to begin massive assistance of railroad construction.[9]

James Ward also notes that the community-oriented idea of railroads was retained in western states for years after its demise in the East.[10] In Kansas this image of railroads was more readily perceptible as the state's economic fate was tied directly to the fortunes of its major railways. Railroads were the region's link to the great markets of the East and Europe, and without their presence the Great Plains may have been uninhabitable.[11] Hence, the coming of the iron horse was a harbinger of prosperity and civilization to the smallest Kansas hamlets. To further progress, the Kansas legislature and the federal government ceded 8,234,013 acres of land to prospective railroads.[12] Cities, townships, and counties bonded themselves and offered the cash to railroad companies as an incentive to construct rail lines in their direction.[13] In the 1880s every town that could bond itself to aid railroad building did so, sending Kansas construction and property values spiraling upwards in the speculative fever which accompanies the promise of progress.[14] By 1890, Kansas had the second largest number of lines of railroad in the nation, much of it incapable of turning a profit.[15]

But the state's partnership with the railroad was not one-sided: just as the people of Kansas supported the great railway companies, the railway corporations helped populate and civilize the Kansas plains. Realizing that their roads could only become profitable if the lands near their rights-of-way were farmed, the companies brought immigrants to the state.[16] The general interests of the state coincided with the private interests of the railroad; and the cooperation between the two brought thousands of settlers to the Kansas prairies, opening these fertile fields to the commerce of the world. The railroads of Kansas thus performed an essential duty in the creation of the state: they populated its vacant spaces and organized the distribution of much of its land.

The relationship of Kansas farmers to the railroad was hence a symbiotic one. The railroad made farming feasible in that fertile but remote region, offering the new inhabitants a method of transporting their produce to cities. Indeed, it would be difficult to exaggerate the importance of the railroads to Kansas. Clearly, they constituted the most vital component of the state's economic structure. Upon them Kansas's prosperity—and even its viability—rested. In that rectangular midwestern land, the image of the railroad as an implement of the commonweal was retained out of necessity.

When the importance of railroads to the development of Kansas is understood, it becomes difficult to accept the notion that Kansas Populists felt a blind, unthinking hatred for the invention which made their state habitable. While the Hofstadter thesis burdens Populists with the ignominious labels "retrogressive" and "reactionary," the Populists in fact harbored little resentment toward the railroad itself. Populist leaders who discussed the railroad issue were careful to distinguish between the potential value of railroads and the negligent manner in which they perceived railways to be operated.[17]

The paramount issue in the minds of Kansas Populists was not the practical concern of railroads—which made up the facade of their critique—but the role of the railroad within the state. Echoing the language of James Ward's "national unity image," Populists asserted that the railroad was inherently public in nature and could only be operated properly by the government. The plethora of problems to which the Populists drew the nation's attention, then, arose from the dichotomy between the railway's actual and theoretical status. The notion of railroads as public highways subsumes the multiplicity of unrelated—and sometimes conflicting—grievances espoused by the People's Party: these complaints were made coherent only by the notion of public utility.

In the literature of Kansas Populism the "national unity image" of the railway, which Ward links to the period before the 1850s, resurfaced with a vengeance. Like their forebears, whose taxes were invested in railroads in the belief that they would serve public needs, Kansas Populists saw the roads which had transformed their state as communal property. Thus James D. Holden, an Emporia, Kansas, businessman and prolific pamphlet writer, asserted in his 1890 pamphlet, *Metallic Money and Hard Times,* that railroads were "closely identified with the interests of each member of society." Furthermore, Holden argued, "railroads are public in character. They exist only by authority of charters granted by the state. They were built largely by the people themselves, and their advantages and emoluments instead of being conferred upon any class of private individuals, should be RETAINED and enjoyed by the public."[18] A later pamphlet, *Free Freight and Government Railways,* which Holden subtitled "A Proposition to restore to Society essential rights of which it has been wrongfully divested," focused specifically on this issue and opened with a powerful statement of the public utility idea. "That indispensable public agencies should not be 'owned' nor controlled by private corporations or individuals, is a truth which . . . but slowly takes root in the minds of men," Holden wrote. "Yet, that a nation . . . cannot be generally prosperous [where] . . . it is *legal* for a few to exercise absolute control over interests or agencies that are essential to the welfare of all, is a fact so apparent that it ought not to require elucidation."[19]

C. Wood Davis, possibly the greatest railroad authority of the Kansas Populists, also recognized that certain industries could be so central to the general welfare that government control was warranted. To prove his point he referred to the preferential treatment accorded railway corporations by the state: "The endowment of the railway company with the exceptional power to enter upon and take private property, and the equally exceptional limitation of the stockholders' liability to the cost of the shares held, implies special duties and obligations to the public; and the people, whose lands have been taken, who furnish the traffic, and provide the revenue, have a right to a voice in determining the justness of the rates charged."[20]

In 1891 Populist senator William A. Peffer claimed that "in course of time, from a private convenience railroading became a public necessity; and, as it has been always with the development of any great industry, as it became more general it attained greater power over the people and their interests." Peffer admitted in *The Farmer's Side* that the principle of public necessity was the central basis of the Populist demands for government ownership.[21] He clarified this position before the Senate on 8 February 1893:

I have no qualms of conscience about commanding the corporations of the country to obey the law, they are the creatures of the law; all that they have the law gives to them; and the people of this country, especially the farmers and the workmen, have been trampled upon by these railway corporations until they are crying out in despair almost, and asking that Congress take hold of this subject and compel respect to the public will. Those corporations are not only the creatures of Congress, but they are public agents.[22]

Peffer linked this theoretical concern to the Pullman strike by introducing his speech on that great industrial spasm with a resolution that "all public functions" should be "exercised by . . . public agencies."[23] The Populist state platform of 1892 also asserted that "public needs should be supplied by public agencies."[24] And, third in a list of six proposals by the editors of the Populist *Topeka Advocate* was the demand "that the people shall own and operate the railroads, telegraphs, and telephones for their own interest and benefit; and that private corporations shall cease to monopolize these *public functions* [author's emphasis] for purposes of public plunder."[25]

The principle of public utility enjoyed articulation in the declining years of the People's Party of Kansas. In 1898 the state platform still demanded "the public ownership of all public utilities."[26] In 1899 ex-Senator Peffer composed "The Trust Problem and Its Solution" for *Forum* magazine, in which he reaffirmed his earlier arguments for this theoretical keystone. He classified railroads as "public functions" because they "are engaged in the business of carrying merchandise for the people generally—for all the people without distinction."[27]

By asserting that the railway was rightfully the servant of the general public instead of a private business venture, the Populists repeated the convictions of their ancestors. The public utility image, as James Ward observes, was as old as the railroad itself but had been eclipsed in mid-century by the fervor of the burgeoning entrepreneurial state. Kansas Populists, though, were not ignorant of this political legacy; indeed, they were very much aware of the attitudes that had accompanied railroad expansion. Frequent references to railroad history punctuate the writings of Kansas leaders, who sought to thereby legitimize their otherwise radical suggestions.

Congressman William A. Harris, who described himself as a former railroad employee, spoke before the House of Representatives on the debt of the Union Pacific in January 1895. During a brief expostulation on the history of the Union Pacific, Harris repeatedly referred to the forgotten promises of public service: "Away back in 1835 the idea was advanced that a railroad should be built by the Government to the Pacific. That same idea was continually being advanced from 1835 to 1840, and from then on until 1850 to 1860 almost every session of Congress had bills introduced for this purpose." The notion of common benefits, Harris maintained, was pervasive in those early years. "There was always the idea that there should be a great national highway constructed. There was always the idea that other relations would exist between the Government and the parties constructing this road other than merely that of debtor and creditor."[28] Harris later tied together the various Populist notions of railroad history, portraying the status of railways in the 1890s as not only a theoretical and practical injustice, but as a betrayal of a historical promise: "Mr. Chairman, as a mere matter of justice, I think the load which has borne so heavily upon these men [farmers] for so long a time should be lightened, and that these settlers should at least have some relief. . . . They should have the benefit of this great national highway that has been promised them for more than a generation . . . in the history of the people of this country."[29]

Congressman "Sockless" Jerry Simpson expressed a similar viewpoint in a speech given several days later, noting that "the Government has aided by a large grant and by the issuing of bonds the building of a great national highway to the Pacific Coast—not alone for the benefit of the people along the line of the road, but for the benefit of all the people."[30]

Populist Governor John Leedy gave his version of railroad history to the Kansas House of Representatives in 1897: "These corporations have received their charter rights from the various states, and these states naturally concluded that they had the right to regulate and control the corporations that they had thus created. This view of the case was constantly combated by the corporations, who claimed that, as they were private corporations, they were not subject to state legislation so far as their charges were concerned."[31] Former Representative John Davis reviewed the grants of land and money to the Union Pacific in 1898 and concluded that "the road should have been turned over to the government as a public highway, free from incumbrance, to be operated in the interest of the people at mere cost of running expenses and repairs."[32]

Kansas Populists were not ignorant of their historical position. Understanding that the idea of public utility had a lengthy past connected with railroads, they sought to revive this principle and thus explain the grievances they had raised. Public ownership of this public utility, it was thought, would lead to reasonable freight rates, the end of stock-watering, arbitrary discrimination, and political corruption, better treatment of employees, and safer conditions for everyone associated with the railroad. The national party's 1892 Omaha platform recognized that "the time has come when the railroad corporations will either own the people or the people must own the railroads" and demanded that, "transportation being a means of exchange and a public necessity, the government should own and operate the railroads in the interest of the people."[33]

But theoretical dissension over the railroad question did exist in Populist ranks, and this division reflects directly on the topic of industrialism and state intervention. Many of the Populists of Kansas, while savagely critical of railroad corporations, remained suspicious of a larger government role in the economy. State ownership or regulation of railroads was justified, perhaps, due to the public nature of this particular industry, but Populists believed that in all other areas laissez-faire capitalism should be the rule.

A distinct capitalist sentiment can be found in the writings of James Holden, who asserted that farm prices should be determined by supply and demand. Exorbitant freight rates interfered with this system— therefore they should be neutralized: "With a sufficient supply of money as proposed, the wages of labor, and the value of its product, would be governed SOLELY BY THE LAW OF SUPPLY AND DEMAND, uninfluenced at present by . . . the obstacle to the ready transfer of the product to market—enormous tribute now exacted by the private owners of THE FRANCHISES of the great transportation lines."[34] Congressman Harris further articulated this concept on 31 January 1895. Capitalism as a whole works well, he argued. The only problem is that railroads, which are a public institution, are privately owned:

> I am not in favor of the intrusion of the Government upon private affairs anywhere. I think it would be a great misfortune. I am in this case in favor of the Government undertaking the operation of a highway which has been from the beginning conceded to be of a different character; . . . I am in favor of seeing to it that these quasi public corporations perform the duties which their charters require them to perform, fairly and honestly, to the people of this country.[35]

Public utilities, then, stand outside the realm of things properly owned by individuals.

Others explicitly portrayed government intervention in the railroad industry as a way of increasing Kansas's and America's profits. Populist congressman Thomas Hudson argued in February 1895 that action against railroads would increase British investment in the United States. To demonstrate this he quoted the *New York Sun:* "The failure to punish the criminal mismanagement of railroad and other great corporations in America is having a disastrous effect upon the English view of the American sense of honor. There can be no revival of English interest in this class of investments until at least some measure is adopted in the United States for the punishment of railway thieves."[36] S. S. King, a lawyer from Kansas City, Kansas, and a Populist candidate for Congress, saw the more efficient railroad arrangement which he proposed in his 1896 pamphlet, *The Gulf Outlet,* as a way of increasing the midwestern farmer's competitiveness. "To-day the American producer is competing with the world's producers in supplying the world's consumers. If the American farmer can get a shorter route and a cheaper rate by way of the Gulf to Europe, he will be in that much better position to compete with the cheap labor of Russia, India, and Egypt in furnishing [w]estern Europe's wheat supplies." To this end King proposed the construction of new roads, not necessarily by the government, but certainly with state aid.[37] Unlike many of his more fervent Populist colleagues, King postulated a possible confluence of interests between capital and government. Undaunted by the overt misdeeds of railway corporations, he perceived their potential worth and advocated construction by private agencies.

In the works of these Populist leaders there were few hints of the cooperative ideal which Lawrence Goodwyn saw at the heart of Populism. More useful in understanding this group of Kansans is the distinction proposed by Peter H. Argersinger, who labels this faction of the Kansas party "developer Populists," noting that they "objected to any proposed restrictions on what they perceived as the engines of economic growth: eastern capital investment and the railroads."[38] These Kansans perceived the railroad as an exceptional industry which needed government intervention, if only to make the nation's capitalist economy function more effectively. They used arguments similar to those employed by advocates of free trade around the world: the most desirable economic arrangement is that which least impedes the flow of capital and commodities.

On the other hand, most prominent leaders of the Kansas People's Party envisioned a state in which certain economic relationships were fundamentally altered. For this group, nationalization of public utilities such as railroads was widely perceived as the first step toward such a goal. While these men cannot be said to have favored government direction or even ownership of the nation's means of production, they clearly sought to protect individuals against the vicissitudes of economic forces. For these Populists, unrestrained competition was not a desirable state of affairs. It necessarily entailed lamentable human costs which society, in their view, was obligated to mitigate. For these Populist leaders, then, government ownership of railroads was merely a starting point for economic intervention by the state.[39] Gene Clanton has noted that adherents of this faction of the party often called themselves "socialists," although not in a Marxian sense. "Perhaps 'Gas and Water,' or Fabian would be an appropriate prefix for the brand of socialism espoused by most Populists; but whatever prefix is applied, socialism received a sympathetic hearing among Kansas Populist leaders."[40]

The *Topeka Advocate* anticipated a logical progression from nationalization of public utilities to broader socialism in an 1893 editorial:

> Municipal ownership of waterworks, gas works, electric light plants, and other public utilities by which the people receive the maximum of service for a minimum of cost afford other examples of pure socialism, by which serious abuses are corrected and great benefits secured to the public. . . . It is undoubtedly true that observing and studious Populists, with such examples before them, have come to believe that a still wider expansion of socialist doctrines and practices would be beneficial to mankind.[41]

In 1897 John Dunsmore, leader of the Populists in the 1893 "Legislative War," further clarified the link between nationalization of this basic industry and broader conceptions of social justice:

> [P]opulism . . . demands the enactment of new laws based on the natural rights of men, and not limited by precedents and accepted theories in relation to property, when such precedents and theories do not meet the requirements of modern life. Populism does not necessarily mean "to nationalize all the essentials of existence, land, labor, transportation and money. . . ." It does mean, however, . . . that not only the means of transportation, but all public utilities, shall be subject to public control, and when necessary, public ownership.[42]

For this faction of Populist leaders, then, public ownership of utilities was the obvious first step in economic restructuring by the state.

While railroads were labeled public agents by Peffer, other Populists referred to them as natural monopolies, a germ common in the language of nineteenth-century economics. Monopolies in general were perhaps the greatest recipients of Populist abuse, and railroads were seen by many as a peculiar type of monopoly in which competition was inherently limited. Percy Daniels wrote in 1896 that "The railroad is of necessity a monopoly, and the tendency to consolidation is natural, and is not in itself an evil. . . . It is the purpose of consolidation that is so offensive, because it is tyrannical because the concentration is one of despotism."[43]

The concept of natural monopolies was further elucidated by Carl Vrooman, a "Harvard- and Oxford-educated farmer-economist" whose 1900 pamphlet, *Taming the Trusts,* focused on the issue of natural monopolies.[44] One character in this essay informed his audience that such vital thoroughfares as railroads, canals, and roads "involve what are called public utilities and as they are not subject to competition it is now substantially agreed among all classes of reformers that they must be classed as natural monopolies." Vrooman's solution to the wrongful possession of these public necessities by private concerns was proposed to the reader by Professor Richard Ely, a well-known Gilded Age economist: "They must be democratized, transformed into government monopolies. The only good monopoly, like the only good government, is one 'of the people, by the people, and for the people.'"[45] For these Populist leaders, then, the public utility concept encompassed the additional dimension of natural monopoly, which only further increased the imperative for nationalization.

With their demands for state control over public utilities and natural monopolies, Kansas Populists aligned themselves with the group of contemporaneous theorists whom historian Sidney Fine labels the "new political economists." Including such luminaries as Ely, Edmund James and Edward Bemis, this school of thinkers made recommendations concerning government's economic duties which paralleled those of the Populists. "[T]he new-school economists called on the state to take positive action in behalf of the general well-being," Fine writes in his work, *Laissez-Faire and the General-Welfare State,* "and from the new-school point of view, the government 'which governs the most wisely' is the one that addresses itself to the amelioration of the conditions under which its citizens live and work, that performs general-welfare functions."[46] Central to these functions was state control of natural monopolies and public utilities. (The terms are used interchangeably by Fine.) The importance of government control of these industries was emphasized by these thinkers in terms that are reminiscent of Populist attacks on railroad corporations. According to Fine, "James favored public ownership because he believed that no prime necessity of life such as gas, water, or electricity, should be entrusted to a private concern, regardless how carefully the conduct of that concern might be watched." Ely and Bemis further argued that nationalization would permit improved treatment of employees and would lower freight rates.[47]

The similarities between the opinions of the intellectuals of the new political economy and those of Kansas Populists are at once remarkable and yet predictable. As Gene Clanton has noted, Kansas reform leaders were well aware of the dominant intellectual trends in American economic circles.[48] Prominent Populist journalist Annie Diggs even asserted in 1895 that Populists were responsible for enlightening the U.S. Congress about the "newer political economy."[49] And indeed, references to the thinkers of this school were common in Populist statements. In his 1889 pamphlet, *A Crisis for the Husbandman*, Percy Daniels quoted at length from Ely to illustrate the flaws in railroad charters.[50] Carl Vrooman, whom Clanton describes as a student of the new political economy,[51] made Ely—as well as Henry Demarest Lloyd— a character in *Taming the Trusts* and quoted Bemis on the subject of natural monopolies for his 1899 *Arena* article, "Twentieth Century Democracy."[52] Like many of his fellow Populists, Vrooman had grandiose visions of his party's intellectual forebears: "In Europe, many of the principles advocated by the Populists have had as their champions such statesmen as Bismarck, Gladstone, Chamberlain, and such writers as Carlyle, Victor Hugo, Ruskin, Mazzini, and the greatest college professors and economists of England and Germany." One appendix to *Taming the Trusts* even sought to prove that "Jefferson Favored Government Ownership of the Means of Transportation."[53]

Vrooman's fellow reformers frequently attacked American railroad corporations using references to political trends around the world. In 1889 Percy Daniels advocated the adoption of "The European Plan" of government-railroad relations. "The European method," he wrote, "is to exact from natural monopolies, using public property or receiving valuable privileges, a definite compensation. . . ."[54] The multiplicity of grievances voiced by C. Wood Davis were also illustrated with examples chosen from other western nations. Australia, in particular, was described as a country where the government possessed proper (i.e., complete) authority over roads. Australian railways, Davis argued, were superior to American railways in every way: There were fewer accidents on Australian roads, they cost considerably less to operate, there were no arbitrary discriminations by self-interested corporations, and employees were treated properly and did not strike. Finally, Davis noted, America was almost alone in its reluctance to nationalize railroads: "There are but three countries of any importance where the railways are operated by corporations permitted to fix rates, as in all others the government is the ultimate rate-making power: these are Great Britain, Canada, and the United States. . . ."[55]

Vrooman, whose Oxford education undoubtedly endowed him with an international perspective, wrote on the similarity of Populist demands to the practices of European states. In his article, "Twentieth Century Democracy," he employed this tactic to demonstrate just how modern and up-to-date Populist doctrine was. On other occasions, such as in "The Diary of a Kansas Republican" and "A Kansas Populist Abroad," Vrooman aimed to turn the tables on his GOP foes by identifying them rather than the reformers, as the true retrogressive enemies of sophistication.[56] "Every civilized nation except the United States owns its own telegraph," he observed in *The Arena*. And he continued: "All but the United States and England own their own railroads, wholly or in part. . . . Even little Japan, the wonder of the closing years of our century, owns and controls her own railroads, telegraphs, telephones, savings-banks, insurance, and loan departments, express companies, and canals."[57]

In "A Kansas Populist Abroad" Vrooman claimed that "the Populists are in control of Switzerland," in the sense that the Swiss government operates all natural monopolies and public utilities. In that most politically mature of nations, Vrooman wrote, "the people run the government and the government runs the monopolies and corporations."[58] One appendix to *Taming the Trusts* consists of descriptions by Joseph Chamberlain of the success of municipal socialism in Birmingham.[59] For Vrooman, these examples of political progress by foreigners revealed Populist ideas of public utility to be in fact part of the international vanguard of economic theory. Vrooman's internationalist inclination is even more significant in historiographical terms.

Populists raised issues in their struggle against railroad corporations which they saw being raised by others as well, both in their own and in other countries. Whether the arguments used by Populists were specifically invented by them or not was immaterial: The central issue of public utility was one which reformers knew to be common to their ancestors, the theorists of the new political economy, and the policies of foreign nations. Kansas Populists perceived themselves as (and in fact they were) participating in a larger debate over the proper role of the government in the economy—a debate which was to influence the political course of the twentieth century.

In his two works on American Populism, Lawrence Goodwyn writes on the "movement culture" generated by the Farmers' Alliance. This culture incorporated, Goodwyn argues, a language and analytical perspective qualitatively different from anything before or since the 1890s. In *The Populist Moment* he asserts that "in intellectual terms, the generating force of this new mass mode of behavior may be rather simply described as 'a new way of looking at things.'" "The language of the Alliance," he continues, "was a language not often heard in mainstream American politics." According to the Goodwyn thesis, Populists isolated themselves from the "received political culture," seeking cultural and political autonomy.[60]

But in the important railroad question, one finds little evidence for a self-imposed cultural isolation of this sort. Many Populist leaders perceived their efforts as part of an international and inexorable movement of social progress. Their statements on the paramount concern of public utility further deflate the idea of Populist cultural autonomy: fond of explaining their ideological descent from Jefferson and Jackson, Populists placed great emphasis on the ideals which had guided railroad construction in previous decades and shared the opinions of the intelligentsia of the new political economy. Kansas Populists, evaluated by their perception of railroads, were not—and did not feel themselves to be—culturally isolated. A certain faction even embraced the capitalist theory of Goodwyn's received culture.

Perhaps a more useful characterization of the culture which facilitated the Populist Revolt is that offered by Stanley B. Parsons and others in a 1983 article in *The Journal of American History*. In a piercing rejoinder to Goodwyn's hypothesis of sequential "movement-building," these scholars point out that Populism arose much too rapidly in Kansas to allow for the development of a highly sophisticated movement culture. The agrarian insurgency of the 1890s, then, is not to be explained by reference to rigid patterns of "democratic movement-building," but rather by the political tenets of the American culture already existing in the late nineteenth century.[61] As Parsons and the others observe: "These often disparate groups [of discontented farmers] responded to their adversity in a manner typical of a people with a long tradition of political participation. Their political culture was in place; it did not need a lengthy period to develop.

Therefore, "Populism did not require the development of a culture significantly different from the culture of the 1890s. Although Americans did not agree on the exact characteristics of a democratic order, they did agree to it in principle."[62] Populists reacted to their hardships by embracing a set of ideas—expressed by the Omaha Platform and other writings of their leaders—which, although rejected by many, were intelligible and even familiar to other Americans.

The Populist critique of railroads consisted of a multifaceted array of grievances which focused on the concepts of public utility and public ownership. There was considerable disagreement among Kansas Populists about the ultimate objective of public ownership: Whether nationalization was simply to revitalize a corrupt capitalist system or lead the way to a more cooperative economy constituted a largely unresolved question. Populists who supported both sides, though, shared concern for the harms wrought by perceived corporate misbehavior. But while one faction believed these depredations to be inherent in the economic system, the other felt that a properly ordered capitalist economy would prevent such wrongs. Both harked back to the policies of earlier days, reminiscing about the times when relations between state and utility were correctly arranged.

While some historians see the Populists as retrogressive malcontents grumbling fruitlessly about the technological changes which had forever marred rural America, others laud them for the constructive, human-oriented critique of industrial society which they are thought to have voiced. Scrutiny of the attacks on railroad corporations made by Kansas Populists reveals considerably more truth in the latter than the former view. Populists, although willing to abide with the vast advances in technology of the nineteenth century, did seek to subject those advances to political restraints which they plucked from earlier notions of governmental obligation. This tendency to apply aged political standards to recent developments can be labeled "retrogressive," but certainly not in the pejorative sense intended by historians such as Richard Hofstadter.

While the more positive perception of Populist intentions is readily applicable to the socialist-inclined wing of the party, it does not explain the views of those Kansas Populists who desired government control of railroads in order to repair American capitalism. The Populists, like any other large political party, divided themselves into conservative and radical factions. Although certain ideas may be said to characterize the thinking of the party as a whole (those of the Omaha Platform, for example), historians who make generalized conclusions about the Populists as a single entity frequently overlook the heterogeneity of the People's Party.

But the progressive framework of interpretation fits the grievances and proposals of the Kansas party's left-leaning leaders well. By applying their ideals of their democratic heritage to the forces which made them miserable, the dominant segment of Kansas Populism sought to force an ethical restructuring on the growing American business culture. Their lengthy enumeration of the harms associated with private control of railroads can be interpreted in no other way: Populists desired to protect humans from the excesses of unrestrained industrialism.

These Kansas leaders both reacted to the simple day-to-day difficulties posed by railroad abuses and accepted theoretical principles which gave their grievances a certain objectivity. Regardless of whether Populists were right or wrong to complain about exorbitant freight rates, their most powerful thrust at railroad corporations—the public utility idea and its logical corollary, nationalization—cannot be judged true or false by statistical analysis. The Populist critique was, in the end, an ethical one, demanding that the government intervene economically to prevent the widespread suffering of American citizens. Having acquired certain political values through the hardships of their daily existence, Kansas Populists advocated changes which both encompassed the ideas of their ancestors and foreshadowed the policies of their grandchildren.

NOTES

1. Quoted in Leo Marx, *The Machine in the Garden: Technology and the Pastoral Idea in America* (New York, 1964), 191.

2. Hallie Farmer, "The Railroads and Frontier Populism," *Mississippi Valley Historical Review*, 13 (December 1925), 387.

3. John Davis, *Public Ownership of Railroads* (Girard, KS, 1898), 63. The passage continues, ". . . whose business it is to confuse people and get their money."

4. "[T]he democratic dreams of the Populists have been difficult for twentieth-century people to imagine," Goodwyn argues, because Populists proposed "a new way of thinking about oneself and about democracy." Lawrence Goodwyn, *The Pop-*

ulist Moment: A Short History of the Agrarian Revolt in America (New York, 1978), xv, xxiv.

5. Ira G. Clark wrote in 1958: "The farmer struck blindly at the railroads, the nearest tangible evidence of what to him was the agent of his misfortunes. The railroads thus became the whipping boy for all the accumulated woes plaguing the West." Ira G. Clark, *Then Came the Railroads: The Century from Steam to Diesel in the Southwest* (Norman, 1958), 216. See also Theodore Solutos, "The Agricultural Problem and Nineteenth-Century Industrialism," *Agricultural History*, 22 (July 1948), 167.

6. Only Bruce Palmer, in his work on southern Populism, explicitly recognizes the importance of the pubic utility concept. He writes that Populist arguments concerning exorbitant freight rates "implied that the railroads were not ordinary property because they had qualities which made them, in some ways, public institutions." Palmer, *"Man over Money": The Southern Populist Critique of American Capitalism* (Chapel Hill, 1989), 77.

7. "Railroad promoters . . . looked at the welfare of the larger public and emphasized, not the potentialities for private gain from the railways, but rather what their construction would do for the body politic." James A. Ward, *Railroads and the Character of America, 1820–1887* (Knoxville, 1986), 80.

8. Peter Lyon, *To Hell in a Day Coach: An Exasperated Look at American Railroads* (Philadelphia, 1968), 11. Lyon describes the 1862 creation of the Union Pacific by Congress in precisely the terms of the commonweal: "The intentions of Congress were clear; they were 'to promote the public interest and welfare by the construction of said railroad. . . .'" (p. 30).

9. Stewart H. Holbrook places the amount of land ultimately handed over to the railroads rather conservatively at 131,350,534 acres. Holbrook, *The Story of American Railroads* (New York, 1947), 157.

10. Ward, *Railroads and the Character of America*, 10.

11. As Gene Clanton writes, "The key to the growth of industry and commercial agriculture in Kansas was clearly the development of railroad transportation. Kansans in all walks of life recognized this, and practically everybody became, in one way or another, railroad promoters." O. Gene Clanton, *Kansas Populism: Ideas and Men* (Lawrence, 1969), 18.

12. Mary A. Rich, "Railroads and the Agricultural Interests of Kansas, 1865–1915" (master's thesis, University of Virginia, 1960), 20.

13. Raymond Curtis Miller writes that "the roads were built largely from grants of land, guaranteed mortgages, gifts, and bonuses from nation, state, county, township, city, and even individuals—gifts which amounted by 1890 to about $50,000,000 and including railroad bonds guaranteed by the state, to almost $75,000,000." Raymond Curtis Miller, "The Background of Populism in Kansas," *Mississippi Valley Historical Review*, 11 (March 1925), 470.

14. The statistics arising from this spasm of optimism are startling. As Miller notes: "By 1888 there was one mile of railroad for every nine and one-third square

miles of land, and five and one-half miles of track for every thousand people in the state." Ibid., 470.

15. Clanton, *Kansas Populism*, 19.

16. Glenn Danford Bradley, *The Story of Santa Fe* (Boston, 1920), 109.

17. See in particular: William A. Peffer, *The Farmer's Side: His Troubles and Their Remedy* (New York, 1891, repr., Westport, CT, 1976), 64–65, 67; C. Wood Davis, "The Farmer, the Investor, and the Railway," *Arena* (February 1891), 291; John Davis, *Public Ownership*, 1; and C. B. Hoffman, "Populism—Its Future," *Agora*, 4 (April 1895), 250.

18. James D. Holden, *Metallic Money and Hard Times: Why They Are Inseparable* (Emporia, KS, 1890), n.p.

19. James D. Holden, *Free Freight and Government Railways: A Proposition to restore to Society essential rights of which it has been wrongfully divested. . .* (Emporia, KS, n.d.), 2.

20. C. Wood Davis, "Farmer, Investor, Railway," 306–307.

21. Peffer, *Farmer's Side,* 176–77.

22. Congress, Senate, William A. Peffer speaking on Safety of Life on Railroads to the Committee of the Whole, H. R. 9350, 52d Cong., 2d sess., *Congressional Record* (8 February 1893), vol. 24, pt. 2, 1323.

23. Congress, Senate, Senator William A. Peffer of Kansas speaking on Public Agencies, 53d Cong., 2d sess., *Congressional Record* (10 July 1894), vol. 26, pt. 7, 7230.

24. Junction City, Kansas, *Tribune,* 28 July 1892.

25. As reprinted in Norman Pollack, ed., *The Populist Mind* (Indianapolis, 1967), 58.

26. As quoted in Clanton, *Kansas Populism*, 214.

27. William A. Peffer, "The Trust Problem and Its Solutions," *Forum* (July 1899), 528.

28. Congress, House, Congressman William A. Harris speaking on Pacific Railroads to the Committee of the Whole, H. R. 7798, 53d Cong., 3d sess., *Congressional Record* (30 January 1895), vol. 27, pt. 2, 1555.

29. Congress, House, Congressman William A. Harris speaking on Pacific Railroads to the Committee of the Whole, H. R. 7798, 53d Cong., 3d sess., *Congressional Record* (31 January 1895), vol. 27, pt. 2, 1591.

30. Congress, House, Congressman Jerry Simpson speaking on Pacific Railroads to the Committee of the Whole, H. R. 7798, 53d Cong., 3d sess., *Congressional Record* (2 February 1895), vol. 27, pt. 2, 1704.

31. John Leedy, "Message to Kansas House of Representatives," *House Journal,* 1897, 32–33.

32. John Davis, *Public Ownership,* 7–8.

33. As reprinted in John Hicks, *The Populist Revolt* (Minneapolis, 1931), 442, 443.

34. Holden, *Metallic Money,* n.p.

35. Congress, House, Congressman William A. Harris speaking on Pacific Railroads to the Committee of the Whole, H. R. 7798, 53d Cong., 3d sess., *Congressional Record* (31 January 1895), vol. 27, pt. 2, 1592.

36. Congress, House, Congressman Thomas Hudson speaking on Pacific Railroads to the Committee of the Whole, H. R. 7798, 53d Cong., 3d sess., *Congressional Record* (2 February 1895), vol. 27, pt. 2, 1703.

37. S. S. King, *The Gulf Outlet* (Kansas City, KS, 1896), 77, 88.

38. Peter H. Argersinger, "Populists in Power," *Journal of Interdisciplinary History,* 18 (Summer 1987), 101. This split in Populist ranks is also observed by O. Gene Clanton, who writes that for many populists, "collectivist methods were simply a legitimate means of restoring free enterprise and small competitive capitalism; in particular, they felt government owned and operated railroads would contribute to that end." Clanton, *Kansas Populism,* 71.

39. Clanton, *Kansas Populism,* 71.

40. Ibid., 147. In the later years of Kansas Populism, a number of the Party's leaders declared outright their support for "socialism." G. C. Clemens was instrumental in the founding of the state socialist party, running as its gubernatorial candidate in 1900. In that campaign he was endorsed by former governor Lewelling. John Briedenthal, the 1900 Populist candidate, also declared himself a "socialist," as did Willits, the 1890 People's Party choice for governor. Ibid., 217–18, 223–24, 227, 236.

41. As quoted in Norman Pollack, *The Populist Response to Industrial America: Midwestern Populist Thought* (Cambridge, MA, 1962), 92–93.

42. Clanton, *Kansas Populism,* 216–17.

43. Daniels, *Gordian Knot,* 11.

44. Clanton, *Kansas Populism,* 222–23. Vrooman was later assistant secretary of agriculture for President Wilson.

45. Carl S. Vrooman, "The Diary of a Kansas Republican," in *Taming the Trusts* (Topeka, 1900), 27–28, 24.

46. Sidney Fine, *Laissez Faire and the General-Welfare State: A Study of Conflict in American Thought, 1865–1901* (Ann Arbor, 1956), 207–208.

47. Ibid., 203–31, 227, 226. Of Ely and Bemis, Fine writes, "Publicly owned monopolies, they believed, would treat their employees better than privately owned businesses, would pay them higher wages, and have them work fewer hours, and, as a result, there would be fewer strikes. Farmers would also benefit in that they would be charged lower rates for moving their crops." Ibid., 227.

48. Gene Clanton, "'Hayseed Socialism' on the Hill: Congressional Populism, 1891–1895," *Western Historical Quarterly,* 15 (April 1984), 146.

49. As quoted in ibid., 146.

50. Percy Daniels, *A Crisis for the Husbandman* (Girard, KS, 1889), 14.

51. Clanton, *Kansas Populism,* 222.

52. Carl S. Vrooman, "Twentieth Century Democracy," *Arena* (November 1899), 293.

53. Vrooman, *Taming the Trusts*, 6, 102–104.

54. Daniels, *Crisis*, 14.

55. C. Wood Davis, "Should the Nation Own the Railways?" *Arena* (July and August 1891), 290–92, 277.

56. These two essays are included in Vrooman, *Taming the Trusts*.

57. Vrooman, "Twentieth Century Democracy," 593.

58. Vrooman, *Taming the Trusts*, 41, 57.

59. Ibid., 107.

60. Goodwyn, *Populist Moment*, xix, 135, 153.

61. Ibid., xviii.

62. Stanley B. Parsons et al. "The Role of Cooperatives in the Development of the Movement Culture of Populism," *Journal of American History*, 69 (March 1983), 884.

Paved with Good Intentions: Good Roads, the Automobile, and the Rhetoric of Rural Improvement in Kansas Farmer, 1890–1914

Paul Sutter

In 1896 a group of perturbed farmers confronted William Allen White on the streets of Emporia and berated him for his criticism of their political goals. Angry and cowed, White retired to his office to compose a piece that helped make his reputation as a journalist. Entitled "What's the Matter with Kansas?," the piece received a national audience and won White fame among Republican leaders. With tongue squarely in cheek, White painted his fellow Kansans into a premodern corner:

> Oh, this is a state to be proud of! . . . What we need is not more money, but less capital, fewer white shirts and brains, fewer men with business judgement, and more of those fellows who can boast that they are "just ordinary clodhoppers. . . ."

"Paved with Good Intentions: Good Roads, the Automobile, and the Rhetoric of Rural Improvement in *Kansas Farmer,* 1890–1914," by Paul Sutter, *Kansas History* 18, 4 (1995–1996): 284–299. Copyright Kansas State Historical Society. Reprinted by permission.

We don't need population, we don't need wealth, we don't need well-dressed men on the streets, we don't need cities on the fertile prairies; you bet we don't! What we are after is the money power. Because we have become poorer and ornerier and meaner than a spavined, distempered mule, we, the people of Kansas, propose to kick; we don't care to build up, we wish to tear down.

With the fervor of a booster, White chastised the agrarian grab for political power by depicting farmers as reactionary opponents to economic modernization. Concerned for the increasingly soiled reputation of the state, White lashed out at the "hayseeds" who, in his mind, were undermining the state's prosperity. His voice was an important one in creating what historian Gene Clanton called the "negative climate of opinion" that stunted the growth of the Populist movement.[1] White's rhetoric rested on a logic that equated modernization—in White's terms a process that included urbanization, increased population, business virtues, a higher standard of living, and even a fashion aesthetic—with rationality and national destiny. In White's mind, farmers were guilty of opposing the inevitable and doubly guilty for being blind to the fact. Ironically the national circulation of the editorial likely accomplished the undesired effect of reinforcing the negative image that White sought to dismantle.[2]

White's editorial was part of the charged rhetoric of an era in which discussions of modernization resonated with symbolic language and emotional appeals. Depictions of the agricultural population as "backward" were rife, although they were not always as vehement or animated as White's diatribe. This article examines how such depictions shaped the discussion about the improvement of rural roads and the acceptance of the automobile in Kansas. It is based on a thorough analysis of the discourse about good roads and the automobile found in the Topeka-based weekly farm journal, the *Kansas Farmer,* between 1890–1920.

Discussions about rural road improvement occurred in two phases. The early good roads movement of the 1880s and 1890s was a contemporary of the agrarian challenge and was profoundly shaped by Populist and anti-Populist rhetoric. A second phase of the good roads movement occurred in the first two decades of the twentieth century, an era in which Populists yielded the mantle of reform to progressive Republicans.[3] The automobile was central to this second phase, shaping the arguments both for and against road improvement. Many of the themes of both the agrarian movement and of the rhetorical backlash against its participants remained a part of this second phase, although they were somewhat transmogrified by Progressive Era concerns. Indeed there is a noticeable shift in the pages of *Kansas Farmer* from a more open and searching dialogue about modernization to a reliance on authoritative notions of progress, efficiency, and expertise.[4] This article looks at how periodical literature encouraged Kansans to empower themselves by modernizing the farm and by challenging the market on its own terms.

Railroad dominance during the mid–nineteenth century stifled serious discussion of road improvement on a national scale. Although rural residents struggled with the poor conditions of the nation's roads, sentiment for road improvement was not effectively mobilized until the 1880s. And when it was, it came from an unlikely source: bicyclists. The bicycle was an important precursor of the automobile. Many of the technological achievements we tend to associate with the automobile are more appropriately credited to the bicycle. These include mass production, accurately machined gears, and pneumatic tires, among other innovations.[5] Above all else, however, cyclists desired passable roads, and as they ventured into the countryside they came into conflict with rural residents over the condition of the roads. To represent their interests, cyclists organized themselves into clubs, including the League of American Wheelmen (LAW), founded in 1880. By 1888, LAW had launched a national campaign for better roads, a campaign that is widely considered the genesis of the modern good roads movement. It was not, however, a movement which fit easily into the agrarian agenda. According to Philip Mason, farmers raised their voices "in bitter opposition" for numerous reasons: fear of increased taxes, threats to their control over highway administration, and the potential meddling of city folks with their notions of expertise.[6] Many saw LAW as a challenge to rural autonomy.

LAW initially manifested some hostility toward the farmer. A LAW publication from 1891, entitled "The Gospel of Good Roads: A Letter to the American Farmer," berated farmers for their backward concerns. In this account its author, Isaac B. Potter, told of a visit to his fictitious farming friend, "Hubmire." Potter depicted Hubmire as irrationally conservative and ignorant because he refused to acknowledge the effects of primitive road conditions in the nation's rural areas.

To Potter, Hubmire was a "typical representative of the farming class," who, true to his name, refused to pull himself out of the literal and symbolic mud of inferior roads. Rather than addressing farmers' fiscal concerns about road improvement as legitimate, Potter opted for rhetorical intimidation. While LAW changed its tune by the end of the century, farmers were slow to forget the condescending tones heard during the movement's early years.[7]

There is no reason to think that Kansas was not equally affected by the proliferation of the bicycle. Joseph Pennell's photographs of Junction City, Kansas, in the 1890s document the bicycle's ubiquitous presence.[8] From the 1890s onward, one finds in the pages of *Kansas Farmer* articles and advertisements discussing the bicycle's merits and drawbacks. An ad for Columbia bicycles claimed that their product provided "just the kind of exercise that stimulates the monotony of country life." An editorial in 1895 suggested that "the bicycle is displacing many horses formerly used, especially in cities and towns."[9] The bicycle provided a quick and simple form of transport, although some were still worried about certain impacts of the bicycle. It was, as the previous quote indicates, a tool of the townsperson, an invader to the agricultural hinterland. In another 1895 editorial came a report of a woman who, while walking along a rural road, had been accosted and robbed by a man on a bicycle. Bicycles, the author implied, brought strangers into the rural landscape; improved roads promised only to facilitate such travel. Luckily in this case the woman was able to lure the bandit off of his bicycle, at which point she grabbed the vehicle and went for help.[10]

Some Kansans were skeptical about cyclists' demands for better roads. In a speech to the Cowley County Farmer's Institute, I. O. Rambo implored those in attendance to submit to the expertise of competent engineers rather than continue to operate with the substandard roads that came with the use of statute labor. (Rural roads in the nineteenth century were built primarily by local officials who lacked training as engineers and were often maintained by local residents who chose to work in the place of tax payments.)[11] But Rambo also issued a warning against catering to cyclists, clearly intimating that they were interlopers of a different economic class. Good roads, Rambo suggested, were meant to meet the needs and standards of the farmers who built and paid for them and not interest groups like LAW that offered farmers little but insult.[12] Rambo foreshadowed a debate about the nature of the road as a public space, a debate that focused on who should properly be using and paying for rural roads.

In 1895, largely because of the efforts of LAW and its affiliates, the U.S. Department of Agriculture (USDA) created the Office of Road Inquiry (ORI) to survey conditions of the nation's rural roads and to provide advice to local authorities. ORI was significant for a number of reasons. First, it represented the federal government's entry into the discussion of road conditions, a presence that gained strength despite an initial wariness to assert influence. Second, the placement of ORI within the USDA suggested the extent to which the argument for good roads became an agricultural one. The pages of *Kansas Farmer* indicated that farmers, with some exceptions, were not against good roads per se; they were worried about the imposition of external authority, concerned that they would have to build roads to suit the standards of wealthy urbanites, and aware of the potentially high cost of road improvement. Although farmers in general, and Kansas farmers in particular, frequently cursed the conditions of their roads, they did not trust the urgency with which many approached improvement.[13] Finally, the ORI was one of a number of federal bureaus in this era that expressed concern, in typically progressive fashion, about the "amateurish" way in which Americans cared for their resources.[14] From the 1890s forward, state and local governments, city and town folk, the press, and a growing number of farmers pushed ideas of progress that rejected earlier concerns about debt and entangling economic alliances.

The federal government, since Kansas' entrance into the Union, had given the state a small percentage of the receipts from land sales to finance internal improvements. Despite such aid, the county was the governmental unit most responsible for building and maintenance of roads in Kansas prior to the advent of the automobile. Traditionally, the county levied road taxes, which residents could either pay in cash or in labor. Road districts were established and supervisors appointed, and charges of corruption and poor administration were frequent. Indeed, much of the sentiment for adopting a system of county engineers and professional road crews played upon these issues. As the ORI evolved into the Office of Public Road Inquiry (1899) and then the Bureau of Public Roads (1905), the ideal of apolitical expertise, embodied by the highway engineer, asserted greater influence over the nation's development of a system of roads.[15] Kansans resisted these trends; the state was one of the last to form a highway commission and was dead last in putting together a system of state aid for road building. It was not until the automobile became a common sight that Kansans were pushed to action.[16]

Along with pressure brought by groups like the League of American Wheelmen and the National League for Good Roads (1892), the advent of rural free delivery (RFD) of mail in 1896 and its corollary that designated routes be properly maintained (1899) chipped away at rural resolve to maintain roads on their own terms. "Nothing else," historian Wayne Fuller argued, "brought the sense of urgency to the good roads movement that rural delivery did." The threat of discontinuing mail service as a result of impassable roads was a powerful one, and mail carriers provided farmers with constant reminders of such a possibility.[17] As national groups, including the federal government, increased their scrutiny of the condition of Kansas roads, and as agrarian political power rose and fell, a more subtle form of rhetorical pressure came to bear on Kansas farmers.

Populism had affected national perceptions of Kansans. An 1898 editorial in *Kansas Farmer* made this explicit: "It was charged at home and abroad that the party was one of repudiation and dishonor, and the bottled up wrath of fools who had foolishly parted with their money was poured in multiplied measure upon our people."[18] Populism was seen, by at least some Kansans, as an embarrassment. The press buttressed the accuracy of such perceptions, and the party's soiled reputation was turned upon Kansans as a matter of conscience—in the above case by a voice that purported to represent the interests of the farmers themselves. As William Allen White had portrayed his own state's farmers as backward in the 1890s, so the government, national organizations, and the press depicted the rural environment as impoverished and an embarrassment to the nation during the first two decades of the twentieth century. Progressives adopted the rhetoric of "backwardness," which the Republicans had so successfully used to combat the Populists, and used it as a tool of persuasion to push rural improvement.

In a letter to *Kansas Farmer* in 1892, Marcus J. Wells, a farmer from Woodston, Kansas, expressed a common reaction to the first phase of ferment for good roads:

What is the meaning of the effort of the metropolitan press to create an interest in good roads? Is the object to get really good roads, or to find investment for the money of our eastern capitalists? The farmers of our country should be cautious about accepting the calculations intended to prove the feasibility of building good roads and bonding our counties to pay for them. . . . Such figuring as this is responsible for much of our farm indebtedness today. . . . The mania for borrowing has resulted in improving farms for others to enjoy, and I submit that if we build public roads with borrowed money, we shall soon find ourselves in the condition to get little benefit from them. . . . Our farmers will do well to beware the voice of the siren speaking through the subsidized press of the large cities. It will lure them onto the rocks of destruction.[19]

Although his rhetoric was replete with distrust, Wells recognized the hazards of speculation, mortgaging, and bond issues, particularly railroad bonds, which had fueled Kansas' boom in the early 1880s and which created havoc when prices bottomed out at the end of the decade.[20] Debt circumscribed agricultural behavior; the deeper a farmer sagged into debt, the more market production became a necessity and the more vulnerable the farmer became to economic and environmental cycles. Wells rejected a consumer ethic that suggested farmers spend their way to prosperity, insisting instead that farmers use fiscal logic to assess the reasonableness of road improvement. But Wells also recognized that the initial impetus for improved roads was in part an urban one. Although Wells may have accepted such a landscape as a goal, he insisted that rural road improvement be an indigenous and thoughtful process. He had to contend, however, with the powerful moral and aesthetic arguments— "the siren"—that connected status with the condition of roads.

While some Kansans formulated an argument for fiscal conservatism, others vilified that argument as an obstacle to progress and offered in its stead a vision of a modern prairie which only the courage to capitalize could achieve. Within a month, readers of *Kansas Farmer* were privy to another side of the story in a lengthy article by former Governor George W. Glick. After pointing out the inevitable increases in land values that accompanied good roads and the monetary losses incurred by farmers due to poor roads, Glick played the booster:

Good highways make all the surroundings more pleasant; the easy inter-communication adds pleasure to the social conditions; friendships are nurtured and preserved; love of home and surroundings are [*sic*] instilled into the minds of the young, and in such localities family homesteads are occupied for years. . . . These conditions are the direct profits that good highways bestow. . . . Poor teams, muddy dooryards, no barns, hungry cattle, and a score of yelping curs, are the unfailing sights exhibited to the unfortunate wanderer who is compelled to pass through that "vale of despond" where poor roads prevail.[21]

Glick appealed to a number of concrete concerns—the transience of the farm population and the flight of the young to cities, land values and the costs entailed due to limited access to markets—but he also conflated questions about rural identity and image with the issue of road improvement. Rather than addressing the legitimate fiscal fears of people like Marcus Wells, Glick tried to embarrass farmers into submission. He did this by placing poor roads within an aesthetic of rural poverty. Poor roads in particular and a disorderly rural environment in general were signs of the farmer's depravity. Glick encouraged farmers to view their surroundings as status writ large. Finally, Glick introduced the outsider as cultural voyeur and judge of moral probity, making it clear that farmers were being scrutinized by the nation. Whether poor or not, the farm family had to avoid the appearance of poverty at all costs, lest the value of their land depreciate and their social standing plummet.

Both Wells and Glick employed manipulative rhetoric, but while Wells depicted a distant enemy, Glick indicted the farmers themselves. And while a large number of farmers were likely more sympathetic to Wells' characterization of the situation, Glick's argument was not without its power. Instead of looking to the government or corporations themselves for regulation of market conditions that created economic inequality, boosters like Glick tried to persuade the farmers of Kansas that they alone were responsible for their predicament and that they alone could choose the path toward resolution. After 1896 many Kansas farmers assessed Populism's political demise in the progressive terms that served their foes so well. The challenge to the direction of American economic growth which the Populists had posed was swallowed by a consensus that sought to incorporate agricultural demands into a larger ethic and rhetoric of progress and modernity. Even before this shift, however, other important themes emerged as part of the discourse on roads.

The logic and aesthetics of suburbanization played a major part in the argument for improving Kansas' roads in the 1890s. In a letter to the *Kansas Farmer,* John Van Voorhis Gould invoked a number of suburban themes. Citing one of the best reasons for promoting better roads, Gould suggested that "farm lands, not too remote from cities, would readily sell for suburban residences." This argument that good roads raised property values was ubiquitous. Continuing, Gould noted that roads "outlined with trees . . . would be very suggestive of boulevards, [and would] make cheerful and brighten the monotony . . . of farm life." Trees were lauded as the primary agents in the pastoralization of the Kansas landscape and betrayed the aesthetic preferences of many who populated the recently settled state. Consonant with one of the main themes of nineteenth-century reform, Gould expressed his faith in the potential moral benefits of a more ordered and attractive environment. Gould ended his exposition with some moralizing characteristic of the arguments for good roads. "I believe," he predicted, "that there would be fewer paupers and less insanity in our land if we had a good system of public roads."[22]

Scholars have tended to stress the urban origins of the suburban impulse, citing how transportation innovations like the streetcar and later the automobile allowed urbanites to reside outside of the city, and how urban life itself created the conditions under which the pastoral ideal of the manicured countryside flourished.[23] Discussions about improving roads in Kansas suggest that the imposition and adoption of these ideals by rural dwellers is a process that deserves more attention. While urbanites sought to infuse the city with the fresh air of rural living, farmers discussed the possibilities of urbanizing and modernizing the countryside in similar terms. In his study of the origins of the American suburb, John Stilgoe suggested that a "subtle shift in language" distinguished agricultural and suburban interests in the Country Life Movement, a distinction between moral and aesthetic progress. Rural reformers bombarded country dwellers with the idea of "improvement," while suburbanites, whose lives apparently were already "improved," were instructed to "beautify" their surroundings.[24] A reading of *Kansas Farmer* suggests the adequacy of Stilgoe's distinction to a certain point. Most of the discussion through the 1890s focuses on improvement, which, although it had a powerful aesthetic component, was more practical in nature. With the arrival of the first automobiles in Kansas in the early 1900s, however, *Kansas Farmer* supported an interest in beautification as well as improvement. And that interest was consistently proffered by women.

Women played an important part in modernizing the countryside. Indeed evidence points to their unique, gendered role as arbiters of beauty and taste. Lucretia Levett insisted that women's efforts remain distinct when she presented her paper, entitled "Roadside Adornment," to a Farmer's Institute meeting in 1904. "I do not wish to discuss the grading, draining, and working of roads," she concluded, eschewing the technical drudgery of road improvement. "I will leave that to the men, but will speak of some things that may be done to beautify what is often an eyesore as well as a harbor of noxious weeds." Levett, leaving the mechanics of improvement to men, embraced the challenge of beautification. Like George Glick before her, Levett invoked the gaze of the outside observer: "When we plant a tree by the highway, we are doing what we can to make the traveler who comes that way happier." The pre-settlement plains and prairies were, in Levett's mind, flat and featureless landscapes. Trees brought variety, beauty, and civility; they domesticated the countryside. After making the point that once Kansas was but a treeless plain, Levett jumped to the conclusion that "to-day its homes are beautiful," leaving the readers to supply the apparently obvious logic that trees equal beauty and that beauty equals prosperity. Levett urged Kansas residents to craft a new level of rural sophistication, one based on the appearance of grace and mastery.[25]

Mary M. Bates, the wife of a Topeka florist and a member of a local forestry club, added leisure to beautification as an appropriate topic of female discourse. Like Levett, Bates insisted that all talk of constructing roads be left to men. In "Women! Talk Good Roads," she urged women to take advantage of the fact that "the Lord gave women the gift of talk with the idea in view that they might keep at the men so they would do the work." Besides suggestions for beautification, like clearing weeds and planting alfalfa by the sides of the road, the pleasures of driving concerned Bates. She wanted a beautiful countryside as a destination for her outings. Women, Bates implied, had a unique role to play in rural improvement, one defined by contemporary notions of gender and separate spheres. Without challenging male roles, Bates suggested that women could encourage and shape rural improvement by making it clear to their husbands how such efforts would increase leisure opportunities and thus female happiness. Bates and Levett illustrate how women's voices became distinct ones in the debate over modernizing and beautifying the rural environment, particularly where roads and the automobile were concerned.[26]

Yet another powerful strand of the argument for good roads combined an urgency to control and improve the environment with a need to think in fiscal terms about the condition of rural roads. These arguments took many forms, but all centered around the idea that bad roads cost farmers more money annually in hauling costs than road improvement itself would. Furthermore, good roads meant that the uncertainties of the natural setting—knee-deep mud, storms, snow and ice—could be mastered, permitting the marketing of products when prices were highest. Instead of eliminating the "gambling in grain" bemoaned by many, farmers were encouraged to grasp control of the system itself by reducing the obstacles between themselves and the market. George Glick stated, "poor roads practically increase the distance to market."[27] Farmers had a choice to make: either continue with roads that frequently were impassable but required minimal investment and therefore minimal debt, or capitalize the roadway and put themselves in a position where they would need the promised savings to repay the debt incurred. Arguments presented in *Kansas Farmer* point to a strengthening of the latter position as farmers entered the twentieth century.

Playing on the familiar Populist theme that poor distribution was behind farmers' economic woes, G. E. Miller of Republic, Kansas, concluded: "[The] remedy is not to be found in a return to the conditions of a century ago. . . . The genius of the past has given us an excellent system of production. We must provide an equitable distribution." Other interests contributed their own logic. The Electric Wheel Company submitted an article that stressed the money-saving aspects of good roads, insisting that lowered shipping costs "would be sufficient to give every farmer an asphalt pavement from his front door to the nearest market."[28] The promise of saving money by spending money gained credence as the shroud of agricultural depression lifted around the turn of the century. But the 1890s saw resistance. Farmers were not always inclined to swallow the logic of improvement. Mortimer Whitehead, a lecturer for the National Grange, warned about the danger of being seduced by arguments for good roads. "The alcohol of the sentiment," he proffered, "is doing its work, aided and abetted by engineers, professors, and manufacturers of stone crushers, machinery men and dealers, and other 'interested' parties."[29] Farmers, according to Whitehead, had to be ever on their guard against commercial predation in the guise of progress.

Others saw it differently. After arguing for the fiscal beneficence of improved roads, Elwood E. Douglas, a farmer from Melvern, Kansas, concluded that, "beside economy from a business standpoint, a luxury of health and pleasure to all classes could be secured by having such public highways as this progressive age requires and is beginning to demand."[30] Douglas implicitly suggested what others later made clearer—good roads were an emerging national priority, perhaps even part of the nation's destiny. To him they were an essential nationalizing force, breaking down the divisive barriers of geography and class. Market access and the encouragement provided by rural free delivery were strong elements in the nationalization of this sentiment. Douglas, far from succumbing to the demands of urbanites or industrialists, saw good roads as part of a sensitive reading of the age itself. Although his comments were made a decade later, George C. Diehl, Chairman of the National Good Roads Board of the American Automobile Association, echoed Douglas' sentiment:

> . . . every mile of improved road anywhere in the United States benefits all the people of the United States in almost equal degree. To improve the road over which the apple-grower of the Yakima Valley hauls his fruit to the packing sheds of the growers' association means cheaper apples for the people of Philadelphia, New Orleans, or Boston. A better road . . . means that the rural mail-carriers can make the trips from these post-offices to the farms along the route more regularly and eventually more frequently, and that by thus bringing the farmer into closer contact with the world markets not only is his selling power increased, but his buying power also.[31]

As the movement for good roads jumped into the present century, the interests of farmers in Kansas and the perceived interests of the nation as a whole were more frequently discussed as if they were one.

Perhaps no one better epitomizes the progressive impulse to improve and standardize the lives of rural Americans, through efforts like the Country Life Movement, than Theodore Roosevelt. In a rousing speech given at the Good Roads Convention, held during the Louisiana Purchase Exposition in St. Louis in 1903, Roosevelt urged the audience to consider the role of good roads in raising the level of American civilization. Invoking the Roman Empire's road-building achievements, Roosevelt launched into a discussion of the conquest good roads would afford:

> And we, to whom space is less of an obstacle than ever before in the history of any nation, we who have spanned a continent . . . we, who take so little account of mere space, must see to it that the best means of nullifying the existence of space are at our command.[32]

Part of the goal of such conquest was economic. But Roosevelt, whose speech was reprinted in *Kansas Farmer*, had social and moral concerns as well. Good roads, Roosevelt concluded, "are needed for their effects on the industrial conditions of the country districts, and I am almost tempted to say that they are needed even more for their effect upon the social conditions of the country."[33] For Roosevelt and many other good-roads advocates, roads were the most representative physical symbol of the nation's strength—of the far-reaching connections between individuals. Their condition spoke directly of the strength of ties between groups, of access to the common goals of prosperity. Poor roads, in Roosevelt's mind, placed a portion of the populace in the retarded condition of spatial separation and isolation. Progressives like Roosevelt cringed at the notion of farmers mired in the mud of nineteenth-century conditions.

Perhaps no one piece of machinery was as responsible for the transformation of rural life in the early twentieth century as the automobile. Much has been written about the social and economic impact of automobiles and the good roads that accompanied them—how they put a significant dent in the cursed rural isolation, led to the rise and transformation of rural towns and economies, and expanded farmers' horizons. But little has been said about the ideological context in which the automobile became a chosen technology. How did farmers in Kansas greet the availability of automotive technology? How did farmers envision, and how were they encouraged to envision, the possibilities the automobile presented? That the farmers of Kansas did accept the automobile into their lives in a dramatic way is easy to establish. In 1914, the *Kansas Farmer* estimated that there were fifty thousand automobiles in Kansas, thirty thousand of which belonged to farmers. In the 1920 Agricultural Census, the first census in which categories like motor vehicle ownership were included, Kansas ranked third in percentage of farms that owned automobiles at 62 percent. Kansas was one of eleven states, all of them west of the Mississippi, that counted 10.7 or more automobiles for every hundred residents.[34]

The promise of technology played a prominent role in Kansans' vision of the future. The *Kansas Farmer* expressed pride in the technological strides farmers had made, at the home and in the fields. "From a mere slave," an editorial concluded:

> the farmer has come, with all these conveniences, to be a respected and intelligent individual. He has been emancipated from severe manual labor and has become independent. By machines his intellect is refreshed, his home made more pleasant. The farm laborer has not been thrown out of employment by the introduction of these machines. His labor is of a different kind, only.[35]

A number of important buttons were pushed in this piece; the farmer's reputation as unintelligent, the appeal of the free labor ideology, a connection between technology and democratic values, and the increased pressure for farmers to improve their surroundings. Machines afforded a new sort of freedom—freedom from excessive manual labor and a fickle natural environment. Respectability and intelligence, this editorial intoned, arrived on the farm with the first friction matches and sewing machines, and above all else with the automobile. The machine meant modernity.

Farmers were no strangers to technology. The *Kansas Farmer* is replete with discussions of the merits of various technologies, from steam and wind power to gasoline and electricity. Frequently isolated from sources of mechanical expertise, farmers had to learn how to do repairs themselves.[36] Farmers were using steam-powered tractors as early as the 1890s, and they had some exposure to and experience with gasoline engines before the automobile appeared on the scene.[37] When the automobile did appear, however, it had to pass a few tests before farmers would admit its usefulness.

Prior to the automobile, the horse was the motive power of choice for transportation and travel on and from the farm. The shift from biological to mechanical power offered a few challenges. The earliest automobiles in the United States were expensive. Usually, farmers first encountered the automobile in the hands of the rich urbanite out in the country for a joy-ride. Aside from the speeds these autos achieved and the annoyance of automobilists trudging through yards in search of water for radiators or the perfect picnic site, there were numerous instances of automobiles spooking horses. Many motorists were not sensitive to complaints that they used, monopolized, and frequently damaged roads which they had no part in maintaining.[38] The farmers, who paid the taxes for these roads, saw them as public in a limited sense; they were open to use for all those who paid for their upkeep. Urban motorists, on the other hand, not only transgressed this informal boundary, but often made themselves at home in farmers' fields for meals or a night's sleep. Compared to the cities and towns of their everyday experience, the vast spaces of the rural countryside seemed unowned. The increased radius of the urban tourist contributed to conflicts over the use of rural public space, conflicts that farmers sometimes settled by littering rural routes with glass, logs, trenches, and the occasional blast of shot.[39]

The challenge to the well-entrenched horse economy was also a major one. Farmers and other rural residents had significant capital tied up in horses and did not always respond positively to the notion of upgrading to an automobile. The automobile also threatened the horse-based economy of blacksmiths, breeders, harness and saddlemakers, and wagon and carriage manufacturers. The city of Lawrence provides an example of this scenario. In 1900, Lawrence had a strong horse economy with horse-drawn streetcars, eleven blacksmiths, five dealers in buggies and wagons, two carriage-makers, five harnessmakers, and two carriage-painting specialists. By 1917, when an interurban line connected downtown Lawrence with Kansas City, no harnessmakers, carriage-makers, or horse dealers were listed. The blacksmith count was down to eight and there were still two carriage-painters, but both groups were likely involved in the automobile economy. In their places were numerous auto dealers and garages as well as supply houses and automobile liveries.[40]

As the automobile age dawned, farmers encountered arguments, many of them quite scientific in their logic, for the economic merits of either the horse or the auto. Some insisted that automobiles, particularly the early ones which were expensive and unreliable, dried up even more of the farmer's capital and often put the farm family deeper in debt. Automobile boosters argued that autos were cheaper than horses to maintain, and that the increased mobility that they afforded allowed farmers to save valuable time and money marketing their goods.

The first notice of the automobile in *Kansas Farmer,* while ripe with suspicion, also gave reason for hope. Appearing in 1899 it began with a reference to the temperamental reactions of horses (a common theme), but proceeded right to the appealing possibility that use of the automobile would undermine the interests of the railroad stockholder. The editorial ends with a message of promise for the disgruntled farmer:

> Whether this frightened stockholder is worse scared than he is likely to be hurt, or whether he has secretly disposed of his stock in the railroad and invested in automobile stock which he wishes to boom, can not be definitely determined at this stage of the proceedings. But the farmer who is somewhat remote from the railroad station, or who is somewhat exasperated by the indifferent service rendered by the "calamity branch," will not be averse to even a remote prospect of better service from the automobile.[41]

The automobile, whether it profited capitalists or not, was a potentially liberating technology once in the hands of farmers. Unlike the railroad it offered the farmer some control over marketing, even if only from farm to railhead. Although it took almost a decade before the automobile arrived in the hands of Kansas farmers in any great numbers, the discourse on good roads and the infusion and successful adoption of other technologies readied the farmer for the auto age.

With the arrival of the automobile, a whole new round in the movement for good roads took shape. Farmers were again suspicious that urbanites and industrialists would have their way in the Kansas countryside. Jim Engle wrote an angry letter to the *Kansas Farmer* in 1906 protesting the Atchison, Topeka and Santa Fe's "Good Roads Train." The train, complete with roadbuilding machinery and labor crews, traveled to numerous communities in Kansas and other states to build "object-lesson" roads. The logic was that once farmers experienced the pleasures of a good road, they would adopt the cause enthusiastically. Engle was not impressed: "if they mean to introduce the building of hard roads . . . by us farmers, they had better wait until we invite them." Moreover, he had an idea of their motives. "No doubt," he concluded, "the auto people would like to have the farmers build hard roads for them to run their automobiles on." The tone of Engle's letter was so contrary to the editors that they felt compelled to follow it with a comment of their own: "The Santa Fe is to be commended for bringing before the people of the territory it traverses practicable methods of maintaining good roads cheaply."[42] Joseph Satran of Wilson, Kansas, shared Engle's suspicion of the strengthening good roads movement. "To my mind," he grumbled, "the chief beneficiaries of the scheme are not the farmers, but the automobile maker, banker, capitalist, and political office-seeker. . . . In proof of my assertion just notice with what persevering persistency and rush they are pushing the scheme along."[43]

Automobile makers, among others, were beginning to target farmers as their major market. Henry Ford presented himself as the farmer's advocate, attacking the evils of Wall Street financiers with an enthusiasm that befitted a struggling tenant farmer, not one of the world's richest men. Reynold Wik points out that Ford even "talked like a Populist."[44] In this sense, he provides a link between the Populist rhetoric of the 1890s and the Progressive concerns for modernization and efficiency in the early 1900s. The federal government's Office of Public Road Inquiry, transformed into the Bureau of Public Roads in 1905, pushed the cause of improving roads for automobiles with abandon and was chastised for inappropriate advocacy. Automobile clubs, like the American Automobile Association, were a strong national force in pushing for an improved domain for the automobile. Finally, railroads were the largest backers of the good roads effort until 1916 when they realized that autos and a burgeoning trucking industry were bypassing rail transport altogether.[45]

Many of the arguments for the purchase of automobiles and for good roads on which to drive them echoed the logic that guided the earlier good roads movement. Again farmers encountered pleas and seduction. A 1909 article encapsulated a number of these arguments: "Besides the returns in making markets more accessible and in comfort and pleasure of going about, the enhancement of land values on account of the good impression upon persons who pass or who may be looking for farms is a consideration of importance." Numerous other articles echoed these and other themes. "Aside from its worth as a pleasure car," reported a 1910 article, "it [the automobile] is an actual agency of progress and prosperity."[46] The automobile's promise was a simple one: to liberate the farm family from the ordinary agricultural constraints of time and space, and to supply the farm with the ultimate symbol of modernity and progress.

When Henry Ford began building inexpensive and durable cars that were ideal for the farmer, he went a long way toward smoothing over the automobile's initially rough reception. The *Kansas Farmer* reinforced this detente between farmers and the automobile, assuring Kansans that the automobile was in the picture to stay. A 1910 editorial sought to persuade farmers that it was "no longer a matter of pride or ostentation of wealth for the farmer to own an automobile but in very many cases is a matter of real economy."[47] The automobile offered to finish the job of modernizing the countryside:

> Life on the farm is undoubtedly pleasanter, more healthful and more nearly ideal than it could ever be under the artificial conditions of the city, and the invention of the automobile has removed from the farm its objectionable features. . . . The automobile will revolutionize both life and labor in rural America.[48]

Farmers were promised that the automobile would bring their business "more closely in touch with the merchants and bankers to [their] advantage." Competition between auto makers for the farm market lowered prices to the farmers' advantage.[49] Finally, the automobile revolutionized the social lives of Kansas farmers by allowing isolated farm families more frequent contact with cultural centers. The automobile promised individual agency, social improvement, and economic prosperity through mastery of environment and market relations. Its arrival tipped the scales in favor of road improvement.

Depictions of the rural environment as backward and progressive promises about the transformative properties of improved roads and the automobile warped the fiscal concerns expressed by many farmers. Such rhetoric, heavily reliant on a modern aesthetic, profoundly shaped the debates over rural road improvement and the adoption of the automobile that appeared in the *Kansas Farmer* between 1890–1914. Certainly the automobile and good roads offered numerous advantages to farmers. This cannot be denied nor should it be trivialized. But those who did choose to resist the advent of the automobile age found themselves in an increasingly untenable position—not because the automobile and the hard-surfaced road were part of the inevitable "next stage" in economic growth, but because so many believed them to be so and expressed their beliefs in language that distorted the logic of dissent.

Farmers' decisions were influenced by many other factors, public and private. Little has been said about other important considerations which may have contributed to the discourse on roads and the automobile. The economic recovery that characterized the first few decades of the twentieth century surely made buying an automobile and supporting good roads appear a better choice. In a 1914 editorial entitled "This and That for Good Roads," the author included a telling remark that "even bankers no longer oppose the motor car," perhaps indicating that the debt involved in purchasing an automobile was less risky in that prosperous era.[50] World War I intensified Plains agriculture and profoundly affected farmers' views of technology and the capacity of the market. The war years also revealed to Americans the limitations of railroad transport, as vital supplies often languished in rail yards awaiting shipment. Nonetheless, the adoption of the automobile and hard-surfaced roads was irreversible. The spatial configuration of the rural environment changed—towns became more centralized and farming operations relied on more frequent visits to these centers—and with these changes the automobile became more of a necessity.[51] The risks involved in making such a shift were painfully clear in another circumscribed choice that many Kansas farmers made in the 1930s—the choice to pack their belongings in their automobiles and leave their farms for the smoothly paved roads that headed west.

NOTES

1. O. Gene Clanton, *Kansas Populism: Ideas and Men* (Lawrence: University Press of Kansas, 1969), 242; White's editorial quoted in *The Autobiography of William Allen White* (New York: Macmillan Co., 1946), 282.

2. Scott McNall, *The Road to Rebellion: Class Formation and Kansas Populism, 1865–1900* (Chicago: University of Chicago Press, 1988), 174–75; Sally Foreman Griffith, *Home Town News: William Allen White and the Emporia Gazette* (New York: Oxford University Press, 1987), 44–49; Robert S. La Forte, *Leaders of Reform: Progressive Republicans in Kansas, 1900–1916* (Lawrence: University Press of Kansas, 1974), 2–3.

3. See La Forte, *Leaders of Reform.*

4. Samuel P. Hayes, *Conservation and the Gospel of Efficiency: The Progressive Conservation Movement, 1890–1920* (New York: Atheneum, 1972).

5. Peter J. Hugill, "Good Roads and the Automobile in the United States 1880–1920," *Geographical Review* 72 (July 1972): 327; see also James J. Flink, *The Automobile Age* (Cambridge: MIT Press, 1988), 4–5.

6. Philip P. Mason, "The League of American Wheelmen and the Good Roads Movement" (Ph.D. diss., University of Michigan, 1957), 90–92; see also Bruce E. Seely, *Building the American Highway System: Engineers as Policy Makers* (Philadelphia: Temple University Press, 1987), 11–13.

7. "The Gospel of Good Roads: A Letter to the American Farmer" is cited in Mason, "The League of American Wheelmen," 101–2.

8. Joseph Pennell Collection, Kansas Collection, University of Kansas Libraries, Lawrence.

9. *Kansas Farmer* (Topeka), June 10, 1897, 367; "The Bicycle," ibid., June 5, 1895, 360.

10. "A Bandit on a Bicycle," ibid., March 6, 1895, 150.

11. Seely, *Building the American Highway System*, 12.

12. I. O. Rambo, "Roads," *Kansas Farmer*, March 31, 1898, 211.

13. For an example of such a reaction, which is cited at length later in the *Kansas Farmer*, see letter from M. J. Wells, ibid., January 27, 1892, 1.

14. Seely, *Building the American Highway System*, 11–23.

15. Ibid.

16. Mary Scott Rowland, "Managerial Progressivism in Kansas, 1916–1930" (Ph.D. diss., University of Kansas, 1980), 63; see also Arman J. Habegger, "Out of the Mud: The Good Roads Movement in Kansas, 1900–1917" (master's thesis, University of Kansas, 1971). Numerous articles in the *Kansas Farmer* are informative of the process by which Kansans came to accept more centralized and professional control over road construction. Rowland's dissertation also contains an important discussion of the politics of road building and maintenance, but she does not cover the years prior to 1916 in any detail.

17. Wayne E. Fuller, "Good Roads and the Rural Free Delivery of Mail," *Mississippi Valley Historical Review* 42 (June 1955), 67–83. The quote is from Fuller, *RFD: The Changing Face of Rural America* (Bloomington: University of Indiana Press, 1964), 189.

18. "Why This Change?" *Kansas Farmer*, February 3, 1898, 76.

19. Letter from M. J. Wells, *Kansas Farmer*, January 27, 1892, 1. Information about Wells' occupation was gleaned from the 1900 U.S. Census, Kansas, Rooks County.

20. McNall, *The Road to Rebellion*, 74–83.

21. George Glick, "Public Highways and Their Improvement," *Kansas Farmer*, February 24, 1892, 4–5.

22. John Van Voorhis Gould, "Good Roads," ibid., April 6, 1892, 5.

23. For an example of this urban interpretation of suburbanization, see Joel A. Tarr, "From City to Suburb: The 'Moral' Influence of Transportation Technology," in *American Urban History*, ed. Alexander B. Callow, 2d ed. (New York: Oxford University Press, 1973), 202–12.

24. John R. Stilgoe, *Borderland: Origins of the American Suburb, 1820–1939* (New Haven: Yale University Press, 1988), 212–13.

25. Lucretia E. Levett, "Roadside Adornment," *Kansas Farmer*, October 6, 1904, 990.

26. Mrs. Walter Bates, "Women! Talk Good Roads," ibid., August 11, 1904, 794–95. Information about Bates' identity was taken from the 1900 U.S. Census, Kansas, Shawnee County, City of Topeka.

27. *Kansas Farmer*, February 24, 1892, 4. The phrase "gambling in grain" is borrowed from William Cronon, *Nature's Metropolis: Chicago and the Great West* (New York: W. W. Norton and Co., 1991).

28. G. E. Miller to *Kansas Farmer*, February 8, 1893, 6; "Good Roads Will Save Big Money," ibid., February 24, 1898, 123.

29. Information on Whitehead's position comes from National Grange of the Patrons of Husbandry, *Journal of the Proceedings of the 27th Session* (Philadelphia: J. A. Wagenseller, 1893); Mortimer Whitehead, "Whence Came the Good Road Craze?" *Kansas Farmer*, June 14, 1893, 9.

30. Elwood E. Douglas, "The Good Roads Agitation," *Kansas Farmer*, May 10, 1900, 394.

31. George C. Diehl, "For Good Roads," *Harper's Weekly* 56 (April 6, 1912): 12.

32. Theodore Roosevelt, "Why Want Good Roads?" *Kansas Farmer*, May 28, 1903, 592.

33. See Cronon, *Nature's Metropolis*, particularly his chapter entitled "Annihilating Space: Meat"; Roosevelt, "Why Want Good Roads?" 592.

34. "This and That for Good Roads," *Kansas Farmer*, December 12, 1914, 3; Bureau of the Census, *Fourteenth Census of the United States, 1920, Volume V, Agriculture* (Washington, D.C.: Government Printing Office, 1920), 514; George Kirkham Jarvis, "The Diffusion of the Automobile in the United States: 1895–1969" (Ph.D. diss., University of Michigan, 1972), 189.

35. "Invention—Its Relation to the Farmer and Farm Laborer," *Kansas Farmer*, July 31, 1895, 485.

36. Michael Berger, *The Devil Wagon in God's Country: The Automobile and Social Change in Rural America* (Hamden, Conn.: Anchor Books, 1979), 46, provides a lengthy discussion about farmers' familiarity with machine technology; see also Joseph Interrante, "You Can't Go to Town in a Bathtub: Automobile Movement and the Reorganization of Rural American Space, 1900–1930," *Radical History Review* 21 (Fall 1979): 151–68.

37. Thomas D. Isern, *Bull Threshers and Bindlestiffs: Harvesting and Threshing on the North American Plains* (Lawrence: University Press of Kansas, 1990), 71–72; see also Harry Morgan Mason, *Life on the Dry Line: Working the Land, 1902–1944* (Golden, Colo.: Fulcrum Publishing, 1992), 5. That same year a discussion was held concerning the importance of Kansas' petroleum reserves, with particular emphasis on the potential of gasoline power. Also around this time, advertisements for gasoline engines started to appear. See "Oil of Importance to Kansas," *Kansas Farmer*, April 15, 1897, 232.

38. Joseph Interrante in "You Can't Go to Town in a Bathtub," 155, concludes that urban tourists "failed to see rural space as a living and working environment."

39. A number of authors discuss these conflicts at length. See Warren Belasco, *Americans on the Road: From Autocamp to Motel, 1910–1945* (Cambridge: MIT Press, 1979); Berger, *The Devil Wagon in God's Country;* Reynold Wik, *Henry Ford and Grass Roots America* (Ann Arbor: University of Michigan Press, 1972).

40. Paul Caviness, "Building More History: The Automobile in Lawrence" (paper, Kansas Collection, University of Kansas Libraries, 1985).

41. "The Automobile," *Kansas Farmer,* July 20, 1899, 484.

42. Seely, *Building the American Highway System,* 11–16; Jim Engle, "The Good Roads Train," *Kansas Farmer,* March 29, 1906, 353.

43. Joseph Satran, "Views on the Good Roads Proposition," *Kansas Farmer,* February 20, 1909, 14.

44. Wik, *Henry Ford and Grass Roots America,* 10.

45. Seely, *Building the American Highway System,* 16–23; see also William R. Childs, *Trucking and the Public Interest: The Emergence of Federal Regulation, 1914–1940* (Knoxville: University of Tennessee Press, 1985), 1–46.

46. "Good Roads," *Kansas Farmer,* April 3, 1909, 5; "The Farm Automobile," ibid., August 27, 1910, 5, 8.

47. "The Farmers Buy Automobiles," ibid., February 19, 1910, 4.

48. "The Automobile Belongs on the Farm," ibid., April 9, 1910, 4.

49. "The Farm Automobile," ibid., August 27, 1910, 5.

50. "This and That for Good Roads," ibid., December 12, 1914, 3.

51. Interrante, "You Can't Go to Town in a Bathtub," 151–68.

Twentieth-Century Kansas

Modernization did not end the influx of new peoples into Kansas and the West, nor did it answer all the questions raised at the end of the nineteenth century. In fact, twentieth-century Americans continued to experience the racism and class conflict that had dominated the previous century. For example, the Ku Klux Klan experienced a resurgence in the 1920s, focusing its attacks not only on African-Americans but also on new, often Catholic, immigrants from southern and eastern Europe. Class conflict also came to a head in the same decade, when an increase in strikes and labor union membership elicited fears of communism. In the 1930s, Americans, and Kansans in particular, suffered one of the most devastating droughts and economic depressions in history. World war struck twice in the century, the second thrusting America into the role of a superpower.

Although America was unquestionably a modern society by the mid–twentieth century, as Elliott West pointed out in the first essay in this collection, modern society contains "echoes of the ways of life before." Some of these echoes can be heard in the power struggles between new immigrant workers and the people who hired them, between competing definitions of "American," over who has the opportunity to attain an education, and over the best ways to feed the ever-growing nation. Power, of course, is a major source of conflict in every society, modern or not. And, as we have seen, power takes many forms. Once again, the questions raised by scholars of the new history help us to understand America's transformation into a modern society and the role of power in that transformation. Focusing on issues of technology, economics, ethnicity, and gender, the six scholars whose work is included in this final part illuminate how struggles for power and empowerment affected every aspect of daily life.

Issues of assimilation and acculturation affected many ethnic communities throughout the twentieth century, just as they had in the nineteenth century. Whichever route they took, individuals in these communities were attempting to gain power in their own lives. The first essay, "Acculturation or Assimilation," by Robert Oppenheimer, examines the experiences of Mexican immigrants who came to Kansas between 1900 and 1940 to find economic opportunity. Many found employment on the railroads, in meatpacking, and on sugar beet farms. They also worked as migrant agricultural laborers for parts of the year, with entire families toiling together in the fields. Although their labor was welcomed, Mexicans as Mexicans were not. They frequently suffered discrimination. At best, they were objects of well-meaning but sometimes misguided Americanization campaigns.

Often from the same provinces in Mexico, these new migrants clustered together in barrios in towns and cities. These close-knit communities provided new immigrants with economic and moral support and allowed them to maintain certain aspects of their traditional culture, but they also hindered their acceptance into wider American society. Mexicans' demographic separation and cultural and linguistic distinctiveness made them easy targets for discrimination, and even repatriation during the financial crisis of the Great Depression. Lack of educational opportunities reinforced their separation from broader American society and kept them from attaining the skills necessary for higher-paying jobs. Oppenheimer's essay provides valuable insight into the "double bind" Mexican immigrants experienced, as well as into how they maintained cultural continuity in the face of pressures to assimilate.

If the Mexicans of Oppenheimer's study were readily identified as "outsiders," ethnic industrial workers were sometimes described as the "enemy within." Although many of these workers were largely assimilated, their attempts to better their working conditions through strikes were seen as a threat to the American way of life. Strikes were important tools workers used to express their dissatisfaction with working conditions and to exert some power in the workplace. But strikes cannot succeed without broader community support, in particular, the support of workers' families. Gender analysis, thus, can prove helpful in understanding the history of these actions. In "An 'Army of Amazons,'" Ann Schofield introduces us to a group of miners' wives in southern Kansas who supported their husbands' strike efforts by staging a march to advocate a family wage. Steeped in their definitions of femininity, these women's actions were aimed at defending their husbands' jobs, as well as their rights as Americans. These women saw themselves as working within the proscribed definitions of femininity and, rising above the divisions of ethnicity, identified themselves as "working-class" Americans. Critics of the march viewed the striking ethnic laborers as the "enemy within" and accused the women of having "violated accepted concepts of femininity." Thus interwoven with definitions of what it meant to be an American were the issues of what it meant to be female and working-class in Kansas.

Like Schofield's analysis along the lines of class and gender, Donald Worster's essay on the Dust Bowl integrates one of the major subjects highlighted by the new approach to history—the environment. Environmental history examines the relationships between humans and the natural world, focusing on how social systems such as capitalism, gender, and race have influenced those relationships. The Dust Bowl of the 1930s offers an instructive example of how human actions, at least in part, caused what has traditionally been described as a "natural disaster." The Dust Bowl was a crucial period in Kansas history largely because few Kansans were spared its devastating effects. Already in the midst of the Great Depression, Kansans were hit with a second blow: the topsoil, their lifeblood, was blowing away in the wind. In asking the question why, many at the time blamed nature. Donald Worster, however, suggests a very different answer. In "The Dirty Thirties," Worster questions the assumption that the Dust Bowl was simply the result of environmental forces. Instead, he argues that farmers, concerned with short-term profits and reliant on new, highly efficient farm machinery, heedlessly plowed up the grasses of the High Plains that held the precious topsoil in place. When drought conditions appeared in the 1930s, there was little to prevent the topsoil from blowing away. It was a "capitalist ethos," paired with new technology and a severe drought, that caused the arid High Plains to transform into the Dust Bowl.

Although agriculture survived the "Dirty Thirties," it faced an equally serious problem in the next decade: labor shortages. Beginning in 1941, many young men left farms and factories to become soldiers. Thousands of jobs came open, and women were called on to fill them.

Much has been written on "Rosie the Riveter," the symbol of female industrial workers, but less is known about those women who took on the patriotic challenge of feeding the nation. As Caron Smith reveals in her essay, "The Women's Land Army During World War II," women who went to work for the WLA in Kansas differed in significant ways from their counterparts in other areas of the country. Most participants of the WLA were urban women who received limited training necessary for helping out temporarily on outlying farms. In Kansas, however, the main crop was wheat, which required skilled machine handlers at harvest time. For this reason, the WLA focused on training farm women, who already had some skills and familiarity with farm life and procedures. Through the WLA, women's roles on the farms expanded to include field work as well as housework, and the WLA was an important force in easing that transition.

A much more difficult transition for Kansans to make after World War II was the desegregation of schools. Mary Dudziak's essay, "The Limits of Good Faith," examines the political and legal arguments surrounding segregation in Kansas. National attention was riveted on Kansas in 1954 when the U.S. Supreme Court agreed to hear the case of *Brown v. Board of Education of Topeka, Kansas,* which challenged the constitutionality of segregated public schools. Segregation had a long but ambiguous history in Kansas, as Dudziak shows. The first state legislature gave school districts permission to segregate. In 1879 the legislature permitted but did not require segregation in elementary grades but forbade it in cities of fifteen thousand or more, the places where most African-Americans lived. Smaller towns and rural areas were exempt, but it is clear that segregation was the rule even there. Although the decision in *Brown v. Board of Education* overturned the "separate but equal" ruling of *Plessy v. Ferguson,* segregation continued, effectively limiting, as Dudziak argues, the bounds of good faith.

The final essay in this part brings home the connections between Kansas's past and its present. Not long after cattle began trailing up from Texas to Kansas in the late nineteenth century, stockyards and packing plants grew up west of Chicago, especially after the development of refrigeration made shipping processed meat over long distances possible. Major packers such as Armour and Cudahay established large plants near railroads in urban areas such as Kansas City and hired numerous unskilled wage workers from recently arrived ethnic groups. Although meatpacking in urban centers has declined in recent years, largely in response to new environmental regulations, a new trend—rural industrialization—has taken its place.

The essay by Donald Stull and Michael Broadway examines the very successful growth of the rural meatpacking industry in Kansas since the 1970s. Meatpacking in Kansas has become increasingly profitable through extensive cost-cutting efforts such as locating plants in close proximity to the meat source and hiring predominantly immigrant, nonunionized workers. With little say in the production process, these workers have little recourse for solving problems of workplace safety and low wages. What Stull and Broadway found in their extensive study of the meatpacking industry is that a high turnover rate, frequently due to worker injury, is an acceptable cost to the packers in light of increased profits.

Obviously, modernization has brought both costs and benefits to Kansas, the West, and America as a whole. New technologies have made both rural and urban industries more productive, but with certain consequences for workers, as well as for the natural environment. Through such efforts as the civil rights and women's rights movements, discrimination and segregation have ended—in law if not in fact. The following six essays begin to illustrate the ambivalent character of modernization and open the door for more thorough and far-reaching analysis of modern society.

Acculturation or Assimilation: Mexican Immigrants in Kansas, 1900 to World War II

Robert Oppenheimer

From 1900 to 1930 Mexicans immigrated in large numbers to the United States.[1] In the early twentieth century, Mexico experienced change under the leadership of the dictator Porfirio Díaz. The traditional rural and neofeudalistic character of society gave way to modernization and the expansion of export agriculture. As railroads opened more land to potential profits from agricultural exports and as land and traditional farm work became more scarce, living and working conditions of peasants deteriorated. Peasants began to migrate to the urban centers of Mexico and the United States to find work. Two major depressions during the first decade of the twentieth century and the violence of the Mexican Revolution during the second exacerbated the situation in Mexico.[2]

Simultaneously, the economy of the western United States was expanding rapidly. Shortages of inexpensive labor created a need for new sources of unskilled workers, and some industries, mining companies, agribusiness, and particularly railroads began active recruitment of

"Acculturation or Assimilation: Mexican Immigrants in Kansas, 1900 to World War II," by Robert Oppenheimer, *Western Historical Quarterly* 16 (October 1985): 429–448. Copyright Western History Association. Reprinted by permission.

Mexican laborers. Although most of the new immigrants settled in the Southwest and Colorado, the Mexican population of the Great Plains, particularly Kansas, increased significantly as well.

Historical examination of this massive migration to the United States falls generally in two periods. The first occurred in the 1920s and 1930s; the second came in the 1970s as a response to the rising demographic, economic and political activity of the Chicano communities of the Southwest.[3] Some of these studies have examined various aspects of the Mexican population in the Midwest, especially Chicago. One historian has reviewed the history of Mexicans in Oklahoma, but Kansas, the plains state with the largest Mexican population, remains largely neglected.[4]

The objectives of this study are to present a historical overview of the Mexican immigration to Kansas prior to World War II, to describe the contribution of Mexicans to the state, and to analyze their relationships and assimilation by the larger Kansas society and culture. It concentrates on two aspects of the Mexican immigrant experience: occupation and education. These areas are indicative of the general circumstances and experiences that Mexicans confronted in pre–World War II Kansas. Mexicans found themselves in something akin to what psychologists call a "double bind." The new immigrants wanted to be assimilated into some aspects of Kansas society but also wished to maintain their own sense of cultural identity in a society that demanded conformity and acculturation.[5]

Mexicans and Mexican-Americans historically have been segregated by the community at large and by their own design from mainstream life. By 1930 the Mexican and Mexican-American population of Kansas was the seventh largest Mexican ancestral group in the United States, and this group comprised the second largest immigrant population in the state, after Germans. While the state's urban population was about 39 percent, approximately 60 percent of the Mexicans resided in urban areas.[6] Mexican colonias formed in the main commercial centers along the rail lines or at the location of rail yards, shops, and roundhouses. The largest colonias, or barrios, were in Kansas City, Topeka, Emporia, Wichita, and Garden City. Recently barrios have been disappearing in Garden City and certain other urban areas, but in Kansas City they continue to flourish.

The first whites to set foot in Kansas passed through in the early 1540s as part of the Francisco Vasquez de Coronado expedition.

Traders and explorers followed including Juan de Oñate of New Mexico in 1601. In the mid–nineteenth century, Mexicans passed through Kansas as merchants and wagoneers on the Santa Fe trail or as cowboys on the cattle drives north from Texas. Because part of their job was greasing wagon wheels, the wagoneers and wheelmen came to be known by the derogatory sobriquet "greasers."[7]

These racial biases reflected both the early nineteenth-century ideals of Manifest Destiny and the later concept of Social Darwinism. Americans considered Mexicans to be inherently inferior racially and culturally.[8] Mexican laborers who came to Kansas in the early twentieth century found that the earlier opinions persisted. A German-American foreman for the Santa Fe Railroad in Kansas and his Anglo-Saxon workers would in 1917, for example, regard Mexican laborers "as more or less animals sufficiently tamed to respond to their handler, but otherwise to be left alone unless they got in the way."[9]

Overt racial bias was common. Throughout Kansas, Mexicans remained segregated, and Anglos viewed Mexicans with suspicion even when they left the confines of the barrios for the day. As a response a weekly Spanish language newspaper, *El Cosmopolita,* began publication in 1915 in Kansas City. Running for more than four years, its stated objectives were to unite elements of the Mexican communities of Kansas City, Kansas and Missouri, to represent the ideals and needs of Mexicans, to create harmony with the Anglo community, and to gain political respect for Mexicans based on United States ideals. The newspaper presented extensive coverage of the Mexican Revolution, World War I, and national news with an emphasis on stories relating to Mexican immigrants. Locally, the newspaper covered community activities and problems, vital statistics, advertising, and features on the colonia and its people. It provides some insight into early attempts to organize the Mexican population of Kansas City as well as information on the colonia's needs, problems, and people.[10]

Until the 1950s, in virtually every Kansas town and city, Mexicans and Mexican-Americans remained segregated in movie theaters and were often restricted from some sections of city parks, churches, and other public facilities. Windows of some businesses contained signs stating "no Mexicans allowed," and Mexicans could not obtain haircuts in local barbershops. In the 1930s, Bell Memorial Hospital of the University of Kansas defined Mexicans by skin color. Darker-skinned Mexicans were put in black wards and light-skinned Mexicans in white wards where the care was appreciably better. Stories abound in every Mexican colonia of such discrimination.[11] One interviewee from western Kansas described a classic example during World War II.

When I came back, I was wearing my uniform and at that time my brother says let's go into the restaurant and eat and see what happens so we went into this restaurant and I was wearing a uniform and he wasn't but he was a little lighter complected than I was . . . the girl that was waiting tables brought him a menu and he ordered his meal and she didn't give me a menu . . . I said ah am I not going to have a menu? She said no. I said well how come. She said well because you're a Mexican. I said well I'm going to tell you something honey this is my older brother here. . . . He is born in Mexico he is not an American citizen I said I'm born here and I have the United States uniform on and you're turning down an American for a Mexican. . . . Anyway she called the cook back there and he stood about 6'6" and he had a meat cleaver in his hands he said what is going on here and she told him what had happened and I told him the same thing that I told her. . . . He said we just don't serve Mexicans period.[12]

A period of Mexican influx began shortly after the turn of the century when the Santa Fe Railroad (SFRR) and other railroad companies actively recruited section gang laborers. Simultaneously, other industries, such as sugar beet farming, also sought inexpensive and unskilled workers. However, it was not until 1907 that the SFRR began to actively recruit Mexicans to come to Kansas. Most cities record their first influx in the period from 1905 to 1910. The usual pattern of employment was for rail companies to hire the laborers to work from May to October on the repair and maintenance of the lines and then the workers usually returned to Mexico. Nevertheless it was estimated that as early as 1907 at least 30 percent of the section gang workers remained in the United States and worked in the fields for the other six months.[13] In 1905, for example, the Garden City Sugar Beet Company began operations and soon had vast holdings in the Finney County region. The company irrigated the land, opened a processing factory and an electric power plant, built the Garden City Western Railroad, and began hiring Mexicans to work the fields and in the factory.[14]

Because of socioeconomic conditions in Mexico, the rail lines and other companies found a ready labor source. In 1907 Mexico's econ-

Table 3. Mexican Population of Kansas and Percentage of State's Population, 1900–1940

Year	Mexican population	Mexican and Mexican-American population	Percentage
1900	71	—	—
1910	8,429	8,597	51%
1920	13,770	16,170	90%
1930	11,183	19,150	100%
1940	5,122	13,060	73%

Source: U.S. Census and Carman, *Language Units,* vol. 1, p. 221.

omy was slowed by a severe depression, and many workers lost their jobs, particularly in the north and north-central plateau mining and ranching regions. Many of the early immigrants to Kansas came from the ranks of these unemployed laborers.[15]

Ignacio Galindo Valenzuela, a railroad employee for forty years in Finney County (Copeland and Garden City), described how he crossed the border and came to reside in Garden City. Valenzuela first came to the United States for six months in 1916 and returned in 1917. An El Paso contractor sent Valenzuela and 750 others to work on a railroad in Illinois. There he met a friend who had spent some time in Garden City, and the two men moved there after their contract period ended.[16]

World War I, the drop in European immigration, and the lack of available labor were external factors in creating continued occupational opportunities for Mexican immigrants in Kansas. Although Mexicans remained a small percentage of the state's population, their numbers increased steadily to the mid-1920s. With the beginning of the Great Depression their numbers declined until after the Second World War. (See Table 3.)

Few of the immigrants had the technical skills or understanding of the English language needed to succeed in the industrialized economy of the United States. On the other hand, they escaped the poverty and the horrors of the Mexican Revolution (1910–1920) and postrevolutionary chaos. Conditions on the great estates and ranches of Mexico were harsh for many peasants, and Indians were often in debt or virtually slaves. One immigrant from rural Mexico described his living and working conditions as a youth: "My father and I worked on this hacienda [great estate] and then we returned to our village and worked there, good hard farm labor. Occasionally, we would travel from our village to Guadalajara with carts full of wood. We did this until harvest season. With God's permission, I married and we moved and worked on the hacienda for the same patron until 1923 when we came here [Garden City]."[17] Another immigrant who had lived in an urban area and worked for a newspaper in Mexico explained how in 1916 the revolution disrupted his life: "That particular press was small, which I moved with my foot and from there on I didn't like it very much but the revolution kept on growing and coming up, going back south and coming back up north it was just terrible. Anyway the place closed up on account of the political changes and that put me out."[18]

Though the immigrants to Kansas came from virtually every state in northern and central Mexico, the majority came from Guanajuato or Michocan. People from the same village or region often settled together in Kansas. For example, many Topeka Mexicans came from Silao, Guanajuato. One immigrant to Topeka estimated that 60 to 70 percent were from Guanajuato. In Kansas City 34 percent of those interviewed stated that their families immigrated from Michoacan and 17 percent from Guanajuato. The "Argentine" barrio of Kansas City, Kansas, included many persons from Tanganicuarco, Michoacan. A survey of 112 Mexicans employed by the SFRR in Kansas City from 1905 to 1940 showed 57 percent from Michoacan and Guanajuato.[19] This helped to create a sense of community identity and culture in an alien environment.

At first male laborers usually came to the United States alone. Later this began to change. By 1912 the SFRR in Kansas started to use Mexican laborers in its shops and on its permanent section maintenance crews. As the laborers found permanent jobs with the railroads or in meat-packing, sugar beets, or mining industries, the workers and their families organized permanent settlements. These communities grew steadily from World War I to the mid-1920s. Increases in the number of Mexican families were indicative of the new permanence of these immigrants. For example, in 1915 in a Kansas City SFRR yard colony that eventually became part of the Argentine barrio, there were thirteen dwellings with 201 occupants, but only ten families. There were 181 males, and 174, or 96 percent, were over twenty years old. The colony had only twenty females, half of whom were under ten years of age. While the same yard camp had only 122 persons in 1925, the number of families had more than doubled to twenty-three, and 20 percent of the camp's population were Kansas-born Mexican-Americans. Similar shifts were evident in colonias in Garden City, Emporia, and Topeka.[20] Though some colonia areas within a town or city declined in population, the overall Mexican immigrant urban population continued to increase.

Once in Kansas, the immigrants often moved about within the state. In Garden City a majority of the Mexican immigrant families or family members participated in some form of migrant labor. They worked the sugar beet, onion, wheat, and potato fields of southwest Kansas, Colorado, and Nebraska. Some families spent the winter laboring in the citrus groves of California.

Many eventual Kansas City residents came initially as itinerant families to small towns or lived in camps outside of a town. The families then migrated to Kansas City or Topeka to work at permanent jobs in the railroad repair shops or other industries that were developing in the city.[21] Jobs existed for Mexican immigrants in the sugar beet factory in Garden City, in salt mining near Lyons and Hutchinson, coal mining and oil in the southeast region of the state, and in meat packing, ice houses, and other industries in Kansas City, Topeka, and Wichita.

However, from the beginning, railroad lines remained the principal employer. The Kansas City colonia was typical. Seventy-two percent of those interviewed in Kansas City stated that they or their immigrant parents came between 1910 and 1920 to work for railroads in Kansas, most for the SFRR. In 1925 at least 75 percent of all employed Mexican males in the Argentine barrio worked for the SFRR. As late as 1930, of the 6,720 male Mexican and Mexican-Americans employed in Kansas, 74.3 percent worked for the railroad companies.[22] Depending on the region's economy, the percentage of Mexicans employed by the rail companies varied. In Emporia virtually all the Mexican laborers worked for the railroad, while in Garden City, with its large sugar beet industry, a smaller percentage were railroad workers.

Jobs for males were almost always at the lowest occupational levels, usually laborer. Most females did not work outside the home, but the occupations of those employed were in the food industry, fields, or domestic service. That little upward mobility was possible is suggested by the fact that Mexican track laborers in Kansas City accounted for 55 percent of the total in 1910, 85 percent by 1915, and over 91 percent by 1927. In the 1915 state census in a Santa Fe yard tenement in Kansas City, all 174 males over the age of 20 were classified as laborers.[23]

Table 4. Mexican Labor in Kansas, 1930

	Male	*Female*
Total number of Mexicans (over ten years of age)	8,142	4,758
Total number employed	6,720	175
Railroad employees	4,954	15
Railroad "laborers"	4,877	15
Manufacturing employees	1,118	12
Manufacturing "laborers"	859	12

Source: U.S. Census, 1930, vol. 5, pp. 87–91.

By 1930 of the 8,142 males of Mexican ancestry over the age of ten in Kansas, 82.5 percent were employed (see Table 4). Over 91 percent of the total Mexican males were classified as laborers, and 98 percent of the railroad employees were classified as laborers. On the rail lines the other 2 percent included forty-five foremen as the highest occupational level. A few Mexicans advanced to skilled jobs in the early 1920s by acting as strikebreakers. The actual number of skilled Mexican workers rose from four to thirteen following a strike in 1922 at the Argentine shop. In manufacturing, 77 percent of the Mexicans were laborers. The percentage of Mexican workers classified as laborers was much greater than for blacks or whites.[24]

Initially laborers on section gangs received from $1.00 to $1.50 per ten-hour day. By 1920 wages had improved to $2.50 to $3.00 per eight-hour day and remained at this level through the 1930s. Since the work was often seasonal, actual annual wages were low and income was not constant. Laborers who moved sides of beef from refrigerated cars to the plant or vice versa received eighty-five cents to a dollar an hour. Moreover, they were hired daily for this backbreaking work and seldom worked more than three days per week.[25]

For Mexicans another important employment sector was agriculture, especially sugar beets in western Kansas. Labor in the fields was arduous. From May to November field hands planted, hoed, thinned, and topped the sugar beets. Families usually worked together tending a field for the season. In some cases wives and children of railroad workers supplemented the family income by working in the sugar beet fields. These women seldom classified themselves as employed but considered their work only as supporting their husband.[26] This helps to explain the low employment figures for females in the census. Workers labored daily from dawn to dusk for wages of two to nine dollars per acre for a season's work. A family might work as many as 100 acres in a season. In the decade 1931 to 1940 wages for sugar beet laborers in Kansas were the lowest among the fifteen major sugar beet–producing states.[27]

The company provided the workers with housing and loans to purchase food or other necessities. At the end of the season a loan was subtracted from the family's pay. As one respondent described it:

> . . . if you needed any money in between time, you decided whether the kids need shoes or you needed some more groceries, some clothing, whatever it was, then you figure it out in your own mind how much you needed—50–75 dollars—and you went to the sugar factory and you asked for this amount and they would write it out after they asked you what store you wanted it or where ever, and uh, they'd make you out a voucher for that amount and then you would go and make your purchases. And at that time the majority of the Mexicanos, the Mexican-Americans did not keep tabs on how much they took out and so at the tail end it depended on the sugar beet factory to take care of the tabs and all the money that they were withdrawn from there so many of them at the tail end of the working season wound up with maybe 10–15 dollars, in some cases they wound up with nothing at all.[28]

Wages were seldom sufficient to meet a family's basic needs. Therefore, young sons often left school to work, women took in laundry or worked as domestics, other relatives or boarders contributed, and families pooled their resources to make ends meet. Of course, many women worked a "double-day" taking care of their own house and family as well as working outside the home. The railroads, for example, hired young boys, especially those who spoke some English, as water boys and translators. Often the eldest children migrated to work in the summer in surrounding states, other parts of Kansas, or the West Coast in order to supplement the family income.[29]

In the late 1930s the United States Department of Labor surveyed the conditions for sugar beet workers in various locations throughout the United States. Although the Arkansas Valley of western Kansas was not included, Colorado and Nebraska workers were studied. Since the Kansas company (Garden City Sugar Beet Company) was a direct off-shoot of the Colorado industry, the government's findings for Colorado were approximate for Kansas as well. Income in 1934 ranged from $4 to $24 per acre, and the median family income was about $340 per year. In Colorado over 95 percent of the families had supplemental incomes of about $50 per year, and an equal percentage lived on credit obtained through a company store. This annual income amounted to about one-third to one-half of the average annual salaries made by workers in retail sales or manufacturing and about one-third the annual salary of a railroad section-crew laborer.[30]

The question of wage discrimination was also paramount. Many interviewees claimed they consistently received less pay than other workers and seldom worked on the same crews with non-Mexicans. A review of the Santa Fe railway payroll records from the mid-1920s to the mid-1930s indicated that the Mexicans' claims contained some truth, but the problem was not wages. Through the period, Mexicans and other workers were paid the same amount for the same job. A few examples existed of Mexican shop laborers, car painters, boiler washers, and others being paid less than non-Mexicans, but these cases can be attributed to function or seniority, and the difference was usually a few cents per hour.[31]

The biggest discrepancies pertained to job status and hours. Few Mexicans rose above common labor status, whether on a gang or in a shop. Most Mexican immigrants came to the United States with little or no knowledge of English, which was a requirement for advancement, and few had technical skills for the United States industrial market. These factors, along with racial prejudice, limited their possibility for employment above laborer or for upward occupational or social mobility. In the shops, Mexicans and non-Mexicans worked together in close proximity. On maintenance crews and section gangs the situation was strikingly different. Although the larger crews through most of the 1920s and 1930s had some Anglos and Mexicans working together, most crews, particularly smaller crews, were either all Mexican or all non-Mexican. In 1930, for example, section crew 46 in Hutchinson had an Anglo foreman and nineteen Mexican laborers, while the crews at Sterling and Raymound were all Anglo. They consisted of crew chiefs and fourteen and fifteen laborers respectively. Extra gangs were more likely to be mixed. In June 1930 extra gang number 11 of Copeland had a Mexican foreman, Antonio Lopez, and forty-three out of seventy-four crewmen who were Mexican. In this case, hours were split relatively evenly among the Anglos and Mexicans. However, an hourly differential was apparent on a gang in Wellington where forty-three Mexicans averaged about 250 hours for the month and eight Anglos averaged about 280 hours.[32]

In 1935 the situation was even more discriminatory. In the Topeka shop in June an Anglo laborer received about $14 more for a two-week pay period than a Mexican doing the same work. On mixed section crew 23 in Emporia a typical situation existed. While all workers received thirty-five cents per hour, twenty Mexicans averaged 134 hours per pay period and the five Anglos averaged 167 hours. On an annual basis the average Mexican laborer on this crew received about $300 less in salary. In 1935 sections 45 to 70 in western Kansas had thirteen Mexican crew chiefs who averaged $120 per month. The Anglo crew chiefs received more than $150 per month.[33]

As the depression worsened after 1930, Mexicans, working for the Santa Fe railroad, clearly received less then their Anglo counterparts. This was largely done, not by wage discrimination, but by occupational level and hours worked. This left a lasting impression on the Mexican laborer and more clearly defined his position in the Kansas labor market. Even with such problems, most interviewees saw occupational mobility and educational opportunities as their means to becoming part of United States society.

Mexican-Americans, like most North Americans, consider education to be an avenue toward upward socioeconomic mobility. This is evident in virtually all the recent interviews, public forums, political demands, or newspaper articles.[34] Here again the Mexican or Mexican-American faced difficulties. Few programs existed to teach adults, and children faced intentional and unintentional discrimination. By the 1920s, for example, "Americanization" was a dominant theme. No language or special programs existed to deal with the difficulties facing migrants. By participating fully and acceptingly in the existing educational structures and in seeking upward mobility, the Mexican family gave up some of its values, language, and culture. In 1925 over half of the Mexican and Mexican-American children of Topeka, Kansas City, Emporia, Garden City, and Hutchinson were attending school. In the Argentine barrio 65 percent of the males over eighteen and 66 percent of the married females were literate in English. In Garden City 92 percent of the adult immigrants were listed as illiterate in English, but over 55 percent of Mexican and Mexican-American school-age children attended school.[35]

Many interviewed for this study related stories of feeling separated, different, and inferior. Typically, Margarita Rodriguez explained how she was taunted by Anglo students because she attended the "Mexican" Clara Barton School and was told by teachers of her inferiority and that of all Hispanic students. These situations created in many a long-term sense of their status in society. From 1920 to 1950 almost 9 percent of the children attending public school in Garden City had Hispanic surnames, but Mexicans represented less than 1 percent of the city's population. However, during these thirty years, only 22 percent of the Hispanic-surnamed students would graduate from grammar school, and all Hispanic students averaged only 2.5 years of schooling, or about one-half the amount for non-Hispanics. In 1940 the Catholic church of Garden City opened its elementary school, and many Mexican-American youth enrolled. Most Mexican-American students left school before the end of the semester each year to plant sugar beets and returned in November following the fall beet harvest. Others stayed in school only short periods because their families migrated during the semester. Some students were forced to leave school to seek permanent work.[36]

Through the 1920s, few Mexicans in Kansas graduated from high school. The first to graduate were in the late 1920s or early 1930s. In Topeka they graduated from Catholic Hayden High School and later from public schools. In Emporia from 1932 to 1941 only fifteen Mexican students (five males and ten females) graduated from high school. Seven of these graduated in 1941. By 1950 only eighteen Mexican-Americans had graduated from Garden City High School. Lucille Ramírez was the first female in 1934, and Frank Rodríguez was the first male in 1950.[37]

In Garden City and Emporia more women graduated from high school than men. This was a consequence of the tendency for males to leave school to find work. While men could be sent to the fields, factories, or labor gangs, families allowed young women to work only in the fields or as domestics. During the depression, domestic service was difficult to find, and field work did not add appreciably to a family's income. Some women became migrant laborers, particularly during the summer, but were allowed to travel only in groups with their fathers or brothers to work fields in Colorado and Nebraska. The best opportunity for many women was to complete school and seek employment near home. Furthermore, a high school diploma apparently contributed little to upward job mobility for males. The SFRR, for example, preferred literate workers, but little more. Eighty percent of the Mexicans employed by the SFRR in 1925 were literate, but few had the eighth-grade education needed to qualify for apprenticeship and eventual foreman jobs. Even though Mexican workers could qualify for apprenticeships, they were denied such advancement. A general reason given to many was the lack of competency in English.[38]

In the larger cities few primary schools, public or private, opened their doors to Mexican children until the late teens or early 1920s. In 1918 the Topeka School Board opened the Branner School Annex for Mexican youth matriculating in kindergarten to the third grade. Clara Barton School was opened in the Argentine (Kansas City) in 1924 essentially for Mexican children. As late as 1938, a school superintendent in Kansas City felt that all Mexican children should attend the same segregated school. The hope in opening separate schools was that the segregated students would learn a command of English and eventually be able to attend school with non-Mexican students. However, none of the annex school teachers in Kansas City or Topeka spoke Spanish or had any bilingual educational training. In Topeka after a number of years of confrontation with the school board, Mexican parents, with support from Anglos, forced the closing of the Branner Annex school in 1942. Since the school was in the National Guard Armory, the beginning of World War II obviously affected the decision.[39]

In smaller communities, such as Garden City, Mexican children attended the same schools as the other children. D. C. García, a city commissioner of Garden City in the early 1970s and mayor in 1974, spent three years in the first grade, because he did not speak enough English to be promoted to the second grade.[40] Beatrice Arteaga elaborated on this problem in an article in the *Wichita Eagle-Beacon:* "I'll never forget how in kindergarten they would write c-a-t on the board. I'd return home and say: 'Mama, que es un c-a-t, cat?' and my mother would say: 'Hija mia, cat es un gato!' We had to take home what we learned and have it explained to us."[41] In many families non-English-speaking parents were unable to help. Therefore, a vicious cycle was perpetuated. Mexicans lacked the necessary preparation for technical industrial labor, but the educational system did little to alleviate the problem. In fact, education aided the existing system by helping to train the Mexican and Mexican-American youth to accept their position at the bottom of Kansas society.

For most Mexican immigrants to Kansas, the most important event in fixing their position in society was the Great Depression. Though conditions always were difficult for the immigrants, hard times magnified their low socioeconomic status. The economic collapse of the Great Depression was difficult for laborers in general but was devastating for most Mexican immigrants and their families. Patterns such as occupational levels, education, discrimination, and attitudes toward Anglo society affected the immigrants' lives even more than usual.

The first major depression that Kansas Mexican immigrants confronted was during the post–World War I years of 1921–1922. Some railroads laid off workers for short periods, and the SFRR reduced its work force by one-half. Meat packers and other urban laborers were the most severely affected. In Kansas City it was reported that 1,500 to 1,700 Mexican meat-packing employees lost their jobs; many slept outdoors and survived on donations of meat from Swift and Armour. Chicago steel mills desperate for labor recruited Mexican workers heavily in the Kansas City area. The railroad companies cut wages by 3 to 12 percent in 1921, forcing many families to split up in order to make ends meet. Some of the younger males became itinerant migrant laborers to help supplement family income, traveling to states adjoining Kansas or Texas and California to work in the fields.[42]

Communities organized to help the unemployed. Families in Garden City and Kansas City shared their earnings, food, and shelter. Colonias held fiestas and dances to raise money, and missions opened to help the unemployed. In both cities the most successful and well received of these missions was that of the Methodist church. They provided food, clothing, shelter, and medical attention, and in Garden City a small, but active, segment of the Mexican population joined the Methodist church.[43]

Relations with the Anglo community became more clearly defined in this period. Some unions demanded that Mexican immigrants be fired. As conditions worsened, the Mexican government and the state and local governments in Kansas suggested a repatriation program. In May 1921 a train left Topeka for Mexico with a reported 1,500 Mexicans, and in June a train with 800 Mexicans left Kansas City. The cost was split between the Mexican government, local governments, and chambers of commerce. Kansas officials supported the program, which lasted from May to October 1921, to rid themselves of a problem.[44]

The sense of isolation and separation continued and grew throughout the twenties. A national railroad shop strike in 1922 added internal ill will. This worked in several ways. Mexican laborers who worked in the shops supported the strike, but most section and gang workers did not. Some Mexicans even became strikebreakers, creating a split with both Mexican and non-Mexican shop workers.[45] In the mid-twenties conflicts between Mexicans and Anglos reported in the Garden City press were consistently blamed on the Mexicans. In such outbreaks all those arrested were Mexican, and a sense of animosity grew between the Mexican and Anglo communities. One interviewee noted that Mexicans knew their position, where they could go, and when and how to deal with the community at large, particularly with the authorities.[46]

The Great Depression magnified and strengthened the Mexican's sense of isolation and separation. In 1928 a representative of the SFRR testified before the House Committee on Naturalization and Immigration that Mexican laborers were important to the company because they willingly undertook jobs that Anglos would not perform.[47] During the depression most workers had their hours shortened or were laid off for short periods, but even under increasing pressure, the SFRR in Kansas maintained its Mexican labor crews.

Elsewhere in the state, efforts were made to force the firing and repatriation of Mexican immigrants. In November 1930 J. F. Lucey, the Southwest regional director of the Emergency Committee for Employment, wrote the governor of Kansas asking that he take action to have the immigrants returned to Mexico.[48]

Governor Clyde Reed immediately sent a letter to the rail lines urging that Mexican workers be fired and repatriated. Although the governor received a few letters opposing such actions, the majority of the responses supported the idea. Support came from across the state, including letters from private citizens, relief agencies, and secretary of the Topeka Federation of Labor.[49]

The railroads generally opposed the firing of Mexican laborers, claiming that they had few Mexican employees and that their willingness to work at jobs few others would undertake for relatively low wages left no choice in the matter.[50] The Rock Island and the SFRR agreed to hire United States citizens wherever possible, but the president of the SFRR explained from experience that whites were reluctant to do section gang work, and the line continued to employ its Mexican workers.[51]

Although relief agencies did little to benefit the Kansas Mexican community, the federal government did channel some funds through the various local missions and welfare agencies. Using federal relief funds, the Methodist missions and Catholic churches expanded programs in housing, food distribution, and medical aid. Most support came through direct relief, rather than from job-related programs such as Works Progress Administration (WPA) and Civil Conservation Corps (CCC) camps. From the Mexican's perspective many factors contributed to nonparticipation in federal job programs: language barriers, lack of understanding of how agencies operated, fear of repatriation if one registered, lack of United States citizenship, and the inability to meet local residency requirements. In a few cases Anglo friends helped Mexicans in getting on program rolls, and local bosses disregarded citizenship and residency requirements until challenged. When the issue came up, the agency usually forced the Mexican to leave unless he could prove citizenship.[52] In 1937, as a consequence of a 1935 federal study of beet workers in the Arkansas River Valley areas of Colorado, Nebraska, and Kansas, the Federal Sugar Act was established to help sugar beet workers. Though late in the depression, it did help many sugar beet workers by improving wages and working and living conditions.[53]

Not unlike the depression of the early twenties, most of the support for Mexicans during the Great Depression came from within the barrio. Besides local church groups, Mexicans created their own mutual societies or unions. There was a sugar beet workers union formed in the late twenties that became very strong during the thirties in the Garden City area. Also, mutual societies, such as the Sociedades Mutuas Benito Juarez in Garden City and Kansas City, sprang up throughout the state. These groups, common in Latin America, provided aid to members' families in times of death, ill health, or unemployment.[54]

Mexican communities became stronger and better organized. A new sense of mutual support and cultural pride was created. Families and friends often moved into one home to share expenses and upkeep. Those who stayed in Kansas took jobs wherever and whenever possible, while some family members migrated to California or other states seeking work. Many worked shortened hours and split a job among two or more workers so that more people would have some income. One Garden City railroad worker explained how he and a friend each worked three days per week on a section gang so that both could have some wage. His two eldest sons (of eleven children) did the same. His wife, older daughters, and younger children took in wash and worked in the sugar beet fields.[55]

Pedro Sandoval of Garden City described how his grandmother ran an open house. Anyone who came was provided with a meal and shelter. He noted that often the meals were meager and sometimes it was difficult to find a place at the table, but no one was turned away. Those who could afford to pay something did, but many could not.[56] Depression conditions forced many young people, like Sandoval, to leave school permanently to find work. Though many planned to return to school, few did. Mexicans got a clear sense of being the first fired in bad economic times and understood their status within the general community.

The impulse to return to Mexico or the attempt to retain Mexican heritage and culture was strong. In the early 1930s in Topeka and Garden City, Mexican colonias organized fiesta days to bring the community closer and to encourage an understanding of Mexican culture and history. Since then they have been continuously and enthusiastically celebrated. Similarly, Chanute has had a Mexican festival for more than sixty years. These events have become popular with the community at large and a source of tremendous pride for Chicanos.

Not all Mexicans in Kansas suffered during the depression. Under favorable circumstances, some Mexicans improved their status. Families able to maintain an annual wage equal to or greater than their pre-depression income benefitted from the deteriorating economic conditions in the state. From 1930 to 1935, for example, the cost of living decreased by more than 30 percent.[57] Therefore, some families found the depression to be an opportune time to purchase a home. Others who benefitted from federal relief programs gained a new respect for the government and became increasingly a part of the state's society. As more contact took place, some Anglos began to change their views of Mexicans. This would be a factor that contributed to the post–World War II integration process. For those who stayed in Kansas, a strong desire existed to acculturate and become part of the state's society. At the same time a new pride in Mexican heritage and culture was created. This left Mexicans with a problem of wanting to retain their Mexican past and also of being accepted into their new environment. This is something that the dominant culture finds difficult to accept and that the Mexican-American must continue to grapple with.

In the period before World War II, Mexicans and Mexican-Americans in Kansas existed in an atmosphere of poverty and hostility. The consequences of these conditions limited, obstructed, and retarded the integration of Mexicans and Mexican-Americans into the mainstream of Kansas life. Because Anglos treated Mexicans as racial inferiors, because Mexican immigrants arrived late in the United States, and because of the socioeconomic level at which Mexicans entered American society, integration occurred slowly at best and often was denied entirely.

The Mexican is a relative newcomer compared to European immigrants. Most Mexican families were still largely first- and second-generation residents by World War II. Like most immigrants to the United States, their mobility was restricted in the first and second generations. The first-generation European immigrants to Kansas found conditions on the job, in housing, and education similar to those that Mexicans confronted. Conditions for Mexicans and Mexican-Americans in Kansas remained, however, largely unchanged to World War II. They generally lagged behind other immigrant groups in being integrated into society. Radical prejudice toward Mexicans is an important factor in this lag. From the nineteenth century, or even before, North Americans perceived Mexicans as racially and culturally inferior. After the influx of Mexicans to Kansas in the early twentieth century, radical prejudices plagued the relationship of Mexicans with the rest of Kansas society. This made acceptance and integration of Mexicans much more tenuous. Coming from a rural, "feudalistic" socioeconomic structure, Mexican immigrants had little education and few skills that enabled them to function except at the lowest economic level of society. Generally, Mexican-Americans remain in large numbers in the lower economic strata of Kansas society.

Kansas Mexicans have not been simply inert victims of society. Kept at the lower socioeconomic levels and finding racial, occupational, and cultural discrimination difficult to combat or overcome, they have reacted by separating themselves from the rest of society. The older generation resisted acculturation, retained their native language and customs, rejected United States citizenship, and created enclave communities. These conditions persist and affect the present position of Mexican-Americans in Kansas.

Today Hispanics are the fastest-growing ethnic group in Kansas. While the state's population from 1970 to 1980 increased by 5 percent, the Hispanic population, largely of Mexican ancestry, increased by 35 percent.[58] Since 1945, socioeconomic conditions of long-term resident Mexicans and Mexican-Americans in Kansas, especially the larger cities, have improved in the areas under discussion. However, many problems still exist both for the Mexican-Americans and the more recent immigrants. The Mexican-Americans' steady influx into the middle-income and "white-collar" sectors adds to their political awareness and increasing concerns over their social status within Kansas society. There is also the growing influence of Mexican immigrants and of the cultural and political activities of Chicanos in the Southwest. This new consciousness is expressed by the growth in the number of political and cultural clubs, by the expansion of statewide organizations, and by demands for bilingual education and English-as-a-second-language programs. In Kansas large segments of the Mexican-American population across the state are seeking and demanding equal opportunity without giving up their heritage and culture.

NOTES

1. For the purpose of this article the term *Mexican* is used to define an immigrant and *Mexican-American* to describe a United States native of Mexican descent. Information for this article is based on a series of ongoing interview projects with "viejitos" or senior citizens. Three projects funded by the Kansas Committee for the Humanities in Kansas City (1979–80), Emporia (1980), and Garden City (1981) have been completed. Copies of all the interviews are available through the Manuscript Department of the Kansas State Historical Society, Topeka. Other such projects for Lawrence, Manhattan, and Topeka are underway or planned. Interviews from the Kansas City project have been collated into a composite and hereafter will be referred to as Kansas City Interviews, 1979–80. Considering the uniformity of experiences and accounts of events in their lives in Kansas, the interviews are being used here as representative of the Mexican immigrant's experiences in Kansas. Unless otherwise noted, the interviews were in English. The accuracy of the population figures for the federal census for the 1900 to 1940 period, and especially the Kansas State Census of 1915 and 1925, is very questionable. This data is used to demonstrate obvious patterns of migration rather than provide accurate counts of the actual number of immigrants.

2. Lawrence A. Cardoso, *Mexican Emigration to the United States, 1897–1931* (Tucson, 1980), 1–70; and Michael C. Meyer and William L. Sherman, *The Course of Mexican History* (New York, 1979), 431–566.

3. Arthur F. Corwin, "Mexican Emigration History, 1900–1970; Literature and Research," *Latin American Research Review,* VIII (Summer 1973), 3–24; and Rose Spalding, "Mexican Immigration: A Historical Perspective," *Latin American Research Review,* XVIII (no. 1, 1983), 201–9.

4. Rodolfo Acuña, *Occupied America: A History of Chicanos,* 2d ed. (New York,

1981), passim; "Mexican-Americans in the Mid-West," *Aztlan,* 6 (Summer 1975); Michael M. Smith, *The Mexicans in Oklahoma* (Norman, 1980); and Michael M. Smith, "Beyond the Borderlands: Mexican Labor in the Central Plains, 1900–1930," *Great Plains Quarterly,* 1 (Fall 1981), 239–51. Some of the works on Mexican-Americans in Kansas include: sections from Justice Neale Carman's published and typescript study, *Foreign Language Units of Kansas,* vol. 1 (Lawrence, 1962); vol. 2 is typescript found in University Archives, University of Kansas, Lawrence; Judith Ann Fincher Laird, "Argentine, Kansas: The Evolution of a Mexican-American Community, 1905–1940" (doctoral dissertation, University of Kansas, 1975); Larry G. Rutter, "Mexican Americans in Kansas: A Survey and Social Mobility Study, 1900–1970" (master's thesis, Kansas State University, 1972); Robert Swan, Jr., "The Ethnic Heritage of Topeka, Kansas" (n.p., 1974), in Institute of Comparative and Ethnic Studies, University of Kansas, Lawrence; Socorro M. Ramírez, "A Survey of the Mexicans in Emporia, Kansas" (master's thesis, Emporia State University, 1942); Hector Franco, "The Mexican People in the State of Kansas" (master's thesis, Wichita State University, 1950); Marian Braun, "A Survey of the American Mexicans in Topeka, Kansas" (master's thesis, Emporia State University, 1970); and Cynthia Mines, "Riding the Rails to Kansas: The Mexican Immigrants" (n.p., 1980), typescript copy in possession of this article's author. Mine's work was funded by the National Endowment for the Humanities and made extensive use of Santa Fe Railroad (SFRR) records and the papers of Governor Clyde Reed.

5. The definition, as used here, is taken from American Psychiatric Association, *A Psychiatric Glossary: The Meaning of Terms Frequently Used in Psychiatry,* 3d ed. (Washington, DC, 1969).

6. U.S. Department of Commerce, Bureau of the Census, *Fifteenth Census of the United States: 1930, Population,* 5 vols., vol. 2 (Washington, DC, 1933), 65–66; and Carroll D. Clark and Roy L. Roberts, *People of Kansas: A Demographic and Sociological Study* (Topeka, 1936), 51. In 1920 Germans accounted for 21.1 percent of immigrants and Mexicans, 12.4 percent, and in 1930 it was 21.5 and 13.8 respectively.

7. Local Kansas mythology of Anglos and Mexicans described the use of the term. For Texas and the Southwest, see Arnoldo De León, *They Called Them Greasers: Anglo Attitudes Toward Mexicans in Texas, 1821–1900* (Austin, 1983), 16–17.

8. J. Rogers Hollingsworth, ed., *American Expansion in the Late Nineteenth Century: Colonialist or Anticolonialist?* (New York, 1968).

9. Carman, *Language Units,* II, 879; and Rutter, "Mexican Americans in Kansas," 109.

10. *El Cosmopolita* was published from August 22, 1914, to November 15, 1919. The owner and director was Jack Danciger, an Anglo, and the editors were J. M. Urbina and M. A. Urbina. The first issue clearly stated the goals and objectives of the paper. Each issue averaged four pages and the cost was one dollar per year. For personal and financial reasons publication ceased in 1919. The newspaper was

adamantly anti–Santa Fe Railroad and consistently printed complaints by Mexican workers.

11. Kansas City Interviews; and Laird, "Argentine," 192.

12. Interview with D. C. Garica, Garden City, KS, May 27, 1981.

13. Carman, *Language Units,* II, 216; Rutter, "Mexican-Americans in Kansas," 36–39; Swan, "Ethnic Heritage of Topeka," 139; Mines, "Riding the Rails"; Paul S. Taylor, *Mexican Labor in the United States,* vol. 2 (Berkeley, 1932), 66–68; Victor Clark, *Mexican Labor in the United States,* U.S. Department of Labor Bulletin no. 78 (Washington, DC, 1908), 472; and State of Kansas, "Decennial Census of the State of Kansas, 1915 and 1925," in Census Division, Kansas State Historical Society, Topeka.

14. Leola Howard Blanchard, *Conquest of Southwest Kansas* (Wichita, 1931), 328–29; *Garden City (KS) Telegram,* June 4, 1971; Barbara Oringderff, "A Short History of the United States Sugar and Land Company: Now Called the Garden City Company," in Kearny County Historical Society, *History of Kearny County, Kansas,* vol. 2 (Lakin, KS, 1973), 171–72.

15. "Decennial Census, 1915 and 1925"; Carman, *Language Units,* 2, 891; Kansas City Interviews; *Topeka Capital Journal,* December 17 and 20, 1961; Laird, "Argentine," 39; Rutter, "Mexican Americans in Kansas," 45–48; Swan, "Ethnic Heritage of Topeka," 139; Braun, "Survey," 12; Meyer and Sherman, *Course of Mexican History,* 432–79; and Cardoso, *Mexican Emigration,* 1–37.

16. Interview with Ignacio Galindo Valenzuela, Garden City, KS, May 23, 1981.

17. Interview in Spanish with Aniseto Herrera and Felipa Martínez de Herrara, Garden City, KS, May 24, 1981.

18. Interview with Ignacio Galindo Valenzuela, Garden City, KS, May 23, 1981.

19. Kansas City Interviews; Laird, "Argentine," 84; and *Topeka Capital Journal,* December 17, 1961.

20. "Decennial Census, 1915 and 1925."

21. Laird, "Argentine," 189–99; and Kansas City Interviews.

22. Kansas City Interviews; "Decennial Census, 1925"; and U.S. Department of Commerce, *Fifteenth Census, Population,* vol. 5, 87–91.

23. "Decennial Census, 1915 and 1925"; and Laird, "Argentine," 117.

24. U.S. Department of Commerce, *Fifteenth Census, Population,* vol. 5, 87–89; and Laird, "Argentine," 139. Some of the males classified as "laborers" may actually have been "helpers," which was a higher ranking job. However, the census did not make the distinction. The 1930 census counted 3.7 percent of female "Mexicans" employed. "Laborer" jobs included hostler helper, coach cleaner, engine watcher, carman, wiper, boiler washer, firebuilder, pitman, locomotive painter, car carpenter, cinder laborer, and shop laborer; U.S. Department of Commerce, *Fifteenth Census: Population,* vol. 4, 556, 565. The census indicated that 14 percent of whites and 30 percent of blacks in manufacturing were laborers and 16 and 55 percent respectively in transportation industries.

25. This attitude of the women was evident in the interviews and confirmed on follow-up questions.

26. Kansas City Interviews; Ramírez, "Mexicans in Emporia," 26; Rutter, "Mexican Americans in Kansas," 17; Laird, "Argentine," 137–46; and SFRR payroll records reviewed every five years throughout the period 1900 to 1949. These records are located in the Manuscript Department, Kansas State Historical Society.

27. Composite from interviews in Garden City, May–June 1981. Statistics for the 1931–40 decade were taken from Department of Agriculture, referred to in Kansas State University, Department of Sociology and Office of Minority Affairs, "Source Book: Mexican Americans in an Anglo World," mimeograph (1974), 4. An article in the *Garden City Herald,* December 3, 1925, described the work in the fields and factory.

28. Interview with Pedro Sandoval, Garden City, KS, May 26, 1981.

29. This was common to most of the interviewees in all locations.

30. Elizabeth S. Johnson, *Welfare of Families of Sugar-Beet Laborers,* U.S. Department of Labor, Children's Bureau Publication no. 247 (Washington, DC, 1939). Other general income figures are from U.S. Department of Commerce, Bureau of the Census, Fifteenth Census of the United States: 1930, *Construction Industry* (Washington, DC, 1933), 476.

31. Kansas City Interviews; Interview in Spanish with Aniseto Herrera and Felipa Martínez de Herrara, Garden City, KS, May 24, 1981; and Laird, "Argentine," 197–98.

32. SFRR Payroll, June 1930.

33. SFRR Payroll, June 1935.

34. *Wichita Eagle Beacon,* September 28–October 1, 1980. Bilingual program demands and organizations like the Mexican American Council on Education (M.A.C.E.) in Garden City and statewide organizations such as LULAC and G.I. Forum are indicative of the importance placed on education.

35. "Decennial Census, 1925"; and Laird, "Argentine," 135.

36. Garden City School District, List of Elementary School Students, 1920–1950, in Student Files, Garden City Unified School District Offices, Garden City, KS. Interview with Father Emil Dinkle, Garden City, KS, May 27, 1981.

37. *Topeka Capital Journal,* December 19, 1961: Rutter, "Mexican Americans in Kansas," 134–36; Swan, "Ethnic Heritage of Topeka," 151; Ramirez, "Mexicans in Emporia," 24, and List of High School Graduates, 1900–50, Garden City School District.

38. Laird, "Argentine," 135, 193–96; and Kansas City Interviews. Such an incident actually occurred with Ignacio Valenzuela, and he related the story in his interview, May 23, 1981, Garden City.

39. Carman, *Language Units,* II, 897; Laird, "Argentine," 193–96; Swan, "Ethnic Heritage of Topeka," 152–53; and Franco, "Mexican People," 54–55.

40. Interview with D. C. García, Garden City, KS, May 27, 1981.

41. *Wichita Eagle Beacon,* September 29, 1980.

42. Mark Reisler, *By the Sweat of Their Brow: Mexican Immigrant Labor in the United States, 1900–1940* (Westport, CT, 1976), 50; Rutter, "Mexican Americans in Kansas," 89; *Topeka Capital Journal,* December 20, 1961; Laird, "Argentine," 72–75, 197–98; and Mines, "Riding the Rails," 51–52.

43. Interviews in Spanish with Francis Ávila de Gonzales, May 21, 1981; and Isabel Negrete de Hernandez and Bartolo Rodríguez, May 23, 1981, all in Garden City, KS; Laird, "Argentine," 199–200; and *Garden City Herald,* September 17, 1925, and September 16, 1926, on fiesta; on May 19, 1927, the newspaper reported a Mexican band concert.

44. Reisler, *By the Sweat of Their Brow,* 49–76; Laird, "Argentine," 197; and *Topeka Capital Journal,* December 20, 1961.

45. Laird, "Argentine," 139–40. Most railroad workers interviewed in western Kansas remembered little about the 1922 strike, and all were section laborers, not shop workers.

46. *Garden City Herald,* June 4, April 15 and 30, September 9 and 23, and October 7, 1925, January 27, and April 7, 1927; and interview in Spanish with Gregorio Mujica, May 22, 1981. Also, the *Kansas City Star* published a number of articles in the mid-1920s on Anglo-Mexican confrontations; and Laird, "Argentine," 140–41.

47. Mines, "Riding the Rails," 54.

48. Ibid., 55.

49. Ibid., 55, 58–59; and Laird, "Argentine," 203.

50. Mines, "Riding the Rails," 56–57; and Laird, "Argentine," 203–4.

51. Mines, "Riding the Rails," 48.

52. Interviews with Ignacio Galindo Valenzuela, May 23, 1981; and Pedro Sandoval, May 22, 1981, Garden City, KS; and Laird, "Argentine," 204–5.

53. Reisler, *By the Sweat of Their Brow,* 248.

54. Interview in Spanish with Gregorio Mujica, May 22, 1981, Garden City, KS. *Garden City Herald,* March 23, 1931, reported that 400 Mexicans held a reunion to celebrate the 125th anniversary of Benito Juarez's birth. The mutual society organized the festivities. *El Cosmopolita* frequently mentioned events in Kansas City sponsored by the Sociedad Mutua in the city.

55. Interview in Spanish with Aniseto Herrera, May 24, 1981, Garden City, KS.

56. Interview with Pedro Sandoval, May 22, 1981, Garden City, KS.

57. "Index of Rental Food Prices in Kansas, 1930–36," in State of Kansas, Commission of Labor and Industry, *Annual Report, Year Ending December 31, 1936* (Topeka, 1937), 32.

58. Census figures for 1980 are from *New York Times,* September 6, 1981, section 4; figures for 1970 are from U.S. Department of Commerce, Bureau of the Census, *General Census Characteristics,* vol. 1, pt. 18 (Washington, DC, 1970), table 48, p. 206.

An "Army of Amazons": The Language of Protest in a Kansas Mining Community, 1921–1922

Ann Schofield

On Sunday, December 11, 1921, five hundred women from the various mining camps of the Kansas "Little Balkans" crowded into a church hall in Franklin. Caught in a protracted strike and faced with dwindling family incomes, they resolved to take action. By the next day their ranks had swelled to several thousand women who, marching behind a billowing American flag and singing patriotic songs, blocked the entrances to mines, threw pepper in workers' eyes and may even have beaten several miners in an attempt to stop strikebreakers from jeopardizing the four-month-old miners' walkout.

Pittsburg, the largest city of Crawford County, braced for an assault by the "army of Amazons." The sheriff frantically assembled a deputized force of one thousand men and recruited veterans who stockpiled rifles and guns in a local hotel. Excitement in the town heightened as three troops of Kansas National Guard cavalry arrived on December 15 to take up positions in the Ringo, Mulberry and Franklin coal camps.

But the "army" never attacked. Restrained by the authorities, the women were subjected to harsh legal reprisals following their march. Forty-nine women were charged with unlawful assembly, assault and disturbing the peace; bond was set at seven-hundred-fifty dollars rather than the customary two hundred dollars. When tried in January the women pleaded guilty and were fined anywhere from one dollar to two hundred dollars, paroled and ordered to pay court costs.

At first glance the women's march seems the stuff that enlivens local history. Its drama pulls us toward the community concerns that inspired its participants—labor solidarity and family wages. But deeper analysis of that drama, most especially of the rhetoric of protest employed by the women, leads to even more substantive questions. The "language" of the march, both nonverbal and spoken, reflected important social tensions of the time; the struggle between modern and traditional values, between the dominant society and an ethnic population, between labor and capital. It depicts as well women's participation in the unique culture of a mining community.

That culture—the values, institutions and shared experience focusing on the mines—connected the public world of work and the private world of domesticity for women in a way that was a specifically working-class experience. Through the march, women expressed their collective stake in the community as wives and mothers in family units whose economic viability was threatened by the public event of the strike. In symbol and rhetoric, the women laid claim to their rights as Americans and defined their concept of femininity. The women's behavior and its description by contemporary observers also reflects the range of political and social conflict that existed in southeastern Kansas and, paradoxically, a consensus as to what constituted appropriate moral behavior. Critics felt the march challenged fundamental values associated with flag and family while participants viewed their actions as a defense of those very same values. Patriotism and domesticity seemed cherished beliefs for each side; conflict consisted in the substantive or behavioral content of those categories. Before turning to the women's march, however, it is important to understand the issues of the strike, the nature of southeastern Kansas mining communities, and the economic context in which the march took place.

The women's march formed but one chapter of a turbulent era in American labor history. In the years following the First World War, John L. Lewis struggled to achieve and then to maintain leadership of the

United Mine Workers of America (UMWA). Alex Howat, the "rambunctious, argumentative, and tempestuous" president of Kansas District 14, repeatedly challenged Lewis; indeed, he led Kansas miners out on strike in September 1921 in defiance of Lewis's orders. That strike, ostensibly over a change in work rules at the Dean and Reliance mine near Pittsburg, Kansas, was complicated by a number of other issues, the foremost of which was Howat's ambition. Idolized in the Kansas coal communities for his consistent pose as a "militant class warrior," Howat demonstrated, nonetheless, a poor understanding of the political situations both in Kansas and in the international union. The Kansas legislature, partially in response to the chaotic situation caused by repeated miners' walkouts, had passed a compulsory arbitration law in 1920 known as the Industrial Court. Although Lewis was opposed to the law in principle, in the interest of stabilizing the Kansas situation he joined Howat to honor a contract which the UMWA had signed with the South Western Coal Operators Association, whose terms forbade strikes until issues were adjudicated by a joint union management committee. When Howat defied both the union demand to honor the contract and the state demand for compulsory arbitration, the union voted to suspend him; the state put him in jail. As Melvyn Dubofsky and Warren Van Tine have written: "Howat . . . proved unable to distinguish between strikes for a good cause and those without reason, between walkouts banned by a law that the UMW challenged in court and those that the UMW pledged to enforce."[1]

While this may be a fair historical assessment of the mercurial Alex Howat, the fact remains that Howat was a folk hero in the Kansas coal fields and his imprisonment was taken as a symbol of the injustice felt by the rank and file miners.[2] Failing to recognize Howat's local importance, Lewis installed Van Bittner as provisional head of District 14 in the fall of 1921. Bittner then used the international union payroll to hire Lewis supporters and he convinced surrounding districts (Oklahoma-Arkansas-Texas, Iowa, Missouri) not to accept transfer cards from Kansas miners. Both actions seriously undermined the strike; by late November the mines were operating at about half their capacity as increasing numbers of miners returned to work. These actions had critical economic repercussions for miners' households because here, as in mining communities elsewhere, the mines were the single source of employment.

Kansas miners and their families knew all too well the impact of strikes on household budgets particularly during a time of steadily declining incomes. Coal was one of America's "sick" industries during the

1920s as reflected in the persistent irregularity of miners' wages. Walter Hamilton and Helen Wright pointed out the implications of wage fluctuations for the family: ". . . if a miner worked the number of days that the industry formerly averaged and earned the average wage at the present union scale, he would earn between $1800 and $2000 a year. Even this wage would not provide the estimate of the Bureau of Labor Statistics for minimum requirements of 'health and decency.'"[3] They correctly concluded that "such incomes would give the housewife an impossible task," for the welfare of the household was totally contingent upon the miner's wage, thus giving wives as household managers a particularly immediate connection to workplace issues.

In many other ways the communities surrounding Pittsburg resembled typical mining communities.[4] Towns with populations ranging from 100 to 1000 made up the coal mining area of southeastern Kansas. Centered primarily in Crawford and Cherokee Counties, the mine field consisted of twenty or so small mining camps located anywhere from two to fifteen miles from the city of Pittsburg.[5] Life was dictated by the rhythms of the mine; sudden death, economic insecurity and a traditional work culture were the norm.[6] For men this work culture consisted of obvious elements: the dangers of the occupation, the underground work environment, the power to effect an immediate work stoppage, a body of myths, songs and superstitions and the focal institution of the union, the United Mine Workers of America. It included also a sporadic pattern of employment and unemployment—miners were idle at least one-third of the year.[7] When asked how miners amused themselves when out of work, one miner testified to the economic and psychic instability of the miner's family with his taciturn reply: "What do we do when we are out of work? . . .Why we sit around or start a fight. There is nothing else to do."[8] Few mining towns provided any outlet for this enforced leisure—evening schools, reading rooms and free libraries were in short supply. For women the towns offered little external to the family or mines that was "stimulating or developing."[9] Unlike the middle-class women of Pittsburg whose activities in such clubs as the Helpers, the Queen Esthers and the Worthwhile filled the pages of local newspapers, miners' wives centered their lives on the camps.

Working-class women shared more with the men of the community than this lack of a cultural outlet, for their distinct roles were shaped by the presence of the mines. The stark figure of the woman at the mine entrance conveyed the immediacy of numerous mine accidents for miners' families, accentuated in an age with few survivor's benefits and inadequate state workmen's compensation acts.[10] A daily ritual was the hot bath which miners' wives were responsible for having ready for the filth-encrusted miners when they returned from the mines. Furthermore, the union sponsored some of the few social events held in the mining camps such as the Dante Allegheri Clubs for wives of Italian miners. Wives shopped in company stores and lived in company houses.

Like the women described by historians Susan J. Kleinberg[11] and Glenna Matthews[12] in other one-company towns, these women were rarely employed outside of the home; the demands of domestic work without modern appliances, in addition to the narrow occupational structure and physical isolation of the camps, precluded wage work for women. Unlike more heterogeneous industrial communities where wives contributed to family income by taking in boarders or doing seasonal work, census data for Pittsburg and its environs indicated an overwhelming majority of nuclear family households, few boarders and a minuscule number of wage-working wives.[13] Women shared the burden of economic insecurity by forming "networks" through trading bread, eggs and garden produce and through midwives' visits from house to house. When asked if she had worked outside the home to help make ends meet one miner's wife replied, "Of course not, no one did—who would take care of the children?"[14] It seems clear that even though there was a strict sexual division of labor in mining towns, the mines themselves were central to the community and had a profound impact on both men and women. Once again, the role of the mines in Kansas coal fields should remind us of the very permeable boundaries that existed between public and private life for working-class people.[15]

In many ways, this interaction between home life and work life characterized mining communities everywhere. June Nash, for example, found in her study of Bolivian tin miners that miners' wives publicly shamed husbands following a domestic quarrel by refusing to bring their lunch buckets to the mine. And wives of miners, organized by community, marched to defend their interests in Maryland in 1894, on the Mesabi Iron Range in 1916 and in Colorado in 1927, to name but a few instances.[16] In some instances, even death, that most individual of experiences, drew the community into a work-related ritual. In 1917, for example, the body of a young Italian miner killed by a gas explosion was taken to Pittsburg where it was met by a band and carried behind an empty hearse to its grave accompanied by several hundred fellow miners.[17] Briefly, then, we can see that the women and men of mining towns shared values and traditions which centered on the mine to a point where we can genuinely expand the definition of work culture beyond the workplace to encompass the entire community.

Ethnicity, however, also colored the culture of the Kansas Balkans. As Kansas coal mines expanded between 1877 and 1879, Welsh coal miners migrated from the coal fields of Pennsylvania to Kansas. Following that date, until 1889, the need for workers was so great that coal companies sent agents to Illinois and Pennsylvania coal fields as well as to the port of New York to recruit miners. Agents met immigrants at the pier and, if they had been miners in Europe, promised them transportation to the Kansas coal fields. Miners also came to Kansas from Indian Territory (now Oklahoma) during labor disputes in that area between the years 1882 and 1895. Once immigrants established themselves in Kansas, they soon sent for family, friends and countrymen to join them. By the turn of the century, southeastern Kansas was a polyglot area peopled by Italians, Germans, French, Belgians and a variety of ethnic groups from the British Isles and the Austro-Hungarian Empire.[18] The contrast which the ethnic population of the mining camps struck with the surrounding environment caused one observer to note in 1911, "at no place west of the Mississippi is there a similar large group of industrial immigrants living in the very midst of a flourishing rural community."[19]

Still, work, rather than ethnicity, ultimately determined community in southeastern Kansas. With the exception of the Italians, immigrants did not cluster together into residential enclaves as they did in eastern urban areas and they formed fewer distinctively ethnic organizations.[20] The Catholic church, for example, never sent priests to minister to one particular ethnic group and encouraged the foreign-born to Americanize as quickly as possible. One study of a local baptismal registry found: ". . . most nationalities married outside of their own nationalities including frequent intermarriage between American and foreign-born."[21] While cross-ethnic, these marriages were rarely cross-class —the "Americans" were usually the children of immigrants or miners themselves.

Thus, the coal companies and the mine itself dominated life in the mining camps. Coal companies built these camps—Franklin, Arma, Mulberry, Camp 50, Chicopee and a host of others—to house workers as close as possible to shaft mines. As one geographer explained this pattern of settlement: "There is thus created near the openings of the mines a sort of artificial city, with houses exactly alike which are the 'result' and the necessary 'sign' of the work underground."[22] Many of these houses, or more appropriately shacks, were owned by the mining companies as were the company stores where miners and their wives bought groceries in exchange for script.[23] Some camps boasted churches, schools and dance halls while others were simply dreary rows of three-room shacks. There was a higher incidence of smallpox, measles, scarlet fever, typhoid, malarial fever, pneumonia and other respiratory illnesses in the camps than in the surrounding area. Nutritional standards were also lower; stews and soups rather than meat provided the main protein source for family's diets. In a poignant testament to this fact, a Dunkirk schoolchild once began an essay on cows with the sentence, "The meat of a cow is called soupbone."[24]

Families dealt with this insecurity in a number of different ways. They frequently planted large vegetable gardens and preserved or canned the produce which they stored in cellars behind their shacks; those without cellars stored vegetables under the house and piled straw or dirt over them. Italians were especially noted for growing herbs, fig trees and grapes for wine.[25] Mining families also kept hogs and chickens for their own use. The sameness of their existence and the shared insecurity drew the people of these camps into tight community networks as uniform poverty circumscribed their lives.

Politics distinguished the "Little Balkans" of southeastern Kansas from other mining areas. Girard, the seat of Crawford County and a familiar name to students of American socialism, was the site of a socialist press which published the national socialist weekly the *Appeal to Reason,* along with *The Coming Nation* and *The Progressive Woman.* Eugene Debs lived in Girard for a number of years and Kate Richards O'Hare, Mother Jones and a number of other socialist luminaries frequently visited the area for camp meetings, union conventions, and Fourth of July celebrations.[26] "Mother," especially, was well known to the members and leaders of UMWA District 14. The Socialist party had an active following in the camps; indeed, many camps had several elected Socialist officials. Arma, for example, boasted all Socialist officials in 1911 while Dunkirk relied on an entirely Socialist school board.[27] The Industrial Workers of the World added to the radical activity in southeastern Kansas although they organized primarily in the oil fields of Butler county and among migratory wheat harvest workers.[28] By 1920, activities of the Kansas Communist party attracted the attention of the state Attorney General's office to Kansas's "red sector."[29]

The area also produced its own "Jennie Higginses," socialist activists who, as Neil Basen reminds us, performed critical roles as "community educators and leaders" in the decentralized southwestern socialist movement. Laura A. Lasater of Pittsburg, for example, "a blue-collar widow," served as district clerk of Crawford County, Luella Roberts Krehbiel of Coffeyville, a state organizer, held "parlor propaganda meetings"[30] and Mary Skubitz of Ringo led the women's march in 1921. Thus trade union and radical politics enriched community life, even for women as isolated as those in southeastern Kansas.

Citizens of Crawford County were clearly distressed by this "enemy within," a fear heightened by the area's involvement in the bitter 1919–20 coal strike, as well as by the postwar "Red scare." Before the 1919 strike ended, mine operators had used the National Guard and college boys from Lawrence and Topeka as strikebreakers. The strike engendered such anti-union feelings throughout the state that in 1920 the Kansas legislature passed the Industrial Court Act which outlawed strikes and subjected all labor disputes to arbitration by an Industrial Court. By 1921, there was sufficient nativist and anti-Catholic sentiment in Crawford County to support the founding of a Ku Klux Klan chapter which numbered 4600 members by 1924.[31] The "army of Amazons," then, exacerbated these tensions between the mining camps and the society around them and, at the same time, expressed the family needs and ethnic unity of the community.

In contemporary descriptions of the march itself, the most striking element is always gender. The very phrase, for example, "army of Amazons," or "maddened Amazons," was used repeatedly by such "establishment" newspapers as the *New York Times, Topeka Journal, Kansas City Times,* and the *Pittsburg Daily Headlight* to convey a disturbance in the natural order of things. The *New York Times* editorialized about the Amazon warriors from the "Red sector" of Kansas under the headline "Extending the Sphere of Women": "What they did was less a demonstration of courage than a willingness to capitalize and exploit the weakness that is ascribed to them."[32]

Similarly, the *Topeka Journal* evoked a military tone as it described the first day of the march. Headed by the girl's band of Arma, playing martial music, "General" Annie Stovich, the Joan of Arc [sic] of the "Amazon army" led her invading hosts, already weary and footsore, into the enemy country this afternoon.[33]

The article went on to describe the "pent-up fury of the women" and claimed that "Men viewed the situation with alarm, for it was believed that even bayonets will not deter the strong, highly temperamental foreign women." The *Kansas City Times* cautioned readers not to underestimate the chaos in the coal fields for "stopping a mob of more than two thousand maddened Amazons is the task confronting [the sheriff]."[34] In a symbolic sense, then, the Amazons posed a threat that went far beyond a few days of disorder in a remote area of Kansas. They represented a social order at risk, the family under siege.

While critics cast the march in a threatening light, the marchers themselves and their supporters were eager to promote the "womanly" meaning of their actions. The marchers' initial manifesto, for example, issued the day before the march (December 11), proudly proclaimed in the name of "the wives of the loyal union men of Kansas" that "it is our duty to stand shoulder to shoulder with our husbands in this struggle."[35] Several days later, the socialist *Appeal to Reason* assured readers of the feminine restraint shown by the marching women.

> The whole episode of the marching women was remarkably peaceful . . . conducted with . . . admirable restraint. . . . The demonstration throughout was more moral than physical in its nature. The wives of the strikers wished to shame the men who had returned to work—to enforce on their consciousness the fact that they had deserted their comrades in a righteous struggle.[36]

Although the march was viewed as "peaceful" by the labor press, mainstream journalists sharply disagreed. The controversy over the women's behavior during the march seems to have centered, then, about the issue of whether the women were acting out of an appropriate family ethic or brazenly displaying unfeminine qualities. The *New York Times* seemed to believe that they were doing the latter, for when it described the women's arrival at the mine on December 13, it included the following charge:

> The workers' dinner buckets were taken and a bombardment of bread, butter, bacon, jelly, eggs and other food was begun. The buckets, as fast as they were emptied were smashed by the rioters. Coffee compartments were opened and the working miners as well as the Sheriff were showered with the drink intended for their lunch. Only two or three of the men resisted the women.[37]

Similar stories of violence were reported after the march. Richard J. Hopkins, the Attorney General of Kansas, complained of the difficulty of finding prosecution witnesses. One potential witness, who was driving to work in one of the mines, ". . . was stopped and badly beaten by several of the women and refused to file a complaint altho [*sic*] he knew and recognized more than one of his assailants."[38] The fear of community sanctions, it would seem, at least in this case, superseded legal or police pressure.

In another explicitly identified incident, Mrs. Nick Bossetti and Mrs. Walter Carbaugh were arrested following the march and accused of assaulting Walter Madden at Central Mine #49. They supposedly dragged him out of the mine office, beat him and tore his clothing.[39] Finally, one paper told of a miner who was stripped and paraded through the town of Frontenac in a motorcar. "Women thrust pins into his flesh and shouted: 'Now, will you go back to work you dirty scab.'"[40]

The two ideological camps stood divided on other issues as well. In addition to highlighting the violence, opponents of the march questioned the leadership and initiation of the women's march. Officials tried to make a case that a few militants coerced many women into participating in the march and down-played the significant size and duration of the three-day disturbance. To this end, they found several women, including one schoolteacher from Ringo, who repudiated their participation in the march and identified the speakers at the December 11 organizational meetings as Mary Skubitz, a Socialist activist, a Mrs. Wilson and Dr. P. L. Howe.[41]

Another effort to discredit the march, at least as an autonomous activity of working-class women, was made by the *New York Times* which claimed "the Howat forces sent their women into the fight. . . ."[42] Journalist Henry J. Haskell also wrote in *The Outlook* that "radical Howat followers undertook a policy of terrorism. Women were incited to lead mobs and threaten miners who stood by the International."[43] Yet another reporter endorsed the opinion that the "women have been skillfully and effectively tutored in their meetings and in their marches."[44] In a similar vein, Van Bittner, provisional president of District 14, censured cowardly men who sent their mothers, wives and sisters out to riot.

The need to identify the march as carefully planned by male leaders reflected mainstream society's ever-present fear of an alien conspiracy, so prevalent in postwar America. Playing perhaps on that fear of the "enemy within," one miner, when asked how the women assembled so quickly, sarcastically replied: "We have a wireless that calls them together just as the superintendents of the mine find out the secrets of our union meetings. It's our own grapevine."[45] In contrast to this sense of subversion, the *Appeal to Reason* stated that "the idea of marching was entirely spontaneous with the women. None of the Howat leaders advised this tactic, and Howat from his jail cell, expressed his regret that the violence had occurred."[46] Another labor paper, the *Workers' Chronicle*, noted that men were barred from the organizational meeting Sunday night[47] and, finally, Fannie Wimler, an active participant in the march, responded to Bittner's charges in a letter to the *Pittsburg Daily Headlight*:

> Husbands, sons and brothers aren't cowards and haven't anything to do with our affairs. We are doing this on our own accord, and what we mean is business. . . . If you don't think us responsible, we'll just have to put the responsibility on you, for you are the one who is driving us to this. We don't want any bloodshed here in Kansas like there was in the Ludlow Strike, and in Alabama and Mingo County, West Virginia. What we want is our industrial freedom and liberty and we want our men to be good, true, loyal union men and 100 percent American citizens, not like you and your dirty bunch of strike breakers. In the World War we bought liberty bonds.[48]

In addition to its proclamation of autonomy, Wimler's letter struck the patriotic tone of the marchers' original statement. It reflected as well a solidarity which linked their action to labor struggles elsewhere and a conception that their cause was truly American.

Despite these seemingly polarized descriptions of the same events, both defenders and detractors agreed that women's natural role was domestic and privatized. However, although gender ideology united these two camps, they divided once again over their interpretation of the sort of behavior the ideology should foster. For the opponents of the march, the women's actions violated appropriate concepts of femininity; for supporters, those same actions upheld the basic tenets of womanhood.

The statement issued by the men before the march expressed their beliefs about women's social role. The proclamation was given by "the wives of the loyal union men of Kansas" and condemned both the

"Alien Industrial Slavery Law" and the international union. Proudly they proclaimed, "it is our duty to stand shoulder to shoulder with our husbands in this struggle." Finally, they defined their struggle as "the fight for our democracy that we was [*sic*] to receive after the World War."[49] In expressing their solidarity with male members of the mining community, the marchers' logic rhetorically linked the miners' struggle to American democratic ideals. They identified with ideals of justice and democracy which they felt should have been defended by the international union and, in a larger sense, by the American government. Undoubtedly, the women considered their cause one of conserving values rather than of revolt, for the marchers felt they were behaving in an appropriately womanly fashion because they were defending their rights and the jobs of their husbands. While their view of the family was holistic, detractors found their behavior inappropriate and not fitting for women.

Their persistent use of the flag—they marched behind the flag, stretched it across the entrance to mines and forced strikebreakers to kneel and kiss the flag—clearly reflects the marchers' acute sensitivity to the labels "foreign" or "subversive." The marchers, it would seem, desperately sought to identify themselves as American, particularly in response to such statements as Governor Allen's proclamation that "the Kansas government does not intend to surrender to foreigners and their female relatives."[50]

The flag conveyed a different meaning to critics of the march, however. One Kansas City paper devoted a lengthy article to the "brazen boldness of a mob of alien[s]" who "compelled miners who are American citizens to kiss the American flag." The xenophobic tone of the article—"They were foreign faces, most of them, and the words that fell from the lips of the men and women were foreign. It was a jargon, and at the head of the fury were two American flags"—drew a sharp contrast between the "loyal citizens and lovers of Americanism" and the "followers of the deposed mine czar Alexander Howat." Religious metaphors evoked a sense of evil ritual akin to a witches' sabbath: "'You kiss the flag, damn you, and say you will not work' . . . amid blasphemy and profane cries the travesty was performed."[51] The flag, in other words, was sacred, the women's actions profane.

The paranoia of local and state officials about subversive female aliens underscored the rift that loomed between Kansans and the mining camps. In two telling examples of that distance, A. J. Curran, the judge of the district court of Pittsburg, wrote to Mrs. John Tracy, chairman of the Americanization committee of the Pittsburg Women's Auxiliary, about the law where naturalization of a male alien conferred citizenship on his wife (especially threatening in light of the political rights and privileges conferred on women by the recently passed Nineteenth Amendment). As Curran stated: "It is a known fact that there are anarchists, communists, and bolsheviks among the alien women in this community. As you know it was the lawlessness of the women in this community a few months ago which made necessary the stationing of the state militia in our country for two months to preserve law and order."[52] In another pronouncement, Al F. Williams, the U.S. District Attorney, threatened to deport the "worst radicals" for he claimed that "when a situation like the present arises they all flock together like so many sheep."[53] Faced with such sentiment, many marchers fled the area; authorities searched in vain for some women when warrants were issued for their arrest.

For Curran, Williams and others, the marching women threatened a political order that included disenfranchised immigrants and an economic order based upon docile workers. Conversely, the marchers staked claim to citizenship and economic equity. Most importantly, each side struggled with a definition of femininity which was used both to condone and to condemn the march. The marchers presented themselves as maternal, patriotic and motivated by family concerns. Their critics labeled them alien, violent and incapable of autonomous action. Both, however, as demonstrated by their words and actions, shared a conception of women as inherently domestic.

On one level, of course, the women's motives were quintessentially domestic, like those of thousands of other women who have engaged in militant activity for traditional goals. History's pages are animated by women who have marched in bread riots, Kosher meat boycotts, as well as in mining strikes, to defend threatened family economies.[54] Rather than isolating women in households, this dependency drew them into the political life of the community, as illustrated by their strength and initiative in the march. As the historian Meredith Tax reminds us, "These women had their own reasons for wanting to fight. In the company towns and migrant labor camps of the West, people were oppressed as members of family units rather than as individuals."[55] And as Mrs. Anna Okorn, a miner's widow, reflected some sixty years after the strike, "People were starving, Mr. Howat was in jail and it wasn't fair."[56]

There are, though, even wider implications in this march for the study of American culture and women's history. As social scientists suggest, in episodes of collective behavior, ideologies and myths which lie beneath the surface of a society emerge. Thus the march discloses information about the roles, values and political consciousness of women in this working-class community. The march itself tells in its own "language" how work, class and politics shaped the subculture of a community suffering hegemonic pressure from the distinct and dominant culture around them. The way in which contemporary observers structured the narrative of the event, evoking images of "Amazons" and foreign hordes, shows that the women's march represented a clear and distinct challenge to a social order based upon separate social roles of men and women as well as upon docile and subservient foreign workers. The marchers symbolically used the traditional American flag to invoke a heritage of American democracy and their claim to the rights of citizens. As women, they went to their kitchens for their weapon, red pepper. By emptying dinner buckets, they further conveyed the message that the food which nurturant women had always given freely they could violently take away.

Several issues about such demonstrations remain problematic, however. The first is the political consciousness of the marching women. Were they aware of the ways in which class determined their situation and of the political issues of the strike? Did they act on that awareness, designing the march as an effective instrument of protest? In the case of the Kansas march, it is clear that miners who returned to work posed a political threat to mining camp communities. They shattered the cohesiveness of the working-class communities and broke the balance of cooperation that sustained these communities in tension with the world around them. Given the radical climate around them, women who marched certainly could have perceived the political dimensions of their actions, or, like Mrs. Okorn, they could have been more simply motivated by the daily reality that "people were starving and it wasn't fair."

A wide array of scholars—anthropologists, sociologists, rhetoricians, historians—have been intrigued by dramatic social behavior.[57] Influenced recently by linguistic theory they have turned their attention to the specific "language" used by participants in mass demonstrations. The French historian Emmanuel LeRoy Ladurie, for example, analyzed a sixteenth-century carnival as a "symbolic revelation of an [emerging] urban consciousness" in the "common people's state of mind."[58] In much the same way, I believe, the women's march reflects women's participation in the unique work culture of the mining community. Just as Ladurie's citizens justified themselves and their actions in religious terms, using a particular religious "code," so did the Kansas women legitimate their behavior with a symbolic lexicon drawn from democratic and domestic ideologies shared by proponents and opponents of the march alike. Each side believed in flag and family, but each defined those ideologies in dramatically different ways. The key issues which concerned both the marchers and their critics—the direction of the march, the definitions of femininity and of appropriate feminine behavior, the role of an American and its corresponding rights—demonstrate important elements in these ideologies and the way in which a particular experience of work, family life and politics led to a uniquely working-class interpretation of fundamental American values.

NOTES

1. Melvyn Dubofsky and Warren Van Tine, *John L. Lewis: A Biography* (New York: Quadrangle, 1979), 115. See also Joseph Skubitz, Jr., "A History of the Development of Deep Mine Production in Crawford County and the Factors That Have Influenced It," M.S. Thesis, Kansas State Teachers College (Pittsburg State University), 1934; Domenico Gagliardo, *The Kansas Industrial Court* (Lawrence: University of Kansas Publication, 1931); Irving Bernstein, *The Lean Years: A History of the American Worker, 1920–1933* (Baltimore: Penguin Books, 1966).

2. Mary Heaten Vorse described Howat as an idol to Kansas miners under whose leadership "people stopped being afraid." Mary Heaton Vorse, "Ma and Mr. Davis," *Survey*, 49 (15 Dec. 1922): 359–60. The 1921 strike, however, became so identified with the local leader that it was known as the "Howat strike." Gagliardo, the Kansas Industrial Court, and one contemporary supporter of the Industrial Court found the "obdurate" Howat was the principal cause of the vicious 1919 strike. See also John Hugh Bowers. *The Kansas Court of Industrial Relations: The Philosophy of the Court* (Chicago: A. C. McClurg & Co., 1922), 28.

3. Walter Hamilton and Helen Wright, *The Case of Bituminous Coal* (New York: Macmillan Co., 1928), 78–80. See also Van Bittner, "Wages in Bituminous Coal Mines as Viewed by the Miners," and Anne Bezanson, "Earnings of Coal Miners," in Cyde L. King, ed., *The Price of Coal: Anthracite and Bituminous* in *The Annals of the American Academy of Political and Social Science*, 111 (Jan. 1924).

4. There is neither an institutional history of the United Mine Workers of America nor a comprehensive social history of mining in the United States. The best guide to the various articles and monographs on mining and life in communities

is Robert F. Munn, *The Coal Industry in America: A Bibliography and Guide to Studies* (Morgantown: West Virginia Univ. Library, 1965). Two studies of mining communities in Great Britain which are suggestive for the analysis of American communities are John Benson, *British Coal Mining in the Nineteenth Century: A Social History* (New York: Holmes and Meier Publishers, Inc., 1980), and Michael Hanies, "Fertility, Nuptiality, and Occupation: A Study of Coal Mining Populations and Regions in England and Wales in the Mid–Nineteenth Century," *Journal of Interdisciplinary History,* 8 (Autumn 1977), 245–80. See also David A. Corbin, *Life, Work and Rebellion in the Coal Fields: The Southern West Virginia Miners, 1880–1922* (Urbana: Univ. of Illinois Press, 1981), and Alan J. Linger, "'What Side Are You On?': Ideological Conflict in the United Mine Workers in America, 1919–1928." Diss. Rutgers Univ. 1982.

5. Strip coal mining began in Crawford Co., Kansas, in 1850 and the first shaft mine was sunk in 1874. By 1898 there were 53 deep pit mines operating in Crawford Co., the leading coal producing area of the state. Production of coal increased in Crawford Co. from 221,741 tons in 1885 to 4,508,747 tons in 1920, the year in which production began to decline. The market for Kansas coal included both domestic and railroad use and was dominated by seven to ten large companies. Vorse, "Ma and Mr. Davis."

6. There were 19 fatal and 836 nonfatal mine accidents in Kansas in 1920. *State of Kansas 35th Annual Report of Department of Labor and Industry,* Topeka, 1920.

7. Annual Report of Coal Mine Inspector and Mine Rescue Departments, State of Kansas, 1921. Mine production slowed during the summer when most miners worked 2–3 days of the week.

8. May Wood-Simons, "Mining Coal and Maiming Men," *The Coming Nation,* 6 (11 Nov. 1911), 4. See also Marie L. Obenauer, "Living Conditions Among Coal Mine Workers of the U.S.," in King, *The Price of Coal,* 12–23.

9. Hamilton and Wright, *The Case of Bituminous Coal,* 82–84.

10. Ibid.

11. Susan J. Kleinberg, "Technology and Women's Work: The Lives of Working Class Women in Pittsburg, 1870–1900," *Labor History,* 17 (Winter 1976), 59–72.

12. Glenna Matthews, "An Immigrant Community in Indian Territory," *Labor History,* 23 (Summer 1982), 374–94.

13. Census, Kansas State 1925, manuscripts for Pittsburg. See also United States Immigration Commission (Dillingham Commission) Immigrants in Industries, United States Senate Documents, 61st Congress, 2nd Session, No. 633. Vol. II, Part I (Hereafter Dillingham Commission). The analysis of Franklin, a representative mining community with a total population of 1409, showed 87.7 percent of the population living in nuclear family households, 6.9 percent of multigenerational households and 5.4 percent in households classified as "other" (indicating the presence of boarders). The homogeneity of the population is indicated by the fact that 25.1 percent were miners, 20.4 percent housewives and 43.0 percent students and children. The Dillingham Commission claims that of 542 households surveyed

in the Kansas coal districts 98.4 percent of native born and 89.4 percent of foreign born women were at home.

14. Interviews with Mrs. Anna Okorn and Mrs. Clemencia DeGrusin, Pittsburg, Ks., 29 Aug. 1981.

15. See Elizabeth Pleck, "Two Worlds in One: Work and Family," *Journal of Social History*, 10 (Winter 1976), 178–95, for an early formulation of the permeability of private/public spheres in working class history.

16. June Nash, *We Eat the Mines and the Mines Eat Us: Dependency and Exploitation in Bolivian Tin Mines* (New York: Columbia Univ. Press, 1979). Katherine A. Harvey, *The Best-Dressed Miners: Life and Labor in the Maryland Coal Region* (Ithaca: Cornell Univ. Press, 1969), 283ff. Charles J. Baynard, "The 1927–1928 Colorado Coal Strike," *Pacific Historical Review*, 32 (1963), 235–50; *Industrial Worker* (5 Aug. 1916), 1.

17. *The Arma Record*, 4 Jan. 1917, 3.

18. Fred N. Howell, "Some Phases of the Industrial History of Pittsburg, Ks.," *Kansas Historical Quarterly*, 18 (1952), 273; William E. Powell, "The Historical Geography of the Impact of Coal Mining upon the Cherokee-Crawford Coal Field of Southeastern Kansas," Diss. Univ. of Nebraska 1970, and idem. "Former Mining Communities of the Cherokee-Crawford Coal Field to Southeastern Kansas," *Kansas Historical Quarterly*, 38 (1972), 187–99.

19. Wood-Simons, "Mining Coal and Maiming Men."

20. Dillingham Commission.

21. Kenneth Melaragno, "Immigrants as Viewed Through the Baptismal Register" (unpub. ms., Pittsburg, Ks., 25 Aug. 1981), studies the *Registrum Baptizatorum in Ecclesia Santa Mariae de Lourdes for 1855–1928*. I am indebted to Eugene DeGruson for bringing this paper to my attention.

22. Jean Brumbes, *Human Geography* (Chicago: Rand McNally Co., 1920), 386.

23. Wood-Simons, "Mining Coal and Maiming Men," describes Kansas miners' homes.

24. Ibid. See also Dillingham Commission.

25. Powell, "Historical Geography," 299.

26. Ray Ginger, *The Bending Cross: A Biography of Eugene V. Debs* (New Brunswick: Rutgers Univ. Press, 1949), 249; Nick Savatore, *Eugene V. Debs: Citizen and Socialist* (Urbana: Univ. of Illinois Press, 1982), 213.

27. Wood-Simons, "Mining Coal and Maiming Men." Until February 1912 the *Girard Times* carried a "Socialist Page" purchased by the local Socialist party. As socialists increased in size and vocality most newspapers in the county including the *Times* started campaigns denouncing the party as a threat to home and church. *Gerard Times*, 31 Oct. 1912; *The Cherokee Sentinel*, 1 Nov. 1912; *The Mulberry News*, 1 Nov. 1912; *Walnut Eagle*, 1 Nov. 1912.

28. Clayton R. Koppes, "The IWW and County Jail Reform in Ks., 1915–1920," *Kansas Historical Quarterly*, 41 (Fall 1975), 63–85. Interview with George Gust, Pittsburg, 30 Aug. 1981. Mr. Gust remembers an organizer from "The Imperial Workers

of the World" who worked with him in the Southeastern Kansas coal mines and intended to set up the "Imperial Wizzard" in the area to dominate the country.

29. Statements by John Eber, 3 July 1920, and by John Hughes, 5 Jan. 1920. Kansas State Historical Society, Topeka, Ks.

30. Neil K. Basen, "The 'Jennie Higginses' of the 'New South in the West': A Regional Survey of Social Activists, Agitators, and Organizers, 1901–1917," in Sally Miller, ed., *Flawed Liberation: Socialism and Feminism* (Westport, Conn.: Greenwood Press, 1981), 91–92. See also James Green, *Grassroots Socialism: Radical Movements in the Southwest, 1895–1943* (Baton Rouge: Louisiana State Univ. Press, 1978).

31. Lila Lee Jones, "The Ku Klux Klan in Eastern Kansas During the 1920's," *Emporia Research Studies*, Emporia State College, 23 (Winter 1975), 22.

32. *New York Times*, 15 Dec. 1921, 16.

33. *Topeka Journal*, 14 Dec. 1921, 1.

34. *Kansas City Times*, 14 Dec. 1921, 2.

35. Reprinted in full with signatures in *Pittsburg Daily Headlight* (hereafter *PDH*), 12 Dec. 1921, 1.

36. *Appeal to Reason*, 14 Jan. 1922, 1.

37. *New York Times*, 13 Dec. 1921. Mrs. Anna Okorn did remember a "Mrs. Nino" hitting a miner on the head with his dinner pail.

38. *Topeka Daily Capital*, 20 Dec. 1921, 1.

39. *PDH*, 19 Dec. 1921, 1.

40. *Kansas City Times*, 17 Dec. 1921, 2.

41. On 29 December 1921, for example, police arrested Mrs. John Morris of Camp 51, the wife of a miner and mother of seven children. Mrs. Morris, along with Mrs. Carrie Didlott of Ringo, expressed their regret at having marched, as did Miss Tillie Roitz, a schoolteacher at Ringo. Roitz protested the revocation of her teacher's certificate and pointed out that wives of members of the school board had participated in the march. Her brother, she said, was in World War I and she herself taught Americanism to her students. *PDH*, 17 Jan. 1922.

42. *New York Times*, 15 Dec. 1921, 16.

43. Henry Haskell in *The Outlook*, 129 (28 Dec. 1921), 680–81.

44. *Kansas City Times*, 15 Dec. 1921, 10.

45. Ibid.

46. John Gunn in the *Appeal to Reason*, 24 Dec. 1921, 1.

47. *Worker's Chronicle*, 16 Dec. 1921, 1.

48. Fannie Wimler in *PDH*, 15 Dec. 1921, 4.

49. See note 35 above.

50. *New York Times*, 16 Dec. 1921, 1.

51. *Kansas City Times*, 17 Dec. 1921, 1–2.

52. Letter A. J. Curran to Mrs. John Tracy, dated 10 May 1922. Pittsburg State University Library, Pittsburg, KS.

53. *PDH*, 29 Dec. 1921, 1.

54. Natalie Z. Davis, "Women in the Crafts in Sixteenth-Century Lyon," *Feminist Studies*, 8 (Spring 1982), 47–80. Paula E. Hyman, "Immigrant Women and Consumer Protest: The New York City Kosher Meat Boycott of 1902," *American Jewish History*, 70 (Sept. 1980), 91–105. Temma Kaplan, "Class Consciousness and Community in 19th Century Andalusia," in Maurize Zeitlin, ed., *Political Power and Social Theory*, vol. 2 (Greenwich, Conn.: JAI Press, 1981). Specific instances of demonstrations by women in mining communities can be found in Harvey, *The Best-Dressed Miners*, 283ff.; Charles J. Bayard, "The 1927–1928 Colorado Coal Strike," *Pacific Historical Review*, 32 (1963), 235–50; *Industrial Worker*, 5 Aug. 1916, 1; Victor Greene, *The Slavic Community on Strike* (Notre Dame, Ind.: Notre Dame Press, 1968), 143–44; Corbin, "Life, Work and Rebellion," 92–93.

55. Tax, *The Rising of the Women: Feminist Solidarity and Class Conflict, 1880–1917* (New York: Monthly Review Press, 1980), 127.

56. Interview with Mrs. Anna Okorn, 29 Aug. 1981, Pittsburg, Ks.

57. Some examples included: Emmanuel LeRoy Ladurie, *Carnival in Romans* (New York: George Braziller, Inc., 1979); George Rude, *Ideology and Popular Protest* (New York: Pantheon, 1980); Louise A. Tilly and Charles Tilly, eds., *Class Conflict and Collective Action* (Beverly Hills: Sage Publications, 1981); Victor Turner, *Dramas, Fields and Metaphors* (Ithaca: Cornell Univ. Press, 1974); Kenneth Burke, *A Grammar of Motives* (New York: Prentice-Hall, 1945); Joseph R. Gusfield, *Symbolic Crusade: Status Politics and the American Temperance Movement* (Urbana: Univ. of Illinois Press, 1963).

58. Ladurie, *Carnival in Romans*.

The Dirty Thirties: A Study in Agricultural Capitalism

Donald Worster

"The history of any land begins with nature, and all histories must end with nature," J. Frank Dobie once wrote.[1] He was eloquently right, but until very recently such a view was not regarded seriously by academic historians, who commonly took nature for granted, beginning and ending their studies with an air of human omnipotence. That attitude, however, is becoming harder to maintain in innocence, as a group of ecologically informed historians challenge it. It is now more acceptable to say, with Dobie, that nature has played a stage-center role in the making of history—the making of its setbacks and tragedies as well as its progress and triumphs. Whether defined as climate, as vegetation, as the presence or absence of water, as soil and topography, or more compositely as ecosystem and biosphere, nature has been a force to be reckoned with in social evolution. Many geographers and anthropologists have long acknowledged that fact. And now historical thinking, if it wants to be taken seriously, must to some extent also become ecological.[2]

There have been some important exceptions to the historians' neglect of environmental perspectives. Strikingly, those exceptions have come mainly out of the Great Plains. Dobie was a well-known son of

"The Dirty Thirties: A Study in Agricultural Capitalism," by Donald Worster, *Great Plains Quarterly* 6 (1986): 107–116. Copyright *Great Plains Quarterly*, Center for Great Plains Studies, University of Nebraska–Lincoln. Reprinted by permission.

this region, growing up and teaching here. So was his University of Texas associate, Walter Prescott Webb, who stitched history and environment together in his writings.[3] And so was the man who, more than any other, anticipated the emerging ecological synthesis in history: James Malin of the University of Kansas. As far back as 1950 Malin was envisioning history as a process of "ecological adaptation" and was promoting the grasslands as an ideal laboratory for tracking that process.[4] These scholars, particularly Webb and Malin, were not always clear about what they meant by adaptation—whether it was a process of yielding to natural exigencies or of surmounting them by means of technology—but they were all convinced of the profound importance of the human dialogue with nature.

The Great Plains have uniquely had an impact on the historical imagination because conditions of settlement there have presented so stark a contrast with those in more humid American environments. But in the case of Malin there was another, more specific influence at work, riveting his attention on the earth. During the 1930s he found himself directly in the midst of the Dust Bowl, as dramatic an example of *maladaption* as any in human ecological experience. Anyone who lived through the "dirty thirties" or the subsequent echoes of it, as he did, could hardly fail to be impressed by the relevance of environmental health to human welfare and happiness. The Dust Bowl made emphatically clear the consequences nature can have for people, the surprises she can bring to those who leave her out of their calculations.

In the traumatic years of the Dust Bowl, the Great Plains offered at once a stimulus to the rise of an ecologically oriented history and a compelling subject for historians to grapple with. My main purpose here is to move toward a cultural explanation for this disaster, one that will, when complete, be adequate to its significance and alert to its complexity. Such an explanation cannot be the work of any single individual, for it demands what no individual alone can achieve: first, a detailed, interdisciplinary investigation of the special environmental conditions of the Plains—their cycles of weather and climate, of drought and rainfall, their grassland ecosystems as a force for moderating and buffering those cycles—and, second, a probing interpretation of the cultural elements introduced here. Of course, the rubric of culture in that account will encompass the tools, the agricultural techniques, devised to make a living from nature, but more basically it must be seen to refer to the values, world views, classes, and institutions active on the Plains. Those social and mental structures have created the tools and determined how they have been used. Finally, it is in the swirling interaction of all these agencies that an adequate explanation of the Dust Bowl is to be found. Ecological history is not monocausal. It assigns neither to nature nor to culture a sole, exclusive authority over the past, its rhythms and events.[5]

James Malin, an early advocate of the field of ecological history, attempted an explanation of the Dust Bowl experience. Or rather, he suggested a couple of explanations, both of them fragmentary and not entirely compatible with each other. Part of their weakness as history comes from Malin's bias and provinciality, which prevented him from taking a detached view of the culture he was seeking to understand. Their value, on the other hand, is that they make any simplistic alternative impossible to sustain. Though I will argue that his explanations do not satisfy the tests of evidence or logic, whether taken singly or in tandem, they still have their supporters and so require some attention.

In the first place, Malin argued that the Dust Bowl was essentially the work of nature, being caused by conditions of severe drought; that therefore it was an inevitable disaster and the plains people its victims, not its perpetrators. In 1946 he published in the *Kansas Historical Quarterly* a series of three articles arguing that dust storms "are a part of the economy of nature and are not in themselves necessarily abnormal."[6] Painstakingly, he tried to show that, long before there was white settlement and plowing of the native sod, dust storms had blown across the region. Some of the dust storms in his examples may in fact have been due to drought and others to prairie fires, both events being capable of destroying natural vegetation and freeing the soil to move. Severe, prolonged drought can ruthlessly destroy the grassland ecosystem; it certainly did so in the distant past, might have done so to some degree in the thirties, and undoubtedly will do so again in the future. Unfortunately, however, Malin could not, from his travelers' reports and newspaper notes, establish conclusively that drought had been the sole and sufficient cause of the pre–Dust Bowl storms. Nor could he demonstrate that any of the earlier storms matched those of the 1930s in intensity or scope, though he did make it incontestable, if anyone doubted the point, that not every puff of dust had a human origin. In arguing that case, he must grant the critical point that dust storms are evidence of ecological disturbance and disequilibrium, whatever the cause. The difficulty he faced was how to assign all, or even most, of that disturbance to natural factors—and he could not, as a historian working with archival evidence, surmount it.

Scientists, climatologists and ecologists in particular, may one day be able to tell the historian why droughts happen. They may eventually be prepared to trace their contribution to wind erosion acre by acre, square mile by square mile, county by county. But neither in the thirties nor in the decade or two after was science able to give a clear, reliable answer as to whether humans or nature was responsible for the Dust Bowl. More recently, however, photographs taken from orbiting earth satellites have begun to supply the kind of data that Malin lacked—and it has not been strong for his case against nature. In the late winter of 1977, when the Plains were roiled again by high winds and dirt, when Oklahoma was stunned by its worst dust storm in twenty years, the meteorologist Edward Kessler demonstrated precisely, with the aid of the new high-level cameras, that the source of the dust was west Texas farms, plowed and planted to seed, while neighboring New Mexico lands left in grass remained stable.[7] The dust could actually be seen picking up from one side of a fence, the plowed side, and streaming eastward. Aerial cameras have documented that it was not the ragged, pervasive specter of drought but the human mind and its ill considered land practices—a mind marking its presence by straight fence lines—that was the main culprit in the 1970s; and the cameras show persuasively that the same was probably true in the 1930s. There can hardly be any doubt now that the destruction by plow of the grass cover on vulnerable lands—semiarid lands where the soil is loose and the horizon flat and open to winds—has been the leading reason for the devastating scale of dust storms in the twentieth century. Malin seems to have realized, even as he was writing, the inadequacy of blaming nature for the Dust Bowl. There was clearly something more at work—in the culture of plains people and the nation. Here is what he wrote at the end of his dust storm series:

> The worst manifestations of soil blowing as related to agricultural operations occurred during the pioneering process. The country was new, the population was not settled-in on a firm and stabilized foundation in harmony with the new environment. . . . The older and better established communities usually kept their soil fairly well under control. In recent times, because of the technological revolution in agriculture and as the result of the initial exploitive stage of power

farming, the period of the late 1920's was analogous in a sense to pioneering. In the light of that experience and well-considered conservation measures, the worst features of those eras need not be repeated. There is no reason to assume that dust storms can be prevented altogether, because without question they were frequent and severe prior to white settlement and the plowing of the sod, but the damage incident to agricultural operations should and can be minimized by careful soil management.[8]

This conclusion took most of the wind, and much of the dust, out of his earlier argument. It was an almost backhanded way of admitting that there had been, after all, significant cultural forces at work creating the Dust Bowl disaster.

Malin's second thesis, when closely examined, had problems of its own. It began with the claim that ecological disequilibrium on the Plains and the dust storms it generated were due, not merely to nature, but to the culture of a "pioneer" people. The settlement of the region was going through a youthful phase when the land was still unfamiliar to its new inhabitants. As newcomers, they did not understand what their environmental limits were nor have the techniques to overcome them. Added to their lack of knowledge was an instability in their social organization; things generally, the soil included, were out of their control. That primitive phase would give way, Malin was sure, to one of "better established communities," when the population would stay put, when farm turnover would come to an end, when generation would begin to follow generation on the same piece of land. Then erosion (except for what was natural and inescapable) would come to an end. In later writings, Malin would do path-breaking work on the phenomenon of frontier instability; in 1946 he associated such instability with the land destruction of the thirties. But there was some uncertainty in his reasoning; he was not at all sure what he meant by "pioneering." Modern power farming in the form of the tractor and the mechanized harvester had appeared on the Plains, he pointed out, immediately before the major dust storms—a state of affairs hardly found on the archetypal American frontier or in classic pioneer life. He described the plainsmen as going through an early "exploitive stage" with that technology; their culture in the late 1920s was only "analogous in a sense to pioneering."[9] With this sentence Malin shifted the terms of his indictment. Advanced technology now became the culprit, undermining at least temporarily the good judgment embedded in a traditional agronomy. But the tractor was not forever to be a bad influence, for once the revolution was assimilated a new plateau of civilization would be reached. Thus no matter what he meant by pioneering, whether he had in mind the entering of a new land or the adoption of a new technology, Malin remained optimistic. The Dust Bowl episode was a brief spot of darkness and chaos on the road to order, and nothing like it would happen again.

In the passage quoted above, conservation appears as a normal activity of a culturally mature region. It is defined not as the preservation of grassland ecosystems but as a regime of "careful management" of the soil, and it will arrive, Malin asserts, with time, with affluence, with more (not less) technology, with population equilibrium. The confidence behind these assurances resembles closely that of the so-called Progressive conservationists, as described by Samuel Hays.[10] Like Malin, they maintained that environmental destruction was a result of a pioneering culture—of poor, ignorant, unsettled people—and that it would disappear with progress. But unlike the Progressive conservationists, for whom the state was the proper agency to assume active command and move the society beyond its pioneering crudities, Malin denied that government was needed to enforce conservation. Careful management would come about inevitably with further development of the private economy.

Was Malin right in this confidence? Was the Dust Bowl merely a passing stage in the plains region's cultural maturing? And is environmental adaptation a product of progress and prosperity? The answer to all those questions must be a qualified no. The dirty thirties were largely the outcome of a well-established, long-maturing economic culture, that of agricultural capitalism. Moreover, its recent apotheosis as agribusiness has not made it a more adaptive or stable culture, nor more preservation-minded. To be sure, in the aftermath of the thirties it has been placed under some restraint by other, countervailing forces in American culture; nonetheless, agricultural capitalism remains the dominant agency on the plains today, and the prospect is less reassuring than Malin wanted us to believe.

Any attempt to understand the cultural roots of the Dust Bowl must begin with a scrutiny of Great Plains rural society in the late 1910s and the 1920s. Before that time there were, of course, forays by farmers into the fragile shortgrass country, the lands lying beyond the hundredth meridian; there was precedent for both agricultural settlement and widespread ecological disruption. And there was a recurrent pattern of crop disaster and farm failure, of retreating to ground representing less risk. But in the teens and twenties there occurred the critical assault on the grasslands that some have called "the Great Plow-up."[11] A brief summary of the history of those years will tell us much about how and why there was a Dust Bowl.

World War I put the American wheat farmer into a happy dither. As the Turks cut off shipments of grain from Russia, the largest producer and exporter of wheat in the world, Europeans turned to the United States, to the Great Plains, for their food supply. Wheat, it was said in Washington and in the western provinces, would help win the war by feeding the Allies and toughening their resolve. When the war ended, Europe for a while still needed food imports, and by 1919 America, under government-set goals, harvested 74 million acres of wheat—yielding 952 million bushels in all, a 38 percent increase over the 1909–13 average, and providing 330 million bushels for shipment abroad. Most of this gain came in winter wheat, the standard variety grown over most of the southern Plains, which was planted in the fall and cut in the following midsummer. From 1914 to 1919 Kansas, Colorado, Nebraska, Oklahoma, and Texas had expanded their wheatlands by 13.5 million acres, mainly by plowing up 11 million acres of native grass.[12]

The Great Plow-up, initially provoked by the wartime mobilization of the national economy, might have been expected to pass with victory. Such was not to be the case. The war integrated the plains farmers more thoroughly than ever before into the national economy—into its network of banks, railroads, mills, implement manufacturers, energy companies—and, moreover, integrated them into an international market system. When the war was over, none of that integration loosened; on the contrary, plains farmers in the 1920s found themselves more enmeshed than ever, as they competed fiercely with each other to pay off their loans and keep intact what they had achieved. By the mid-twenties that integration did begin to pay off; having squeezed through the postwar depression, many plains farmers began to rake in substantial fortunes. There was, for instance, Ida Watkins, the "wheat queen" of Haskell County, Kansas, farming two thousand acres; in 1926, she made a profit on her wheat of $76,000, more than President Coolidge's salary. Down in the Texas panhandle the movie mogul Hickman Price set about to show plainsmen what modern commercial farming could really do, how it could apply the large-scale business methods of Henry Ford to the mass production of wheat. His factory farm stretched over fifty-four square miles and required twenty-five combines at harvest time. In every part of the Plains there were pacesetters like this man and woman who fervently believed in capitalistic enterprise and sought to apply it to the unproductive grasslands. These two were among the largest and most successful entrepreneurs; the less aggressive were forced by the competitive marketplace to follow their lead.[13]

The mobility of Malin's machines not only allowed these large-scale enterprises to develop but also encouraged widely dispersed holdings. It was now possible to drive one's equipment to another county or even to another state, plant wheat, return home in a few weeks, and wait until the next spring before visiting the land again—in other words, to become a "suitcase farmer." This was particularly attractive to wheat speculators, many of whom were city bankers, druggists, or teachers; they put in their seed, went back to their regular work, and waited to see what would happen to the Chicago grain futures. In a year of high prices they might make a killing, paying for an entire farm with one crop, then selling the land at a tidy sum to another fast-buck chaser. Not all suitcase farmers were looking for such quick returns; some of them were more concerned about their investment's long-range security.[14] But the machine made possible, as it made common, an exploitative relationship with the earth—a bond predominately commercial—so that the land became little more than a form of capital that must be made to pay as much as possible.

All across the flat open spaces the tractors steadily plowed away, especially in the second half of the twenties and up until the very eve of the dust storms. Occasionally they even worked at night, their headlights moving like fireflies in the grass. Near Perryton, Texas, H. B. Urban, an altogether typical wheat farmer of the day, arrived in 1929 and cranked up his two International tractors; each day he and his hired man broke out twenty acres of native prairie, until virtually his whole section of land was stripped of its grama and buffalo grass. In thirteen southwestern Kansas counties, where there had been two million crop acres in 1925, there were three million in 1930. Altogether in that period farmers tore up the vegetation on 5,260,000 acres in the southern Plains—an area nearly seven times as large as Rhode Island. Most of the freshly plowed ground went into wheat, so that over the decade of the twenties the production of that cereal jumped three hundred percent, creating a severe glut by 1931. That, in sum, was the environmental history immediately preceding the dirty thirties. When the black blizzards began to roll across the region in 1935, one third of the Dust Bowl region—thirty-three million acres—lay naked, ungrassed, and vulnerable to the winds.[15]

This Great Plow-up was not dictated by Malthusian population pressures, which in many parts of the world have been responsible for decisions to put marginal land into food production. Nor was it exclusively or primarily drought that disrupted the ecological system of the Plains; it was humans and the economic culture pushing them ahead. Nor was their push carried out in ignorance or inexperience. For over a century men had been coming into the shortgrass country, observing it, and writing about its risks. For a half-century before the Dust Bowl, cattlemen had trailed their animals to railheads there, and farmers had repeatedly tried breaking the sod to make houses and crops, leaving a record of devastating reverses as well as some years of bounty. Furthermore, by the second and third decades of the twentieth century the region could by no means be labeled an intellectual frontier; an extensive scientific literature was available on it, and the hard realities of the country had permeated widely into common consciousness.[16] All of this information was almost studiously disregarded in the 1920s plow-up. To describe those who did that disregarding as backward, primitive folk, as a hard-living rabble of frontiersmen, simply will not do. On the contrary, they were, especially the leaders among them, people with access to capital and expertise; some of them were in fact men and women of education and broad sophistication. The historical problem to be solved is why such people used their capital as they did, why they demanded and quickly deployed the new machinery, why they chose to hear what they did from the past and present, shutting out what did not appeal to them—what, in other words, they were after and why. If we call them hungry, then we must be careful to specify what they were hungry for. If we call them pioneers, then we must go further to distinguish them from other pioneers in national and world history.

Essentially, the Great Plow-up was the work of a generation of aggressive entrepreneurs, embued with the values and world view of American agricultural capitalism. They smelled an opportunity to create a profit on the Plains and, in the classic way of entrepreneurs, they charged out to create that profit—to derive from the land both personal wealth and status. No matter that others had failed or that the

risks were high; these entrepreneurs were convinced they would succeed, as indeed they did in the short run. For a few years at least they
made the region say money instead of grass. Throughout the twenties
a scattering of reporters came to watch them succeed, writing up their
achievements in glowing prose for newspapers and magazines. Many
of these farmers had once been lowly clodhoppers; now they were
making their mark on the world, were getting celebrated as "kings"
and "queens" of wheat. And justly so, for the food that poured from
the erstwhile grasslands was, if the environmental costs are disregarded, a positive gain for the nation and the world as well as for the
entrepreneurs. They heard little criticism. Standing behind them all
the way, trumpeting their contribution to humanity repeatedly so that
it was not lost on the American public or on the farmers, was a vast
chorus of bankers, millers, railroad executives, and government officials, all of them looking forward themselves to sharing in the abundance being created. It is, of course, the nature of entrepreneurs, in
agriculture as in industry, to disregard the voices of caution and criticism, to show themselves venturesome where others have been ruined,
and to court disaster.

Entrepreneurialism was not a new cultural innovation on the Plains.
It had been around, gathering force, seeking territory for its expression, for several centuries—indeed it had been the animating ethos of
the economic culture of capitalism since its rise to hegemony.[17] Out of
that imported cultural heritage we can single out several influential
ideas about nature and farming, all of them endlessly reiterated and repeatedly acted on by Europeans and Americans long before anyone
had contemplated plowing the high Plains. Each of these would be an
idea with bleak consequences in the 1930s.

First, the agricultural entrepreneur stood for the idea that the land's
true and only end was to become a commodity—something to be used,
bought and sold, for human gain. The land itself, divided into property
and made an object of speculation, was the first part of nature to be
commodified by this culture, then came its products. That drive toward
commodification was never uncontested or universally accepted. On
the Plains there were, as there had been elsewhere, many rival cultural
values present; often these had been brought over from Old World
farming or religious traditions, or from some obscurely intertwined,
peasant-grounded combination of the two.[18] These rivals for moral authority found their way into much of the literature and art of the region;

327

into, for example, the novels of Willa Cather, who spoke often of the mysterious spiritual power of the Plains, of an indwelling presence in nature there, one particularly accessible to many women and to recent immigrants.[19] But it is safe to say that the typical wheat entrepreneur did not read Cather or put much stock in peasant modes of thought. None of that, he was quick to insist, was rationally compatible with his drive to dominate and commodify.

Second, entrepreneurialism was part and parcel of the social ideal of economic individualism. It deliberately made, with no end of paradox, the pursuit of private wealth into a social ethic. The implications in that individualism for the ecological communities of the Plains were predictable: farmers would not be expected to accommodate their ambitions to the whole of nature, or recognize and use those ecological interdependencies for their own survival. Likewise, they would, and did, reject any restraint on their economic freedom to get what they could from the Plains in their own terms now, in their own generation. All others, future and present, must look out for themselves. Here again Malin was simply wrong; it was the entrepreneurial culture, not frontier life, that was destructive to communal bondedness and social stability.[20]

Third, risk was treated in this economic culture almost as a positive value, as a needed spur to success. Without risk, there could be no gain. This idea has been emphasized earlier; what should be added now is the insistent search by the bearers of entrepreneurial culture to find ways to pass the risks on to someone else. Since they saw themselves as taking chances that, if profitable, would enrich the entire society, entrepreneurs hoped that others would pay some of their costs. In the case of the Dust Bowl those costs included the damage that the dust storms did to health and property and the rehabilitation they necessitated. More than $2 billion was spent by New Deal agencies in the thirties to keep the farmers of the plains region in business.[21] As risk-spreaders, these federal programs signified the maturation of the national capitalist economy: the coming of a new era when entrepreneurial drives need not entail such severe penalties for failure. Back in the 1890s, when little outside assistance had existed, the plains settler had learned that he had either to adapt to nature or leave. The generation that came to plow in the twenties and ate their own dust in the thirties successfully evaded much of that disciplining. They lived in a more humane and protective age that allowed them considerable economic freedom while removing some of the old anxiety and the bitterness of defeat.

Bring these ideas, this economic culture, into a volatile environment where intermittent drought was a fact of life—and the outcome could hardly be anything different from the dirty thirties. That such an outcome would seem to be unavoidable is clear in the famous government report, *The Future of the Great Plains (1937)*. Its chief author, the economist Lewis Cecil Gray of the Resettlement Administration, one of the country's leading agricultural historians, made an analysis of the cultural roots of the Dust Bowl similar to the one suggested here, of "the attitudes of mind" inherent in an expansionary, entrepreneurial society.[22] The evidence was clear to Gray that the disaster could not be wholly laid at the door of nature, of imperfect technique, of inadequate knowledge, or of "frontier society." As in the case of that other great tragedy of the decade, the Depression, the Dust Bowl was a crisis made and delivered by socially destructive forces in modern American culture.

In 1946 James Malin vigorously rejected Gray's cultural analysis of the plains debacle, and he was not alone. His was a common response in the region, somewhat so in the thirties and unabashedly so by the time he wrote. A resurgent national economy, a new war raging in Europe, the success of the federal relief programs in helping people hang on until better times—all these elements made deeper critical inquiry unpopular. Most important of all, nature contributed to the renewal of self-assurance. The return of rains, accompanied by bumper wheat crops in the early 1940s, demonstrated that the environmental damage had not been permanent—and, indeed, it has been difficult until the present nuclear age for humans anywhere to inflict irreversible destruction on the earth and its fabric of life. Nature has extraordinary powers of recuperation, a fact that has been proved many, many times in the long geological history of the Great Plains. When the healing comes, it is easy and altogether human to suppress the memory of misjudgment and loss; to revert to old, familiar ways and deny responsibility. That was precisely what Malin hoped would happen: a renewal of faith in the culture of entrepreneurial farming. Any effort to find a different path for the Plains he harshly identified with "totalitarianism."[23]

Despite assurances that the Plains would achieve a mature agricultural capitalism in the post–World War II period; that the land and society would come under firm, enlightened control; that no radical reform in the culture would be necessary, the region's recent ecological history has seen some disturbing chapters. High crop prices and great profit expectations have again and again produced waves of profit-seeking enterprise when grasslands have been destroyed to make more crops. In the aftermath of each of those waves have come new cycles of dust storms, some of them as grueling as anything in the thirties. Then, so the familiar pattern goes, the blowing dust brings in its train warnings from federal soil scientists, larger budget requests from federal agencies, and talk of new state and national laws to reform the culture. Perhaps these frequent replays of the thirties have produced a cumulative reform of the culture. One might argue, though not precisely in the terms Malin did, that the capitalistic agriculture has in fact been substantially altered since the 1930s; that it no longer enjoys the power and influence it once held in the region; that today it is strictly hedged about with governmental authority; and that these reforms, these countervailing pressures, have successfully prevented another Dust Bowl from occurring.[24] It will take a few serious, prolonged droughts to test thoroughly the accuracy of such an argument. Very recent evidence, however, indicates that the entrepreneur is still around, still sitting tall in the tractor seat—and the old danger is not over.

In the late spring and early summer of 1983 the national news again announced the impending threat of western wind erosion. For example, *Time* reported that wheat operators had torn up the sod on 6.4 million acres of marginal grasslands in Montana and Colorado. Depressed livestock prices and favorable federal wheat support programs were responsible for this frenzy. "I want to make a buck," is the way one Montanan expressed his motives to *Time*. He and his neighbors had broken 250,000 acres of grazing land over the preceding decade. "We face the possibility of another Dust Bowl," said the executive vice president of the Montana association of conservation districts. So serious was the threat that the conservative senator from Colorado, William Armstrong, with backing from the Reagan administration and the Montana Stockgrowers Association, introduced a "sodbuster" bill that would deny federal payments of any kind for crops grown on highly erodible land. And a Colorado county began contemplating the issuing of permits by its commissioners before any more sod could be plowed up.[25] Unmistakably, leaders of the region were being forced to admit that they did not yet have sufficient public authority to restrain risk-taking entrepreneurs, nor could they depend on capitalistic maturity to achieve soil conservation. Whether they now had the will to establish that authority remained to be decided.

The ecological history of the future Great Plains is still to be accomplished, still to find its historians. When they come to write it, they will have a subject of international significance, for these days the dry lands of the earth are everywhere under pressure and scrutiny. In that future history, as in past accounts, we may expect the key issue to be the fit of the Plains's economic culture to its environment. And we can predict that historians will return often to the dirty thirties to understand what that culture has been and what it is in the process of becoming.

NOTES

1. Quoted in David A. Dary, *The Buffalo Book* (New York: Avon, 1974), 4.

2. This sentence is a paraphrase of Lewis Mumford, *The Power of the Pentagon* (New York: Harcourt, Brace, Jovanovich, Harvest ed., 1974), 393. For a discussion of the new ecological history, see my article, "Nature as Natural History: An Essay on Theory and Method," *Pacific Historical Review* 53 (Feb. 1984): 1–19.

3. Both Webb's major works, *The Great Plains* (Boston: Ginn, 1931) and *The Great Frontier* (Boston: Houghton Mifflin, 1952), are landmark studies in the environmental impact on culture.

4. Malin, "Ecology and History," *Scientific Monthly* 70 (May 1950): 295–98.

5. A useful discussion of this problem is in John Bennett's *The Ecological Transition: Cultural Anthropology and Human Adaptation* (New York: Pergamon, 1976), esp. 162–67, 209–42.

6. Malin, "Dust Storms: Part One, 1850–1860," *Kansas Historical Quarterly* 14 (May 1946): 129–44.

7. Edwin Kessler, Dorothy Alexander, and Joseph Rarick, "Duststorms from the High Plains in Late Winter 1977—Search for Cause and Implications," *Proceedings of the Oklahoma Academy of Science* 58 (1978): 116–28.

8. Malin, "Dust Storms: Part Three, 1881–1890," *Kansas Historical Quarterly* 14 (Nov. 1946): 391–413.

9. Ibid. The distinction between pioneering and entrepreneurialism is commonly obscured in American historical writing as it is in popular mythology; indeed, they are often conflated, especially in the West, producing a "cowboy capitalism." Malin's writing is replete with the confusion.

10. See Hays, *Conservation and the Gospel of Efficiency: The Progressive Conservation Movement, 1890–1920* (Cambridge: Harvard Univ. Press, 1959).

11. See, for example, Vance Johnson, *Heaven's Tableland: The Dust Bowl Story* (New York: Farrar, Straus, 1947), chap. 12.

12. A. B. Genung, "Agriculture in the World War Period," in U.S. Department of Agriculture, *Farmers in a Changing World* (Washington, D.C., 1940), 280–84; Lloyd Jorgenson, "Agriculture Expansion into the Semiarid Lands of the West North Central States During the First World War," *Agricultural History* 23 (Jan. 1949): 30–40; *Kansas City Star,* 19 April 1935.

13. Johnson, *Heaven's Tableland,* 136–37; *Topeka Capital,* 3 Aug. 1925; *Panhandle Herald* (Guymon, Okla.), 13 Dec. 1928. See also Garry Nall, "Specialization and Expansion: Panhandle Farming in the 1920's," *Panhandle-Plains Historical Review* 47 (1974): 66–67. The largest operator of all on the Plains was located in Montana: see Hiram Dache, "Thomas B. Campbell—The Plower of the Plains," *Agricultural History* 51 (Jan. 1977): 78–91. Campbell's ambition was to be a "manufacturer of wheat"; he farmed, with House of Morgan backing, over 100,000 acres, most of it on Indian reservations.

14. Leslie Hewes, in *The Suitcase-Farming Frontier: A Study in the Historical Geography of the Central Great Plains* (Lincoln: Univ. of Nebraska Press, 1973), gives a thorough accounting of this phenomenon, and one strongly supportive of its entrepreneurial characteristics.

15. H. B. Urban, transcribed interview, 15 June 1974, Panhandle-Plains Historical Museum, Canyon, Texas; *The Dust Bowl,* U.S. Department of Agriculture, Editorial Reference Series No. 7 (Washington, D.C., 1940), 44; Clifford Hope, "Kansas in the 1930's," *Kansas Historical Quarterly* 36 (Spring 1970), 2–3; Johnson, *Heaven's Tableland,* 146.

16. A number of excellent studies of popular understanding of the Plains have been published by geographers and historians; see, for example, Brian Blouet and Merlin Lawson, eds., *Images of the Plains: The Role of Human Nature in Settlement* (Lincoln: Univ. of Nebraska Press, 1975).

17. Entrepreneurialism is essential to all forms of agricultural capitalism, whether it be potato farming in Maine or rice growing in California. But the strength of this drive may, of course, vary from time to time and place to place. Not all of American agriculture has been so unstable or risk-taking as that of the semiarid plains.

18. Frederick Luebke, "Ethnic Group Settlement on the Great Plains," *Western Historical Quarterly* 8 (Oct. 1977): 405–30.

19. One thinks, for example, of the Swedish immigrant Alexandra Bergson in Willa Cather's *O Pioneers!* (Boston: Houghton Mifflin, 1913). Though eager to acquire more and more property, Bergson responds to the land with a powerful love and yearning. "It seemed beautiful to her," writes Cather, "rich and strong and glorious. Her eyes drank in the breadth of it, until her tears blinded her" (p. 65).

20. A provocative discussion of this set of ideas is C. B. Macpherson's *The Political Theory of Possessive Individualism: Hobbes to Locke* (Oxford: Oxford Univ. Press, 1962).

21. This figure includes, in addition to ecological restoration efforts, all programs of farm price supports, rural relief, and public works expenditures.

22. Great Plains Committee, *The Future of the Great Plains,* U.S. House Document 144, 75th Congress (Washington, D.C., 1937), 63–67.

23. Malin, *The Grassland of North America: Prolegomena to Its History* (Lawrence, Kansas: privately published, 1956), 335.

24. As John Borchert has written, the flurry of federal soil and water conservation programs since the thirties has "encouraged a widespread belief that, though there will be future droughts, there need be no future dust bowl." See "The Dust Bowl in the 1970s" *Annals of the Association of American Geographers* 61 (March 1971): 13.

25. *Time* (27 June 1983): 27.

The Women's Land Army During World War II

Caron Smith

World War II called thousands of farmers and their workers away from food production to military service. Even before America entered the war, statistics published by the U.S. Department of Agriculture on October 1, 1941, showed that there were two hundred thousand fewer agricultural workers than the year before.[1] After America went to war and as the war continued, gasoline and tire shortages combined to complicate the farmers' labor problems by reducing the flow of migratory workers along the entire Atlantic Seaboard, while on the West Coast, the supply of Japanese workers was stopped completely when they were placed in relocation camps.

One non-depleted labor supply was women. Though a great deal has been written about the part women played in war industries during World War II, people tend to forget the vital part they played in agriculture. This lack of interest is surprising since large numbers participated. For example, more than three hundred thousand non-farm women worked on farms in 1943 alone.[2]

At times of shortages of manpower or at harvesting times, farm women had always helped out. During World War II, farm women in-

"The Women's Land Army During World War II," by Caron Smith, *Kansas History* 14 (summer 1991): 82–88. Copyright Kansas State Historical Society. Reprinted by permission.

creased their roles in food production, but eventually city women had to be mobilized to maintain output levels. Many organizations were formed to match city women to farmers needing workers. The most important of these organizations was probably the Women's Land Army of America (WLA), which became a national organization on April 28, 1943, when Congress appropriated funds and named the Extension Service of the U.S. Department of Agriculture as the agency to mobilize and allocate farm labor.

The term "Women's Land Army" usually conjures up pictures of urban women spending their vacations on farms, helping farmers in times of need. This was indeed the case on the eastern and western seaboards where women could easily pick fruit and vegetables and sort and pack produce. A case study of Kansas, however, shows that the Women's Land Army in the midwestern states had significant differences. In Kansas the main crop was wheat. It was not a labor-intensive crop and at harvest time the need was for skilled machine-handlers, not unskilled pickers. For this reason, farmers were loath to hire raw recruits with non-farm backgrounds to handle their expensive machinery. The burden of the work therefore fell upon the farmer's own family, who had some understanding of harvesting and of the machinery used. Thus, the Women's Land Army in Kansas directed most of its attention toward farm women. Its primary function was to teach women to handle machinery safely, proper clothing, work-simplification methods in the home, and nutrition. It was not assumed that simply because a woman lived on a farm, she knew all that was necessary to its operation.

The Women's Land Army dated from World War I, the idea of mobilizing women as agricultural workers originating in Great Britain. In 1918, forty thousand women served in the British Women's Land Army, which was a government-directed scheme. Similar wartime programs operated in countries such as France, Italy, and Canada. In America the labor scarcity in rural areas led some people to try to adapt the European solution to American circumstances. During World War I, however, the WLA was organized by private women's organizations and it was not until peacetime that the government accepted direction of the project.[3]

During World War II, it was not until mid-1942 that the farm labor problem became acute and progressive farmers and women's leaders began organizing agencies to recruit farm workers. On February 3,

1943, the secretary of the Department of Agriculture, Claude R. Wickard, requested that the Cooperative Extension Service of the Department of Agriculture and the State Extension Service take responsibility for the development and supervision of programs to recruit non-farm women for appropriate tasks. The Women's Land Army was set up under the U.S. Extension Service, and in April 1943, Congress appropriated funds. The WLA became a national service and Land Army leaders were appointed by the Extension Service in each state, working directly under the state farm labor supervisor, who was an employee of the Extension Service.

The WLA of America was a decentralized organization with county agents of the State Extension Services working with the U.S. Employment Service, state colleges, civic groups, clubs, and local farmers in recruiting and placing women. By the end of the war the Extension Service and the U.S. Employment Service were the major recruitment agencies. They printed circulars and posters and advertised extensively in newspapers and on the radio. A uniform and insignia were designed and adopted and certificates of service were printed.

In April 1943, it was envisaged that the women's division of the U.S. Crop Corps would number 360,000. Of these, 60,000 would compose the Women's Land Army, of whom 10,000 would be permanent year-round workers living where they worked. An additional 50,000 were expected to enroll for a period of one month or more to harvest perishable crops that required quick handling. The other 300,000 female farm workers were to wear armbands which designated them as members of the U.S. Crop Corps; their service would be given during weekends or for a week or so at a time.[4]

On the eastern and western seaboards, the farmers' early skepticism as to the worth of city women depleted as the labor shortage became more critical. Most farmers were astonished by the quantity and quality of the women's work. According to Florence Hall, head of the WLA, prejudice against employing women broke down first in the northwestern states because the women had pitched in so effectively in 1942 when the Japanese workers were placed in relocation camps. By August 1943, there were approximately seventeen thousand women field hands in Oregon and ten thousand in California.[5]

The women of the Atlantic and Pacific areas usually worked in units, traveling from one farm to another. These women came from a variety of backgrounds and included students and teachers from colleges and high schools, business and professional women, housewives, and industrial women workers.[6] In the midwestern states the situation was quite different. The WLA in Kansas, while still attempting to recruit and place town women on farms, spent the majority of its time organizing training for farmers' wives on machine handling, safety, proper clothing, time-saving methods, and nutrition. The main aim was improving the efficiency of farm women as these women were taking on much more outside work than they had previously. If the farmer had to entrust his machinery to anyone, his best option seemed to be his immediate family who were at least familiar with farm life. Therefore, farm women were spending more time doing outside work but were still responsible for domestic chores. The WLA realized that these women needed training to develop skills in time management and heavy machinery operation.

The need for women farm laborers became more pronounced as the war wore on. The armed services and war industry made deep inroads into farm labor in the Midwest. Draft regulations changed in 1943, resulting in the deferment of many farmers and workers. Yet in Kansas many farmers' sons and workers were enlisting believing it was their patriotic duty to do so. At the same time, workers discovered they could earn larger wages by working at war plants or factories such as the aircraft plants in Wichita. Gas shortages too effectively cut off the supply of transient labor which some had relied upon.

Despite labor shortages, Kansas farmers succeeded in planting and harvesting record crops and rearing record numbers of livestock. Much of the praise for this must go to the farmers' wives, daughters, and relatives, both male and female, who helped out. The Kansas Farm Labor Report for 1942 and 1943 notes that despite female workers providing a small part of the farm labor in 1942 and 1943, "the proportion of the farm workers who were females increased two thirds from 1942 to 1943."[7] Table 5 shows the percentage distribution of farm workers (excluding operators) in Kansas in 1942 and 1943. About two-fifths of all farm workers were related to the operator and the percentage was larger in 1943 than 1942. This reflects the greater dependence on labor within the family and among relatives. Because of military exemptions for farmers, most of the immediate family labor was supplied by operators' sons, but this number fell between 1942 and 1943 as many entered the armed services. The compilers of the Kansas Farm Labor Report sampled 1,902 farms and found 183 female workers in

Table 5. Percentage Distribution of Farm Workers (Excluding Operators)
According to Their Relation to the Operator in 1942 and 1943 in Kansas

Relation to operator	1942 % total employed	1943 % total employed
None	64.2	61.0
Wife	1.5	2.9
Son	15.3	14.7
Daughter	1.2	2.1
Other relation	17.8	19.3

1942 and 283 in 1943, representing 3.6 percent of farm workers in 1942 and 6 percent in 1943. Of the female workers, only 12 percent were not related to the farm operator. In 1942, 95 percent of female farm workers were farm reared, while in 1943, 90 percent were farm reared.[8]

In 1942 and 1943, the majority of female farm workers were performing tasks such as driving tractors, running combines, hauling grain, and operating other machinery. Hauling grain was by far the most frequent job performed by female workers; 30.5 percent in 1942 and 28.25 percent in 1943.[9] By the very nature of these tasks one can see why the farmer preferred to employ farm-related rather than non-farm women. Farm machinery could be dangerous for those unfamiliar with its use, and parts were difficult to obtain if broken by mismanagement. Many Kansas farm women were passingly familiar with the operation of farm equipment, although their usual tasks before the war had consisted of chores such as feeding chickens or milking cows.

In an interview in 1985, Mrs. Ray Sayler from Topeka, Kansas, related some of her wartime experiences. These probably were mirrored by many hundreds of other farm women across the state at this time. During the war, the Saylers owned a two-hundred-acre farm near Manhattan where the family raised hogs, a few cattle, some chickens, corn and alfalfa. Help on the farm was usually provided by the Saylers' eldest son, but in March 1943 he enlisted, leaving a serious shortage of manpower. As well as her usual chores of gathering eggs and feeding and milking the cows, Mrs. Sayler's services were enlisted in driving a tractor and a horse-pulled mowing machine. Her day began at 4:30 a.m. and ended at 5:00 p.m. or later. Besides those tasks, she had meals to prepare and a small child to care for. It was to ease these burdens and to ensure safety that the WLA generally concentrated upon in Kansas.

By 1943, the Extension Service described farm labor as one of the nation's most serious problems. The farm labor supply was "seriously depleted" because of the induction of men of military age into the armed services, the employment of skilled farm workers in war plants, the introduction of farm women into auxiliary branches of the armed services, and the employment of farm women in war plants and allied industries.[10]

It was decided that all 105 Kansas counties should have a WLA. Recruitment was to be made by visiting schools, women's groups, and by house-to-house visits to attract enlistees. Training of recruits was to be provided by short courses held at Kansas State Agricultural College (now Kansas State University) and other colleges throughout the state. The training would be in gardening, poultry work, dairying and housework which were all farm homemaker tasks. The aim of the training was to teach non-farm women how to help in and around the farm home, freeing farmers' wives to operate heavy farm equipment and to aid in the fields.

By the end of 1943, the Extension Service realized that farmers were not responding to the call to hire non-farm women, even for housework. It was discovered that most farm women solved their home labor problems by exchanging help with neighbors during harvesting and by only doing tasks of major importance, neglecting many regular duties. In response, the WLA became even more strongly directed toward recruiting farm women. The 1943 Farm Labor Report of the Extension Service described enrollment progress as follows:

In general, farm women assisting their husbands did not respond until the end of the year to the idea of enrolling with the Women's Land Army. Their husbands resisted the plan also. The uppermost thought in their minds was that they did not want to have their womenfolk working in the fields if any other source of labor could be located. This resistance was softening, however. A general change in attitude was being felt and the outlook for progress in 1944 was much better, especially in the western half of the state.[11]

Home economics agents began to play a large part in the Farm Labor Program. They helped teach local leaders the skills that the farmers' wives needed to know. Extension specialists traveled extensively around the state holding training sessions for local leaders in county seats. Many of the changes introduced by the agents were simple to apply, but very effective in saving women time and labor. They cut chairs to correct heights or put them on casters, adapted milking stools as garden stools, and invented a service cart that made it unnecessary to walk continually between the kitchen and dining area. All of these small changes were intended to conserve time and energy. Agents also taught fire drills, kitchen organization, and meal management. Efficiency in shopping was emphasized because of the gasoline and rubber shortages that limited travel to market.

Vera Ellithorpe, former extension specialist in the Family Housing and Safety Unit, described some of her wartime experiences.

> The Extension Foods and Nutrition Specialist who worked in the western half of the state, and I, taught "Meal Management in Wartime" in those counties. She taught leaders how to prepare quick, attractive and nutritious dinners for harvesters and family. I taught methods of organizing for meal service, improved methods for dishwashing, and the "new" way of washing the cream separator. They did have fun making a silverware drainer, modelled after the tin juice can which I carried to meetings. I used an ice pick to punch holes in the bottom of the can. Silver could be "fed" into it from the sudsy water, the can could be lowered into scalding water and later removed to the drain board. This saved laundering of tea towels.[12]

Home health experts helped women plan their work to allow time for rest periods, avoiding fatigue. These experts demonstrated how to maintain one's posture and to lift properly and how to care for one's feet by choosing the correct type of shoes for outdoor work. Local leaders would pass on to farm wives the skills they already possessed. For example, Mrs. Sayler became a local leader and often held demonstrations for groups of ten to fifteen ladies in a church kitchen.

> I taught the young farm wives to make cheese, homemade soup, food from corn yeast for bread making and how to dry fruits for winter use. Towards the end of the war, cotton was a surplus crop so I taught how to make mattresses for beds.[13]

The major proportion of training for outdoor work was given by farmers to farm and non-farm women. In some cases this was adequate since the women already were experienced. In other cases it caused a safety hazard as those unused to helping outside did not have proper instruction or work clothing. The Extension Service responded by setting up seven training schools to teach women to safely operate and care for heavy farm machinery. To safeguard women against accidents caused by inappropriate clothing, many Home Demonstration agents ordered the Women's Land Army work outfit. This was modelled at Home Demonstration meetings with the hope that women would adopt the uniform. Many women ordered the outfit, while others made similar outfits for themselves.

By 1944, up to 80 percent of the farm women in some counties were helping out because of farm labor shortages. A Geary County agent reported:

The farm wife and younger children are doing most of the chores so that the men can work from daylight to sundown in the fields. They are helping with fieldwork after the chores are done on two-thirds of our farms. Thus 900 grown men on our farms with help from farm women and children are doing what 1,500 did before the war and our production has increased 40 percent.[14]

The 1944 Farm Labor Report of Kansas describes the type of women working in agriculture as first, the farmer's wife; second, the farmer's daughter; third, the daughter who "is in business but who can get two weeks off to help her dad with the job she is somewhat familiar with"; fourth, the relative who "likes to spend a short vacation on the farm"; fifth, friends of the family eager to help; and finally, those urban women who "desire to help if they are accepted into the farm family."[15]

In most cases family members were not paid for their help at harvest time. It was customary for harvest to be a family project, and patriotism and the war effort fuelled this trend. Before and during World War II, it was customary for the farm homemaker to prepare and serve at least one meal a day for all those working on the farm. This was usually served at noon. The farm homemaker would usually provide midmorning and mid-afternoon refreshments, which she would take to the fields. Board was normally provided for all workers, whether they were relatives or not. Non-family workers were either provided bedrooms or haymows if they were unable to return to their own homes at night.[16]

In 1945, the term "Women's Land Army" was changed to "Women's Division of Farm Labor Program" since Land Army was not a popular title. It was anticipated that enough farm boys and workers would return in 1946 to ease the situation, and the 1945 Kansas Labor Report noted:

> That part of the Labor Program where women were urged to work in the fields was sound during the war but our farm economy after the war should be on a plane which would not necessitate women working in the fields.[17]

Women's roles as operators of farm machinery and field hands decreased in importance after 1945 with the veterans' return. The women of Kansas, however, had played a vital part in alleviating the labor shortage and in increasing agricultural production during the war years. At least 215,000 men, between the ages of eighteen and thirty-five, had joined the armed forces;[18] an estimated sixty percent were from farms. The loss of crops, which would have occurred without the women's help, would have had serious consequences at a time when the maximum amount of food was needed for American and Allied armed forces.

The Women's Land Army in the eastern and western states and in Kansas showed striking differences. Along the seaboards mainly urban women enrolled, whereas in Kansas the emphasis was upon farm women. Kansas farmers were not as used to hiring migrant workers as were farmers in the truck garden/orchard states, having relied mostly on sons and trusted year-round workers. In the wartime emergency farmers turned to those they trusted—their immediate family and friends. The WLA in Kansas focused upon the needs of the farm women who attempted to meet the wartime crisis by continuing to maintain their homes while carrying on the jobs of the absent male farm laborers.

NOTES

1. *New York Times,* October 29, 1941.

2. Ibid., September 30, 1943.

3. Penny Martelet, "The Women's Land Army, World War One," in *Clio Was a Woman: Studies in the History of American Women,* edited by Mabel E. Deutrich and

Virginia C. Purdy (Washington, D.C.: Howard University Press, 1980), 136. For discussion of general rural mobilization during World War I see David B. Danbom, *The Resisted Revolution: Urban America and the Industrialization of Agriculture, 1900–1930* (Ames: Iowa State University Press, 1979), 103–4.

4. *New York Times*, April 18, 1943; Chester W. Gregory, *Women in Defense Work During World War II: An Analysis of the Labor Problem and Women's Rights* (New York: Exposition Press, 1974), 123–24.

5. *New York Times*, October 13, 1944.

6. Frances W. Valentine, "Successful Practices in the Employment of Nonfarm Women on Farms in the Northeastern States, 1943," *Bulletin of the Women's Bureau*, No. 199 (Washington, D.C.: 1944), 5.

7. *Kansas Farm Labor in 1942 and 1943* (Manhattan: Kansas State College of Agriculture and Applied Science, 1944), 23.

8. Ibid., 42.

9. Ibid., 47.

10. *Annual Report. Farm Labor Project, 1 May 1943 to 30 November 1943* (Manhattan: Kansas State College of Agriculture and Applied Science, 1943), 7.

11. Ibid., 61.

12. Mrs. Vera Ellithorpe to author, Topeka, Kansas, August 5, 1988.

13. Mrs. Ray Sayler to author, Topeka, Kansas, April 3, 1985.

14. *Annual Report. Farm Labor Project, 1 December 1943 to 30 November 1944* (Manhattan: Kansas State College of Agriculture and Applied Science, 1944), 31.

15. Ibid., 32.

16. Ellithorpe to author.

17. *Annual Report. Farm Labor Project, 1 December 1944 to 30 November 1945* (Manhattan: Kansas State College of Agriculture and Applied Science, 1945), 88.

18. *Annual Report. Project No 32—Farm Labor, 1 December 1945 to 30 November 1945* (Manhattan: Kansas State College of Agriculture and Applied Science, 1946), 4.

The Limits of Good Faith: Desegregation in Topeka, Kansas, 1950–1956

Mary L. Dudziak

I. INTRODUCTION

In September of 1953, eight months before *Brown v. Board of Education of Topeka, Kansas*[1] would be decided, the Topeka Board of Education voted to abolish segregation in its schools.[2] Some Topekans thought it curious that the school board would vote to abolish segregation when its case defending segregation was pending in the U.S. Supreme Court. When Edward Goss of the Topeka Civic Club asked the board why it hadn't waited for the Court's decision, board member Harold Conrad responded: "We feel that segregation is not an American practice.". . .[3]

In the 1950s, the State of Kansas was not allowed the luxury of blaming somebody else, as the state and the city of Topeka found themselves on the wrong side of *Brown v. Board of Education*. Many Kansans were quite uncomfortable with the state's role in *Brown* and wondered why Kansas the "free state" was involved in a struggle that really concerned the South. In its policies on race, Kansas had maintained a middle ground between the widespread enforced segregation in the South and the comparative lack of legally mandated segregation in the

North.[4] For Kansas, civil rights and segregation were compatible concepts, and the state maintained laws which permitted segregation in some aspects of public life, yet prohibited it in others.[5] Granting too great a legal status to racial prejudice would conflict with the heritage of "bleeding Kansas," born amidst a struggle against slavery within its borders.[6]

In the early 1950s, Kansas' middle-of-the-road approach did not exempt it from the growing national controversy over racial segregation. In 1951, the NAACP brought suit against the Board of Education of Topeka, Kansas, challenging the constitutionality of the Kansas law permitting segregated schools.[7] Caught in the embarrassing position of supporting a policy which was coming into increasing disfavor in other parts of the country, state and local officials waffled on the question of whether to defend the segregation statute when the NAACP appealed a lower court judgment to the U.S. Supreme Court. Some considered Kansas a "hapless defendant" in a suit that was really concerned with practices in the deep South.[8] The state reluctantly defended its statute, while in 1953, when the appeal was pending, the Topeka school board voted to abolish segregation in its schools.[9]

Taking what it considered to be an important and progressive step, the school board moved slowly and carefully to dismantle its system of enforced racial segregation. All along the way, it was careful to provide parents who preferred to avoid integration with the time and the means to do so. Such private choice, board members came to believe, was not for the school board to oppose, but rather to facilitate in the interests of protecting associational rights of whites as well as blacks. The school board's plan would leave formerly all-black schools exclusively black. Some formerly all-white schools were integrated to varying degrees, and five schools remained exclusively white. The remaining racial isolation was not the school board's problem, the board believed, as it was the result of private choice and residence patterns, even though the board's plan maximized the effect residential patterns might have on school segregation, and affirmatively accommodated private efforts to avoid integration. As far as the Topeka school board was concerned, once they stopped enforcing a clear color line in school attendance, segregation no longer existed.[10]

The efforts of the Topeka Board of Education and other boards of education in Kansas during the 50s [however] did not end the phenomenon of one-race schools in the state. . . .[11]

This article considers what the school board sought to accomplish in desegregating its schools, as illustrated by the actions it would take and the way it would justify them. Of particular interest is the question of how it is that, once the board defined segregation as a wrong, its ideas about the actions it should take to redress the wrong came to be limited in the way they were. . . .

II. THE LEGAL HISTORY OF SCHOOL SEGREGATION IN KANSAS

In the years prior to *Brown,* the state of Kansas maintained an ambivalent posture toward school segregation, at least as far as its legal status was concerned.[12] In enacting its first school law in 1861, the Kansas State Legislature granted school districts the authority "to make such orders as they deem proper for the separate education of white and colored children, securing to them equal advantages."[13] This authority to segregate was retained for several years in varying forms.[14] However, when Kansas codified its school laws in 1876, it deleted the authority to segregate from its statutes with no recorded debate or explanation.[15] This temporary aberration apparently had no effect on the practice of segregation.[16]

In 1879, the Kansas state legislature enacted the law which would shape the course of permissible school segregation in Kansas for the next seventy-five years. The legislature distinguished between "cities of the first class" with populations of 15,000 and over, and smaller cities of the second and third classes. First-class cities were explicitly granted the authority to segregate students in the elementary grades. Such segregation was permitted, but not required, and "no discrimination . . . on account of color" was allowed in high school.[17] The legislature was silent on the question of whether smaller cities could segregate school children.

Whether, under Kansas law, "cities of the second class" could provide segregated schooling without legislative authorization was considered by the Kansas Supreme Court in 1881 in a case involving the schools in Ottawa, Kansas.[18] Leslie Tinnon, a black second grader, sued the Ottawa Board of Education, arguing that Kansas law requiring communities to maintain a system of "common schools free to all children residing in such city"[19] prohibited the establishment of separate schools for blacks. In addition, he claimed that school segregation violated the Fourteenth Amendment.[20]

Noting that the law on the subject was unclear, the Kansas Supreme Court did not consider the constitutionality of segregation per se. It limited its inquiry to the question of whether, in the absence of state legislation authorizing segregation, smaller "cities of the second class" had the authority to establish separate schools. . . . [T]he court strictly construed Kansas school laws on the question of whether authority to segregate had been granted. It held that boards of education did not have the power to segregate students by race unless the legislature clearly authorized such segregation, and it did not find such a clear authorization for segregation in cities of the second class. Rather, "by the clearest implication, if not in express terms, [the legislature] has prohibited the boards from establishing any such [segregated] schools."[21]

In 1903, in a case involving the schools in Topeka, the Kansas Supreme Court addressed the question it had reserved in *Tinnon:* whether legislatively authorized school segregation violated the state and federal constitutions. In *Reynolds v. Board of Education of the City of Topeka,*[22] which involved school segregation in a city of the first class, the court first considered whether segregation violated the provision of the state constitution requiring the establishment of "a uniform system of common schools."[23] The court found it "perfectly plain" that a uniform system of schools did not imply integrated schools, but rather uniform educational facilities. . . .

The court then turned to the validity of the Kansas law under the U.S. Constitution, quoting at length from opinions by other state courts holding that the Fourteenth Amendment was not violated when states provided separate-but-equal schooling for blacks.[24] The court grounded its view of the Fourteenth Amendment on the U.S. Supreme Court's ruling in *Plessy v. Ferguson,*[25] which found that

> [t]he object of the amendment was undoubtedly to enforce the absolute equality of the two races before the law, but in the nature of things it could not have intended to abolish distinctions based upon color, or to enforce social, as distinguished from political equality, or a commingling of the races upon terms unsatisfactory to either.[26]

According to *Plessy,* segregation statutes did not necessarily "imply the inferiority of either race to the other," and were generally recognized to be within the police power of the states. The most common instance of such segregation was "the establishment of separate schools for white and colored children, which has been held to be a valid exercise of the legislative power even by courts of states where the political rights of the colored race have been longest and most earnestly enforced."[27] Following *Plessy,* the Kansas court held that the Kansas statute permitting segregation did not violate the U.S. Constitution. It further held that the educational facilities provided to blacks in Topeka were not unequal and, consequently, segregation in the Topeka schools was consistent with state and federal law.[28]

In upholding segregation in *Reynolds,* the Kansas Supreme Court validated the dichotomy in Kansas law which would remain in effect until segregation was outlawed in *Brown v. Board of Education* in 1954.[29] Segregation was lawful in larger cities where it was authorized by the legislature, and unlawful in smaller cities where it was not explicitly authorized. As the legislature would not choose to materially alter the school segregation laws in the intervening years,[30] the only legal questions between *Reynolds* and *Brown* would be concerned with the refinement and application of these principles.[31] Litigation continued even though the law was so clearly settled by 1903. Smaller cities continued to segregate their elementary schools until ordered by the courts to comply with the law.[32] And black students and their parents in larger cities continued to seek access to the white schools from which they were legally excluded. . . .[33]

Because the definition of first- and second-class cities remained the same, as Kansas communities grew in population, an increasing number would gain the authority to segregate.[34] By 1954, ninety percent of black Kansans would live in cities of the first class, so that the state's seemingly ambiguous policy would mean widespread permissible segregation in practice.[35]

III. SEGREGATION AND BLACK EDUCATION IN TOPEKA

For the first superintendent of schools of Topeka, Kansas, black education was an important priority. In 1867, one hundred blacks were enrolled in an overcrowded one-room elementary school in which one teacher would teach all subjects to the fifty or so who attended each day. In addition, working people crowded into the segregated evening school which was maintained for several weeks during the winter. As Topeka expanded and improved its educational facilities and programs for the increasing population of white students, Superintendent L. C. Wilmarth urged the Board of Education to "fully recognize the claims that the colored race have upon us for educational privileges," and to act promptly to provide additional facilities for black schools. . . .[36] Whether or not Wilmarth's successors provided black Topekans with an equal education, by the 1880s the city did provide four black schools.[37]

In one part of Topeka, there was partial elementary school integration as late as 1900. When the Lowman Hill area was annexed to the City of Topeka in 1890, only one school house existed in that new part of the city. It was attended by all children in the district regardless of race.[38] After the school burned down in 1900, the Topeka school board purchased a new site upon which to rebuild, claiming that the old site was unsanitary and inconvenient. It built a modern, two-story brick school building on the new site, and equipped it with new furniture and modern plumbing. The board then moved an old one-story structure to the original school site, equipping that two-room building with second-hand furniture. As the water mains for the city water stopped two blocks short of the old site, well water remained its sole water supply.[39] Once school was re-opened in the Lowman Hill District in early 1902, only white children were admitted to the new school building. Although the one-hundred and thirty whites occupied only four of the eight school rooms, black students were directed to the two room building on the old site.[40]

Black parents in the Lowman Hill District were outraged by the school board's action, and many responded by keeping their children out of school. According to the Women's League, an organization of black women in the Lowman Hill area, black parents would boycott the schools "until the trouble is adjusted in some satisfactory way." As they wrote to the *Topeka Plaindealer,* a local black community newspaper,

> if the board had given us equal school facilities for our children we would have had no grounds for complaint, though we were not in favor of separate schools, because we have not had one heretofore and it is not pleasant to have even the school house doors closed in one's face.[41]

The group did not want "to appear stubborn or unreasonable, but simply ask for equal school facilities."[42]

According to the *Plaindealer*, the black community was willing "to agree to almost any sort of a compromise if the board had shown any spirit of conciliation and would have let the matter drop if the colored children had been admitted to the sixth grade at the Lowman Hill School."[43] However, when it met to consider the segregated schools controversy, the Topeka Board of Education was not in a compromising mood. The Board's "attitude" foreclosed "all possibility of compromise or setting the matter on any basis which has hitherto been proposed."[44] Instead, Topeka blacks took the school controversy to the courts, as the Board's hard-line position on segregation polarized the community. G. C. Clement, the attorney representing the black parents, vowed to "see these people through to the Supreme Court of the United States, if need be, and spare my state this disgrace, if it takes the remainder of my life. I shall fight this miserable spirit of caste, and fight it to the last ditch."[45]

Two months later, Clement filed a Writ of Mandamus in the Kansas Supreme Court on behalf of William Reynolds, a black parent whose son was excluded from the Lowman Hill School. Clement's most important legal argument was that racial segregation violated the state and federal constitutions. With the constitutional standard set by *Plessy v. Ferguson*,[46] he would not get far. The Kansas Supreme Court upheld the constitutionality of the Kansas school segregation statute, paving the way for an increasingly rigid and pervasive system of segregation in Topeka.[47]

Although *Reynolds* established the constitutionality of segregation in the Topeka schools, it was not the last time the city would be called upon to defend its practices in the Kansas courts.[48] For example, black education in Topeka was challenged as unequal in 1941. When the city established junior high schools,[49] it continued to segregate students through eighth grade, but not ninth grade, as Kansas law permitted.[50] White school children attended elementary school through sixth grade, junior high school for grades seven to nine and high school for grades ten to twelve. Black children, on the other hand, attended black elementary schools through the eighth grade, attended junior high for ninth grade only, and then attended the integrated high school. In *Graham v. Board of Education of the City of Topeka*,[51] blacks successfully challenged this pattern of schooling as providing unequal education for blacks in the seventh and eighth grades. Amid dissention in the black community stemming from the effect integration might have on the jobs of black teachers, the school board complied with the Kansas

Supreme Court ruling by integrating black seventh and eighth graders into the junior high schools. Six black teachers lost their jobs, and two more were reduced to half-time.[52]

One year after the *Graham* ruling, Topeka hired a new school superintendent. Kenneth McFarland, a young, ambitious Kansan, was a gifted speaker who would provide forceful, perhaps overbearing, leadership in the Topeka school system during his tenure. Considered prejudiced and arrogant by many Topeka blacks, he held a hard line on segregation. In his racial ideology, McFarland invoked Booker T. Washington, suggesting that the only way to gain equality was to get a job and earn it. While he believed in segregation, he also believed in keeping separate schools equal, and tried to ensure that black students in Topeka were provided with equal opportunities.[53]

To enforce his policies on race, McFarland hired a black assistant, Harrison Caldwell, to supervise black education in Topeka. Caldwell used strong tactics to enforce a segregationist philosophy on black teachers, capitalizing on the insecurity created when blacks were fired as a result of *Graham*. Caldwell suggested that elementary school integration would lead to the elimination of black teachers from the Topeka schools. Shortly after he arrived, black teachers, responding to his pressure, increased segregation within their profession by forming a separate black teachers association.[54]

A focus of Caldwell's attention was Topeka High School. Topeka's only high school was considered "a segregated school within an integrated school."[55] Through 1949, classes were integrated but activities were not. Caldwell was ever vigilant to keep black and white students apart outside the classroom. He held separate 'good-nigger assemblies' for black high school students while whites attended chapel.[56] As one student later recalled,

> Caldwell would tell us not to rock the boat and how to be as little offensive to whites as possible—to be clean and study hard and accept the status quo—and things were getting better. Those who went along got the good after-school and summer jobs, the scholarships, and the choice spots on the athletic teams.[57]

Blacks were segregated from music groups, sports and student government. There was a separate black student council which sent the only black representative to the student government body composed of representatives from all student groups. Blacks had their own school "kings and queens."[58] One sport open to blacks was basketball through a separate black league. The black team, the "Ramblers," could not use the Topeka High team name or colors. They played home games at East Topeka Junior High.[59] Separate black teams were abolished when, with little fanfare, the school board rescinded its formal policy of internal segregation at the high school in 1949.[60]

By mid-century, Topeka was a city of over 100,000, and approximately 7.5 percent of its residents were black.[61] Segregation in the city was not limited to its schools. Most of its public accommodations were segregated, even though Kansas law formally prohibited it.[62] Only one Topeka hotel, the Dunbar, would serve blacks, and most restaurants would not seat them. Of the seven movie theaters in town, five served only whites, one provided balcony seating only for blacks, and one theater was for blacks only. The municipal swimming pool at Gage Park was for whites only, with the exception of one day a year when it was open to the black community. Not everything in Topeka was segregated, however. There was no racial segregation in bus or train transportation.[63] And while many blacks lived in eastern Topeka, residential segregation was not absolute. Blacks also lived in mixed-race neighborhoods scattered through the rest of Topeka.[64]

After repeatedly requesting that the Board of Education reconsider its elementary school segregation policy, the Topeka NAACP, in conjunction with the NAACP national office, brought suit against the Board in 1951.[65] The district court ruled in favor of the Board. Although it found that segregation was harmful to black children, the three judge panel believed that it remained constitutional under *Plessy* until the Supreme Court reconsidered the wisdom of that ruling.[66] As the NAACP appealed, and, in the fall of 1952, the *Brown* case was consolidated with cases from South Carolina, Virginia and the District of Columbia, the focus of the legal battle shifted to Washington.[67]

IV. THE SCHOOL SEGREGATION CONTROVERSY

A. The Politics of Ambivalence

Back in Kansas, a different battle was being waged, as state and local government officials awoke to the political implications of defending segregation. Proud of the Kansas free-state heritage, many citizens were displeased that their state was involved in legal action which they associated with Southern racism. As school superintendent H. H. Robinson of Augusta, Kansas, wrote Governor Edward Arn,

I am surprised and I must say chagrined to learn that Kansas now classifies itself as one of the White Supremacy states as indicated by the case now before the United States Supreme Court. I have just finished reading a new and fine history of Kansas and found much of it thrilling and glorious. As I review those historical events which caused us to be called 'bleeding Kansas', I wonder how we suddenly find ourselves represented before the Supreme Court opposed to those human rights for which our early settlers bled.[68]

Robinson was concerned that, through defending *Brown,* "we are throwing the influence of our state against those principles for which we have always stood."[69]

Many shared Robinson's view that participation in the *Brown* case involved the city of Topeka and the state of Kansas in matters that really concerned the South. It was in the South, after all, that "real" segregation occurred, as far as many Topekans were concerned. While the white community[70] in Topeka paid little attention to black criticism of their own schools, they were outraged at Southern racial practices. For example, in June of 1950, the *Topeka Daily Capital* ran an editorial criticizing Georgia Governor Herman Talmadge for his vow to defy Supreme Court decisions finding certain forms of segregation in higher education to be unconstitutional.[71] According to the paper, "[a]s was to be expected, certain southernors [*sic*] are perturbed" about the decisions.[72] "Southern states have ignored the 14th Amendment almost since it was adopted in 1868. Educational facilities available to white students have been denied colored boys and girls." Further, blacks were "shamefully segregated" on trains. Following the Supreme Court rulings affecting their states, Texas and Oklahoma would now 'be obliged to admit colored students to classrooms on equality with whites. They have no other alternative.'[73] Notwithstanding historic racially discriminatory practices in Topeka and Kansas laws permitting segregation, the editorial characterized segregation as a peculiarly Southern phenomenon. "Northern states have never practiced discrimination to the extent it has been prevalent in the South. . . .

353

Only in the die-hard South have Negroes been segregated and thus denied their constitutional rights." The recent Supreme Court decisions "open the way for a square deal for a race that has been woefully mistreated in the southern states."[74]

As a general rule, the local press simply ignored the black schools when reporting on educational matters in Topeka.[75] Black education was acknowledged only when something significant occurred that specifically concerned segregated education.[76] For example, one of the only news stories in the *Topeka Daily Capital* in 1950 that considered black education was a front page article announcing a "new step to end school segregation."[77] The article reported that the school board had voted to abolish the Office of Director of Colored Schools. This step would mean that black schools would not have their own administrator, but would be governed by the same administrative structure as the white schools.[78] Coming only a week after the editorial that had identified segregation as something practiced "[o]nly in the die-hard South,"[79] the article would seem to contradict the paper's characterization of the peculiarly Southern nature of segregation. However, according to the paper, while school segregation in Topeka was permitted under state law, "'arbitrary segregation,' as interpreted by the board, is not." Abolishing the separate administrative office was the "final policy step in the board's program to stop arbitrary segregation," which had also included an end to segregation at high school dances and in athletic competition.[80] Taken together, the article and editorial suggest that, for this newspaper, the form of segregation practiced in Topeka was somehow not of the Southern variety that so clearly violated the constitutional rights of Southern blacks.

Given the ambivalence of many toward school segregation in general, and the *Brown* case in particular, it is not surprising that neither the Topeka Board of Education nor the State Attorney General wished to be associated with the controversy. In a split vote, the school board decided not to defend itself on appeal. Board members justified their decision by the fact that the court had ruled in their favor on the question of the equality of educational opportunities. As purely local matters were no longer at issue, they felt that the Attorney General should be responsible for defending the constitutionality of the Kansas law.[81] Attorney General Harold Fatzer waffled in his response. During the summer of 1952, he told the Topeka school board that he intended to argue the case. He later changed his mind, insisting that the school board was responsible for defending its own practices.[82] With the Kansas case and three other school cases set for argument in the Supreme Court that December,[83] attorneys for the other states were concerned that the Topeka case would be decided by default.[84]

As state and local officials refused to budge, the Supreme Court forced the issue. On November 24, 1952, the Court issued an extraordinary per curiam order. The Court noted that no appearance had been entered by any of the Kansas defendants, and that counsel for the Topeka Board of Education had informed the court that the board did not intend to appear in oral argument or present a brief. The order continued,

> Because of the national importance of the issue presented and because of its importance to the State of Kansas, we request that the State present its views at oral argument. If the State does not desire to appear, we request the Attorney General to advise whether the State's default shall be construed as a concession of invalidity.[85]

Harold Fatzer was not happy with the Supreme Court's order. The day after it was issued he rushed to Washington to confer with the Clerk of the Supreme Court. As he later reported to the *Topeka Daily Capital*, Fatzer told the Clerk that the Court's order was "not a fair request. It is not the prerogative of the state executive department to concede the invalidity of any legislative act. That is for the courts to decide."[86] Backed into a corner, Fatzer was forced to abandon his neutral stance. He first agreed to file a brief and later decided that the state would also participate in oral argument. . . .[87]

Fatzer wished to make it clear that his decision to defend the suit did not mean that he, personally, or the State of Kansas favored a policy of racial segregation. "Segregation, in the first place, is a local matter in Kansas," he insisted. Further, the state statute "is permissive and it is not of major importance as it appears to be in the Southern States." Fatzer believed that 'segregation in Kansas is rapidly being ended where practiced. Kansas has been making strides to abolish the injustice of segregation in the public school system and elsewhere.'[88] Perhaps in an effort to protect his political reputation from tarnish, Fatzer announced that "I have never advocated or championed segregation and will not do so before the Supreme Court." The state would restrict its arguments to the constitutional question of whether segregation was within the power of the state legislature in regulating education. Kansas would leave emotional appeals about the goodness or badness of racial segregation to other participants in the case.[89]

To further distance himself from the controversy, Fatzer would send Assistant Attorney General Paul Wilson to argue the case for Kansas. Wilson was new to the Attorney General's Office. After some eight years of legal practice, he had come to work for Fatzer in part to gain appellate experience. He would present the first oral argument of his career before the U.S. Supreme Court.[90]

Not everyone on the Topeka school board agreed with the board's hands-off posture toward the case. At the October 6, 1952, school board meeting, board member Marlin Casey read a prepared statement criticizing his colleagues for their inaction. Casey felt that, as defendant in the *Brown* litigation, the board had a duty to defend its policies. He felt that the board's failure to take action reflected a desire to take an easy way out of a sticky political controversy. He suggested that

> [i]f the majority of the board is against segregation, as I assume they are by not defending this suit, then action should be taken to abolish it as the board can do under the present statute, and not take the weak position of letting the Supreme Court do it. Apparently the board would like to be in a position of saying to the colored people, if the Supreme Court holds the statute unconstitutional, "We have helped abolish segregation by not defending this suit." While on the other hand, they could say to the white people, 'We are sorry, there is nothing we could do, the Supreme Court has held the statute unconstitutional and therefore segregation must be abolished.'[91]

The Board of Education was not willing to follow Casey's suggestion, preferring a low profile on the substantive issue of segregation. However, the board did begin to prepare for the possibility that the Court might strike down segregation. The school board would not act on its own, but if the Supreme Court should abolish segregation, the board would be ready.

B. *The Teacher Problem*

In the spring of 1953, the Topeka papers reported that a "purge" of black teachers had begun. Throughout the state "a mass unannounced weeding-out of Negro teachers" was taking place in anticipation of a possible desegregation decision that might affect the upcoming school year.[92] In Topeka, the six newest black teachers were notified that their contracts would not be renewed. Wendell Godwin, the new Superintendent of the Topeka Schools, wrote the teachers that

> [d]ue to the present uncertainty about enrollment next year in schools for Negro children, it is not possible at this time to offer you employment for next year. If the Supreme Court should rule that segregation in the elementary grades is unconstitutional, our Board will proceed on the assumption that the majority of people in Topeka will not want to employ Negro teachers next year for white children. . . . If it turns out that segregation is not terminated, there will be nothing to prevent us from negotiating a contract with you a[t] some later date this spring.[93]

The board only terminated the black teachers hired within the past year or two, as "[i]t is presumed that, even though segregation should be declared unconstitutional, we would have need for some schools for Negro children and we would retain our Negro teachers to teach them."[94]

In response to pressure from the community and from one of its own members, the Board of Education reconsidered the firing of black teachers shortly after the initial decision hit the press. Nine Topeka NAACP members made an "impassioned plea" that the teachers be reinstated.[95] Marlin Casey, the board's most outspoken advocate of segregation, moved that they be rehired.[96] Jacob Dickenson, Casey's "arch antagonist,"[97] tried unsuccessfully to table the motion regarding the teachers while the board reconsidered its segregation policy. When that move failed, he voted against the rehiring on the grounds that the board was not entitled to rehire teachers unless it had a place for them, and in order to have a place for them the board had to establish a policy on segregation and the employment of black teachers. Other board members refused to reconsider the Topeka policy until after the Supreme Court ruling came down. With a vote of three to three, the motion to rehire the teachers did not pass. Later during the same meeting the board hired seven new white teachers.[98]

The six black Topeka teachers would at least temporarily retain their jobs. In June of 1953, the Supreme Court called for reargument in the school segregation cases to be held the following October.[99] Under the assumption that a subsequent desegregation decree would not affect the 1953–54 school year, on June 15 the board rehired the teachers.[100]

C. Desegregation Kansas Style

When the Topeka Board of Education decided to postpone a reconsideration of its school segregation policy until after the Supreme Court ruling, the board had anticipated a resolution to the problem by the end of the 1952–53 school year. The Court's postponement of the case and request for reargument caught the board by surprise. Its posture of neutrality would be difficult to maintain through another year. According to Superintendent Godwin, "the board has sort of an agreement to take up the matter of segregation policy after the Supreme Court's decision was known, but I think the members may want to discuss whether the Supreme Court's failure to give a decision soon may change the board's course of action."[101]

A newly constituted school board would meet to consider these questions in the fall of 1953. Marlin Casey, the board's most vocal supporter of segregation, Charles Bennett, Casey's closest ally, and Mrs. David Neiswanger[102] were replaced by three new members as a result of elections during the spring of 1953. The outgoing board members were the remaining three of the original six from the days of the McFarland administration.[103]

Very late one evening near the end of an unusually lengthy board meeting, the Topeka Board of Education considered the question of whether to continue segregation in the schools. It was 12:30 A.M. on September 4 when the bussing contract was about to be considered to continue transporting black children to segregated schools.[104] Jacob Dickenson, the new board president, offered a motion not on the agenda: "Be it resolved that it is the policy of the Topeka Board of Education to terminate the maintenance of segregation in the elementary grades as rapidly as practicable."[105] The motion was seconded, and Dr. Harold Conrad offered an amendment that no action to end segregation be taken until the fall of 1954. The amendment was defeated, which the *Topeka Daily Capital* took as "indicating the board may not see fit even at that time to completely abolish the system of separate classes."[106] Dickenson's motion passed with a vote of five to one. Former board president M. C. Oberhelman cast the only negative vote. He felt that the decision was "ill timed." Oberhelman was careful to note that he was "not opposed to integration," however he thought "we should have an orderly program in mind and a much more definite goal before we pass the resolution."[107] Before adjourning, the board approved the bus contract for the 1953–54 school year, ensuring that, for the coming year at least, black children would still be bussed to achieve racial segregation.[108]

Just what the Topeka Board of Education intended to do to desegregate its schools was clarified somewhat at a board meeting the following week. Superintendent Godwin presented a report to the board, recommending a first step in the desegregation process. First, he emphasized four general points governing his recommendation:

1) That the termination of segregation should be done in a gradual and orderly manner.
2) That in his judgment it is a social impossibility to terminate segregation suddenly.
3) That speed with which segregation is terminated depends largely on the forebearance [*sic*] and self-discipline of both white and colored people.
4) That it is not possible to set an accurate time in which segregation is terminated completely.[109]

As a first step, Godwin recommended that black children residing in the Southwest and Randolph districts be allowed to attend those schools. However, any black student who wished to continue to attend black Buchanan School could do so, although bus transportation would not be provided. This move would affect approximately fifteen black students, and would take effect immediately. The board unanimously approved the Superintendent's recommendation.[110]

At the September 8 meeting, the board was called on to defend its decision to desegregate the schools. Edward Goss of the Topeka Civic Club asked the board how they could end segregation before the Supreme Court decided the issue. Board member Conrad explained that "[w]e feel that segregation is not an American practice."[111] As the *Topeka Journal* reported, Conrad noted that

the subject had been under discussion for two years and there had been an informal agreement that segregation could not be continued because of the general trends in social and human development and that some time in the future, whether or not the Supreme court decided to end segregation, the board would do so in the best interests of the public schools and Topeka.[112]

The Topeka school board took further action to end segregation in its schools on January 20, 1954. Superintendent Godwin proposed that segregation be terminated at an additional ten elementary schools and partially terminated at another two. Under this second step, all black children residing in the ten districts could attend the white schools near their home, although they would "be given the privilege of attending the nearest Negro school" if their parents desired. No transportation would be provided these students. The districts partially desegregated each had three black children geographically isolated from other blacks in the district. These children would be allowed to attend the white schools; the others would not. The justification given for this distinction was that the white schools had space limitations, so more integration was not possible.[113]

Step two of the Topeka program would affect up to 123 of the city's 824 black school children. It would leave nine of Topeka's twenty-two elementary schools completely segregated, four black and five white. The school board unanimously approved the plan, which would go into effect at the beginning of the 1954–55 school year. The primary problem with integrating the remaining white schools was reported to be the overcrowded conditions at the white schools, indicating that desegregation in Topeka was clearly contemplated as a one-way proposition.[114] In a matter-of-fact news story, the *Topeka Journal* reported the plan under the headline "Segregation Ended in Twelve More Elementary Schools Here." If there was any pronounced public reaction to the plan, the local papers did not choose to report it.[115]

D. *The* Brown *Decision*

When the *Brown* case was reargued before the Supreme Court in December of 1953, the Topeka school board filed a brief. This time they wished to have their say.

The board's brief dealt only with the remedial questions before the Court. They recommended that the Court not end segregation immediately, arguing that completely ending segregation would require "difficult and far-reaching administrative decisions" which would affect nearly all school children, teachers, buildings and attendance boundaries, making "a hurried and summary" change "both impossible and impractical." The board believed that under immediate desegregation, "the attendant confusion and interruption of the regular school program would be against the public interest and would be damaging to the children, both Negro and white alike."[116] Since the board had voted to desegregate, they felt they no longer had an active interest in the constitutional questions before the Court.[117]

The Supreme Court finally decided *Brown v. Board of Education* on May 17, 1954.[118] The Court found that the *Brown* cases squarely presented the question of whether school segregation, by itself, deprived non-white students of their constitutional rights, for in *Brown* the separate schools were equal or were being equalized.[119] In considering the constitutional question, the Court looked broadly at the effect of segregation on public education and the role education played in contemporary society. The Court found that "[t]oday, education is perhaps the most important function of state and local governments." Education is "required in the performance of our most basic public responsibilities," and is "the very foundation of good citizenship." Consequently, "[i]n these days, it is doubtful that any child may reasonably be expected to succeed in life if he is denied the opportunity of an education. Such an opportunity, where the state has undertaken to provide it, is a right which must be made available to all on equal terms."[120] The court found that the intangible factors that had produced educational inequality in previous cases "apply with added force to children in grade school and high school." Relying on social science evidence that segregation harms children, the Court found that "[t]o separate [non-white] children from others of similar age and qualifications solely because of their race generates a feeling of inferiority as to their status in the community that may affect their hearts and minds in a way unlikely ever to be undone." Therefore, "in the field of public education the doctrine of 'separate but equal' has no place. Separate educational facilities are inherently unequal."[121] The Court reserved the question briefed by the Topeka Board of Education. More time, more briefs and more argument were needed before the Court would decide on an appropriate remedy.[122]

In Topeka, school officials hailed the ruling. School board president Jacob Dickenson felt it was "in the finest spirit of the law and true democracy"....[123]

The Topeka NAACP was overjoyed with the *Brown* decision. Chapter President Burnett was "completely overwhelmed." "[T]hank God for the Supreme court. Their decision will enable me to pay my taxes with a little more grace. . . . We will celebrate and leave the rest to the court," he added. "We believe we can depend on them". . . .[124]

It would be one full year before the Supreme Court would rule on the implementation of *Brown*. By that time the Topeka school board would adopt one more step in their desegregation plan, a step which they would initially believe fully terminated school segregation in Topeka.

E. Topeka Takes Another Step

In February of 1955, the Topeka Board of Education considered step three of the Topeka desegregation plan. The proposal, which would go into effect in the fall of 1955, was designed to end segregation in all remaining schools. Black students within the remaining white districts would be able to attend the white school near them. Three black schools, Buchanan, Monroe and Washington, would be assigned attendance boundaries, and all children within a school's boundaries could attend that school. McKinley Elementary School, the fourth black school, was to be closed and placed "on a stand-by basis." No bus transportation would be provided for any children.[125]

Step three would change Topeka to a school system governed by neighborhood attendance boundaries, with two important exceptions. The plan allowed that "any child who is affected by the changes in district lines herein recommended, be given the option of finishing elementary grades in the school which he attended in 1954–55, McKinley excepted." Further it provided "[t]hat entering kindergarten children in 1955–56, who are affected by the change in school boundaries as herein recommended, be given the option of attending the same school in 1955–56 that they would have attended in 1954–55 if they had been old enough to enter."[126] The plan would get the Topeka school board out of the business of making attendance decisions based overtly on race alone. However, it would leave room for individuals to avoid radical integration by exercising an attendance option. The board estimated that one third of the black students and all of the whites affected would opt to attend their old schools. The plan would increase the strain on already crowded previously white schools, while reducing enrollment at the black schools which, prior to desegregation, had more than enough space.[127]

Given the progress in Topeka toward desegregation, when argument was held for the third time in *Brown v. Board of Education,* Harold Fatzer was proud to go. The Attorney General told the Court in April of 1955 that no order would be required to end segregation in Kansas, as the state was complying with the previous year's ruling "in good faith and with dispatch." In Topeka, school segregation would be fully terminated by the fall of 1955.[128] However, the "end of segregation" did not mean that some semblance of racial balance might be achieved in the Topeka schools. In a follow-up letter to the Supreme Court, Fatzer explained that the estimated school population in the formerly black schools was one hundred percent black. According to Fatzer, this phenomenon was the result of several factors, including:

1. The schools were originally built in predominantly colored neighborhoods because they were originally for segregated Negro children.
2. After the schools were built the Negro people who could do so, tended to move nearer to the Negro schools where their children were required to attend.[129]

Further, the options provided by the school board would enable any whites living in black areas to attend their old white school. In addition, "persons who are dissatisfied with the schools their children will be required to attend during the school year of 1955–56 may have at least a year to move to a district of their choice."[130]

As the Attorney General unabashedly told the Court, the former black schools in Topeka would remain black schools because previous school board policies had fostered residential segregation, and because the board now provided white people with a way out. Yet in spite of the fact that many of Topeka's black school children continued to attend all-black schools, Fatzer and the Board of Education believed that segregation had ended. Clearly, racial isolation, by itself, did not constitute segregation in their eyes. However, it remains to be considered what the "segregation" was that they had eliminated from the Topeka schools.

F. The Question of Good Faith

On May 31, 1955, the U.S. Supreme Court announced the remedial order in *Brown v. Board of Education.*[131] Because it believed that the implementation of *Brown* I would require attention to local conditions, the Court remanded the cases to the lower courts. In fashioning specific decrees, the lower courts would be guided by equitable principles, balancing the "personal interest" of the plaintiffs in admission to non-segregated schools against the "public interest" in eliminating a variety of administrative obstacles in an orderly manner. The Court noted that school authorities had the primary responsibility for solving local school problems, and consequently "courts will have to consider whether the action of school authorities constitutes good faith implementation of the governing constitutional principles." Once defendants had made a "prompt and reasonable start toward full compliance," the Court felt that additional time might be required to handle administrative problems. However, "[t]he burden rests upon the defendants to establish that such time is necessary in the public interest and is consistent with good faith compliance at the earliest practical date." And the lower courts were to ensure that the parties to the cases were admitted to non-segregated schools "with all deliberate speed."[132]

Brown II would be a license for delay and evasion in some Southern states, as the South prepared for a long period of resistance.[133] For Kansas, the Court had offered a welcome pat on the back, finding that "substantial progress" had been made toward the elimination of segregation.[134] As the Topeka case was remanded to the district court, the defendants set out to show that they had acted in good faith to dismantle segregation. Judge Huxman and his colleagues in the district court set the terms of the discussion for argument on remand when they informed the parties that the only question at issue was whether the school board had acted in good faith to desegregate the schools. In a hearing on September 15, 1955, the court expressed reservations about the attendance options provided by the board, and requested both parties to submit briefs on the question of whether the board's plan was a good faith effort toward compliance.[135]

The board argued, first, that "at the present time no child who resides within the Topeka public school system or district is denied admission to any school on the basis of race." Therefore, "the Board of Education has fully complied . . . in that race is no longer a determinative factor to the right to attend any school in the Topeka public school system."[136] However, they recognized that desegregation might not be fully achieved under their plan and that the effects of the implementation of step three warranted study. Nevertheless, the board strongly defended its plan, particularly the questionable options. . . .[137]

The Topeka school board's plan left five schools all-white and three schools all-black as of September, 1955.[138] Even without the attendance options, much of this racial isolation would continue. The board maintained that it was not responsible for the racial composition of the schools when it resulted from the fact that blacks "have chosen to reside and remain in" certain districts.[139]

In essence, the board understood its responsibilities under *Brown* II as ending overtly compulsory race-conscious pupil assignment. Once it got out of the business of enforcing a formal color line, it was no longer engaged in "segregation." For the school board, the remaining racial isolation in the school system was the result of voluntary, private choice. Even when motivated by a desire to avoid integration, the board believed that such choice should be facilitated. To impede private, racially-motivated choice would again engage the school board in compulsion. Forcing integration on parents of school children became, for the board, an evil of the degree that forced segregation had so recently achieved.

As far as the plaintiffs were concerned, the "crucial problem" to be considered by the court was "whether there are any valid reasons of school administration which would warrant a delay in fully putting into effect a policy of nonsegregation in the public schools in Topeka." The NAACP criticized the attendance options as facilitating white student transfers out of the remaining black districts. The effect of the options was that Buchanan, Monroe and Washington remained 100 percent black. They were simply no longer called black schools. Because the racial composition of these schools remained the same, "[s]egregation has not been terminated in the public schools in Topeka." The plaintiffs felt that

> the problem that the defendants do not want to face up to is that of really integrating these former Negro schools into the total school system. Until they face that problem and make these schools a part of the total school system, in our opinion, they have not met their obligation under the Supreme Court decision.[140]

. . . In a brief per curiam opinion issued on October 28, 1955, the district court upheld the school board's actions. The panel felt that, in a number of respects, "the plan does not constitute full compliance with the mandate of the Supreme Court, but that mandate implies that some time will be required to bring that about." The elements of the plan which were problematic were "mostly of a minor nature," and the court believed that "no useful purpose would be served" by going into any of the details of the plan. However, the court did discuss one specific provision: the attendance option for kindergartners. The court did not "look with favor" upon that rule, but because the school board had claimed it was a temporary measure, the court did "not feel that it requires a present condemnation of an overall plan which shows a good faith effort to bring about full desegregation. . . ."[141]

The court did not consider the existence of all-black and all-white schools as evidence of continuing segregation.

> Desegregation does not mean that there must be intermingling of the races in all school districts. It means only that they may not be prevented from intermingling or going to school together because of race or color.
>
> If it is a fact, as we understand it is, with respect to Buchanan School that the district is inhabited entirely by colored students, no violation of any constitutional right results because they are compelled to attend the school in the district in which they live.[142]

The court approved the board's plan as a "good faith beginning to bring about complete desegregation," and retained jurisdiction for the purpose of entering a final decree.[143]

G. A Fourth and Final Step

The district court's ruling surely came as a relief to Topeka school officials. The court approved their handiwork and protected their autonomy regarding future school policy. The court also refrained from invalidating their efforts to facilitate parental avoidance of desegregation, although it was clear that the board would be required to take some further action to limit the frustration of desegregation resulting from private preferences.

Although the superintendent and the school board had, at one point, argued that segregation was completely terminated with step three, they now recognized that, at least in the court's eyes, something further was needed. Within two months, Superintendent Godwin came up with a plan to satisfy the district court's reservations. On December

21, 1955, he presented a proposed step four to the Board of Education. Godwin suggested, first, that the kindergarten option be eliminated for the 1956–57 school year, so that entering school children would be assigned to the school in the district in which they lived, regardless of preference to attend another school. . . .

Secondly, all children moving into an elementary school district would be required to attend the school in the district in which they lived. . . .[144]

For students in grades one through six, the options previously granted would remain unchanged. . . . Superintendent Godwin recommended that no action be taken on step four until the January 18 board meeting so that the board could solicit views from the community.[145]

Representatives from the Topeka NAACP were not pleased with step four. They felt the options it retained would perpetuate racial segregation. Such delay in implementing full desegregation was harmful to the students segregated, and was "creating a feeling of insecurity" among the black teachers at Buchanan, Monroe and Washington Schools.[146] At the January 18 board meeting, Mr. Burnett, President of the local chapter, appealed to the Board of Education to end segregation immediately by eliminating the options in step four. He claimed that, under the proposed plan, "it would take seven long years to terminate racial segregation." Burnett also commented that while the board spoke of the need to hire one hundred new teachers, "nothing has been said about the integration of negro teachers." These teachers "had been completely left out of desegregation."[147]

No discussion followed Burnett's remarks. Instead, school board member Nelda Shriner "moved that Step IV in the gradual and systematic termination of racial segregation, as recommended by the Superintendent, and in compliance with the mandate of the U.S. Supreme Court and the U.S. District Court, be adopted." The board unanimously approved its final step to desegregate the Topeka schools.[148]

Topeka's desegregation plan would, even in the eyes of the school board, retain some vestiges of racial segregation for several years.[149] However, Topeka school officials stood behind their remaining attendance options. They considered their policy as well within their rights under *Brown* II, for it protected the private interests of students who did not "want the sudden disruption of their elementary school pattern." As Superintendent Godwin noted, by proposing to remove these options "[w]hat you are talking about is compelling people to go to a school where they do not want to go."[150]

The Topeka Board of Education had been compelling black children to attend certain schools against their will for many years. Successive school boards had based their decision to segregate on what they felt was best for white and black children alike.[151] Now that the board was getting out of the business of segregation, it wished to get out of the business of compulsion as well. When it meant controlling the choices that whites might make, compulsion became a dirty word.

V. CONCLUSION: THE LIMITS OF GOOD FAITH

It would be quite a while before the Topeka school board found itself before the district court on the question of school segregation again. In the interim, step four would quietly progress. Judge Huxman and his district court panel had had their last word on the adequacy of the Topeka plan. They had entrusted desegregation to the school board's good faith efforts, and it was in the school board's hands that the authority and autonomy to enforce desegregation would remain.[152] Twenty years later, when the question of continuing segregation was raised by Topeka blacks and federal authorities, the board would claim that the court's acquiescence to their plan was evidence that they had fully complied with the law. . . .[153]

Even in implementing this limited, one-way integration plan, the Topeka Board of Education adopted a gradualist strategy, arguing that gradualism was the most sensible, rational means to achieve integration in Topeka. And while the board made passing reference to administrative difficulties that would require delay, the primary purpose behind the options in the plan was to facilitate parental avoidance of desegregation. . . .

In an effort to distance themselves from the racial practices they identified with the "die-hard South,"[154] the Topeka school board embraced an approach to race and school assignment which essentially assumed that the ideal society in which racism was not a factor in human motivation had already arrived in Kansas. From this perspective, any continuing racial isolation in the public schools could be seen as benign. Because racism had presumptively been eliminated from school policies, the board considered blacks to have no special claim to the school board's attention. As blacks and whites were now on equal footing, the desires of each group were entitled to equal weight. Color-blindness had become the order of the day. In the future society that had arrived in Kansas, whites and blacks had associational rights of an equivalent moral character. They could not be compelled to attend segregated schools or to attend integrated schools. In order to avoid such compulsion in violation of associational rights, the board constructed its policies to accommodate private prejudices. . . .

NOTES

1. Brown v. Bd. of Educ., 347 U.S. 483 (1954).

2. Topeka Bd. of Educ. Minutes, Sept. 3, 1953.

3. "Segregation Is Terminated at Randolph and Southwest," *Topeka Journal*, Sept. 9, 1953.

4. See generally Pauli Murray, *States Laws on Race and Color* (Cincinnati, 1950).

5. Ibid. at 8, 10. For example, elementary school segregation in cities with populations over 15,000 was permitted; school segregation in smaller cities was prohibited. High school segregation was only permitted in Kansas City, Kansas. See infra at . . . [348–49].

6. See generally, Kenneth S. Davis, *Kansas* (New York, 1976) 35–71.

7. Brown v. Bd. of Educ., 98 F. Supp. 797 (1951).

8. "In Court Paradox," *Kansas City Star*, Nov. 29, 1953.

9. See infra at . . . [355–56, 358–60].

10. See infra at . . . [359–60, 362–68].

11. See infra note . . . [88]. The effectiveness of the Topeka school board's desegregation plan would later be questioned by federal authorities and members of the black community. In 1974, the Department of Health, Education, and Welfare found that the schools remained racially segregated and that the predominately black schools were of poorer quality, and consequently the school board was in violation of the Civil Rights Act of 1964. However, HEW was enjoined by the federal district court from terminating the city's federal funding because the city was acting under a court order in *Brown*, and was therefore not subject to the enforcement provisions of the Civil Rights Act. Unified School Dist. #501 v. Weinberer, No. 74-160-C5 (D. Kan. August 23, 1974); see Brown v. Bd. of Educ., 84 F.R.D. 383, 390–91 (D. Kan. 1979); see also "How Much Integration?" *Topeka Capital-Journal*, May 12, 1974. A group of black parents later moved to intervene in the *Brown* case. Although the suit had lain dormant for years, the district court had never relinquished jurisdiction over the case, and had never found that complete compliance

with the Supreme Court's ruling had been achieved. Among the intervening plaintiffs was Linda Brown Smith, one of the original plaintiffs, now suing on behalf of her children. Intervention was granted in 1979. Brown v. Bd. of Educ., 84 F.R.D. 383, 405 (1979). The case was tried in October of 1986, and on April 8, 1987, the district court ruled in favor of the defendants. Brown v. Bd. of Educ., No. T-316, slip op. at 50 (D. Kan. April 8, 1987). . . .

12. Ambivalence, or outright hostility toward blacks, appeared in other areas as well. Although, in the 1850s, opposition to slavery was a motivating force in the battle for control of what would become the state of Kansas, the state's first official constitution did not extend equal rights to free blacks. Suffrage was extended only to white male citizens. Kan. Const. art. 5§1 (1859). The framers of the Kansas Constitution considered and rejected a proposal to make Kansas "not only a free state, but a free white state" by forbidding black immigration. Kan. Const. Debates at 178. The convention was divided on the question of black education. In discussing a provision regarding a system of "common schools" for the children of the state, several delegates argued that blacks should be excluded entirely from public schooling. Their opponents argued that, since blacks could be living in Kansas, "they should be made as intelligent and moral as education can make them." Further, the white majority in a community could "protect itself," from blacks, if need be, by providing racially segregated schools. Ibid. at 176. In its final form, the Kansas Constitution did not expressly address the question of black education, leaving discretion over the matter to the state legislature. Kan. Const. Art. 6 (1859).

13. 1861 Kan. Laws, ch. 76, art. III, sect. I.

14. In 1862, the Kansas legislature required separate taxation of white and non-white persons for the purpose of supporting segregated schools. All white taxes would go for the support of white schools, and non-white taxes would support non-white schools. 1862 Kan. Laws, Ch. 46, Art. IV, Sect. 18–19. This measure was repealed two years later, and discretion over school taxes was vested in boards of education. 1864 Kan. Laws, ch. 67, sect. 14–16. The 1864 school law retained for school boards the power to segregate school children, but contained no proviso that separate schools had to be equal. Ibid., sec. 4.

15. 1876 Kan. Laws, ch. 122, art. X, sec. 4.

16. But see Richard Kluger, [*Simple Justice* (New York, 1977)]. . . . Kluger suggests, I believe erroneously, that the process of desegregation began after passage of the 1876 law. This is unlikely as, in 1876, it was not at all clear that legislative authorization was necessary for local school officials to segregate their schools. Further, even after the illegality of certain forms of segregation was settled in 1881, a court mandate was usually required to dismantle illegally segregated schools. See infra note . . . [30]. Some, if not all, school districts were unaffected by the temporary change in the law. See Board of Education of the City of Ottawa v. Tinnon, 26. Kan. 1, 18 (1881). Kluger refers to the existence of some mixed-race schools in 1876. Most likely, these schools began as integrated schools, rather than changing

their racial composition due to legislative action. Cf. Reynolds v. Bd. of Educ. of the City of Topeka, 66 Kan. 672 (1903) (elementary school integrated until 1900): Bd. of Educ. of the City of Ottawa v. Tinnon, 26 Kan. 1 (1881) (elementary school integrated until 1880).

17. 1879 Kan. Laws, ch. 81. sec. 1. This statute withstood a constitutional challenge in Reynolds v. Bd. of Educ. of the City of Topeka, 66 Kan. 672 (1903). See discussion infra at . . . [346–47].

18. Until September of 1880 the city of Ottawa, a city of the second class, educated all city school children, grades one through twelve, in one school building. By 1880 the accommodations had become somewhat crowded, and the Board of Education moved all black children to a separate building. Bd. of Educ. of the City of Ottawa v. Tinnon, 26 Kan. 1. 3. 8–10 (1881).

19. 1879 Kan. Gen. Stat., ch. 92, sec. 151.

20. Tinnon, 26. Kan. 1 at 3, 8–10.

21. Kan. at 20. Justice Valentine's majority opinion prompted Justice Brewer to file the term's only dissent. Brewer found Valentine's analysis to turn on matters more properly reserved for the legislature. For him, the question was not the wisdom of segregation as an educational policy, but rather the scope of the power the legislature had conferred upon boards of education. In addition, although Valentine had reserved the question of the constitutionality of legislatively authorized segregation, Brewer "dissent[ed] entirely from the suggestion" that school segregation might be unconstitutional. He would have held that "free schools mean equal school advantages to every child, leaving questions of classification by territory, sex, or color, to be determined by the wisdom of the local authorities." 26 Kan. at 25.

Tinnon would remain good law throughout the history of legislatively authorized school segregation in Kansas. . . .

22. 66 Kan. 672 (1903). Topeka, Kansas, segregated its elementary schools in accordance with the Kansas statute permitting such segregation. 1879 Kan. Laws, ch. 81. In the fall of 1902, William Reynolds, a black resident of Topeka, sought admission of his son to a white school. When he was refused, Reynolds sought a Writ of Mandamus in the Kansas Supreme Court to compel the Topeka school board to admit his son to the school. Reynolds claimed that school segregation in Topeka violated state law and the federal constitution. Affidavit for Alternative Writ of Mandamus at 4, Reynolds v. Bd. of Educ. of the City of Topeka, 66 Kan. 672 (1903). . . .

23. Kan. at 679; Kans. Const. art. VI, sec. 2. The court also considered and rejected technical arguments that the statute permitting segregation had not been properly enacted. 66 Kan. at 673–79.

24. Kan. at 686–90, quoting The States, ex. rel. Garnes v. McCann, et al., 21 Ohio St. 198 (1871); People, ex rel. King v. Gallagher, 93 N.Y. 438 (1883); Ward v. Flood, 48 Cal. 36 (1874).

25. 163 U.S. 537 (1896).

26. Ibid. at 544.

27. 163 U.S. at 543–44, quoted in 66 Kan. at 691.

28. 66 Kan. at 692. See infra at . . . [348–49] regarding the disparity in school facilities.

29. 347 U.S. 483 (1954).

30. The only change in the segregation statutes between 1903 and 1954 was a 1905 law permitting high school segregation, but only in Kansas City, Kansas. 1905. Kan. Laws, ch. 414, sec. I. See Richardson v. Bd. of Educ. of Kansas City, 72 Kan. 629 (1906). There was at least one unsuccessful attempt to extend high school segregation to other cities. In 1911, a bill was introduced to amend the 1905 law to allow segregated high schools in all cities of the first class. The bill was reported favorably out of the House Committee on Cities of the First Class, but ultimately failed to become law. Kan. House Bill No. 264 (1911).

Legislation to expand the scope of permissible segregation to include cities of the second class was introduced in 1919. Kan. House Bill No. 9 (1919); Kan. Senate Bill No. 567 (1919). The bills engendered strong public reaction in favor of and against expanded segregation. See Kan. State Historical Society, Archives Dept., Governor Allen's Papers, Box 26, file no. 22, "School Segregation" (1919). The legislation failed in both houses.

Although segregation in second- and third-class cities was never authorized by the Kansas State Legislature, it was practiced in many such cities through most of Kansas history. See Bd. of Educ. of the City of Ottawa v. Tinnon, 26 Kan. 1 (1881); Cartwright v. Bd. of Educ. of the City of Coffeyville, 73 Kan. 32 (1906); Woolridge v. Bd. of Educ. of the City of Galena, 98 Kan. 397 (1916); Webb v. School Dist. No. 90 in Johnson County, 167 Kan. 395 (1949) (cases involving segregation in cities of the second class).

31. The most important application of Kansas segregation law through the courts came with the introduction of junior high schools, as they were not mentioned in the Kansas school laws. Thurman-Watts v. Bd. of Educ. of the City of Coffeyville, 115 Kan. 328 (1924), held that ninth grade was part of high school under Kansas law, and therefore junior high school students could not be segregated in the ninth grade.

To comply with *Thurman-Watts,* the Topeka school board sent white students to junior high schools for grades seven, eight and nine, but sent black students to black elementary schools through the eighth grade, then to integrated junior high school for ninth grade only. This pattern of school attendance was challenged in 1941 as violating the requirement that separate schools must be equal. Graham v. Bd. of Educ. of the City of Topeka, 153 Kan. 840 (1941). The Kansas Supreme Court found that, due to the great differences in educational programs and facilities between grades seven and eight in the black elementary schools and the white junior high school, Topeka was not providing black students with an equal education. However, because grades seven and eight were considered elementary grades, the court did not require junior high school integration. It only held that if Topeka was to provide junior high schools for white children, it must do the same for blacks. 153 Kan. at 844–48. Topeka complied with the court order by integrating black seventh and eighth graders into the junior high schools. Kluger, supra note . . . [16] at 379.

32. See cases cited in supra note . . . [30].

33. Williams v. Bd. of Educ. of the City of Parsons [I], 79 Kan. 202 (1908); Williams v. Bd. of Educ. of the City of Parsons [II], 81 Kan. 593 (1910); Wright v. Bd. of Educ. of the City of Topeka, 153 Kan. 840 (1941) (school integration sought due to unequal conditions in cities of the first class).

34. Compare Cartwright v. Bd. of Educ. of the City of Coffeyville, 73 Kan. 32 (1906) (Coffeyville as a city of the second class) with Thurman-Watts v. Bd. of Educ. of the City of Coffeyville, 115 Kan. 328 (1924) (Coffeyville as a city of the first class).

35. Joint Comm. of the National Educ. Assn. and the American Teachers Assn., *Legal Status of Segregated Schools* (Montgomery, Alabama, 1954) 14.

36. Topeka Bd. of Educ., *History of the Topeka Schools* (1954) 110–11.

37. Ibid. at 113.

The teaching staffs of the black schools were initially white. As Superintendent D. C. Tillotson noted in his report for the year 1886–87, "[s]ix years ago, with two exceptions, all the teachers in our colored schools were white," however white teachers were transferred once black teachers could be found. Quoted in ibid. at 115–16. After the first black students graduated from integrated Topeka High School in 1882, that school began to provide "a small consistent flow of colored teachers to the community." Ibid. at 116. Through hiring local and outside black teachers, Topeka eventually achieved completely segregated teaching staffs. Kluger, supra note . . . [16] at 379.

38. Defendant's Return to Alternative Writ of Mandamus at 2–3 (May 1902), Reynolds v. Bd. of Educ. of the City of Topeka, 66 Kan. 672 (1903). There may have been occasional instances of school integration in other parts of the city as well. For example, after his mother petitioned the school board, Langston Hughes, the black writer, attended first grade in 1908 at Harrison School, which was considered a white school. Faith Berry, *Langston Hughes: Before and Beyond Harlem* (Westpoint, CT, 1983).

39. Plaintiff's Affidavit for Alternative Writ of Mandamus at 1–4, *Reynolds;* Defendant's Return to Alternative Writ of Mandamus at 4–5, *Reynolds;* "Lowman Hill School," *The Topeka Plaindealer,* Feb. 1902.

40. There are conflicting accounts as to the number of black children involved. The plaintiff claimed there were fifty in the district. Plaintiff's Affidavit for Alternative Writ of Mandamus at 2, *Reynolds.* According to the defendants, there were about thirty-four black children enrolled in the two-room school, a larger number of black children than had ever been enrolled in the Lowman Hill district. Defendants' Return to Alternative Writ of Mandamus at 5, *Reynolds.* The difference may

be due to a boycott of the segregated school by black parents. "That School Question," *The Topeka Plaindealer,* Feb. 1902.

41. Ibid., quoting a letter to the *Topeka Daily Capital.*

42. Ibid.

43. "The Lowman Hill School," *The Topeka Plaindealer,* Feb. 1902.

44. Ibid.

45. Ibid.

46. 163 U.S. 537 (1896).

47. Reynolds v. Bd. of Educ. of the City of Topeka, 66 Kan. 672 (1903). See discussion supra at . . . [347–48].

48. As the city's school system expanded in the early decades of the twentieth century, it maintained a limited number of black schools, so that many black children had to travel some distance to attend school. In 1930, Wilhelmina Wright sued the Topeka school board, claiming that the distance she had to travel to get to school constituted unequal treatment in violation of the *Plessy* standard. Wright lived a few blocks from Randolph School for whites, but was assigned to Buchanan School twenty blocks away. She claimed that her assignment to Buchanan was unreasonable due to the distance and the number of busy intersections she would have to cross. Wright did not argue that the facilities at the schools were unequal. Wright v. Bd. of Educ. of the City of Topeka, 129 Kan. 852 (1930). In a brief opinion, the court noted that, as a city of the first class, Topeka had maintained segregated schools for many years in accordance with state law. The city provided the plaintiff with bus transportation to and from Buchanan School, and the plaintiff did not allege that the transportation was inadequate. Consequently, the court held that Wright's assignment to Buchanan was not unreasonable. 128 Kan. at 853. Here and in other unequal treatment cases the Kansas Court did not compare the school board's treatment of whites with their treatment of blacks to determine whether the treatment of blacks was unequal. The sole question was whether the board's action regarding blacks, in isolation, was unreasonable. See Williams v. Bd. of Educ. of the City of Parsons [I], 79 Kan. 202 (1908); Williams v. Bd. of Educ. of the City of Parsons [II], 81 Kan. 593 (1910).

49. Topeka's first junior high school was established in 1914 or 1915. Plaintiff's Brief at 6 Graham v. Bd. of Educ., 153 Kan. 840 (1941).

50. See discussion at note . . . [31], supra.

51. 153 Kan. 840 (1941). See note . . . [30] supra, for a discussion of the ruling.

52. Christopher A. McElgunn, "Graham v. Board of Education of Topeka: A Hobson's Choice" (1984) (unpublished paper, Washburn Univ. Law School) 20–21. Three of the teachers whose jobs were affected had some connection to the *Graham* litigation.

53. Kluger, supra note 16 at 379–83.

54. Ibid. at 381.

55. Isabell Masters, *The Life and Legacy of Oliver Brown* (Ph.D. diss., U. of Okla.,

1981), 31. Masters's dissertation overstates the importance of Oliver Brown's role in *Brown*. She presents some interesting information, however, including her own recollections from her experience as a black student at Topeka High and as a resident of Topeka during the 1930s and 40s.

56. Kluger, supra note . . . [16] at 382.

57. Samuel C. Jackson, quoted in Kluger, ibid.

58. Ibid. at 382; Topeka High School, *The 1947 Sunflower* (1947) 54, 56, 69 (school yearbook); Masters, supra note . . . [55] at 31.

59. Julia Etta Parks, *The Development of All-Black Basketball Teams in Topeka High School, 1929–1949* (1982); Kluger, supra note . . . [16] at 382.

60. Topeka Bd. of Educ. Minutes, Sept. 26, 1949.

61. Kluger, supra note . . . [16] at 372.

62. 1935 Kan. Gen. Stat. 21-2424. Kansas law provided civil and criminal penalties against any person making "any distinction on account of race, color, or previous condition of servitude" in the operation of a public accommodation licensed by a municipality. 1935 Kan. Gen. Stat. 21-2424.

To circumvent the law, Topeka repealed its city ordinance which required the licensing of theaters and opera houses in the fall of 1947. Shortly thereafter, two black Topekans were refused admission to a Topeka theater. As they could not sue the theater owners for discrimination in what was now an unlicensed private business, they brought suit against the City of Topeka, challenging its authority to repeal its licensing requirement. Stovall v. City of Topeka, 166 Kan. 35 (1948). The Kansas Supreme Court found that the "[a]ppellants had no vested rights in the continued existence of the licensing ordinance and the city was at liberty to repeal it whenever it so desired." 166 Kan. at 36.

63. Kluger, supra note . . . [16] at 374–75.

64. See ibid. at 377, 408; Transcript of Record at 81–109, Brown v. Bd. of Educ., 347 U.S. 483 (1954).

65. Brown v. Bd. of Educ., 98 F. Supp. 797 (D. Kan. 1951). . . .

66. Brown v. Bd of Educ., 98 F. Supp. 797, 800 (D. Kan. 1951); Transcript of Record at 245–46, Brown v. Bd. of Educ. 347 U.S. 483 (1954).

67. See Brown v. Bd. of Educ., 347 U.S. 483, 486–88 n. 1 (1954). A fifth case, from the state of Delaware, would later be included. Ibid.

68. H. H. Robinson, Superintendent, Augusta Public Schools, letter to Kan. Governor Edward Arn. Dec. 10, 1953, Kan. State Historical Society, Archives Dept., Governor Arn's Papers, Box 62.

69. Ibid.

70. I recognize that the use of a term like "the white community" reifies a group of individual human beings who, in fact, held a variety of views, some of which might conflict with my characterization of dominant white ideology in Topeka during this period. I do not intend to infer that all of white Topeka shared an identical consciousness. Similarly, in referring to "the black community," I do not intend

to downplay the variety of perspectives Topeka blacks held. Rather, I use such terms as shorthand to refer to those who have made their voices heard in the sources I have used. Given my sources, primarily school board minutes, newspaper accounts and court records, those whose ideas are represented are largely elites who were active in the city's political life.

71. "Anti-Segregation Decisions," *Topeka Daily Capital*, June 8, 1950. The cases that Talmadge was concerned with were Sweatt v. Painter, 339 U.S. 629 (1950), and McLaurin v. Oklahoma, U.S. 637 (1950). . . .

72. "Anti-Segregation Decisions," *Topeka Daily Capital*, June 8, 1950.

73. Ibid.

74. Ibid.

75. See, e.g., "School Executives into Second Day of Conference," *Topeka Daily Capital*, Feb. 3, 1950, at 6; "Aim at Flag Hanging in Every School," *Topeka Daily Capital*, March 7, 1950, at 1; "Teachers Face Tough Tests," *Topeka Daily Capital*, April 13, 1950, at 1. The black newspaper, *The Plaindealer*, had moved from Topeka to Kansas City, Kansas, by this time. It would occasionally report on matters concerning the Topeka schools when something particularly significant happened. See *The Plaindealer*, April 1953.

76. See "Colored P.-T.A. Board to Meet," *Topeka Daily Capital*, Nov. 3, 1950, at 21; "Honors Today from Colored P.-T.A.'s," *Topeka Daily Capital*, May 7, 1950, at 6C. When Oliver Brown attempted to enroll his daughter Linda in a white school, the incident was mentioned briefly in a routine story on the opening of the 1950–51 school year. The article appeared on page twelve next to the movie advertisements. "Schools Get Down to Work Today," *Topeka Daily Capital*, Sept. 12, 1950, at 12.

77. "New Step to End School Segregation," *Topeka Daily Capital*, June 15, 1950.

78. Ibid.

79. *Topeka Daily Capital*, supra note 72.

80. *Topeka Daily Capital*, supra note 77.

81. "Segregation Suit to Make History," *Topeka Daily Capital*, November 30, 1952. The vote was apparently taken during the summer of 1951.

82. Ibid.

83. Brown v. Bd. of Educ., 344 U.S. 1 (1952).

84. Paul Wilson, "Speech on *Brown v. Board of Education*, May 1, 1981," 30 *Kansas Law Review* 15, 21 (1981).

85. Brown v. Bd. of Educ., 344 U.S. 141, 142 (1952).

86. "Segregation Suit to Make History," *Topeka Daily Capital*, Nov. 30, 1952.

87. "State to Defend School Statute on Segregation," *Topeka Daily Capital*, Dec. 5, 1952.

88. At that point Wichita and Pittsburg, Kansas, had already "desegregated" their schools. Pittsburg closed its black school for financial reasons in 1950, firing its three black teachers and integrating black students into its white schools. Wichita went from a race-based to a residence-based attendance system. However, the

school board drew attendance boundaries in such a way that the black schools remained all black and the white schools remained predominately or exclusively white. Because it retained substantial school segregation, Wichita did not fire any of its twenty-six black teachers. "Future of State's Negro Teachers Found Uncertain," *Topeka Journal,* Jan. 14, 1954; "Calm At School Ruling," *Kansas City Times,* May 18, 1954.

89. "State to Defend School Statute on Segregation," *Topeka Daily Capital,* Nov. 30, 1952.

90. Wilson, supra note 84 at 20, 22–23.

91. Marlin Casey, Statement Presented to the Board of Education, Topeka Bd. of Educ. Minutes, Oct. 6, 1952.

92. "Negro Teacher Purge Begins in Kansas," *Topeka Daily Capital,* April 6, 1953.

93. Wendell Gordon, letter to unidentified black teacher, reprinted in *The Plaindealer,* Apr. 1953.

94. Ibid.

95. "Board Rejects Bid to Rehire Negroes Here," *Topeka Daily Capital,* April 21, 1953.

96. Topeka Bd. of Educ. Minutes, Apr. 20, 1953.

97. "Firing Negro Teachers to Be Contested," *Topeka Daily Capital,* April 7, 1953.

98. "Board Rejects Bid to Rehire Negroes Here," *Topeka Daily Capital,* April 21, 1953.

99. Brown v. Bd. of Educ., 345 U.S. 972 (1953). Reargument was scheduled following the death of Supreme Court Chief Justice Fred Vinson. Kluger, supra note . . . [16] at 656.

100. "Segregation Decision Reaction Is Mixed," *Topeka Daily Capital,* June 9, 1953; "School Board Rehires Negro Teachers," *Topeka Daily Capital,* June 16, 1953; Topeka Bd. of Educ. Minutes, June 15, 1953.

101. "Segregation Decision Reaction Is Mixed," *Topeka Daily Capital,* June 9, 1953.

102. Unfortunately neither the newspapers nor the school board minutes disclose Neiswanger's first name.

103. The school board election in the spring of 1953 was very quiet on the segregation issue, at least according to the coverage provided in the *Topeka Daily Capital.* The newspaper's stories portrayed a bland campaign focusing on the candidates' records of community service, and ignoring the problems that the *Brown* case might create for the new board. See, e.g., "Mrs. Shiner in School Board Race," *Topeka Daily Capital,* Feb. 1, 1953, at 1; "Sheetz Enters School Race," *Topeka Daily Capital,* Feb. 12, 1953.

104. The only school bus transportation provided in Topeka was for the purpose of bussing black students to segregated schools.

105. Topeka Bd. of Educ. Minutes, Sept. 3, 1953.

106. "School Board Votes End to Topeka Segregation," *Topeka Daily Capital,* Sept. 4, 1953.

107. Ibid.

108. Ibid.

109. Topeka Bd. of Educ. Minutes, Sept. 8, 1953. See also, "Segregation Is Terminated at Randolph and Southwest," *Topeka Journal,* Sept. 9, 1953.

110. Topeka Bd. of Educ. Minutes, Sept. 8, 1953.

111. "Segregation Is Terminated at Randolph and Southwest," *Topeka Journal,* Sept. 9, 1953.

112. Ibid.

113. Topeka Bd. of Educ. Minutes, Jan. 20, 1954.

114. Ibid.

115. "Segregation Ended in Twelve More Elementary Schools Here," *Topeka Journal,* Jan. 21, 1954.

116. "'Gradual' Segregation End Sought," *Topeka Daily Capital,* Nov. 19, 1953.

117. "In Court Paradox," *Kansas City Star,* Nov. 29, 1953.

118. 347 U.S. 483 (1954).

119. Ibid. at 492. The Kansas case was the only case where the lower court had found "substantial equality." Ibid. at 492 n. 9.

120. Ibid. at 493.

121. Ibid. at 494–95.

122. Ibid. at 495–96.

123. "Segregation Already Ending Here, Say School Officials," *Topeka Journal,* May 17, 1954.

124. "Negroes Mark Court Victory Tuesday Night," *Topeka Journal,* May 17, 1954.

125. Topeka Bd. of Educ. Minutes, Feb. 7, 1955. In 1987, the district court found that "[t]he boundaries set around the former *de jure* black elementary schools after this case was remanded by the Supreme Court appear to have perpetuated the racial identity of those schools." Brown v. Bd. of Educ., No. T-316, slip op. at 23 (D. Kan. April 8, 1987). See supra note . . . [11].

126. Ibid.

127. "Board Takes Third Step in Integration," *Topeka Daily Capital,* Feb. 8, 1955; Casey, supra note . . . [91].

128. "High Court Told State Complying," *Topeka Daily Capital,* April 12, 1955.

129. Harold Fatzer, et al., letter to Harold B. Willey, Clerk of the U.S. Supreme Court, May 10, 1955. Kan. State Historical Society, Records of the Attorney General, File 851. "Brown—Segregation."

130. Ibid.

131. Brown v. Bd. of Educ. [II], 349 U.S. 294 (1955).

132. Ibid. at 299–301.

133. See Francis M. Wilhoit, *The Politics of Massive Resistance* (New York, 1973).

134. 349 U.S. at 299.

135. "Segregation Brief Filed," *Topeka Daily Capital*, Oct. 21, 1955.

136. Defendant's Memorandum Brief on Plaintiff's Motion for Formulation of a Decree and Judgment at 3. Brown v. Bd. of Educ., 139 F. Supp. 469 (D. Kan. 1955) [hereinafter cited as Defendant's Memorandum].

137. Ibid. at 5.

138. "Segregation Brief Filed," *Topeka Daily Capital*, Oct. 21, 1955.

139. Defendant's Memorandum, supra note . . . [136] at 6–7.

140. Memorandum in Support of Plaintiffs' Claim That Defendants Have Failed to Meet Their Obligations Under the Supreme Court's Ruling at 5, *Brown v. Bd. of Educ.*, 139 F. Supp. 468 (D. Kan. 1955).

141. Brown v. Bd. of Educ., 139 F. Supp. 468, 469–70 (D. Kan. 1955).

142. Ibid. at 470.

143. Ibid. On April 8, 1987, the district court found that the case had finally "reached an appropriate denouement," and held that the school district was not responsible for the continuing racial imbalance in the schools, Brown v. Bd. of Educ., No. T-316, slip op. at 50 (D. Kan. April 8, 1897). See supra note . . . [11].

144. The "traditional exceptions" were as follows:

   1. A kindergarten or first grade child whose parents reside in Topeka and are both employed, may be granted permission to attend the kindergarten or first grade located in the district in which the adult who cares for the child during the day resides.

   2. A child whose parents move into a different elementary school attendance district during the school year, may finish the year in the school he has been attending.

   3. A child who has finished the fifth grade in an elementary school, and whose parents move into a different Topeka school attendance district, may attend the sixth grade of the school he attended in the fifth grade.

   4. A crippled child may be given permission to attend an elementary school which is suitable in view of the nature of his handicap.

   5. Pupils who are eligible for any phase of our special educational program which is not housed in the school district in which they reside may be asked to attend the school which does house that particular part of our program which meets the needs of those particular individuals.

Topeka Bd. of Educ. Minutes, Dec. 21, 1955.

145. Ibid.

146. Ibid.

147. Topeka Bd. of Educ. Minutes, Jan. 18, 1956.

148. Ibid.

149. The school board claimed segregation would be fully terminated in five years, while the NAACP claimed it would take seven years. Compare "City School Segregation Nears End," *Topeka Daily Capital*, Dec. 22, 1955 (school board view), with Topeka Bd. of Educ. Minutes. Jan. 18, 1956 (NAACP view). It would actually

take five and one-half years for those first graders exercising an attendance option in the 1955–56 school year to matriculate out of the elementary schools and into junior high schools.

150. "City School Segregation Nears End," *Topeka Daily Capital*, Dec. 22, 1955.

151. See, e.g., Bd. of Educ. Minutes, Dec. 12, 1944; Return to Alternative Writ of Mandamus at 2, Reynolds v. Bd. of Education of the City of Topeka, 66 Kan. 672 (1903).

152. In granting nearly absolute autonomy to the Topeka school board in desegregating its schools, the district court was necessarily leaving room for majority interests to frustrate the enforcement of recognized minority rights. See generally [Jennifer] Hochschild, . . . [*The New American Dilemma: Liberal Democracy and School Deseregation* (New Haven, 1984)]. Hochschild argues that data on school desegregation since *Brown* indicates that "normal democratic politics" do not produce effective desegregation plans because desegregation strategies based upon popular control of the desegregation process tend to favor the white middle-class who, within the constraints of local political processes, tend to be the participants who are more likely to gain power and whose voices are more likely to be heard.

153. See supra note . . . [11].

154. See . . . [Alan Freeman "Legitimizing Racial Discrimination Through Antidiscrimination Law: A Critical Review of Supreme Court Doctrine," 62 *Minnesota Law Review* 1049 (1978) at 370.]

The Effects of Restructuring
on Beefpacking in Kansas

Donald D. Stull and Michael J. Broadway

Since the 1950s America's meatpacking industry has declined both in the number of jobs and in the number of plants (Tables 6 and 7). The biggest declines in employment have been in the eastern half of the United States in such traditional railroad terminal locations as Chicago, New York City, Jersey City, and Philadelphia. Kansas, by contrast, has increased its share of U.S. meatpacking employment, and since the mid-1970s has had a net gain of 3,000 meatpacking jobs (Table 6). Accompanying this growth in employment, the state has also increased its share of cattle slaughtered. In 1965 Kansas accounted for just 4.6 percent of the U.S. slaughter market, but by 1987 it had captured 18.2 percent of the market and become the leading beef producing state (Table 8). Indeed, beefpacking has become the brightest spot in the state's otherwise sagging economic fortunes. In 1987 Kansas beefpackers contributed $5.2 billion in economic output—an enviable example of successful economic development through value adding. Better still, the packers have brought jobs, and lots of them—more than 6,100 have been added in Garden City, Dodge City, and Liberal since 1980 (Austin 1988a).

Table 6. U.S. and Kansas Meatpacking Employment (in Thousands of Jobs)

Year	U.S.	Kansas	Kansas as a % of U.S.
1959	196.526	8.015	4.1
1974	161.882	7.676	4.7
1987	126.125	10.795	8.6

Source: U.S. Bureau of the Census, *County Business Patterns,* 1959, 1974, 1987.

This article explains the growth of beefpacking in Kansas and discusses how packers maximize profits by reducing costs and increasing productivity both at the industry and plant levels. We begin with recent changes in the structure of the U.S. meatpacking industry.

RECENT CHANGES IN MEATPACKING

Over the past 30 years meatpacking has been transformed from an urban to a rural industry. The driving force behind this transformation has been the emergence of three new meatpacking companies. IBP, Excel, and ConAgra Red Meats. The "Big Three" have replaced the old line packers—Swift, Armour, Cudahy, and Wilson—by vigorous cost cutting. Meatpacking is a marginally profitable industry—an average of 81 cents for every $100 of sales in 1986—and for every $100 in sales $93 were eaten up in direct production costs. To survive in this highly competitive industry, let alone expand, packers must increase productivity and reduce operating costs. Large-capacity plants are much more economical than smaller plants: the estimated cost of slaughter is reduced by nearly 50 percent at a plant which operates at 325 head/hour compared with one operating at 25 head/hour (Miller 1986). As a result, the number of large-capacity plants has increased since the mid-1970s, while the smaller plants are rapidly disappearing (Table 7).

The principal strategy of the new packers has been to locate large-capacity plants in rural areas close to feedlots in right-to-work states (Skaggs 1986). Live animals deteriorate in value through shrinkage, bruising, and crippling while being shipped long distances. Cattle lose 1.7 percent of their weight when in transit for only an hour; on a three-hour journey they lose 5 percent (Smalley 1978). Shipping costs have been reduced by removing the fat and bone at the plant and trucking out boxed beef rather than hanging sides, enabling the new packing

Table 7. U.S. and Kansas Meatpacking by Size of Plant

Year		1–19	20–49	50–99	100–249	250–499	500–999	>1,000	Total
		Size of Plant (Number of Employees)							
1959	U.S.	1,633	454	211	165	77	78*		2,618
	Kansas	41	6	2	7	—	5*		61
1974	U.S.	1,447	335	207	162	82	38	24	2,295
	Kansas	35	6	5	6	—	6	1	59
1987	U.S.	979	230	118	117	54	26	31	1,555
	Kansas	25	3	3	1	2	1	5	40

*These figures include plants employing 1,000 or more workers.
Source: U.S. Bureau of the Census, *U.S. Summary of County Business Patterns* and *Kansas County Business Patterns, 1959, 1974, 1987.*

companies to locate further away from their major markets. Labor costs have been reduced by avoiding costly union contracts and locating in rural areas where land, labor, and general living costs are cheaper.

IBP has been at the forefront of many of these cost-cutting innovations, and since the company's founding in 1960 it has acquired nearly one-third of the U.S. beef slaughter market (Miller 1990). The company's rural industrialization strategy is exemplified by its recent decision to build a beefpacking plant in Lexington, Nebraska. Lexington has a population of approximately 6,480 persons (1988 est.) and is situated in Dawson County, 225 miles west of Omaha on Interstate 80. Dawson County has one of the largest feedlot capacities in Nebraska and lies atop the Ogallala Aquifer, which will provide a plentiful supply of water to the plant when it opens in the fall of 1990. And the local Council for Economic Development (1990) proudly boasts of "no strikes, work stoppages or labor disputes . . . ever!"

BEEFPACKING IN KANSAS

The structural changes at the national level are also found in Kansas. Between 1959 and 1987 the number of meatpacking plants in the state fell from 61 to 40 (Table 7). Most of this decline occurred in the urbanized counties of Sedgwick (Wichita) and Wyandotte (Kansas City).

Table 8. Kansas Cattle Slaughtered, 1965–87

Year	Number	Kansas as a % of U.S.
1965*	1,447,000	4.6
1970*	2,014,000	5.7
1975	2,684,000	7.3
1980	2,900,000	9.1
1985	6,081,000	17.6
1987	6,179,000	18.2

*Figures include total commercial slaughter; federally inspected plant data were not published separately.
Source: *Annual Livestock Slaughter,* U.S. Department of Agriculture, 1965–1987.

In 1959 Wyandotte County contained 11 plants, by 1987 none remained; of the 5 plants operating in Sedgwick County in 1959 only 2 were left in 1987 (U.S. Bureau of the Census 1959, 1987). Urban packing plants have been replaced by large-capacity plants in small towns. In 1969, IBP opened a plant in Emporia (Lyon County); since then four large plants have been built in southwest Kansas (Table 9).

IBP began slaughtering cattle at its Finney County plant in December 1980, and by the following June it was processing carcasses as well; in the spring of 1982 the company added a second or "B" shift to become fully operational (long-time IBP employee 6/7/89). In 1983, Val-Agri, Inc. purchased Garden City's idle Kansas Beef Processors plant and more than doubled its capacity. This plant was later sold to Swift Independent Packing Company and is now owned by Monfort, a division of ConAgra Red Meats Companies and the nation's second largest beefpacker. Today these two packing plants employ approximately 4,000 workers and slaughter and process up to 8,400 head per day, six days a week— their total reached 2,400,000 cattle in 1987 (Laudert 1988).

The packers were attracted to southwest Kansas by a variety of factors, including plentiful water and cattle, and a low level of unionization. The introduction of center-pivot irrigation systems in the mid-1960s let local farmers draw upon the vast underground reserves in the Ogallala Aquifer and cultivate a variety of feed grains. Between 1964 and 1969 irrigated land in Finney and surrounding counties increased by over 175,000 acres. Sorghum production grew by over 90 million bushels or 63 percent, compared with a 1 percent increase for the state as a whole. The widespread availability of both water and feed led in turn to the introduction of feedyards. In 1964 there were 196,000 cattle fattened on grain in nine counties in southwest Kansas; five years later the number was 506,000 (U.S. Bureau of the Census 1969). This number has continued to increase (Table 10), and by the mid-1970s southwest Kansas was exporting its surplus cattle (Ingrassia 1980).

Packing plants need a plentiful and steady supply of cattle. Because southwest Kansas has become a major cattle feeding center, local packing plants are able to obtain their cattle from feedyards within a 150-mile radius. Modern plants also require an abundant water supply: 400–450 gallons for each cattle slaughtered. The availability of water from the Ogallala Aquifer was critical in IBP's decision to build the world's largest beefpacking plant (1990 capacity of 6,000 head/day) in Finney County rather than Lamar, Colorado.

Kansas's status as a right-to-work state and the lower costs associated with operating plants in rural areas were also important to packers. At the local level, incentives were frequently used to attract the packers. In the case of IBP's plant at Holcomb, the Finney County Commissioners provided the company with $3.5 million in property tax relief for 10 years and helped finance the construction of the plant with $100 million in industrial revenue bonds.

Kansas has benefited from structural changes in the meatpacking industry. Nationally, meatpacking has been transformed from an urban to a rural industry, reflecting the cost-cutting strategies of the new packers, who wish to avoid the high costs of operating in an urban environment with a unionized labor force. Instead, the new packers try to minimize the distance cattle travel to plants, and they avoid costly union contracts. Southwest Kansas provides large feedlots, a plentiful water supply, and a low level of unionization, but it does not offer a traditional attraction for a large manufacturing plant—an available labor force. The absence of sufficient labor meant that many workers would have to move into the region for the plants to operate.

Packinghouse recruiters ranged far and wide—Birmingham, Alabama; San Antonio, Texas; Las Vegas, New Mexico—wherever there were pools of unskilled, unemployed labor. Packinghouses paid well by regional standards, starting at between $6.00 and $6.40 an hour for production workers and climbing as high as $9.58 an hour. Few previous skills—not even a command of English—are required. The "push"

Table 9. Location, Date of Construction, Capacity, and Ownership
of Meatpacking Plants Employing More Than 1,000 Workers, 1987

Town	Date	Ownership	Employees	Maximum slaughter capacity
Emporia	1969	IBP	1,800	3,255
Liberal	1969	National	2,400	4,000
Dodge City	1980	Excel	1,600	4,800
Holcomb	1980	IBP	2,600	5,200
Garden City	1983	Monfort	1,100	3,500

Source: Wichita Eagle Beacon, "Our Beef Boom: What's at Stake," Sept. 11, 1988,
and IBP Common Stock Prospectus.

of a sustained recession and the "pull" of an expanding industry soon
made Garden City the fastest growing community in Kansas. From
1980 to 1985 it grew by an estimated 6,000 people, or 33 percent! The
majority of newcomers were Southeast Asian refugees and Latinos,
many from Mexico.

METHODOLOGY

To understand how these structural changes affected workers in the
plants, we investigated work in the packinghouses as part of a two-year
research project, funded by the Ford Foundation, on the relations between newcomers and established residents in Garden City. Broadway
collected data on macro-level changes in the meatpacking industry;
Stull conducted ethnographic research on work and interethnic relations in packing plants and feedyards. Monfort and IBP declined an invitation to participate in the study, thus forcing a reliance on indirect
methods of data collection. Stull conducted formal interviews with a
cross-section of packinghouse line workers and supervisors, with feed-
yard managers, and others familiar with meatpacking and cattle feeding. He took every opportunity to go on tours of the plants; enrolled in
a meat and carcass evaluation class at the community college to learn
about the industry, make contacts, and gain regular entry to "the
cooler" where carcasses are graded; assisted his meats instructor on several occasions in tagging cattle on the killfloor; regularly attended
workers compensation hearings; and spent many hours as a patron and
sometimes bartender at one of the packinghouse workers' favorite bars.

Table 10. Cattle Fattened on Grain and Concentrates in Southwest Kansas, 1964, 1974, 1987

County	1964	1974	1987
Finney	47,826	174,366	455,331
Ford	59,482	89,605	294,269
Grant	4,940	31,611	*
Gray	13,404	102,446	259,636
Haskell	9,049	163,487	302,285
Hodgeman	16,796	62,444	89,787
Kearny	2,805	105,052	118,113
Scott	37,273	102,710	309,059
Wichita	4,776	103,333	277,148
Total	196,351	935,065	2,413,426**
% of State	15.0	35.0	53.0**

*Data withheld to avoid identifying individual farms.
**Estimate based on Grant County's missing data. Grant County estimate based on the number of cattle sold.
Source: U.S. Bureau of the Census, *Census of Agriculture, Kansas, 1964, 1974, 1987.*

"GETTING IT OUT THE DOOR"

Productivity, in the eyes of management, means "getting it out the door." Production quotas, driven by daily fluctuations in the fat-cattle and boxed-beef markets, appear to take precedence over other considerations, including safety:

The people that are actually overseeing and running the operations: they quote safety, they push safety, and safety is nice until it comes down to a point of whether they're getting a product out the door. And at that point in time, sometimes they kind of drop the safety thing and get the product out the door (maintenance worker 5/9/89).

Productivity is measured by "chain speed"—the number of carcasses processed in an hour. Chain speed is regulated by management—they can speed it up or slow it down. This frustrates workers who often sacrifice safety and quality to keep up. But they must keep pace, and do the job right, or face reprimand, even termination:

. . . so far I have never heard anybody complaining. I just know I don't have time to sweep my sweat from my face, but I haven't heard anybody complaining about how fast it's going. We know it is going fast, and they want to still go faster. But . . . [we] just take it . . . a good way to slow it down would be to do a bad job . . . but then they catch you, they watch you, and you can get written up for that, they take you to the office, and three times, they [fire you] (slaughter worker 6/4/89).

The packers have successfully increased productivity—21 percent from 1980 to 1986 (Austin 1988c). They are able to get more out of each worker in part through technological innovations which allow machines to do more of the work. But more importantly, by "speeding up the chain" workers must produce more just to keep up—and to keep their jobs.

CUTTING COSTS

The second strategy open to packers in their pursuit of profits is reducing costs. We have already discussed how restructuring reduces production costs. The packers also cut costs with low wages, minimum benefits, and, critics argue, by high turnover.

Estimated gross annual income for processing line workers at IBP ranges from about $15,500 for a Grade 1 (lowest level) job after one year to about $22,000 for a Grade 7 (highest level) at the end of two years; slaughter workers start at $.30 more per hour. At the nearby unionized Monfort plant, gross income is somewhat less (starting wage is $.40/hour lower, fewer hours are worked, and union dues must be deducted). Many workers, especially those who must support large families, are forced to rely on social service agencies for supplemental food, medical care, and other basic needs. During the winter and spring packing plants cut back on their hours to compensate for the seasonal decline in consumer demand for beef.

In fact, wages in the meatpacking industry have actually declined in recent years. In the 1980s, led by IBP, packers vigorously slashed wages even as they increased production (Skaggs 1986: 204–208). In 1971 wages in meatpacking were 117 percent of those in manufacturing in general; by 1987 they had fallen to 84 percent of the overall manufacturing wage (Stanley 1988: 9).

The packers provide insurance for medical, dental, and eye care, with paid vacations and yearly bonuses, but hourly workers are not eligible for insurance until they have been on the job for between two and six months, depending on the employer. Bonuses are not paid until employees have worked for a full calendar year. Many do not make it that long.

TURNOVER

Turnover is a problem of astounding dimensions throughout the industry. All the beef plants in southwest Kansas report average *monthly* turnover of between 6 percent and 8 percent (Wood 1988: 76); such turnover, 72–96 percent annually, is "low" in beefpacking. Turnover is said to decline, and worker longevity increase, the longer a plant is in operation. At IBP's Finney County plant, touted as the "Cadillac of all packing plants," turnover remains fairly constant at about 7 percent a month, and approximately one-third of its workers have been at the plant for two or more years; when it first opened, and for several years thereafter, turnover reached levels as high as 60 percent a month (Stull fieldnotes 6/17/88: 9; 7/22/88: 9; 5/6/89: 23)!

Packers decry their "turnover problem" but accept it as "part of the business":

> Our turnover rate is probably 7% a month. . . . But we have 1750 hourly employees, so it's still a pretty good number of people that turn over. . . . [T]he work is physical in nature and it's difficult to do, and we do need people with good physical skills to participate in this type employment. . . . [I]t's very tough work as compared to some other industries, even such as the aircraft industries (director of personnel at an area packing plant interviewed by L. Boitano, KANZ Radio 6/12/89).

Turnover in meatpacking, as in any industry, includes workers who do not make probation, those who are fired, and those who quit. Managers and workers alike agree that working on the line is hard—not everyone can "pull their count." To "hang with it" you must soon learn to do your work properly—how to keep your knife sharp, how to make your cuts cleanly—and you must work rapidly:

> [T]hose guys know what they're doing, because if they don't do it right, boy, that gets hard. Any job that you do, if you don't do it right,

389

you get tired in a flash, because that chain is going too fast to keep up with it if you're not doing it right (slaughter worker 6/19/89).

Working conditions are often unpleasant and the work distasteful:

I didn't want to stick around removing pecks because it gets so hot you can see the steam right there, in the gut table. And, I mean, you feel it, that steam. And you just can't stop sweating there, it's just impossible. Your clothes get all wet, all of it, and they have a fan over there right in front of my station where I was working, but when I moved from the night shift into the day shift, it never worked. It never worked. . . . They moved me into that other job, chiseling heads. Now, we had a fan about that close, I mean, really nice. Now it has been a whole week it doesn't work either, and, boy, it gets hot in there, too (slaughter worker, 6/4/89).

Workers must "hang with it"—or quit. It is a tough business and little sympathy is given to those who cannot "pull their count." Strict rules and rigid sanctions govern work on the floor. Probationary employees may be discharged without notice or recourse. Employees are "written up" for being late or absent without an excuse, excessive excused absenses [*sic*], failure to report on-the-job injuries, overstaying lunch or relief breaks, deliberate discourtesy, horseplay, substandard job performance. Workers with four writeups in a calendar year are discharged. More serious offenses bring even quicker termination—malicious mischief which results in property damage or injury, gambling, alcohol or drug use, theft, abusive or threatening language. Fighting, even in the parking lot, results in immediate discharge—with so many knives so close at hand, it cannot be otherwise (National Beef Packing Company n.d.: 14).

Management, from line supervisors to plant managers, wants efficient and compliant employees, workers who will do as they are told:

They want somebody that naturally will work hard. I think everybody looks for someone like that. But they want somebody that will follow—I mean true to the line follow. Whatever they say, you do. And I express that not just in the fact of they tell you to do something, do it. I mean that in terms of they don't want you to think or bring up other ideas or anything or question their ideas or question their methods or anything, they want you to just do. . . .[T]hey want you to work blind. You just do what they tell you to do, and that's all they want. And if you don't, then they try and make it rough for you (maintenance worker 5/9/89).

For hourly workers, the threat of being written up or fired is always there. Supervisors, with production quotas for their crews, are constantly under pressure to "get it out the door." When the chain speeds up, or when the product does not meet the standards of Quality Control, supervisors have little recourse but to push their crews harder. And if a supervisor has it in for a worker, it is not hard to find a reason to "write him up."

Yet, hard work and ambition are rewarded. Packers look first within their own ranks to fill supervisory positions:

Q: How exactly did you get to be a supervisor?
A: Hard work. I worked my [tail] off out there and I was there every day, on time, and I had a lot of initiative there. I learned jobs that I really wasn't required to know. I just kind of took the initiative to learn them, and my superiors recognized that and promoted me (former material handling supervisor 5/29/89).

Industry critics and many workers say that high turnover benefits the packers, and they encourage it:

What you get in this business . . . is that because they make so much money on turnover, you don't really [care] about the employee except to manipulate him. That's it. So you don't spend any money on supervisory training that teaches human relations. You spend as few dollars as you can on that aspect of the business. And so most of the supervisory people that you see come out of the gang. That's where they got their experience. That's where they learned how to be a boss, by watching what the boss did. If you don't train him and change him, they're not going to be any different. So that's what you have. You have an inbred industry, with very few innovative thinkers. . . .

Q: [A]t the mid-level or the lower-level management it would seem in your best interest to keep your people, to get a good workforce and keep those people around.
A: But the lower-level management doesn't control the fringes and the wages or the outcome.

Q: [D]o you think it pays the packer to turn over the workforce rapidly?

A: It must or he wouldn't do it. . . .The tradeoff there is that the packer is paying a tremendously high cost in workman's compensation claims. So you take his workman's comp claim experience and add that to lost product and slower chain speed if he suffers that, or damaged product by inexperienced people. I mean, once you damage a cut of meat it's damaged, you can't hide it. I think the packer would be better off to work more toward a stable workforce, but then of course you get into the problem of the higher wages (respondent with wide industry experience 3/30/89).

Industry executives deny such charges:

I've heard the old song that high turnover benefited packers because . . . people didn't stay long enough to where they had two weeks vacation, etc. If there was that thought 10 years ago, there sure . . . isn't now. Surely now, particularly as labor is getting harder to find, I don't think anyone thinks they benefit from high turnover. . . . [But] I think the tendency is for most employees, even those that don't mind their job, to feel this is an 8- or 10-year job. Then they'll move on. . . . So that's part of what we get to deal with, you know (meatpacking executive 4/29/80).

SAFETY

At the heart of the turnover debate is worker safety. Meatpacking has always been a dangerous business. Today's workers wear hardhats, earplugs, stainless steel mesh gloves, plastic wrist guards, chainmail aprons and chaps, leather weight-lifting belts, and/or baseball-catcher's shin guards to reduce the ever-prevent risk of injury. But meatpacking remains America's most hazardous industry, with an annual injury rate of 33.4 per 100 workers (U.S. Bureau of Labor Statistics 1988). It is also the most dangerous industry in Kansas. From 1980 to 1988, 17,000 Kansas meatpacking workers were injured on the job—more than one-third lost work time—8 died. One-third of these injuries involved cuts and punctures; almost one-quarter were due to carpal tunnel syndrome or cumulative trauma disorder.

392

Record OSHA fines for underreporting injuries and unsafe practices, coupled with declines in their labor pool, have forced packers to pay more attention to safety. Ergonomists try to improve equipment and tool design, new workers receive training and conditioning to protect them from injury, supervisors are held accountable for accidents on their crews, and incentives are offered for reducing accidents.

But "getting it out the door" is still the order of the day. Packers readily admit that injuries cost them money—but the cost is a minor, acceptable one. Industrywide, payment for workers compensation benefits, insurance, and hospitalization averaged $1.47 per $100 of sales in 1986 (Austin 1988d).

CONCLUSION

In less than a decade beefpacking became a major manufacturing industry in Kansas, pointing the way to economic growth in food products through value adding. Packing plants have infused the economy of southwest Kansas. Eight thousand meatpacking workers in Garden City, Liberal, and Dodge City earn more than $118 million a year, one-third of the wages in Finney, Seward, and Ford counties. Each of their dollars adds another $1.30 in wages to local economies. Packers have invested more than $1 billion in buildings and equipment in southwest Kansas (Austin 1988c). They buy thousands of cattle from area feedyards each day, and each year they spend millions in Kansas on transportation, boxes, utilities, business and banking services.

State and local officials have tried hard to attract the packers and to accommodate them once they arrived. Kansas does not restrict corporate ownership of cattle operations as it does for hogs and poultry. The 1988 legislature chose not to tax industrial cleaning businesses to satisfy packers trying to hold down costs. They also revised the workers compensation law to reduce payments for carpal tunnel syndrome and other industrial injuries (Austin 1988a). The packinghouse towns in southwest Kansas have approved more than $200 million in bond issues, tax abatements, and improved services. State and local governments have paid for road expansions to accommodate the hundreds of trucks that haul cattle and boxed beef in and out of these plants every day (Austin 1988a).

Clearly the beef industry is very important to Kansas. Beefpacking has created new jobs and added value to Kansas's traditional agricultural output. But such development has social and economic costs which must be paid. The new jobs are low paying and dangerous. The opening of new plants brings not only rapid growth but continued high mobility from worker turnover.

State and local governments are willing to subsidize the construction of beef plants through tax abatements and bond issues. However, they often fail to consider, and the public generally resents, the increased and continual burden such industries and their workers place on infrastructure, and on social, medical, and educational services.

The rise of the beefpacking industry in Kansas clearly shows that development is more than annual outputs, new jobs, and multiplier effects. It is change—and change is more complicated than economic forecasters and community boosters are often willing to admit. Those who plot the state's economic course must begin to consider not only the benefits of economic development, but also its costs—not just what must be given away to attract new industry, but more importantly what that industry will cost the people of the state and local communities after it arrives. In a subsequent issue of the *KBR* we look more closely at the social and economic consequences of the rural industrialization beefpacking has brought to Garden City, Kansas.

REFERENCES

Austin, L. "Rich Potential for Kansas Carries Risk." *Wichita Eagle-Beacon,* 11 Sept. 1988a.
Austin, L. "Packers Put Everything But the Moo Up for Sale." *Wichita Eagle-Beacon,* 12 Sept. 1988b.
Austin, L. "Riskiest Job in Kansas Escapes Close Scrutiny." *Wichita Eagle-Beacon,* 4 Dec. 1988c.
Austin, L. "Fines Push Packers to Forefront of Worker Safety." *Wichita Eagle-Beacon,* 11 Dec. 1988d.
Broadway, M. J. "Recent Changes in the Structure and Location of the U.S. Meatpacking Industry." *Geography,* 75. No. 1 (1990) pp. 76–79.
Council for Economic Development–Greater Lexington Corporation. *Industrial and Business Facts. Lexington, Nebraska.* 1990.
Ingrassia, P. "As Iowa Beef Builds a Huge Kansas Plant, Area Packers Get Set for a Battle for Cattle." *Wall Street Journal,* 17 July 1980.
Laudert, S. B. "Information on Feedlot Capacity, Annual Feed Needs for Fed Cattle, and 1987 Finney County Production." Personal communication to M. Warren, Finney County Museum, 1988. Changing Relation Project files.

Miller, B. "Why the Packer Crunch Will Continue." *Farm Journal.* Beef Extra. June/July, 1986.

Miller B. "End of the Trail: Packer Concentration and Vertical Integration Could Drive Cattlemen Out of Business." *Farm Journal,* April (1990), pp. 22–24.

National Beef Packing Company. *Employee Policy Manual,* n.d.

Skaggs, J. M. *Prime Cut: Livestock Raising and Meatpacking in the United States, 1607–1983.* College Station, Texas A&M Press, 1986.

Smalley, H. R. *Guidelines for Establishing Beefpacking Plants in Rural Areas.* Washington, DC: U.S. Dept. of Agriculture, 1978.

Stanley, K. *The Role of Immigrant and Refugee Labor in the Restructuring of the Midwestern Meatpacking Industry.* Binghamton: State University of New York, Department of Sociology, 1988.

U.S. Bureau of the Census. *Census of Agriculture, Volume I. Area Reports. Part 15: Kansas, 1964, 1974, 1987.* Washington, DC: U.S. Government Printing Office.

U.S. Bureau of the Census. *County Business Patterns, Kansas, and U.S. Summary, 1969, 1974, 1987.* Washington, DC: U.S. Government Printing Office.

U.S. Bureau of Labor Statistics. *Occupational Injuries and Illnesses in the United States by Industry.* Washington, DC: U.S. Government Printing Office, 1988.

Wood, A. *The Beef Packing Industry: A Study of Three Communities in Southwestern Kansas: Dodge City, Liberal and Garden City, Kansas. Final Report to the Department of Migrant Education.* Flagstaff, AZ: Wood and Wood Association, 1988.

Contributors

MICHAEL J. BROADWAY is professor of geography at the State University of New York at Geneseo.

JAMES C. CARPER is professor of education at the University of South Carolina.

BILL CECIL-FRONSMAN was professor of history at Washburn University. He died in 1998.

MARY L. DUDZIAK is the Judge Edward J. and Ruey L. Guirado Professor of Law and History at the University of Southern California Law School.

THOMAS FRANK is the editor of *Baffler* magazine.

MICHAEL GOLDBERG is professor of interdisciplinary arts and sciences at the University of Washington.

JOSEPH B. HERRING is an archivist at the National Archives and Records Administration in Washington DC.

ANGEL KWOLEK-FOLLAND is director of the Center for Women's Studies and Gender Research and professor of history at the University of Florida.

RITA NAPIER is professor of American history at the University of Kansas.

ROBERT OPPENHEIMER was professor of history at the University of Kansas. He died in 1988.

ANN SCHOFIELD is professor of women's studies and courtesy professor of history at the University of Kansas.

RICHARD SHERIDAN was professor of history at the University of Kansas. He died in 2002.

CARON SMITH studied at the University of Kansas and now lives in England.

DONALD D. STULL is professor of anthropology at the University of Kansas.

PAUL SUTTER is professor of history at the University of Georgia.

ELEANOR TURK is professor of history at Indiana University.

ELLIOTT WEST is Distinguished Professor of History at the University of Arkansas.

RICHARD WHITE is the Margaret Byrne Professor of American History at Stanford University.

DONALD WORSTER is Distinguished Professor of History at the University of Kansas.

Index

Abbott, James B., 160
Abbott, Nelson, 191
Abolitionists, 104, 107, 112, 140, 143, 144, 150, 160, 166, 175; attack on, 151–52, 154n13
Acculturation, 42, 44, 272, 277, 293
Adaptation, 3, 4, 7; to bison, 6; to horses, 5, 6, 43, 66–68, 70
African Americans, 1, 2, 52; attacks on, 271; Bleeding Kansas and, 25; as cowboys, 9; diversity and, 21; education and, 137, 181–87, 193, 195, 348–52, 354, 370n12; equal rights and, 136, 190; exodus of, 20; segregation and, 26; self-reliance/industriousness of, 195; vote for, 24
Afro-American Advocate, 194, 226n50
Agrarian movement, 193, 251
Agricultural Census, 261
Agriculture: automobiles and, 265; capitalistic, 330; commercial, 10–11, 245n11; culture and, 319; development of, 14–15; entrepreneurs and, 327–28; labor shortages for, 273–74; Mexicans and, 276, 283–84; Native American, 4, 52, 63, 64; pioneering and, 321; railroads and, 229, 267; subsidies for, 17; women and, 334, 335, 341, 342
Alien Industrial Slavery Law, 309
Allen, Forest C. "Phog," 26
Allen, Governor, 310
Allis, Samuel, 68
Allotment, 92, 94; resistance to, 97, 98, 99
American Automobile Association, 260, 265
American Citizen, Scott in, 185
Americanization, 272, 286, 310, 316n41

Anderson, R. C., 171
Anthony, Daniel R., 171
Anthony, George T., 183, 184
Anthony, Susan B., 203, 215; politics and, 223n8; Republicans and, 213–14, 217, 218
Anti-fusionists, 214, 218
Antislavery groups, 136, 143, 147, 160, 170
Apaches, 67
Appeal to Reason, 305, 307, 309
Arena, The, 240, 241
Argentine barrio, 281, 282, 286, 288
Argentine shop, strike at, 283
Argersinger, Peter H., 220, 237
Arkansas River: Cheyennes at, 51; irrigation/industrial use of, 14; Mexicans at, 284, 291
Arma mining camp, 304, 305, 306
Armour, 274, 289, 382
Armstrong, William, 330
Army Corps of Engineers, 17
Arn, Edward, 353
Arteaga, Beatrice, 288
Ashley, William, 69
Assimilation, 27, 44, 87, 194, 272
Associational rights, 345, 369
Atchison: blacks in, 166, 170; Free-State cause and, 110; Germans in, 29, 45, 105, 114n5; slavery issue and, 107–8
Atchison, David Rice, 142, 152
Atchison Champion, 188
Atchison County, Germans in, 103, 111–12
Atchison Patriot, 191, 192
Atchison, Topeka, and Santa Fe Railroad: criticism of, 149–50; Good Roads Train of, 264; surplus lands and, 92

Welsh, 29, 304
Weltfish, Gene, 5, 69
West, Elliott, 21, 22, 42, 271
West, Fanny, 191
Western Historical Quarterly, 8
Westward Expansion (Billington), 18
Wetlands, 14
"What's the Matter with Kansas?" (White), 249
Wheat, 324, 325
White, Richard, 7, 10, 13, 15; on Pawnees, 4–5, 42–43; on suffrage/West, 223n5
White, William Allen, 249, 250, 254
Whitehead, Mortimer, 259
White population, 375n70; growth of, 166(table)
Whitney, Ella, 129, 130
Wichita: desegregation in, 376n88; meatpacking in, 383; Mexicans in, 277, 282
Wichita Eagle-Beacon, on Mexicans/education, 288
Wickard, Claude R., 336
Wik, Reynold, 265
Wilder, D. W., 183, 186
Willard, Frances, 204
Williams, Al F., 311
Willing, Mrs., 121–22
Wilmarth, L. C., 349
Wilson, Julie, 8, 14, 28
Wilson, Mrs., 308
Wilson, Paul, 356, 382
Wimler, Fannie, 309
Winter, Jacob, 188, 189
Winthrop, John, 47
Wise, Henry A., 144
Woman Movement, 137, 138, 201, 209, 212; exclusionism of, 205, 224n14; ideology of, 203, 204; politics and, 206, 218; Populists and, 209, 218, 220–21; prohibition and, 206–7; strategies of, 202, 224n14; suffrage and, 210, 215, 221; WCTU and, 224n14
Woman's Friend, 212, 226n30
Woman suffrage, 24, 126, 201, 202–3, 206, 219; Democrats and, 221; extending, 202, 370n12; farm women and, 205; middle class and, 203; municipal, 207, 221; politics and, 219; Populists and, 211, 221; Republicans and, 218, 221, 224n18; struggle for, 137–38, 215; Woman Movement and, 210, 215, 221
Women: agriculture and, 21, 334, 335, 341, 342; black, 136, 224n14; citizenship and, 311; civilization and, 23, 127, 203,

223n9; complex society and, 22; culture and, 22, 23, 118, 119, 130, 131, 300, 302; domesticity and, 117–18, 119, 130, 300, 309, 313; equality for, 119; home economics and, 125–27; labor and, 300, 303; labor shortages and, 334–35, 337, 342; marriage and, 23–24; Mexican, 284, 297n25; middle-class, 22, 137, 223nn4,9, 224n11; mining and, 299, 300, 303, 317n54; mobilization of, 335; modernization and, 258; non-farm, 334, 338, 339, 341; politics and, 24, 25, 118, 137, 138, 201, 206–7, 208, 221, 222, 300, 306, 311, 312; settlement and, 118, 119; social conflict and, 300; social roles of, 312; strikes and, 31–32, 273, 299, 300, 307–8, 312; unions and, 310; working-class, 312, 313. *See also* Farm women
Women's Christian Temperance Union (WCTU), 201, 202, 204, 205, 220; suffrage and, 206, 211; Woman Movement and, 224n14
Women's Columns, 218
Women's Land Army of America (WLA), 337, 339, 341; farm women and, 274, 335; name change for, 342
Women's League, Lowman Hill and, 349
Women's march, 310, 311–12, 313
Women's Progressive Political League, *Farmer's Wife* and, 210
Women's Relief Corps, 210
Women's rights, 1, 20, 139, 218–19, 275
"Women! Talk Good Roads" (Bates), 258
Wood, John B., 168
Workers' Chronicle, 309
Working class, 31, 144, 273, 302, 303, 312, 313; growth of, 32; private/public spheres and, 315n15
Workmen's compensation, 392, 393
Works Progress Administration (WPA), 291
World War I, 310, 316n41; Mexicans and, 280; rural mobilization during, 343n3; WLA and, 335
World War II: farmers and, 334; federal government and, 18; labor shortages during, 335–36; Mexicans and, 277, 280, 293
Worster, Donald, 13, 15, 273
Worthwhile club, 302
Wounded Knee, 97
Wright, Helen, 301